THE WORST JOURNEY IN THEWORLD (VOLUME I)

LECTOR HOUSE PUBLIC DOMAIN WORKS

THE WORST JOURNEY IN THE WORLD
(VOLUME I)

APSLEY CHERRY-GARRARD

ISBN: 978-93-5344-522-5

First Published: 1922

LECTOR HOUSE LLP
E-MAIL: lectorpublishing@gmail.com

**MCMURDO SOUND FROM ARRIVAL HEIGHTS IN AUTUMN.
THE SUN IS SINKING BELOW THE WESTERN MOUNTAINS.**

THE WORST JOURNEY IN THE WORLD
ANTARCTIC 1910-1913

BY

APSLEY CHERRY-GARRARD

WITH PANORAMAS, MAPS, AND ILLUSTRATIONS BY THE
LATE
DOCTOR EDWARD A. WILSON AND OTHER MEMBERS OF
THE EXPEDITION

IN TWO VOLUMES
VOL. I.

FIRST PUBLISHED 1922

This volume is a narrative of Scott's Last Expedition from its departure from England in 1910 to its return to New Zealand in 1913.

It does not, however, include the story of subsidiary parties except where their adventures touch the history of the Main Party.

It is hoped later to publish an appendix volume with an account of the two Geological Journeys, and such other information concerning the equipment of, and lessons learned by, this Expedition as may be of use to the future explorer.

APSLEY CHERRY-GARRARD.

PREFACE

This post-war business is inartistic, for it is seldom that any one does anything well for the sake of doing it well; and it is un-Christian, if you value Christianity, for men are out to hurt and not to help—can you wonder, when the Ten Commandments were hurled straight from the pulpit through good stained glass. It is all very interesting and uncomfortable, and it has been a great relief to wander back in one's thoughts and correspondence and personal dealings to an age in geological time, so many hundred years ago, when we were artistic Christians, doing our jobs as well as we were able just because we wished to do them well, helping one another with all our strength, and (I speak with personal humility) living a life of co-operation, in the face of hardships and dangers, which has seldom been surpassed.

The mutual conquest of difficulties is the cement of friendship, as it is the only lasting cement of matrimony. We had plenty of difficulties; we sometimes failed, we sometimes won; we always faced them—we had to. Consequently we have some friends who are better than all the wives in Mahomet's paradise, and when I have asked for help in the making of this book I have never never asked in vain. Talk of ex-soldiers: give me ex-antarcticists, unsoured and with their ideals intact: they could sweep the world.

The trouble is that they are inclined to lose their ideals in this complicated atmosphere of civilization. They run one another down like the deuce, and it is quite time that stopped. What is the use of A running down Scott because he served with Shackleton, or B going for Amundsen because he served with Scott? They have all done good work; within their limits, the best work to date. There are jobs for which, if I had to do them, I would like to serve under Scott, Amundsen, Shackleton and Wilson—each to his part. For a joint scientific and geographical piece of organization, give me Scott; for a Winter Journey, Wilson; for a dash to the Pole and nothing else, Amundsen: and if I am in the devil of a hole and want to get out of it, give me Shackleton every time. They will all go down in polar history as leaders, these men. I believe Bowers would also have made a great name for himself if he had lived, and few polar ships have been commanded as capably as was the Terra Nova, by Pennell.

In a way this book is a sequel to the friendship which there was between Wilson, Bowers and myself, which, having stood the strain of the Winter Journey, could never have been broken. Between the three of us we had a share in all the big journeys and bad times which came to Scott's main landing party, and what follows is, particularly, our unpublished diaries, letters and illustrations. I, we, have tried to show how good the whole thing was—and how bad. I have had a freer hand than many in this, because much of the dull routine has been recorded already and can be found if wanted: also because, not being the leader of the expedition, I had no duty to fulfil in cataloguing my followers' achievements. But there was plenty of work left for me. It has been no mere gleaning of the polar field. Not half the story had been told, nor even all the most interesting documents. Among these, I have had from Mrs. Bowers her son's letters home, and from Lashly his diary of the Last Return Party on the Polar Journey. Mrs. Wilson has given her husband's diary of the Polar Journey: this is especially valuable because it is the only detailed account in existence from 87° 32′ to the Pole and after, with the exception of Scott's Diary already published. Lady Scott has given with both hands any records I wanted and could find. No one of my companions in the South has failed to help. They include Atkinson, Wright, Priestley, Simpson, Lillie and Debenham.

To all these good friends I can do no more than express my very sincere thanks.

I determined that the first object of the illustrations should be descriptive of the text: Wright and Debenham have photographs, sledging and otherwise, which do this admirably. Mrs. Wilson has allowed me to have any of her husband's sketches and drawings reproduced that I wished, and there are many hundreds from which to make a selection. In addition to the six water-colours, which I have chosen for their beauty, I have taken a number of sketches because they illustrate typical incidents in our lives. They are just unfinished sketches, no more: and had Bill been alive he would have finished them before he allowed them to be published. Then I have had reproduced nearly all the sketches and panoramas drawn by him on the Polar Journey and found with him where he died. The half-tone process does not do them justice: I wish I could have had them reproduced in photogravure, but the cost is prohibitive.

As to production, after a good deal of experience, I was convinced that I could trust a commercial firm to do its worst save when it gave them less trouble to do better. I acknowledge my mistake. In a wilderness of firms in whom nothing was first class except their names and their prices, I have dealt with R. & R. Clark, who have printed this book, and Emery Walker, who has illustrated it. The fact that Emery Walker is not only alive, but full of vitality, indicates why most of the other firms are millionaires.

When I went South I never meant to write a book: I rather despised those who did so as being of an inferior brand to those who did things and said nothing about them. But that they say nothing is too often due to the fact that they have nothing to say, or are too idle or too busy to learn how to say it. Every one who has been through such an extraordinary experience has much to say, and ought to say it if he has any faculty that way. There is after the event a good deal of criticism, of stock-taking, of checking of supplies and distances and so forth that cannot really be done without first-hand experience. Out there we knew what was happening to us too well; but we did not and could not measure its full significance. When I was asked to write a book by the Antarctic Committee I discovered that, without knowing it, I had intended to write one ever since I had realized my own experiences. Once started, I enjoyed the process. My own writing is my own despair, but it is better than it was, and this is directly due to Mr. and Mrs. Bernard Shaw. At the age of thirty-five I am delighted to acknowledge that my education has at last begun.

APSLEY CHERRY-GARRARD.

LAMER, WHEATHAMPSTEAD,

1921.

CONTENTS

LIST OF ILLUSTRATIONS

LIST OF MAPS

INTRODUCTION

Polar exploration is at once the cleanest and most isolated way of having a bad time which has been devised. It is the only form of adventure in which you put on your clothes at Michaelmas and keep them on until Christmas, and, save for a layer of the natural grease of the body, find them as clean as though they were new. It is more lonely than London, more secluded than any monastery, and the post comes but once a year. As men will compare the hardships of France, Palestine, or Mesopotamia, so it would be interesting to contrast the rival claims of the Antarctic as a medium of discomfort. A member of Campbell's party tells me that the trenches at Ypres were a comparative picnic. But until somebody can evolve a standard of endurance I am unable to see how it can be done. Take it all in all, I do not believe anybody on earth has a worse time than an Emperor penguin.

Even now the Antarctic is to the rest of the earth as the Abode of the Gods was to the ancient Chaldees, a precipitous and mammoth land lying far beyond the seas which encircled man's habitation, and nothing is more striking about the exploration of the Southern Polar regions than its absence, for when King Alfred reigned in England the Vikings were navigating the ice-fields of the North; yet when Wellington fought the battle of Waterloo there was still an undiscovered continent in the South.

For those who wish to read an account of the history of Antarctic exploration there is an excellent chapter in Scott's Voyage of the Discovery and elsewhere. I do not propose to give any general survey of this kind here, but complaints have been made to me that Scott's Last Expedition plunges the general reader into a neighbourhood which he is supposed to know all about, while actually he is lost, having no idea what the Discovery was, or where Castle Rock or Hut Point stand. For the better understanding of the references to particular expeditions, to the lands discovered by them and the traces left by them, which must occur in this book I give the following brief introduction.

From the earliest days of the making of maps of the Southern Hemisphere it was supposed that there was a great continent called Terra Australis. As explorers penetrated round the Cape of Good Hope and Cape Horn, and found nothing but stormy oceans beyond, and as, later, they discovered Australia and New Zealand, the belief in this continent weakened, but was not abandoned. During the latter half of the eighteenth century eagerness for scientific knowledge was added to the former striving after individual or State aggrandizement.

Cook, Ross and Scott: these are the aristocrats of the South.

It was the great English navigator James Cook who laid the foundations of our knowledge. In 1772 he sailed from Deptford in the Resolution, 462 tons, and the Adventure, 336 tons, ships which had been built at Whitby for the coal trade. He was, like Nansen, a believer in a varied diet as one of the preventives of scurvy, and mentions that he had among his provisions "besides Saur Krout, Portable Broth, Marmalade of Carrots and Suspissated juice of Wort and Beer." Medals were struck "to be given to the natives of new discovered countries, and left there as testimonies of our being the first discoverers."[1] It would be interesting to know whether any exist now.

After calling at the Cape of Good Hope Cook started to make his Easting down to New Zealand, purposing to sail as far south as possible in search of a southern continent. He sighted his first 'ice island' or iceberg in lat. 50° 40' S., long. 2° 0' E., on December 10, 1772. The next day he "saw some white birds about the size of pigeons, with blackish bills and feet. I never saw any such before."[2] These must have been Snowy Petrel. Passing through many bergs, where he notices how the albatross left them and penguins appeared, he was brought up by thick pack ice along which he coasted. Under the supposition that this ice was formed in bays and rivers Cook was led to believe that land was not far distant. Incidentally he remarks that in order to enable his men to support the colder weather he "caused the sleeves of their jackets (which were so short as to expose their arms) to be lengthened with baize; and had a cap made for each man of the same stuff, together with canvas; which proved of great service to them."[3]

For more than a month Cook sailed the Southern Ocean, always among bergs and often among pack. The weather was consistently bad and generally thick; he mentions that he had only seen the moon once since leaving the Cape.

It was on Sunday, January 17, 1773, that the Antarctic Circle was crossed for the first time, in longitude 39° 35' E. After proceeding to latitude 67° 15' S. he was stopped by an immense field of pack. From this point he turned back and made his way to New Zealand.

Leaving New Zealand at the end of 1773 without his second ship, the Adventure, from which he had been parted, he judged from the great swell that "there can be no land to the southward, under the meridian of New Zealand, but what must lie very far to the south." In latitude 62° 10' S. he sighted the first ice island on December 12, and was stopped by thick pack ice three days later. On the 20th he again crossed the Antarctic Circle in longitude 147° 46' W. and penetrated in this neighbourhood to a latitude of 67° 31' S. Here he found a drift towards the north-east.

On January 26, 1774, in longitude 109° 31' W., he crossed the Antarctic Circle for the third time, after meeting no pack and only a few icebergs. In latitude 71° 10' S. he was finally turned back by an immense field of pack, and wrote:

"I will not say it was impossible anywhere to get farther to the south; but the attempting it would have been a dangerous and rash enterprise, and what, I be-

[1] Cook, *A Voyage towards the South Pole*, Introduction.
[2] Cook, *A Voyage towards the South Pole*, vol. i. p. 23.
[3] *Ibid.* p. 28.

lieve, no man in my situation would have thought of. It was, indeed, my opinion, as well as the opinion of most on board, that this ice extended quite to the Pole, or perhaps joined to some land, to which it had been fixed from the earliest time; and that it is here, that is to the south of this parallel, where all the ice we find scattered up and down to the north is first formed, and afterwards broken off by gales of wind, or other causes, and brought to the north by the currents, which are always found to set in that direction in the high latitudes. As we drew near this ice some penguins were heard, but none seen; and but few other birds, or any other thing that could induce us to think any land was near. And yet I think there must be some to the south beyond this ice; but if there is it can afford no better retreat for birds, or any other animals, than the ice itself, with which it must be wholly covered. I, who had ambition not only to go farther than any one had been before, but as far as it was possible for man to go, was not sorry at meeting with this interruption; as it, in some measure, relieved us; at least, shortened the dangers and hardships inseparable from the navigation of the Southern Polar regions."[4]

And so he turned northwards, when, being "taken ill of the bilious colic," a favourite dog belonging to one of the officers (Mr. Forster, after whom Aptenodytes forsteri, the Emperor penguin, is named) "fell a sacrifice to my tender stomach.... Thus I received nourishment and strength, from food which would have made most people in Europe sick: so true it is that necessity is governed by no law."[5]

"Once and for all the idea of a populous fertile southern continent was proved to be a myth, and it was clearly shown that whatever land might exist to the South must be a region of desolation hidden beneath a mantle of ice and snow. The vast extent of the tempestuous southern seas was revealed, and the limits of the habitable globe were made known. Incidentally it may be remarked that Cook was the first to describe the peculiarities of the Antarctic icebergs and floe-ice."[6]

A Russian expedition under Bellingshausen discovered the first certain land in the Antarctic in 1819, and called it Alexander Land, which lies nearly due south of Cape Horn.

Whatever may have been the rule in other parts of the world, the flag followed trade in the southern seas during the first part of the nineteenth century. The discovery of large numbers of seals and whales attracted many hundreds of ships, and it is to the enlightened instructions of such firms as Messrs. Enderby, and to the pluck and enterprise of such commanders as Weddell, Biscoe and Balleny, that we owe much of our small knowledge of the outline of the Antarctic continent.

"In the smallest and craziest ships they plunged boldly into stormy ice-strewn seas; again and again they narrowly missed disaster; their vessels were racked and strained and leaked badly, their crews were worn out with unceasing toil and decimated with scurvy. Yet in spite of inconceivable discomforts they struggled on, and it does not appear that any one of them ever turned his course until he was driven to do so by hard necessity. One cannot read the simple, unaffected narra-

[4] Cook, *A Voyage towards the South Pole*, vol. i. p. 268.
[5] *Ibid.* p. 275.
[6] Scott, *Voyage of the Discovery*, vol. i. p. 9.

tives of these voyages without being assured of their veracity, and without being struck by the wonderful pertinacity and courage which they display."[7]

The position in 1840 was that the Antarctic land had been sighted at a few points all round its coasts. On the whole the boundaries which had been seen lay on or close to the Antarctic Circle, and it appeared probable that the continent, if continent it was, consisted of a great circular mass of land with the South Pole at its centre, and its coasts more or less equidistant from this point.

Two exceptions only to this had been found. Cook and Bellingshausen had indicated a dip towards the Pole south of the Pacific; Weddell a still more pronounced dip to the south of the Atlantic, having sailed to a latitude of 74° 15′ S. in longitude 34° 16′ W.

Had there been a Tetrahedronal Theory in those days, some one might have suggested the probability of a third indentation beneath the Indian Ocean, probably to be laughed at for his pains. When James Clark Ross started from England in 1839 there was no particular reason for him to suppose that the Antarctic coast-line in the region of the magnetic Pole, which he was to try to reach, did not continue to follow the Antarctic Circle.

Ross left England in September 1839 under instructions from the Admiralty. He had under his command two of Her Majesty's sailing ships, the Erebus, 370 tons, and the Terror, 340 tons. Arriving in Hobart, Tasmania, in August 1840, he was met by news of discoveries made during the previous summer by the French Expedition under Dumont D'Urville and the United States Expedition under Charles Wilkes. The former had coasted along Adélie Land, and for sixty miles of ice cliff to the west of it. He brought back an egg now at Drayton which Scott's Discovery Expedition definitely proved to be that of an Emperor penguin.

All these discoveries were somewhere about the latitude of the Antarctic Circle (66° 32′ S.) and roughly in that part of the world which lies to the south of Australia. Ross, "impressed with the feeling that England had ever *led* the way of discovery in the southern as well as in the northern region, ... resolved at once to avoid all interference with their discoveries, and selected a much more easterly meridian (170° E.), on which to penetrate to the southward, and if possible reach the magnetic Pole."[8]

The outlines of the expedition in which an unknown and unexpected sea was found, stretching 500 miles southwards towards the Pole, are well known to students of Antarctic history. After passing through the pack he stood towards the supposed position of the magnetic Pole, "steering as nearly south by the compass as the wind admitted," and on January 11, 1841, in latitude 71° 15′ S., he sighted, the white peaks of Mount Sabine and shortly afterwards Cape Adare. Foiled by the presence of land from gaining the magnetic Pole, he turned southwards (true) into what is now called the Ross Sea, and, after spending many days in travelling down this coast-line with the mountains on his right hand, the Ross Sea on his left, he discovered and named the great line of mountains which here for some five

[7] *Ibid.* p. 14.
[8] Ross, *Voyage to the Southern Seas*, vol. i. p. 117.

hundred miles divides the sea from the Antarctic plateau. On January 27, "with a favourable breeze and very clear weather, we stood to the southward, close to some land which had been in sight since the preceding noon, and which we then called the High Island; it proved to be a mountain twelve thousand four hundred feet of elevation above the level of the sea, emitting flame and smoke in great profusion; at first the smoke appeared like snowdrift, but as we drew nearer its true character became manifest.... I named it Mount Erebus, and an extinct volcano to the eastward, little inferior in height, being by measurement ten thousand nine hundred feet high, was called Mount Terror." That is the first we hear of our two old friends, and Ross Island is the land upon which they stand.

"As we approached the land under all studding-sails we perceived a low white line extending from its eastern extreme point as far as the eye could discern to the eastward. It presented an extraordinary appearance, gradually increasing in height as we got nearer to it, and proving at length to be a perpendicular cliff of ice, between one hundred and fifty and two hundred feet above the level of the sea, perfectly flat and level at the top, and without any fissures or promontories on its even seaward face."[9]

Ross coasted along the Barrier for some 250 miles from Cape Crozier, as he called the eastern extremity of Ross Island, after the commander of the Terror. This point where land, sea and moving Barrier meet will be constantly mentioned in this narrative. Returning, he looked into the Sound which divides Ross Island from the western mountains. On February 16 "Mount Erebus was seen at 2.30 A.M., and, the weather becoming very clear, we had a splendid view of the whole line of coast, to all appearance connecting it with the main land, which we had not before suspected to be the case." The reader will understand that Ross makes a mistake here, since Mounts Erebus and Terror are upon an island connected to the mainland only by a sheet of ice. He continues: "A very deep bight was observed to extend far to the south-west from Cape Bird [Bird was the senior lieutenant of the Erebus], in which a line of low land might be seen; but its determination was too uncertain to be left unexplored; and as the wind blowing feebly from the west prevented our making any way in that direction through the young ice that now covered the surface of the ocean in every part, as far as we could see from the mast-head, I determined to steer towards the bight to give it a closer examination, and to learn with more certainty its continuity or otherwise. At noon we were in latitude 76° 32′ S., longitude 166° 12′ E., dip 88° 24′ and variation 107° 18′ E.

"During the afternoon we were nearly becalmed, and witnessed some magnificent eruptions of Mount Erebus, the flame and smoke being projected to a great height; but we could not, as on a former occasion, discover any lava issuing from the crater; although the exhibitions of to-day were upon a much grander scale....

"Soon after midnight (February 16-17) a breeze sprang up from the eastward and we made all sail to the southward until 4 A.M., although we had an hour before distinctly traced the land entirely round the bay connecting Mount Erebus with the mainland. I named it McMurdo Bay, after the senior lieutenant of the Terror,

---

[9] Ross, *Voyage to the Southern Seas*, vol. i. pp. 216-218.

a compliment that his zeal and skill well merited."[10] It is now called McMurdo Sound.

In making the mistake of connecting Erebus with the mainland Ross was look-ing at a distance upon the Hut Point Peninsula running out from the S.W. corner of Erebus towards the west. He probably saw Minna Bluff, which juts out from the mainland towards the east. Between them, and in front of the Bluff, lie White Island, Black Island and Brown Island. To suppose them to be part of a line of con-tinuous land was a very natural mistake.

Ross broke through the pack ice into an unknown sea: he laid down many hundreds of miles of mountainous coast-line, and (with further work completed in 1842) some 400 miles of the Great Ice Barrier: he penetrated in his ships to the extraordinarily high latitude of 78° 11′ S., four degrees farther than Weddell. The scientific work of his expedition was no less worthy of praise. The South Magnetic Pole was fixed with comparative accuracy, though Ross was disappointed in his natural but "perhaps too ambitious hope I had so long cherished of being permit-ted to plant the flag of my country on both the magnetic Poles of our globe."

Before all things he was at great pains to be accurate, both in his geograph-ical and scientific observations, and his records of meteorology, water tempera-tures, soundings, as also those concerning the life in the oceans through which he passed, were not only frequent but trustworthy.

When Ross returned to England in 1843 it was impossible not to believe that the case of those who advocated the existence of a South Polar continent was con-siderably strengthened. At the same time there was no proof that the various blocks of land which had been discovered were connected with one another. Even now in 1921, after twenty years of determined exploration aided by the most modern ap-pliances, the interior of this supposed continent is entirely unknown and unchart-ed except in the Ross Sea area, while the fringes of the land are only discovered in perhaps a dozen places on a circumference of about eleven thousand miles.

In his Life of Sir Joseph Hooker, Dr. Leonard Huxley has given us some in-teresting sidelights on this expedition under Ross. Hooker was the botanist of the expedition and assistant surgeon to the Erebus, being 22 years old when he left En-gland in 1839. Natural history came off very badly in the matter of equipment from the Government, who provided twenty-five reams of paper, two botanizing vascu-la and two cases for bringing home live plants: that was all, not an instrument, nor a book, nor a bottle, and rum from the ship's stores was the only preservative. And when they returned, the rich collections which they brought back were never fully worked out. Ross's special branch of science was terrestrial magnetism, but he was greatly interested in Natural History, and gave up part of his cabin for Hooker to work in. "Almost every day I draw, sometimes all day long and till two and three in the morning, the Captain directing me; he sits on one side of the table, writing and figuring at night, and I on the other, drawing. Every now and then he breaks off and comes to my side, to see what I am after ..." and, "as you may suppose, we have had one or two little tiffs, neither of us perhaps being helped by the best

[10] Ross, *Voyage to the Southern Seas*, vol. i. pp. 244-245.

of tempers; but nothing can exceed the liberality with which he has thrown open his cabin to me and made it my workroom at no little inconvenience to himself."

Another extract from Hooker's letters after the first voyage runs as follows:

"The success of the Expedition in Geographical discovery is really wonderful, and only shows what a little perseverance will do, for we have been in no dangerous predicaments, and have suffered no hardships whatever: there has been a sort of freemasonry among Polar voyagers to keep up the credit they have acquired as having done wonders, and accordingly, such of us as were new to the ice made up our minds for frost-bites, and attached a most undue importance to the simple operation of boring packs, etc., which have now vanished, though I am not going to tell everybody so; I do not here refer to travellers, who do indeed undergo unheard-of hardships, but to voyagers who have a snug ship, a little knowledge of the Ice, and due caution is all that is required."

In the light of Scott's leading of the expedition of which I am about to tell, and the extraordinary scientific activity of Pennell in command of the Terra Nova after Scott was landed, Hooker would have to qualify a later extract, "nor is it probable that any future collector will have a Captain so devoted to the cause of Marine Zoology, and so constantly on the alert to snatch the most trifling opportunities of adding to the collection...."

Finally, we have a picture of the secrecy which was imposed upon all with regard to the news they should write home and the precautions against any leakage of scientific results. And we see Hooker jumping down the main hatch with a penguin skin in his hand which he was preparing for himself, when Ross came up the after hatch unexpectedly. That *has* happened on the Terra Nova!

Ross had a cold reception on his return, and Scott wrote to Hooker in 1905:

"At first it seems inexplicable when one considers how highly his work is now appreciated. From the point of view of the general public, however, I have always thought that Ross was neglected, and as you once said he is very far from doing himself justice in his book. I did not know that Barrow was the bête noire who did so much to discount Ross's results. It is an interesting sidelight on such a venture."[11]

In discussing and urging the importance of the Antarctic Expedition which was finally sent under Scott in the Discovery, Hooker urged the importance of work in the South Polar Ocean, which swarms with animal and vegetable life. Commenting upon the fact that the large collections made chiefly by himself had never been worked out, except the diatoms, he writes:

"A better fate, I trust, awaits the treasures that the hoped-for Expedition will bring back, for so prolific is the ocean that the naturalist need never be idle, no, not even for one of the twenty-four hours of daylight during a whole Antarctic summer, and I look to the results of a comparison of the oceanic life of the Arctic and Antarctic regions as the heralding of an epoch in the history of biology."[12]

---

[11] Leonard Huxley, *Life of Sir J. D. Hooker*, vol. ii. p. 443.
[12] *Ibid.* p. 441.

When Ross went to the Antarctic it was generally thought that there was neither food nor oxygen nor light in the depths of the ocean, and that therefore there was no life. Among other things the investigations of Ross gave ground for thinking this was not the case. Later still, in 1873, the possibility of laying submarine cables made it necessary to investigate the nature of the abyssal depths, and the Challenger proved that not only does life, and in quite high forms, exist there, but that there are fish which can see. It is now almost certain that there is a great oxidized northward-creeping current which flows out of the Antarctic Ocean and under the waters of the other great oceans of the world.

It was the good fortune of Ross, at a time when the fringes of the great Antarctic continent were being discovered in comparatively low latitudes of 66° and thereabouts, sometimes not even within the Antarctic Circle, to find to the south of New Zealand a deep inlet in which he could sail to the high latitude of 78°. This inlet, which is now known as the Ross Sea, has formed the starting-place of all sledging parties which have approached the South Pole. I have dwelt upon this description of the lands he discovered because they will come very intimately into this history. I have also emphasized his importance in the history of Antarctic exploration because Ross having done what it was possible to do by sea, penetrating so far south and making such memorable discoveries, the next necessary step in Antarctic exploration was that another traveller should follow up his work on land. It is an amazing thing that sixty years were allowed to elapse before that traveller appeared. When he appeared he was Scott. In the sixty years which elapsed between Ross and Scott the map of the Antarctic remained practically unaltered. Scott tackled the land, and Scott is the Father of Antarctic sledge travelling.

This period of time saw a great increase in the interest taken in science both pure and applied, and it had been pointed out in 1893 that "we knew more about the planet Mars than about a large area of our own globe." The Challenger Expedition of 1874 had spent three weeks within the Antarctic Circle, and the specimens brought home by her from the depths of these cold seas had aroused curiosity. Meanwhile Borchgrevink (1897) landed at Cape Adare, and built a hut which still stands and which afforded our Cape Adare party valuable assistance. Here he lived during the first winter which men spent in the Antarctic.

Meanwhile, in the Arctic, brave work was being done. The names of Parry, M'Clintock, Franklin, Markham, Nares, Greely and De Long are but a few of the many which suggest themselves of those who have fought their way mile by mile over rough ice and open leads with appliances which now seem to be primitive and with an addition to knowledge which often seemed hardly commensurate with the hardships suffered and the disasters which sometimes overtook them. To those whose fortune it has been to serve under Scott the Franklin Expedition has more than ordinary interest, for it was the same ships, the Erebus and Terror, which discovered Ross Island, that were crushed in the northern ice after Franklin himself had died, and it was Captain Crozier (the same Crozier who was Ross's captain in the South and after whom Cape Crozier is named) who then took command and led that most ghastly journey in all the history of exploration: more we shall never know, for none survived to tell the tale. Now, with the noise and racket of London all round them, a statue of Scott looks across to one of Franklin and his men of the Erebus and Terror, and surely they have some thoughts in common.

Englishmen had led the way in the North, but it must be admitted that the finest journey of all was made by the Norwegian Nansen in 1893-1896. Believing in a drift from the neighbourhood of the New Siberian Islands westwards over the Pole, a theory which obtained confirmation by the discovery off the coast of Greenland of certain remains of a ship called the Jeannette which had been crushed in the ice off these islands, his bold project was to be frozen in with his ship and allow the current to take him over, or as near as possible to, the Pole. For this purpose the most famous of Arctic ships was built, called the Fram. She was designed by Colin Archer, and was saucer-shaped, with a breadth one-third of her total length. With most of the expert Arctic opinion against him, Nansen believed that this ship would rise and sit on the top of the ice when pressed, instead of being crushed. Of her wonderful voyage with her thirteen men, of how she was frozen into the ice in September 1893 in the north of Siberia (79° N.) and of the heaving and trembling of the ship amidst the roar of the ice pressure, of how the Fram rose to the occasion as she was built to do, the story has still, after twenty-eight years, the thrill of novelty. She drifted over the eightieth degree on February 2, 1894. During the first winter Nansen was already getting restive: the drift was so slow, and sometimes it was backwards: it was not until the second autumn that the eighty-second degree arrived. So he decided that he would make an attempt to penetrate northwards by sledging during the following spring. As Nansen has told me, he felt that the ship would do her job in any case. Could not something more be done also?

This was one of the bravest decisions a polar explorer has ever taken. It meant leaving a drifting ship which could not be regained: it meant a return journey over drifting ice to land; the nearest known land was nearly five hundred miles south of the point from which he started northwards; and the journey would include travelling both by sea and by ice.

Undoubtedly there was more risk in leaving the Fram than in remaining in her. It is a laughable absurdity to say, as Greely did after Nansen's almost miraculous return, that he had deserted his men in an ice-beset ship, and deserved to be censured for doing so.[13] The ship was left in the command of Sverdrup. Johansen was chosen to be Nansen's one companion, and we shall hear of him again in the Fram, this time with Amundsen in his voyage to the South.

The polar traveller is so interested in the adventure and hardships of Nansen's sledge journey that his equipment, which is the most important side of his expedition to us who have gone South, is liable to be overlooked. The modern side of polar travel begins with Nansen. It was Nansen who first used a light sledge based upon the ski sledge of Norway, in place of the old English heavy sledge which was based upon the Eskimo type. Cooking apparatus, food, tents, clothing and the thousand and one details of equipment without which no journey nowadays stands much chance of success, all date back to Nansen in the immediate past, though beyond him of course is the experience of centuries of travellers. As Nansen himself wrote of the English polar men: "How well was their equipment

[13] Nansen, *Farthest North*, vol. i. p. 52.

thought out and arranged with the means they had at their disposal! Truly, there is nothing new under the sun. Most of what I prided myself upon, and what I thought to be new, I find they had anticipated. M'Clintock used the same things forty years ago. It was not their fault that they were born in a country where the use of snowshoes is unknown....".[14]

All the more honour to the men who dared so much and travelled so far with the limited equipment of the past. The real point for us is that, just as Scott is the Father of Antarctic sledge travelling, so Nansen may be considered the modern Father of it all.

Nansen and Johansen started on March 14 when the Fram was in latitude 84° 4′ N., and the sun had only returned a few days before, with three sledges (two of which carried kayaks) and 28 dogs. They reached their northern-most camp on April 8, which Nansen has given in his book as being in latitude 86° 13.6′ N. But Nansen tells me that Professor Geelmuyden, who had his astronomical results and his diary, reckoned that owing to refraction the horizon was lifted, and if so the observation had to be reduced accordingly. Nansen therefore gave the reduced latitude in his book, but he considers that his horizon was very clear when he took that observation, and believes that his latitude was higher than that given. He used a sextant and the natural horizon.

They turned, and travelling back round pressed-up ice and open leads they failed to find the land they had been led to expect in latitude 83°, which indeed was proved to be non-existent. At the end of June they started using the kayaks, which needed many repairs after their rough passage, to cross the open leads. They waited long in camp, that the travelling conditions might improve, and all the time Nansen saw a white spot he thought was cloud. At last, on July 24, land was in sight, which proved to be that white spot. Fourteen days later they reached it to find that it consisted of a series of islands. These they left behind them and, unable to say what land they had reached, for their watches had run down, they coasted on westwards and southwards until winter approached. They built a hut of moss and stones and snow, and roofed it with walrus skins cut from the animals while they lay in the sea, for they were too heavy for two men to drag on to the ice. When I met Nansen he had forgotten all about this, and would not believe that it had happened until he saw it in his own book. They lay in their old clothes that winter, so soaked with blubber that the only way to clean their shirts was to scrape them. They made themselves new clothes from blankets, and sleeping-bags from the skins of the bears which they ate, and started again in May of the following year to make Spitzbergen. They had been travelling a long month, during which time they had at least two very narrow escapes—the first due to their kayaks floating away, when Nansen swam out into the icy sea and reached them just before he sank, and Johansen passed the worst moments of his life watching from the shore; the second caused by the attack of a walrus which went for Nansen's kayak with tusks and flippers. And then one morning, as he looked round at the cold glaciers and naked cliffs, not knowing where he was, he heard a dog bark. Intensely excited, he started towards the sound, to be met by the leader of the English Jack-

[14] Nansen, *Farthest North*, vol. ii. pp. 19-20.

son-Harmsworth Expedition whose party was wintering there, and who first gave him the definite news that he was on Franz Josef Land. Nansen and Johansen were finally landed at Vardo in the north of Norway, to learn that no tidings had yet been heard of the Fram. That very day she cleared the ice which had imprisoned her for nearly three years.

I cannot go into the Fram's journey save to say that she had drifted as far north as 85° 55′ N., only eighteen geographical miles south of Nansen's farthest north. But the sledge journey and the winter spent by the two men has many points in common with the experience of our own Northern Party, and often and often during the long winter of 1912 our thoughts turned with hope to Nansen's winter, for we said if it had been done once why should it not be done again, and Campbell and his men survive.

Before Nansen started, the spirit of adventure, which has always led men into the unknown, combined with the increased interest in knowledge for its own sake to turn the thoughts of the civilized world southwards. It was becoming plain that a continent of the extent and climate which this polar land probably possessed might have an overwhelming influence upon the weather conditions of the whole Southern Hemisphere. The importance of magnetism was only rivalled by the mystery in which the whole subject was shrouded: and the region which surrounded the Southern Magnetic Pole of the earth offered a promising field of experiment and observation. The past history, through the ages, of this land was of obvious importance to the geological story of the earth, whilst the survey of land formations and ice action in the Antarctic was more useful perhaps to the physiographer than that of any other country in the world, seeing that he found here in daily and even hourly operation the conditions which he knew had existed in the ice ages of the past over the whole world, but which he could only infer from vestigial remains. The biological importance of the Antarctic might be of the first magnitude in view of the significance which attaches to the life of the sea in the evolutionary problem.

And it was with these objects and ideals that Scott's first expedition, known officially as the British Antarctic Expedition of 1901-1904, but more familiarly as 'The Discovery Expedition,' from the name of the ship which carried it, was organized by the Royal Society and the Royal Geographical Society, backed by the active support of the British Government. The executive officers and crew were Royal Navy almost without exception, whilst the scientific purposes of the expedition were served in addition by five scientists. These latter were not naval officers.

The Discovery left New Zealand on Christmas Eve 1901, and entered the belt of pack ice which always has to be penetrated in order to reach the comparatively open sea beyond, when just past the Antarctic Circle. But a little more than four days saw her through, in which she was lucky, as we now know. Scott landed at Cape Adare and then coasted down the western coast of Victoria Land just as Ross had done sixty years before. As he voyaged south he began to look for safe winter quarters for the ship, and when he pushed into McMurdo Sound on January 21, 1902, it seemed that here he might find both a sheltered bay into which the ship could be frozen, and a road to the southland beyond.

The open season which still remained before the freezing of the sea made progress impossible was spent in surveying the 500 miles of cliff which marks the northern limit of the Great Ice Barrier. Passing the extreme eastward position reached by Ross in 1842, they sailed on into an unknown world, and discovered a deep bay, called Balloon Bight, where the rounded snow-covered slopes undoubtedly were land and not, as heretofore, floating ice. Farther east, as they sailed, shallow soundings and gentle snow slopes gave place to steeper and more broken ridges, until at last small black patches in the snow gave undoubted evidence of rock; and an undiscovered land, now known as King Edward VII.'s Land, rose to a height of several thousand feet. The presence of thick pack ahead, and the advance of the season, led Scott to return to McMurdo Sound, where he anchored the Discovery in a little bay at the end of the tongue of land now known as the Hut Point Peninsula, and built the hut which, though little used in the Discovery days, was to figure so largely in the story of this his last expedition.

The first autumn was spent in various short journeys of discovery—discovery not only of the surrounding land but of many mistakes in sledging equipment and routine. It is amazing to one who looks back upon these first efforts of the Discovery Expedition that the results were not more disastrous than was actually the case. When one reads of dog-teams which refused to start, of pemmican which was considered to be too rich to eat, of two officers discussing the ascent of Erebus and back in one day, and of sledging parties which knew neither how to use their cookers or lamp, nor how to put up their tents, nor even how to put on their clothes, then one begins to wonder that the process of education was gained at so small a price. "Not a single article of the outfit had been tested; and amid the general ignorance that prevailed the lack of system was painfully apparent in everything."[15]

This led to a tragedy. A returning sledge party of men was overtaken by a blizzard on the top of the Peninsula near Castle Rock. They quite properly camped, and should have been perfectly comfortable lying in their sleeping-bags after a hot meal. But the primus lamps could not be lighted, and as they sat in leather boots and inadequate clothing being continually frost-bitten they decided to leave the tent and make their way to the ship—sheer madness as we now know. As they groped their way in the howling snow-drift the majority of the party either slipped or rolled down a steep slippery snow slope some thousand feet high ending in a precipitous ice-cliff, below which lay the open sea. It is a nasty place on a calm summer day: in a blizzard it must be ghastly. Yet only one man, named Vince, shot down the slope and over the precipice into the sea below. How the others got back heaven knows. One seaman called Hare, who separated from the others and lay down under a rock, awoke after thirty-six hours, covered with snow but in full possession of his faculties and free from frost-bites. The little cross at Hut Point commemorates the death of Vince. One of this party was a seaman called Wild, who came to the front and took the lead of five of the survivors after the death of Vince. He was to take the lead often in future expeditions under Shackleton and Mawson, and there are few men living who have so proved themselves as polar

[15] Scott, *Voyage of the Discovery*, vol. i. p. 229.

travellers.

I have dwelt upon this side of the early sledging deficiencies of the Discovery to show the importance of experience in Antarctic land travelling, whether it be at first or second hand. Scott and his men in 1902 were pioneers. They bought their experience at a price which might easily have been higher; and each expedition which has followed has added to the fund. The really important thing is that nothing of what is gained should be lost. It is one of the main objects of this book to hand on as complete a record as possible of the methods, equipment, food and weights used by Scott's Last Expedition for the use of future explorers. "The first object of writing an account of a Polar voyage is the guidance of future voyagers: the first duty of the writer is to his successors."[16]

The adaptability, invention and resource of the men of the Discovery when they set to work after the failures of the autumn to prepare for the successes of the two following summers showed that they could rise to their difficulties. Scott admitted that "food, clothing, everything was wrong, the whole system was bad."[17] In determining to profit by his mistakes, and working out a complete system of Antarctic travel, he was at his best; and it was after a winter of drastic reorganization that he started on November 2, 1902, on his first southern journey with two companions, Wilson and Shackleton.

It is no part of my job to give an account of this journey. The dogs failed badly: probably the Norwegian stock-fish which had been brought through the tropics to feed them was tainted: at any rate they sickened; and before the journey was done all the dogs had to be killed or had died. A fortnight after starting, the party was relaying—that is, taking on part of their load and returning for the rest; and this had to be continued for thirty-one days.

---

[16] Scott, *Voyage of the Discovery*, vol. i. p. vii.
[17] *Ibid.* p. 273.

THE LAST OF THE DOGS—E. A. WILSON, DEL.

The ration of food was inadequate and they became very hungry as time went on; but it was not until December 21 that Wilson disclosed to Scott that Shackleton had signs of scurvy which had been present for some time. On December 30, in latitude 82° 16′ S., they decided to return. By the middle of January the scurvy signs were largely increased and Shackleton was seriously ill and spitting blood. His condition became more and more alarming, and he collapsed on January 18, but revived afterwards. Sometimes walking by the sledge, sometimes being carried upon it, Shackleton survived: Scott and Wilson saved his life. The three men reached the ship on February 3, after covering 960 statute miles in 93 days. Scott and Wilson were both extremely exhausted and seriously affected by scurvy. It was a fine journey, the geographical results of which comprised the survey of some three hundred miles of new coast-line, and a further knowledge of the Barrier upon which they travelled.

While Scott was away southwards an organized attempt was made to discover the nature of the mountains and glaciers which lay across the Sound to the west. This party actually reached the plateau which lay beyond, and attained a height of 8900 feet, when "as far as they could see in every direction to the westward of them there extended a level plateau, to the south and north could be seen isolated nunataks, and behind them showed the high mountains which they had passed": a practicable road to the west had been found.

I need note no more than these two most important of the many journeys carried out this season: nor is it necessary for me to give any account of the continuous and fertile scientific work which was accomplished in this virgin land. In the meantime a relief ship, the Morning, had arrived. It was intended that the Discovery should return this year as soon as the sea-ice in which she was imprisoned should break up and set her free. As February passed, however, it became increasingly plain that the ice conditions were altogether different from those of the previous year. On the 8th the Morning was still separated from the Discovery by eight miles of fast ice. March 2 was fully late for a low-powered ship to remain in the Sound, and on this date the Morning left. By March 13 all hope of the Discovery being freed that year was abandoned.

The second winter passed much as the first, and as soon as spring arrived sledging was continued. These spring journeys on the Barrier, with sunlight only by day and low temperatures at all times, entailed great discomfort and, perhaps worse, want of sleep, frost-bites, and a fast accumulation of moisture in all one's clothing and in the sleeping-bags, which resulted in masses of ice which had to be thawed out by the heat of one's body before any degree of comfort could be gained. A fortnight was considered about the extreme limit of time for such a journey, and generally parties were not absent so long; for at this time a spring journey was considered a dreadful experience. "Wait till you've had a spring journey" was the threat of the old stagers to us. A winter journey lasting nearly three times as long as a spring journey was not imagined. I advise explorers to be content with imagining it in the future.

The hardest journey of this year was carried out by Scott with two seamen of whom much will be written in this history. Their names are Edgar Evans and Lashly. The object of the journey was to explore westwards into the interior of the plateau. By way of the Ferrar Glacier they reached the ice-cap after considerable troubles, not the least of which was the loss of the data necessary for navigation contained in an excellent publication called Hints to Travellers, which was blown away. Then for the first time it was seen what additional difficulties are created by the climate and position of this lofty plateau, which we now know extends over the Pole and probably reaches over the greater part of the Antarctic continent. It was the beginning of November: that is, the beginning of summer; but the conditions of work were much the same as those found during the spring journeys on the Barrier. The temperature dropped into the minus forties; but the worst feature of all was a continuous head-wind blowing from west to east which combined with the low temperature and rarefied air to make the conditions of sledging extremely laborious. The supporting party returned, and the three men continued alone, pulling out westwards into an unknown waste of snow with no landmarks to vary the rough monotony. They turned homewards on December 1, but found the pulling very heavy; and their difficulties were increased by their ignorance of their exact position. The few glimpses of the land which they obtained as they approached it in the thick weather which prevailed only left them in horrible uncertainty as to their whereabouts. Owing to want of food it was impossible to wait for the weather to clear: there was nothing to be done but to continue their eastward march. Threading their way amidst the ice disturbances which mark the head of the glaciers, the party pushed blindly forward in air which was becoming thick with snow-drift. Suddenly Lashly slipped: in a moment the whole party was flying downwards with increasing speed. They ceased to slide smoothly; they were hurled into the air and descended with great force on to a gradual snow incline. Rising they looked round them to find above them an ice-fall 300 feet high down which they had fallen: above it the snow was still drifting, but where they stood there was peace and blue sky. They recognized now for the first time their own glacier and the well-remembered landmark, and far away in the distance was the smoking summit of Mount Erebus. It was a miracle.

Excellent subsidiary journeys were also made of which space allows no mention here: nor do they bear directly upon this last expedition. But in view of the Winter Journey undertaken by us, if not for the interest of the subject itself, some account must be given of those most aristocratic inhabitants of the Antarctic, the Emperor penguins, with whom Wilson and his companions in the Discovery now became familiar.

There are two kinds of Antarctic penguins—the little Adélie with his blue-black coat and his white shirt-front, weighing 16 lbs., an object of endless pleasure and amusement, and the great dignified Emperor with long curved beak, bright orange head-wear and powerful flippers, a personality of 6½ stones. Science singles out the Emperor as being the more interesting bird because he is more primitive, possibly the most primitive of all birds. Previous to the Discovery Expedition nothing was known of him save that he existed in the pack and on the fringes of the continent.

We have heard of Cape Crozier as being the eastern extremity of Ross Island, discovered by Ross and named after the captain of the Terror. It is here that with immense pressures and rendings the moving sheet of the Barrier piles itself up against the mountain. It is here also that the great ice-cliff which runs for hundreds of miles to the east, with the Barrier behind it and the Ross Sea beating into its crevasses and caves, joins the basalt precipice which bounds the Knoll, as the two-knobbed saddle which forms Cape Crozier is called. Altogether it is the kind of place where giants have had a good time in their childhood, playing with ice instead of mud—so much cleaner too!

But the slopes of Mount Terror do not all end in precipices. Farther to the west they slope quietly into the sea, and the Adélie penguins have taken advantage of this to found here one of their largest and most smelly rookeries. When the Discovery arrived off this rookery she sent a boat ashore and set up a post with a record upon it to guide the relief ship in the following year. The post still stands. Later it became desirable to bring the record left here more up to date, and so one of the first sledging parties went to try and find a way by the Barrier to this spot.

They were prevented from reaching the record by a series of most violent blizzards, and indeed Cape Crozier is one of the windiest places on earth, but they proved beyond doubt that a back-door to the Adélie penguins' rookery existed by way of the slopes of Mount Terror behind the Knoll. Early the next year another party reached the record all right, and while exploring the neighbourhood looked down over the 800-feet precipice which forms the snout of Cape Crozier. The sea was frozen over, and in a small bay of ice formed by the cliffs of the Barrier below were numerous little dots which resolved themselves into Emperor penguins. Could this be the breeding-place of these wonderful birds? If so, they must nurse their eggs in mid-winter, in unimagined cold and darkness.

Five days more elapsed before further investigation could be made, for a violent blizzard kept the party in their tents. On October 18 they set out to climb the high pressure ridges which lie between the level barrier and the sea. They found that their conjectures were right: there was the colony of Emperors. Several were nursing chicks, but all the ice in the Ross Sea was gone; only the small bay of ice remained. The number of adult birds was estimated at four hundred, the number of living chicks was thirty, and there were some eighty dead ones. No eggs were found.[18]

Several more journeys were made to this spot while the Discovery was in the south, generally in the spring; and the sum total of the information gained came to something like this. The Emperor is a bird which cannot fly, lives on fish which it catches in the sea, and never steps on land even to breed. For a reason which was not then understood it lays its eggs upon the bare ice some time during the winter and carries out the whole process of incubation on the sea ice, resting the egg upon its feet pressed closely to a patch of bare skin in the lower abdomen, and protected from the intense cold by a loose falling lappet of skin and feathers. By September 12, the earliest date upon which a party arrived, all the eggs which were not broken or addled were hatched, and there were then about a thousand adult Emperors in the rookery. Arriving again on October 19, a party experienced a ten days' blizzard which confined them during seven days to their tents, but during their windy visit they saw one of the most interesting scenes in natural history. The story must be told by Wilson, who was there:

"The day before the storm broke we were on an old outlying cone of Mount Terror, about 1300 feet above the sea. Below us lay the Emperor penguin rookery on the bay ice, and Ross Sea, completely frozen over, was a plain of firm white ice to the horizon. There was not even the lane of open water which usually runs along the Barrier cliff stretching away as it does like a winding thread to the east and out of sight. No space or crack could be seen with open water. Nevertheless the Emperors were unsettled owing, there can be no doubt, to the knowledge that bad weather was impending. The mere fact that the usual canal of open water was not to be seen along the face of the Barrier meant that the ice in Ross Sea had a southerly drift. This in itself was unusual, and was caused by a northerly wind

[18] See Scott, *Voyage of the Discovery*, vol. ii. pp. 5, 6, 490.

with snow, the precursor here of a storm from the south-west. The sky looked black and threatening, the barometer began to fall, and before long down came snowflakes on the upper heights of Mount Terror.

"All these warnings were an open book to the Emperor penguins, and if one knew the truth there probably were many others too. They were in consequence unsettled, and although the ice had not yet started moving the Emperor penguins had; a long file was moving out from the bay to the open ice, where a pack of some one or two hundred had already collected about two miles out at the edge of a refrozen crack. For an hour or more that afternoon we watched this exodus proceeding, and returned to camp, more than ever convinced that bad weather might be expected. Nor were we disappointed, for on the next day we woke to a southerly gale and smother of snow and drift, which effectually prevented any one of us from leaving our camp at all. This continued without intermission all day and night till the following morning, when the weather cleared sufficiently to allow us to reach the edge of the cliff which overlooked the rookery.

THE EMPERORS ROOKERY

"The change here was immense. Ross Sea was open water for nearly thirty miles; a long line of white pack ice was just visible on the horizon from where we stood, some 800 to 900 feet above the sea. Large sheets of ice were still going out and drifting to the north, and the migration of the Emperors was in full swing. There were again two companies waiting on the ice at the actual water's edge, with some hundred more tailing out in single file to join them. The birds were waiting far out at the edge of the open water, as far as it was possible for them to walk, on a projecting piece of ice, the very next piece that would break away and drift to the north. The line of tracks in the snow along which the birds had gone the day before was now cut off short at the edge of the open water, showing that they had gone, and under the ice-cliffs there was an appreciable diminution in the number of Emperors left, hardly more than half remaining of all that we had seen there six days before."[19]

Two days later the emigration was still in full swing, but only the unemployed seemed to have gone as yet. Those who were nursing chicks were still huddled under the ice-cliffs, sheltered as much as possible from the storm. Three days later (October 28) no ice was to be seen in the Ross Sea: the little bay of ice was gradually being eaten away: the same exodus was in progress and only a remnant of penguins was still left.

Of the conditions under which the Emperor lays her eggs, the darkness and cold and blighting winds, of the excessive mothering instinct implanted in the heart of every bird, male and female, of the mortality and gallant struggles against almost inconceivable odds, and the final survival of some 26 per cent of the eggs, I hope to tell in the account of our Winter Journey, the object of which was to throw light upon the development of the embryo of this remarkable bird, and through it upon the history of their ancestors. As Wilson wrote:

"The possibility that we have in the Emperor penguin the nearest approach to a primitive form not only of a penguin but of a bird makes the future working out of its embryology a matter of the greatest possible importance. It was a great disappointment to us that although we discovered their breeding-ground, and although we were able to bring home a number of deserted eggs and chicks, we were not able to procure a series of early embryos by which alone the points of particular interest can be worked out. To have done this in a proper manner from the spot at which the Discovery wintered in McMurdo Sound would have involved us in endless difficulties, for it would have entailed the risks of sledge travelling in mid-winter with an almost total absence of light. It would at any time require that a party of three at least, with full camp equipment, should traverse about a hundred miles of the Barrier surface in the dark and should, by moonlight, cross over with rope and axe the immense pressure ridges which form a chaos of crevasses at Cape Crozier. These ridges, moreover, which have taken a party as much as two hours of careful work to cross by daylight, must be crossed and re-crossed at every visit to the breeding site in the bay. There is no possibility even by daylight of conveying over them the sledge or camping kit, and in the darkness of mid-winter the impracticability is still more obvious. Cape Crozier is a focus for wind and storm, where every breath is converted, by the configuration of Mounts Erebus and Terror, into a regular drifting blizzard full of snow. It is here, as I have already stated, that on one journey or another we have had to lie patiently in sodden sleeping-bags for as many as five and seven days on end, waiting for the weather to change and make it possible for us to leave our tents at all. If, however, these dangers were overcome there would still be the difficulty of making the needful preparations from the eggs. The party would have to be on the scene at any rate early in July. Supposing that no eggs were found upon arrival, it would be well to spend the time in labelling the most likely birds, those for example that have taken up their stations close underneath the ice-cliffs. And if this were done it would be easier then to examine them daily by moonlight, if it and the weather

[19] Wilson, *Nat. Ant. Exp., 1901-1904*, "Zoology," Part ii. pp. 8-9.

generally were suitable: conditions, I must confess, not always easily obtained at Cape Crozier. But if by good luck things happened to go well, it would by this time be useful to have a shelter built of snow blocks on the sea-ice in which to work with the cooking lamp to prevent the freezing of the egg before the embryo was cut out, and in order that fluid solutions might be handy for the various stages of its preparation; for it must be borne in mind that the temperature all the while may be anything between zero and -50° F. The whole work no doubt would be full of difficulty, but it would not be quite impossible, and it is with a view to helping those to whom the opportunity may occur in future that this outline has been added of the difficulties that would surely beset their path."[20]

We shall meet the Emperor penguins again, but now we must go back to the Discovery, lying off Hut Point, with the season advancing and twenty miles of ice between her and the open sea. The prospects of getting out this year seeming almost less promising than those of the last year, an abortive attempt was made to saw a channel from a half-way point. Still, life to Scott and Wilson in a tent at Cape Royds was very pleasant after sledging, and the view of the blue sea framed in the tent door was very beautiful on a morning in January when two ships sailed into the frame. Why two? One was of course the Morning; the second proved to be the Terra Nova.

It seemed that the authorities at home had been alarmed at the reports brought back the previous year by the relief ship of the detention of the Discovery and certain outbreaks of scurvy which had occurred both on the ship and on sledge journeys. To make sure of relief two ships had been sent. That was nothing to worry about, but the orders they brought were staggering to sailors who had come to love their ship "with a depth of sentiment which cannot be surprising when it is remembered what we had been through in her and what a comfortable home she had proved."[21] Scott was ordered to abandon the Discovery if she could not be freed in time to accompany the relief ships to the north. For weeks there was little or no daily change. They started to transport the specimens and make the other necessary preparations. They almost despaired of freedom. Explosions in the ice were started in the beginning of February with little effect. But suddenly there came a change, and on the 11th, amidst intense excitement, the ice was breaking up fast. The next day the relief ships were but four miles away. On the 14th a shout of "The ships are coming, sir!" brought out all the men racing to the slopes above Arrival Bay. Scott wrote:

"The ice was breaking up right across the Strait, and with a rapidity which we had not thought possible. No sooner was one great floe borne away than a dark streak cut its way into the solid sheet that remained, and carved out another, to feed the broad stream of pack which was hurrying away to the north-west.

"I have never witnessed a more impressive sight; the sun was low behind us, the surface of the ice-sheet in front was intensely white, and in contrast the distant sea and its leads looked almost black. The wind had fallen to a calm, and not a

[20] Wilson, *Nat. Ant. Exp., 1901-1904,* "Zoology," Part ii. p. 31.
[21] Scott, *Voyage of the Discovery,* vol. ii. p. 327.

sound disturbed the stillness about us.

"Yet in the midst of this peaceful silence was an awful unseen agency rending that great ice-sheet as though it had been naught but the thinnest paper. We knew well by this time the nature of our prison bars; we had not plodded again and again over those long dreary miles of snow without realizing the formidable strength of the great barrier which held us bound; we knew that the heaviest battle-ship would have shattered itself ineffectually against it, and we had seen a million-ton iceberg brought to rest at its edge. For weeks we had been struggling with this mighty obstacle ... but now without a word, without an effort on our part, it was all melting away, and we knew that in an hour or two not a vestige of it would be left, and that the open sea would be lapping on the black rocks of Hut Point."[22]

Almost more dramatic was the grounding of the Discovery off the shoal at Hut Point owing to the rise of a blizzard immediately after her release from the ice. Hour after hour she lay pounding on the shore, and when it seemed most certain that she had been freed only to be destroyed, and when all hope was nearly gone, the wind lulled, and the waters of the Sound, driven out by the force of the wind, returned and the Discovery floated off with little damage. The whole story of the release from the ice and subsequent grounding of the Discovery is wonderfully told by Scott in his book.

Some years after this I met Wilson in a shooting lodge in Scotland. He was working upon grouse disease for the Royal Commission which had been appointed, and I saw then for the first time something of his magnetic personality and glimpses also of his methods of work. He and Scott both meant to go back and finish the job, and I then settled that when they went I would go too if wishing could do anything. Meanwhile Shackleton was either in the South or making his preparations to go there.

He left England in 1908, and in the following Antarctic summer two wonderful journeys were made. The first, led by Shackleton himself, consisted of four men and four ponies. Leaving Cape Royds, where the expedition wintered in a hut, in November, they marched due south on the Barrier outside Scott's track until they were stopped by the eastward trend of the range of mountains, and by the chaotic pressure caused by the discharge of a Brobdingnagian glacier.

But away from the main stream of the glacier, and separated from it by land now known as Hope Island, was a narrow and steep snow slope forming a gateway which opened on to the main glacier stream. Boldly plunging through this, the party made its way up the Beardmore Glacier, a giant of its kind, being more than twice as large as any other known. The history of their adventures will make anybody's flesh creep. From the top they travelled due south toward the Pole under the trying conditions of the plateau and reached the high latitude of 88° 23′ S. before they were forced to turn by lack of food.

While Shackleton was essaying the geographical Pole another party of three men under Professor David reached the magnetic Pole, travelling a distance of 1260 miles, of which 740 miles were relay work, relying entirely on man-haulage,

---

[22] Scott, *The Voyage of the Discovery*, vol. ii. pp. 347-348.

and with no additional help. This was a very wonderful journey, and when Shackleton returned in 1909 he and his expedition had made good. During the same year the North Pole was reached by Peary after some twelve years of travelling in Arctic regions.

Scott published the plans of his second expedition in 1909. This expedition is the subject of the present history.

The Terra Nova sailed from the West India Dock, London, on June 1, 1910, and from Cardiff on June 15. She made her way to New Zealand, refitted and restowed her cargo, took on board ponies, dogs, motor sledges, certain further provisions and equipment, as well as such members of her executive officers and scientists as had not travelled out in her, and left finally for the South on November 29, 1910. She arrived in McMurdo Sound on January 4, 1911, and our hut had been built on Cape Evans and all stores landed in less than a fortnight. Shortly afterwards the ship sailed. The party which was left at Cape Evans under Scott is known as the Main Party.

But the scientific objects of the expedition included the landing of a second but much smaller party under Campbell on King Edward VII.'s Land. While returning from an abortive attempt to land here they found a Norwegian expedition under Captain Roald Amundsen in Nansen's old ship the Fram in the Bay of Whales: reference to this expedition will be found elsewhere.[23] One member of Amundsen's party was Johansen, the only companion of Nansen on his famous Arctic sledge journey, of which a brief outline has been given above.[24] Campbell and his five companions were finally landed at Cape Adare, and built their hut close to Borchgrevinck's old winter quarters.[25] The ship returned to New Zealand under Pennell: came back to the Antarctic a year later with further equipment and provisions, and again two years later to bring back to civilization the survivors of the expedition.

The adventures and journeyings of the various members of the Main Party are so numerous and simultaneous that I believe it will help the reader who approaches this book without previous knowledge of the history of the expedition to give here a brief summary of the course of events. Those who are familiar already with these facts can easily skip a page or two.

Two parties were sent out during the first autumn: the one under Scott to lay a large depôt on the Barrier for the Polar Journey, and this is called the Depôt Journey; the other to carry out geological work among the Western Mountains, so called because they form the western side of McMurdo Sound: this is called the First Geological Journey, and another similar journey during the following summer is called the Second Geological Journey.

Both parties joined up at the old Discovery Hut at Hut Point in March 1911, and here waited for the sea to freeze a passage northwards to Cape Evans. Meanwhile the men left at Cape Evans were continuing the complex scientific work of

[23] See pp. 128-134.
[24] See pp. xxxi-xxxii.
[25] See p. xxviii.

the station. All the members of the Main Party were not gathered together at Cape Evans for the winter until May 12. During the latter half of the winter a journey was made by three men led by Wilson to Cape Crozier to investigate the embryology of the Emperor penguin: this is called the Winter Journey.

The journey to the South Pole absorbed the energies of most of the sledging members during the following summer of 1911-12. The motor party turned back on the Barrier; the dog party at the bottom of the Beardmore Glacier. From this point twelve men went forward. Four of these men under Atkinson returned from the top of the glacier in latitude 85° 3′ S.: they are known as the First Return Party. A fortnight later in latitude 87° 32′ S. three more men returned under Lieutenant Evans: these are the Second Return Party. Five men went forward, Scott, Wilson, Bowers, Oates and Seaman Evans. They reached the Pole on January 17 to find that Amundsen had reached it thirty-four days earlier. They returned 721 statute miles and perished 177 miles from their winter quarters.

The supporting parties got back safely, but Lieutenant Evans was very seriously ill with scurvy. The food necessary for the return of the Polar Party from One Ton Camp had not been taken out at the end of February 1912. Evans' illness caused a hurried reorganization of plans, and I was ordered to take out this food with one lad and two dog-teams. This was done, and the journey may be called the Dog Journey to One Ton Camp.

We must now go back to the six men led by Campbell who were landed at Cape Adare in the beginning of 1911. They were much disappointed by the small amount of sledge work which they were able to do in the summer of 1911-1912, for the sea-ice in front of them was blown out early in the year, and they were unable to find a way up through the mountains behind them on to the plateau. Therefore, when the Terra Nova appeared on January 4, it was decided that she should land them with six weeks' sledging rations and some extra biscuits, pemmican and general food near Mount Melbourne at Evans Coves, some 250 geographical miles south of Cape Adare, and some 200 geographical miles from our Winter Quarters at Cape Evans. Late on the night of January 8, 1912, they were camped in this spot and saw the last of the ship steaming out of the bay. They had arranged to be picked up again on February 18.

Let us return to McMurdo Sound. My two dog-teams arrived at Hut Point from One Ton Depôt on March 16 exhausted. The sea-ice was still in from the Barrier to Hut Point, but from there onwards was open water, and therefore no communication was possible with Cape Evans. Atkinson, with one seaman, was at Hut Point and the situation which he outlined to me on arrival was something as follows:

The ship had left and there was now no possibility of her returning owing to the lateness of the season, and she carried in her Lieut. Evans, sick with scurvy, and five other officers and three men who were returning home this year. This left only four officers and four men at Cape Evans, in addition to the four of us at Hut Point.

The serious part of the news was that owing to a heavy pack the ship had been absolutely unable to reach Campbell's party at Evans Coves. Attempt after attempt had made without success. Would Campbell winter where he was? Would he try to sledge down the coast?

In the absence of Scott the command of the expedition under the extraordinarily difficult circumstances which arose, both now and during the coming year, would naturally have devolved upon Lieutenant Evans. But Evans, very sick, was on his way to England. The task fell to Atkinson, and I hope that these pages will show how difficult it was, and how well he tackled it.

There were now, that is since the arrival of the dog-teams four of us at Hut Point; and no help could be got from Cape Evans owing to the open water which intervened. Two of us were useless for further sledging and the dogs were absolutely done. As time went on anxiety concerning the non-arrival of the Polar Party was added to the alarm we already felt about Campbell and his men; winter was fast closing down, and the weather was bad. So little could be done by two men. What was to be done? When was it to be done with the greatest possible chance of success? Added to all his greater anxieties Atkinson had me on his hands—and I was pretty ill.

In the end he made two attempts.

The first with one seaman, Keohane, to sledge out on to the Barrier, leaving on March 26. They found the conditions very bad, but reached a point a few miles south of Corner Camp and returned. Soon after we knew the Southern Party must be dead.

Nothing more could be done until communication was effected with Winter Quarters at Cape Evans. This was done by a sledge journey over the newly frozen ice in the bays on April 10. Help arrived at Hut Point on April 14.

The second attempt was then made, and this consisted of a party of four men who tried to sledge up the Western Coast in order to meet and help Campbell if he was trying to sledge to us. This plucky attempt failed, as indeed it was practically certain it would.

The story of the winter that followed will be told, and of the decision which had to be taken to abandon either the search for the Polar Party (who must be dead) and their records, or Campbell and his men (who might be alive). There were not enough men left to do both. We believed that the Polar Party had come to grief through scurvy, or through falling into a crevasse—the true solution never occurred to us, for we felt sure that except for accident or disease they could find their way home without difficulty. We decided to leave Campbell to find his way unaided down the coast, and to try and find the Polar Party's records. To our amazement we found their snowed-up tent some 140 geographical miles from Hut Point, only 11 geographical miles from One Ton Camp. They had arrived there on March 19. Inside the tent were the bodies of Scott, Wilson and Bowers. Oates had willingly walked out to his death some eighteen miles before in a blizzard. Seaman Evans lay dead at the bottom of the Beardmore Glacier.

Having found the bodies and the records the Search Party returned, proposing to make their way up the Western Coast in search of Campbell. On arrival at Hut Point with the dog-teams, I must have gone to open the hut door and found pinned on to it a note in Campbell's handwriting; but my recollection of this apparently memorable incident is extraordinarily vague. It was many long months since we had had good news. This was their story.

When Campbell originally landed at Evans Coves he brought with him sledging provisions for six weeks, in addition to two weeks' provisions for six men, 56 lbs. sugar, 24 lbs. cocoa, 36 lbs. chocolate and 210 lbs. of biscuit, some Oxo and spare clothing. In short, after the sledge work which they proposed, and actually carried out, the men were left with skeleton rations for four weeks. They had also a spare tent and an extra sleeping-bag. It was not seriously anticipated that the ship would have great difficulty in picking them up in the latter half of February.

Campbell's party had carried out successful sledging and useful geological work in the region of Evans Coves. They had then camped on the beach and looked for the ship to relieve them. There was open water lashed to fury by the wind so far as they could see, and yet she did not come. They concluded that she must have been wrecked. The actual fact was that thick pack ice lay beyond their vision through which Pennell was trying to drive his ship time after time, until he had either to go or to be frozen in. He never succeeded in approaching nearer than 27 miles.

It was now that a blizzard wind started to blow down from the plateau behind them out into the continually open sea in front. The situation was bad enough already, but of course such weather conditions made it infinitely worse. Evans Coves is paved with boulders over which all journeys had to be fought leaning against the wind as it blew: when a lull came the luckless traveller fell forward on to his face. Under these circumstances it was decided that preparations must be made to winter where they were, and to sledge down the coast to Cape Evans in the following spring. The alternative of sledging down the coast in March and April never seems to have been seriously considered. At Hut Point, of course, we were entirely in the dark as to what the party would do, hence Atkinson's journey over to the western side in April 1912.

Meanwhile the stranded men divided into two parties of three men each. The first under Campbell sank a shaft six feet down into a large snow-drift and thence, with pick and shovel, excavated a passage and at the end of it a cave, twelve feet by nine feet, and five feet six inches high. The second under Levick sought out and killed all the seal and penguin they could find, but their supply was pitifully small, and the men never had a full meal until mid-winter night. One man always had to be left to look after the tents, which were already so worn and damaged that it was unsafe to leave them in the wind.

By March 17 the cave was sufficiently advanced for three men to move in. Priestley must tell how this was done, but it should not be supposed that the weather conditions were in any way abnormal on what they afterwards called Inexpressible Island:

"March 17. 7 p.m. Strong south-west breeze all day, freshening to a full gale at night. We have had an awful day, but have managed to shift enough gear into the cave to live there temporarily. Our tempers have never been so tried during the whole of our life together, but they have stood the strain pretty successfully.... May I never have such another three trips as were those to-day. Every time the wind lulled a little I fell over to windward, and at every gust I was pitched to leeward, while a dozen times or more I was taken off my feet and dashed against the ground or against unfriendly boulders. The other two had equally bad times. Dickason hurt his knee and ankle and lost his sheath knife, and Campbell lost a compass and some revolver cartridges in the two trips they made. Altogether it was lucky we got across at all."[26]

It was a fortunate thing that this wind often blew quite clear without snowfall or drift. Two days later in the same gale the tent of the other three men collapsed on top of them at 8 A.M. At 4 P.M. the sun was going down and they settled to make their way across to their comrades. Levick tells the story as follows:

"Having done this [securing the remains of the tent, etc.], we started on our journey. This lay, first of all, across half a mile of clear blue ice, swept by the unbroken wind, which met us almost straight in the face. We could never stand up, so had to scramble the whole distance on 'all fours,' lying flat on our bellies in the gusts. By the time we had reached the other side we had had enough. Our faces had been rather badly bitten, and I have a very strong recollection of the men's countenances, which were a leaden blue, streaked with white patches of frost-bite. Once across, however, we reached the shelter of some large boulders on the shore of the island, and waited here long enough to thaw out our noses, ears, and cheeks. A scramble of another six hundred yards brought us to the half-finished igloo, into which we found that the rest of the party had barricaded themselves, and, after a little shouting, they came and let us in, giving us a warm welcome, and about the most welcome hot meal that I think any of us had ever eaten."

---

[26] Priestley, *Antarctic Adventure*, pp. 232-233.

PRIESTLEY AND CAMPBELL

Priestley continues:

"After the arrival of the evicted party we made hoosh, and as we warmed up from the meal, we cheered up and had one of the most successful sing-songs we had ever had forgetting all our troubles for an hour or two. It is a pleasing picture to look back upon now, and, if I close my eyes, I can see again the little cave cut out in snow and ice with the tent flapping in the doorway, barely secured by ice-axe and shovel arranged crosswise against the side of the shaft. The cave is lighted up with three or four small blubber lamps, which give a soft yellow light. At one end lie Campbell, Dickason and myself in our sleeping-bags, resting after the day's work, and, opposite to us, on a raised dais formed by a portion of the floor not yet levelled, Levick, Browning and Abbott sit discussing their seal hoosh, while the primus hums cheerily under the cooker containing the coloured water which served with us instead of cocoa. As the diners warm up jests begin to fly between the rival tents and the interchange is brisk, though we have the upper hand to-day, having an inexhaustible subject in the recent disaster to their tent, and their forced abandonment of their household gods. Suddenly some one starts a song with a chorus, and the noise from the primus is dwarfed immediately. One by one we go through our favourites, and the concert lasts for a couple of hours. By this time the lamps are getting low, and gradually the cold begins to overcome the effects of the hoosh and the cocoa. One after another the singers begin to shiver, and all thoughts of song disappear as we realize what we are in for. A night with one one-man bag between two men! There is a whole world of discomfort in the very thought, and no one feels inclined to jest about that for the moment. Those jests will come all right to-morrow when the night is safely past, but this evening it is anything but a cheery subject of contemplation. There is no help for it, however, and each of us prepares to take another man in so far as he can."[27]

In such spirit and under very similar conditions this dauntless party set about passing through one of the most horrible winters which God has invented. They were very hungry, for the wind which kept the sea open also made the shore almost impossible for seals. There were red-letter days, however, such as when Browning found and killed a seal, and in its stomach, "not too far digested to be still eatable," were thirty-six fish. And what visions of joy for the future. "We never again found a seal with an eatable meal inside him, but we were always hoping to do so, and a kill was, therefore, always a gamble. Whenever a seal was sighted in future, some one said, 'Fish!' and there was always a scramble to search the beast first."[28]

They ate blubber, cooked with blubber, had blubber lamps. Their clothes and gear were soaked with blubber, and the soot blackened them, their sleeping-bags, cookers, walls and roof, choked their throats and inflamed their eyes. Blubbery clothes are cold, and theirs were soon so torn as to afford little protection against the wind, and so stiff with blubber that they would stand up by themselves, in spite of frequent scrapings with knives and rubbings with penguin skins, and always there were underfoot the great granite boulders which made walking difficult even in daylight and calm weather. As Levick said, "the road to hell might be paved with good intentions, but it seemed probable that hell itself would be paved something after the style of Inexpressible Island."

But there were consolations; the long-waited-for lump of sugar: the sing-songs—and about these there hangs a story. When Campbell's Party and the remains of the Main Party forgathered at Cape Evans in November 1912, Campbell would give out the hymns for Church. The first Sunday we had 'Praise the Lord, ye heavens adore Him,' and the second, and the third. We suggested a change, to which Campbell asked, "Why?" We said it got a bit monotonous. "Oh no," said Campbell, "we always sang it on Inexpressible Island." It was also about the only one he knew. Apart from this I do not know whether 'Old King Cole' or the Te Deum was more popular. For reading they had David Copperfield, the Decameron, the Life of Stevenson and a New Testament. And they did Swedish drill, and they gave lectures.

---

[27] Priestley, *Antarctic Adventure*, pp. 236-237.
[28] Priestley, *Antarctic Adventure*, p. 243.

Their worst difficulties were scurvy[29] and ptomaine poisoning, for which the enforced diet was responsible. From the first they decided to keep nearly all their unused rations for sledging down the coast in the following spring, and this meant that they must live till then on the seal and penguin which they could kill. The first dysentery was early in the winter, and was caused by using the salt from the sea-water. They had some Cerebos salt, however, in their sledging rations, and used it for a week, which stopped the disorder and they gradually got used to the sea-ice salt. Browning, however, who had had enteric fever in the past, had dysentery almost continually right through the winter. Had he not been the plucky, cheerful man he is, he would have died.

In June again there was another bad attack of dysentery. Another thing which worried them somewhat was the 'igloo back,' a semi-permanent kink caused by seldom being able to stand upright.

Then, in the beginning of September, they had ptomaine poisoning from meat which had been too long in what they called the oven, which was a biscuit box, hung over the blubber stove, into which they placed the frozen meat to thaw it out. This oven was found to be not quite level, and in a corner a pool of old blood, water and scraps of meat had collected. This and a tainted hoosh which they did not have the strength of mind to throw away in their hungry condition, seems to have caused the outbreak, which was severe. Browning and Dickason were especially bad.

They had their bad days: those first days of realization that they would not be relieved: days of depression, disease and hunger, all at once: when the seal seemed as if they would give out and they were thinking they would have to travel down the coast in the winter—but Abbott killed two seals with a greasy knife, losing the use of three fingers in the process, and saved the situation.

But they also had their good, or less-bad, days: such was mid-winter night when they held food in their hands and did not want to eat it, for they were full: or when they got through the Te Deum without a hitch: or when they killed some penguins; or got a ration of mustard plaster from the medical stores.

Never was a more cheerful or good-tempered party. They set out to see the humorous side of everything, and, if they could not do so one day, at any rate they determined to see to it the next. What is more they succeeded, and I have never seen a company of better welded men than that which joined us for those last two months in McMurdo Sound.

On September 30 they started home—so they called it. This meant a sledge journey of some two hundred miles along the coast, and its possibility depended upon the presence of sea-ice, which we have seen to have been absent at Evans Coves. It also meant crossing the Drygalski Ice Tongue, an obstacle which bulked very formidably in their imaginations during the winter. They reached the last rise of this glacier in the evening of October 10, and then saw Erebus, one hundred and

---

[29] Atkinson has no doubt that the symptoms of the Northern Party were those of early scurvy. Conditions of temperature in the igloo allowed of decomposition occurring in seal meat. Fresh seal meat brought in from outside reduced the scurvy symptoms.

fifty miles off. The igloo and the past were behind: Cape Evans and the future were in front—and the sea-ice was in as far as they could see.

Dickason was half crippled with dysentery when they started, but improved. Browning, however, was still very ill, but now they were able to eat a ration of four biscuits a day and a small amount of pemmican and cocoa which gave him a better chance than the continual meat. As they neared Granite Harbour, a month after starting, his condition was so serious that they discussed leaving him there with Levick until they could get medicine and suitable food from Cape Evans.

But their troubles were nearly over, for on reaching Cape Roberts they suddenly sighted the depôt left by Taylor in the previous year. They searched round, like dogs, scratching in the drifts, and found—a whole case of biscuits: and there were butter and raisins and lard. Day and night merged into one long lingering feast, and when they started on again their mouths were sore[30] with eating biscuits. More, there is little doubt that the change of diet saved Browning's life. As they moved down the coast they found another depôt, and yet another. They reached Hut Point on November 5.

The story of this, our Northern Party, has been told in full by the two men most able to tell it: by Campbell in the second volume of Scott's book, by Priestley in a separate volume called Antarctic Adventure.[31] I have added only these few pages because, save in so far as their adventures touch the Main Party or the Ship, it is better that I should refer the reader to these two accounts than that I should try and write again at second hand what has been already twice told. I will only say here that the history of what these men did and suffered has been overshadowed by the more tragic tale of the Polar Party. They are not men who wish for public applause, but that is no reason why the story of a great adventure should not be known; indeed, it is all the more reason why it should be known. To those who have not read it I recommend Priestley's book mentioned above, or Campbell's equally modest account in Scott's Last Expedition.[32]

The Terra Nova arrived at Cape Evans on January 18, 1913, just as we had started to prepare for another year. And so the remains of the expedition came home that spring. Scott's book was published in the autumn.

The story of Scott's Last Expedition of 1910-13 is a book of two volumes, the first volume of which is Scott's personal diary of the expedition, written from day to day before he turned into his sleeping-bag for the night when sledging, or in the intervals of the many details of organization and preparation in the hut, when at Winter Quarters. The readers of this book will probably have read that diary and the accounts of the Winter Journey, the last year, the adventures of Campbell's Party and the travels of the Terra Nova which follow. With an object which I will explain presently I quote a review of Scott's book from the pen of one of Mr. Punch's staff:[33]

[30] This tenderness of gums and tongue is additional evidence of scurvy.
[31] Published by Fisher Unwin, 1914.
[32] Vol. ii., Narrative of the Northern Party.
[33] A. A. Milne.

"There is courage and strength and loyalty and love shining out of the second volume no less than out of the first; there were gallant gentlemen who lived as well as gallant gentlemen who died; but it is the story of Scott, told by himself, which will give the book a place among the great books of the world. That story begins in November 1910, and ends on March 29, 1912, and it is because when you come to the end, you will have lived with Scott for sixteen months, that you will not be able to read the last pages without tears. That message to the public was heartrending enough when it first came to us, but it was as the story of how a great hero fell that we read it; now it is just the tale of how a dear friend died. To have read this book is to have known Scott; and if I were asked to describe him, I think I should use some such words as those which, six months before he died, he used of the gallant gentleman who went with him, 'Bill' Wilson. 'Words must always fail when I talk of him,' he wrote; 'I believe he is the finest character I ever met—the closer one gets to him the more there is to admire. Every quality is so solid and dependable. Whatever the matter, one knows Bill will be sound, shrewdly practical, intensely loyal, and quite unselfish.' That is true of Wilson, if Scott says so, for he knew men; but most of it is also true of Scott himself. I have never met a more beautiful character than that which is revealed unconsciously in these journals. His humanity, his courage, his faith, his steadfastness, above all, his simplicity, mark him as a man among men. It is because of his simplicity that his last message, the last entries in his diary, his last letters, are of such undying beauty. The letter of consolation (and almost of apology) which, on the verge of death, he wrote to Mrs. Wilson, wife of the man dying at his side, may well be Scott's monument. He could have no finer. And he has raised a monument for those other gallant gentlemen who died—Wilson, Oates, Bowers, Evans. They are all drawn for us clearly by him in these pages; they stand out unmistakably. They, too, come to be friends of ours, their death is as noble and as heartbreaking. And there were gallant gentlemen, I said, who lived—you may read amazing stories of them. Indeed, it is a wonderful tale of manliness that these two volumes tell us. I put them down now; but I have been for a few days in the company of the brave ... and every hour with them has made me more proud for those that died and more humble for myself."

I have quoted this review at length, because it gives the atmosphere of hero-worship into which we were plunged on our return. That atmosphere was very agreeable; but it was a refracting medium through which the expedition could not be seen with scientific accuracy—and the expedition was nothing if not scientific. Whilst we knew what we had suffered and risked better than any one else, we also knew that science takes no account of such things; that a man is no better for having made the worst journey in the world; and that whether he returns alive or drops by the way will be all the same a hundred years hence if his records and specimens come safely to hand.

In addition to Scott's Last Expedition and Priestley's Antarctic Adventures, Griffith Taylor, who was physiographer to the Main Party, has written an account of the two geological journeys of which he was the leader, and of the domestic life of the expedition at Hut Point and at Cape Evans, up to February 1912, in a book called With Scott: The Silver Lining. This book gives a true glimpse into the more boisterous side of our life, with much useful information about the scientific part.

Though it bears little upon this book I cannot refrain from drawing the reader's attention to, and earning some of his thanks for, a little book called Antarctic Penguins, written by Levick, the Surgeon of Campbell's Party. It is almost entirely about Adélie penguins. The author spent the greater part of a summer living, as it were, upon sufferance, in the middle of one of the largest penguin rookeries in the world. He has described the story of their crowded life with a humour with which, perhaps, we hardly credited him, and with a simplicity which many writers of children's stories might envy. If you think your own life hard, and would like to leave it for a short hour I recommend you to beg, borrow or steal this tale, and read and see how the penguins live. It is all quite true.

So there is already a considerable literature about the expedition, but no connected account of it as a whole. Scott's diary, had he lived, would merely have formed the basis of the book he would have written. As his personal diary it has an interest which no other book could have had. But a diary in this life is one of the only ways in which a man can blow off steam, and so it is that Scott's book accentuates the depression which used to come over him sometimes.

We have seen the importance which must attach to the proper record of improvements, weights and methods of each and every expedition. We have seen how Scott took the system developed by the Arctic Explorers at the point of development to which it had been brought by Nansen, and applied it for the first time to Antarctic sledge travelling. Scott's Voyage of the Discovery gives a vivid picture of mistakes rectified, and of improvements of every kind. Shackleton applied the knowledge they gained in his first expedition, Scott in this, his second and last. On the whole I believe this expedition was the best equipped there has ever been, when the double purpose, exploratory and scientific, for which it was organized, is taken into consideration. It is comparatively easy to put all your eggs into one basket, to organize your material and to equip and choose your men entirely for one object, whether it be the attainment of the Pole, or the running of a perfect series of scientific observations. Your difficulties increase many-fold directly you combine the one with the other, as was done in this case. Neither Scott nor the men with him would have gone for the Pole alone. Yet they considered the Pole to be an achievement worthy of a great attempt, and "We took risks, we knew we took them; things have come out against us, and therefore we have no cause for complaint...."

It is, it must be, of the first importance that a system, I will not say perfected, but developed, to a pitch of high excellence at such a cost should be handed down as completely as possible to those who are to follow. I want to so tell this story that the leader of some future Antarctic expedition, perhaps more than one, will be able to take it up and say: "I have here the material from which I can order the articles and quantities which will be wanted for so many men for such and such a time; I have also a record of how this material was used by Scott, of the plans of his journeys and how his plans worked out, and of the improvements which his parties were able to make on the spot or suggest for the future. I don't agree with such and such, but this is a foundation and will save me many months of work in preparation, and give me useful knowledge for the actual work of my expedition." If this book can guide the future explorer by the light of the past, it will not have been written in vain.

But this was not my main object in writing this book. When I undertook in 1913 to write, for the Antarctic Committee, an Official Narrative on condition that I was given a free hand, what I wanted to do above all things was to show what work was done; who did it; to whom the credit of the work was due; who took the responsibility; who did the hard sledging; and who pulled us through that last and most ghastly year when two parties were adrift, and God only knew what was best to be done; when, had things gone on much longer, men would undoubtedly have gone mad. There is no record of these things, though perhaps the world thinks there is. Generally as a mere follower, without much responsibility, and often scared out of my wits, I was in the thick of it all, and I know.

Unfortunately I could not reconcile a sincere personal confession with the decorous obliquity of an Official Narrative; and I found that I had put the Antarctic Committee in a difficulty from which I could rescue them only by taking the book off their hands; for it was clear that what I had written was not what is expected from a Committee, even though no member may disapprove of a word of it. A proper Official Narrative presented itself to our imaginations and sense of propriety as a quarto volume, uniform with the scientific reports, dustily invisible on Museum shelves, and replete with—in the words of my Commission—"times of starting, hours of march, ground and weather conditions," not very useful as material for future Antarcticists, and in no wise effecting any catharsis of the writer's conscience. I could not pretend that I had fulfilled these conditions; and so I decided to take the undivided responsibility on my own shoulders. None the less the Committee, having given me access to its information, is entitled to all the credit of a formal Official Narrative, without the least responsibility for the passages which I have studied to make as personal in style as possible, so that no greater authority may be attached to them than I deserve.

I need hardly add that the nine years' delay in the appearance of my book was caused by the war. Before I had recovered from the heavy overdraft made on my strength by the expedition I found myself in Flanders looking after a fleet of armoured cars. A war is like the Antarctic in one respect. There is no getting out of it with honour as long as you can put one foot before the other. I came back badly invalided; and the book had to wait accordingly.

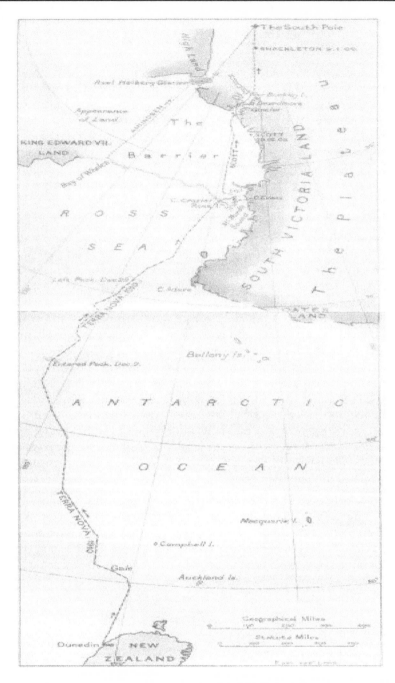

FROM NEW ZEALAND TO THE SOUTH POLE—APSLEY CHER-
RY-GARRARD, DEL.—EMERY WALKER LTD., COLLOTYPERS.

VOLUME I

CHAPTER I

FROM ENGLAND TO SOUTH AFRICA

Take a bowsy short leave of your nymphs on the shore,
And silence their mourning with vows of returning,
Though never intending to visit them more.

Dido and Aeneas.

Scott used to say that the worst part of an expedition was over when the preparation was finished. So no doubt it was with a sigh of relief that he saw the Terra Nova out from Cardiff into the Atlantic on June 15, 1910. Cardiff had given the expedition a most generous and enthusiastic send-off, and Scott announced that it should be his first port on returning to England. Just three years more and the Terra Nova, worked back from New Zealand by Pennell, reached Cardiff again on June 14, 1913, and paid off there.

From the first everything was informal and most pleasant, and those who had the good fortune to help in working the ship out to New Zealand, under steam or sail, must, in spite of five months of considerable discomfort and very hard work, look back upon the voyage as one of the very happiest times of the expedition. To some of us perhaps the voyage out, the three weeks in the pack ice going South, and the Robinson Crusoe life at Hut Point are the pleasantest of many happy memories.

Scott made a great point that so far as was possible the personnel of the expedition must go out with the Terra Nova. Possibly he gave instructions that they were to be worked hard, and no doubt it was a good opportunity of testing our mettle. We had been chosen out of 8000 volunteers, executive officers, scientific staff, crew, and all.

We differed entirely from the crew of an ordinary merchant ship both in our personnel and in our methods of working. The executive officers were drawn from the Navy, as were also the crew. In addition there was the scientific staff, including one doctor who was not a naval surgeon, but who was also a scientist, and two others called by Scott 'adaptable helpers,' namely Oates and myself. The scientific staff of the expedition numbered twelve members all told, but only six were on board: the remainder were to join the ship at Lyttelton, New Zealand, when we made our final embarcation for the South. Of those on the ship Wilson was chief of the scientific staff, and united in himself the various functions of vertebral zoologist, doctor, artist, and, as this book will soon show, the unfailing friend-in-need of all on board. Lieutenant Evans was in command, with Campbell as first officer.

Watches were of course assigned immediately to the executive officers. The crew was divided into a port and starboard watch, and the ordinary routine of a sailing ship with auxiliary steam was followed. Beyond this no work was definitely assigned to any individual on board. How the custom of the ship arose I do not know, but in effect most things were done by volunteer labour. It was recognized that every one whose work allowed turned to immediately on any job which was wanted, but it was an absolutely voluntary duty—Volunteers to shorten sail? To coal? To shift cargo? To pump? To paint or wash down paintwork? They were constant calls—some of them almost hourly calls, day and night—and there was never any failure to respond fully. This applied not only to the scientific staff but also, whenever their regular duties allowed, to the executive officers. There wasn't an officer on the ship who did not shift coal till he was sick of the sight of it, but I heard no complaints. Such a system soon singles out the real willing workers, but it is apt to put an undue strain upon them. Meanwhile most of the executive officers as well as the scientific staff had their own work to do, which they were left to fit in as most convenient.

The first days out from England were spent in such hard and crowded work that we shook down very quickly. I then noticed for the first time Wilson's great gift of tact, and how quick he was to see the small things which make so much difference. At the same time his passion for work set a high standard. Pennell was another glutton.

We dropped anchor in Funchal Harbour, Madeira, about 4 P.M. on June 23, eight days out. The ship had already been running under sail and steam, the decks were as clear as possible, there was some paintwork to show, and with a good harbour stow she looked thoroughly workmanlike and neat. Some scientific work, in particular tow netting and magnetic observations, had already been done. But even as early as this we had spent hours on the pumps, and it was evident that these pumps were going to be a constant nightmare.

In Madeira, as everywhere, we were given freely of such things as we required. We left in the early morning of June 26, after Pennell had done some hours' magnetic work with the Lloyd Creak and Barrow Dip Circle.

On June 29 (noon position lat. 27° 10′ N., long. 20° 21′ W.) it was possible to write: "A fortnight out to-day, and from the general appearance of the wardroom we might have been out a year."

We were to a great extent strangers to one another when we left England, but officers and crew settled down to their jobs quickly, and when men live as close as we did they settle down or quarrel before very long. Let us walk into the cabins which surround the small wardroom aft. The first on the left is that of Scott and Lieutenant Evans, but Scott is not on board, and Wilson has taken his place. In the next cabin to them is Drake, the secretary. On the starboard side of the screw are Oates, Atkinson and Levick, the two latter being doctors, and on the port side Campbell and Pennell, who is navigator. Then Rennick and Bowers, the latter just home from the Persian Gulf—both of these are watchkeepers. In the next cabin are Simpson, meteorologist, back from Simla, with Nelson and Lillie, marine biologists. In the last cabin, the Nursery, are the youngest, and necessarily the best behaved, of this community, Wright, the physicist and chemist, Gran the Norwegian ski-expert, and myself, Wilson's helper and assistant zoologist. It is difficult to put a man down as performing any special job where each did so many, but that is roughly what we were.

Certain men already began to stand out. Wilson, with an apparently inexhaustible stock of knowledge on little things and big; always ready to give help, and always ready with sympathy and insight, a tremendous worker, and as unselfish as possible; a universal adviser. Pennell, as happy as the day was long, working out sights, taking his watch on the bridge, or if not on watch full of energy aloft, trimming coal, or any other job that came along; withal spending hours a day on magnetic work, which he did as a hobby, and not in any way as his job. Bowers was proving himself the best seaman on board, with an exact knowledge of the whereabouts and contents of every case, box and bale, and with a supreme contempt for heat or cold. Simpson was obviously a first-class scientist, devoted to his work, in which Wright gave him very great and unselfish help, while at the same time doing much of the ship's work. Oates and Atkinson generally worked together in a solid, dependable and somewhat humorous way.

Evans, who will always be called Lieutenant Evans in this book to distinguish him from Seaman Evans, was in charge of the ship, and did much to cement together the rough material into a nucleus which was capable of standing without any friction the strains of nearly three years of crowded, isolated and difficult life, ably seconded by Victor Campbell, first officer, commonly called The Mate, in whose hands the routine and discipline of the ship was most efficiently maintained. I was very frightened of Campbell.

Scott himself was unable to travel all the way out to New Zealand in the Terra Nova owing to the business affairs of the expedition, but he joined the ship from Simon's Bay to Melbourne.

The voyage itself on the sailing track from Madeira to the Cape was at first uneventful. We soon got into hot weather, and at night every available bit of deck space was used on which to sleep. The more particular slung hammocks, but generally men used such deck space as they could find, such as the top of the icehouse, where they were free from the running tackle, and rolled themselves into their blankets. So long as we had a wind we ran under sail alone, and on those days men would bathe over the side in the morning, but when the engines were going we could get the hose in the morning, which was preferred, especially after a shark was seen making for Bowers' red breast as he swam.

The scene on deck in the early morning was always interesting. All hands were roused before six and turned on to the pumps, for the ship was leaking considerably. Normally, the well showed about ten inches of water when the ship was dry. Before pumping, the sinker would show anything over two feet. The ship was generally dry after an hour to an hour and a half's pumping, and by that time we had had quite enough of it. As soon as the officer of the watch had given the order, "Vast pumping," the first thing to do was to strip, and the deck was dotted with men trying to get the maximum amount of water from the sea in a small bucket let down on a line from the moving ship. First efforts in this direction would have been amusing had it not been for the caustic eye of the 'Mate' on the bridge. If the reader ever gets the chance to try the experiment, especially in a swell, he will soon find himself with neither bucket nor water. The poor Mate was annoyed by the loss of his buckets.

Everybody was working very hard during these days; shifting coal, reefing and furling sail aloft, hauling on the ropes on deck, together with magnetic and meteorological observations, tow-netting, collecting and making skins and so forth. During the first weeks there was more cargo stowing and paintwork than at other times, otherwise the work ran in very much the same lines all the way out—a period of nearly five months. On July 1 we were overhauled by the only ship we ever saw, so far as I can remember, during all that time, the Inverclyde, a barque out from Glasgow to Buenos Ayres. It was an oily, calm day with a sea like glass, and she looked, as Wilson quoted, "like a painted ship upon a painted ocean," as she lay with all sail set.

We picked up the N.E. Trade two days later, being then north of the Cape Verde Islands (lat. 22° 28′ N., long. 23° 5′ W. at noon). It was a Sunday, and there was a general 'make and mend' throughout the ship, the first since we sailed. During the day we ran from deep clear blue water into a darkish and thick green sea. This remarkable change of colour, which was observed by the Discovery Expedition in much the same place, was supposed to be due to a large mass of pelagic fauna called plankton. The plankton, which drifts upon the surface of the sea, is distinct from the nekton, which swims submerged. The Terra Nova was fitted with tow nets with very fine meshes for collecting these inhabitants of the open sea, together with the algae, or minute plant organisms, which afford them an abundant food supply.

The plankton nets can be lowered when the ship is running at full speed, and a great many such hauls were made during the expedition.

July 5 had an unpleasant surprise in store. At 10.30 A.M. the ship's bell rang and there was a sudden cry of "Fire quarters." Two Minimax fire extinguishers finished the fire, which was in the lazarette, and was caused by a lighted lamp which was upset by the roll of the ship. The result was a good deal of smoke, a certain amount of water below, and some singed paper, but we realized that a fire on such an old wooden ship would be a very serious matter, and greater care was taken after this.

Such a voyage shows Nature in her most attractive form, and always there was a man close by whose special knowledge was in the whales, porpoises, dolphins, fish, birds, parasites, plankton, radium and other things which we watched through microscopes or field-glasses. Nelson caught a Portuguese man-of-war (Arethusa) as it sailed past us close under the counter. These animals are common, but few can realize how beautiful they are until they see them, fresh-coloured from the deep sea, floating and sailing in a big glass bowl. It vainly tried to sail out, and vigorously tried to sting all who touched it. Wilson painted it.

From first to last the study of life of all kinds was of absorbing interest to all on board, and, when we landed in the Antarctic, as well as on the ship, everybody worked and was genuinely interested in all that lived and had its being on the fringe of that great sterile continent. Not only did officers who had no direct interest in anything but their own particular work or scientific subject spend a large part of their time in helping, making notes and keeping observations, but the seamen also had a large share in the specimens and data of all descriptions which have been brought back. Several of them became good pupils for skinning birds.

Meanwhile, perhaps the constant cries of "Whale, whale!" or "New bird!" or "Dolphins!" sometimes found the biologist concerned less eager to leave his meal than the observers were to call him forth. Good opportunities of studying the life of sea birds, whales, dolphins and other forms of life in the sea, even those comparatively few forms which are visible from the surface, are not too common. A modern liner moves so quickly that it does not attract life to it in the same way as a slow-moving ship like the Terra Nova, and when specimens are seen they are gone almost as soon as they are observed. Those who wish to study sea life—and there is much to be done in this field—should travel by tramp steamers, or, better still, sailing vessels.

Dolphins were constantly playing under the bows of the ship, giving a very good chance for identification, and whales were also frequently sighted, and would sometimes follow the ship, as did also hundreds of sea birds, petrels, shearwaters and albatross. It says much for the interest and keenness of the officers on board that a complete hourly log was kept from beginning to end of the numbers and species which were seen, generally with the most complete notes as to any peculiarity or habit which was noticed. It is to be hoped that full use will be made, by those in charge of the working out of these results, of these logs which were kept so thoroughly and sometimes under such difficult circumstances and conditions of weather and sea. Though many helped, this log was largely the work of Pennell, who was an untiring and exact observer.

We lost the N.E. Trade about July 7, and ran into the Doldrums. On the whole we could not complain of the weather. We never had a gale or big sea until after leaving South Trinidad, and though an old ship with no modern ventilation is bound to be stuffy in the tropics, we lived and slept on deck so long as it was not raining. If it rained at night, as it frequently does in this part of the world, a number of rolled-up forms could be heard discussing as to whether it was best to stick it above or face the heat below; and if the rain persisted, sleepy and somewhat snappy individuals were to be seen trying to force themselves and a maximum amount of damp bedding down the wardroom gangway. At the same time a thick wooden ship will keep fairly cool in the not severe heat through which we passed.

One want which was unavoidable was the lack of fresh water. There was none to wash in, though a glass of water was allowed for shaving! With an unlimited amount of sea water this may not seem much of a hardship; nor is it unless you have very dirty work to do. But inasmuch as some of the officers were coaling almost daily, they found that any amount of cold sea water, even with a euphemistically named 'sea-water soap,' had no very great effect in removing the coal dust.

The alternative was to make friends with the engine-room authorities and draw some water from the boilers.

Perhaps therefore it was not with purely disinterested motives that some of us undertook to do the stoking during the morning watch, and also later in the day during our passage through the tropics, since the engine-room staff was reduced by sickness. A very short time will convince anybody that the ease with which men accustomed to this work get through their watch is mainly due to custom and method. The ship had no forced draught nor modern ventilating apparatus. Four hours in the boiling fiery furnace which the Terra Nova's stokehold formed in the tropics, unless there was a good wind to blow down the one canvas shaft, was a real test of staying power, and the actual shovelling of the coal into the furnaces, one after the other, was as child's play to handling the 'devil,' as the weighty instrument used for breaking up the clinker and shaping the fire was called. The boilers were cylindrical marine or return tube boilers, the furnaces being six feet long by three feet wide, slightly lower at the back than at the front. The fire on the bars was kept wedge-shape, that is, some nine inches high at the back, tapering to about six inches in front against the furnace doors. The furnaces were corrugated for strength. We were supposed to keep the pressure on the gauge between 70 and 80, but it wanted some doing. For the most part it was done.

We did, however, get uncomfortable days with the rain sluicing down and a high temperature—everything wet on deck and below. But it had its advantages in the fresh water it produced. Every bucket was on duty, and the ship's company stripped naked and ran about the decks or sat in the stream between the laboratories and wardroom skylight and washed their very dirty clothes. The stream came through into our bunks, and no amount of caulking ever stopped it. To sleep with a constant drip of water falling upon you is a real trial. These hot, wet days were more trying to the nerves than the months of wet, rough but cooler weather to come, and it says much for the good spirit which prevailed that there was no friction, though we were crowded together like sardines in a tin.

July 12 was a typical day (lat. 4° 57′ N., long. 22° 4′ W.). A very hot, rainy night, followed by a squall which struck us while we were having breakfast, so we went up and set all sail, which took until about 9.30 A.M. We then sat in the water on the deck and washed clothes until just before mid-day, when the wind dropped, though the rain continued. So we went up and furled all sail, a tedious business when the sails are wet and heavy. Then work on cargo or coal till 7 P.M., supper, and glad to get to sleep.

On July 15 (lat. 0° 40′ N., long. 21° 56′ W.) we crossed the Line with all pomp and ceremony. At 1.15 P.M. Neptune in the person of Seaman Evans hailed and stopped the ship. He came on board with his motley company, who solemnly paced aft to the break of the poop, where he was met by Lieutenant Evans. His wife (Browning), a doctor (Paton), barber (Cheetham), two policemen and four bears, of whom Atkinson and Oates were two, grouped themselves round him while the barrister (Abbott) read an address to the captain, and then the procession moved round to the bath, a sail full of water slung in the break of the poop on the starboard side.

Nelson was the first victim. He was examined, then overhauled by the doctor, given a pill and a dose, and handed over to the barber, who lathered him with a black mixture consisting of soot, flour and water, was shaved by Cheetham with a great wooden razor, and then the policemen tipped him backwards into the bath where the bears were waiting. As he was being pushed in he seized the barber and took him with him.

Wright, Lillie, Simpson and Levick followed, with about six of the crew. Finally Gran, the Norwegian, was caught as an extra—never having been across the Line in a British ship. But he threw the pill-distributing doctor over his head into the bath, after which he was lathered very gingerly, and Cheetham having been in once, refused to shave him at all, so they tipped him in and wished they had never caught him.

The procession re-formed, and Neptune presented certificates to those who had been initiated. The proceedings closed with a sing-song in the evening.

These sing-songs were of very frequent occurrence. The expedition was very fond of singing, though there was hardly anybody in it who could sing. The usual custom at this time was that every one had to contribute a song in turn all round the table after supper. If he could not sing he had to compose a limerick. If he could not compose a limerick he had to contribute a fine towards the wine fund, which was to make some much-discussed purchases when we reached Cape Town. At other times we played the most childish games—there was one called 'The Priest of the Parish has lost his Cap,' over which we laughed till we cried, and much money was added to the wine fund.

As always happens, certain songs became conspicuous for a time. One of these I am sure that Campbell, who was always at work and upon whom the routine of the ship depended, will never forget. I do not know who it was that started singing

"Everybody works but Father,
That poor old man,"

but Campbell, who was the only father on board and whose hair was popularly supposed to be getting thin on the top of his head, may remember.

We began to make preparations for a run ashore—a real adventure on an uninhabited and unknown island. The sailing track of ships from England round the Cape of Good Hope lies out towards the coast of Brazil, and not far from the mysterious island of South Trinidad, 680 miles east of Brazil, in 20° 30′ S. and 29° 30′ W.

This island is difficult of access, owing to its steep rocky coast and the big Atlantic swell which seldom ceases. It has therefore been little visited, and as it is infested with land crabs the stay of the few parties which have been there has been short. But scientifically it is of interest, not only for the number of new species which may be obtained there, but also for the extraordinary attitude of wild sea birds towards human beings whom they have never learnt to fear. Before we left England it had been decided to attempt a landing and spend a day there if we should pass sufficiently near to it.

Those who have visited it in the past include the astronomer Halley, who occupied it, in 1700. Sir James Ross, outward bound for the Antarctic in 1839, spent a day there, landing "in a small cove a short distance to the northward of the Nine Pin Rock of Halley, the surf on all other parts being too great to admit of it without hazarding the destruction of our boats." Ross also writes that "Horsburgh mentions ... 'that the island abounds with wild pig and goats; one of the latter was seen. With the view to add somewhat to the stock of useful creatures, a cock and two hens were put on shore; they seemed to enjoy the change, and, I have no doubt, in so unfrequented a situation, and so delightful a climate, will quickly increase in numbers.' I am afraid we did not find any of their descendants, nor those of the pig and goats."[34] I doubt whether fowls would survive the land crabs very long. There are many wild birds on the island, however, which may feed the shipwrecked, and also a depôt left by the Government for that purpose. Another visitor was Knight, who wrote a book called The Cruise of the Falcon, concerning his efforts to discover the treasure which is said to have been left there. Scott also visited it in the Discovery in 1901, when a new petrel was found which was afterwards called 'Œstrelata wilsoni,' after the same 'Uncle Bill' who was zoologist of both Scott's Expeditions.

And so it came about that on the evening of July 25 we furled sail and lay five miles from South Trinidad with all our preparations made for a very thorough search of this island of treasure. Everything was to be captured, alive or dead, animal, vegetable or mineral.

At half-past five the next morning we were steaming slowly towards what looked like a quite impregnable face of rock, with bare cliffs standing straight out of the water, which, luckily for us, was comparatively smooth. As we coasted to try and find a landing-place the sun was rising behind the island, which reaches to a height of two thousand feet, and the jagged cliffs stood up finely against the rosy sky.

---

[34] Ross, *Voyage to the Southern Seas*, vol. i. pp. 22-24.

SOUTH TRINIDAD—E. A. WILSON, DEL.

We dropped our anchor to the south of the island and a boat's crew left to prospect for a landing-place, whilst Wilson seized the opportunity to shoot some birds as specimens, including two species of frigate bird, and the seamen caught some of the multitudinous fish. We also fired shots at the sharks which soon thronged round the ship, and about which we were to think more before the day was done.

The boat came back with the news that a possible landing-place had been found, and the landing parties got off about 8.30. The landing was very bad—a ledge of rock weathered out of the cliff to our right formed, as it were, a staging along which it was possible to pass on to a steeply shelving talus slope in front of us. The sea being comparatively smooth, everybody was landed dry, with their guns and collecting gear.

The best account of South Trinidad is contained in a letter written by Bowers to his mother, which is printed here. But some brief notes which I jotted down at the time may also be of interest, since they give an account of a different part of the island:

"Having made a small depôt of cartridges, together with a little fluffy tern and a tern's egg, which Wilson found on the rocks, we climbed westward, round and up, to a point from which we could see into the East Bay. This was our first stand, and we shot several white-breasted petrel (Œstrelata trinitatis), and also black-breasted petrel (Œstrelata arminjoniana). Later on we got over the brow of a cliff where the petrel were nesting. We took two nests, on each of which a white-breasted and a black-breasted petrel were paired. Wilson caught one in his hands and I caught another on its nest; it really did not know whether it ought to fly away or not. This gives rise to an interesting problem, since these two birds have been classified as different species, and it now looks as though they are the same.

"The gannets and terns were quite extraordinary, like all the living things there. If you stay still enough the terns perch on your head. In any case they will not fly off the rocks till you are two or three feet away. Several gannets were caught in the men's hands. All the fish which the biologist collected to-day can travel quite fast on land. When the Discovery was here Wilson saw a fish come out of the sea, seize a land crab about eighteen inches away and take it back into the water.

"The land crabs were all over the place in thousands; it seems probable that their chief enemies are themselves. They are regular cannibals.

"Then we did a real long climb northwards, over rocks and tufty grass till 1.30 P.M. From the point we had reached we could see both sides of the island, and the little Martin Vas islands in the distance.

"We found lots of little tern and terns' eggs, lying out on the bare rock with no nest at all. Hooper also brought us two little gannets—all fluffy, but even at this age larger than a rook. As we got further up we began to come across the fossilized trees for which the island is well known.

"Four or five Captain biscuits made an excellent lunch, and afterwards we started to the real top of the island, a hill rising to the west of us. It was covered with a high scrubby bush and rocks, and was quite thick; in fact there was more vegetation here than on all the rest we had seen, and in making our way through it we had to keep calling in order to keep touch with one another.

"The tree ferns were numerous, but stunted. The gannets were sleeping on the tops of the bushes, and some of the crabs had climbed up the bushes and were sunning themselves on the top. These crabs were round us in thousands—I counted seven watching me out of one crack between two rocks.

"We sat down under the lee of the summit, and thought it would not be bad to be thrown away on a desert island, little thinking how near we were to being stranded, for a time at any rate.

"The crabs gathered round us in a circle, with their eyes turning towards us—as if they were waiting for us to die to come and eat us. One big fellow left his place in the circle and waddled up to my feet and examined my boots. First with one claw and then with the other he took a taste of my boot. He went away obviously disgusted: one could almost see him shake his head.

"We collected, as well as our birds and eggs, some spiders, very large grasshoppers, wood-lice, cockchafers, with big and small centipedes. In fact, the place teemed with insect life. I should add that their names are given rather from the general appearance of the animals than from their true scientific classes.

"We had a big and fast scramble down, and about half way, when we could watch the sea breaking on the rocks far below, we saw that there was a bigger swell running. It was getting late, and we made our way down as fast as we could—denting our guns as we slipped on the rocks.

"The lower we got the bigger the sea which had risen in our absence appeared to be. No doubt it was the swell of a big disturbance far away, and when we reached the débris slope where we had landed, flanked by big cliffs, we found everybody gathered there and the boats lying off—it being quite impossible for them to get near the shore.

"They had just got a life-line ashore on a buoy. Bowers went out on to the rocks and secured it. We put our guns and specimens into a pile, out of reach, as we thought, of any possible sea. But just afterwards two very large waves took us—we were hauling in the rope, and must have been a good thirty feet above the base of the wave. It hit us hard and knocked us all over the place, and wetted the guns and specimens above us through and through.

"We then stowed all gear and specimens well out of the reach of the seas, and then went out through the surf one by one, passing ourselves out on the line. It was ticklish work, but Hooper was the only one who really had a bad time. He did not get far enough out among the rocks which fringed the steep slope from which he started as a wave began to roll back. The next wave caught him and crashed him back, and he let go of the line. He was under quite a long time, and as the waves washed back all that we could do was to try and get the line to him. Luckily he succeeded in finding the slack of the line and got out.

"When we first got down to the shore and things were looking nasty, Wilson sat down on the top of a rock and ate a biscuit in the coolest possible manner. It was an example to avoid all panicking, for he did not want the biscuit.

"He remarked afterwards to me, apropos to Hooper, that it was a curious thing that a number of men, knowing that there was nothing they could do, could quietly watch a man fighting for his life, and he did not think that any but the British temperament could do so. I also found out later that he and I had both had a touch of cramp while waiting for our turn to swim out through the surf."

The following is Bowers' letter:

"Sunday, 31st July.

"The past week has been so crowded with incident, really, that I don't know where to start. Getting to land made me long for the mails from you, which are such a feature of getting to port. However, the strange uninhabited island which we visited will have to make up for my disappointment till we get to Capetown—or rather Simon's Town. Campbell and I sighted S. Trinidad from the fore yardarm on 25th, and on 26th, at first thing in the morning, we crept up to an anchorage in a sea of glass. The S.E. Trades, making a considerable sea, were beating on the eastern sides, while the western was like a mill-pond. The great rocks and hills to over 2000 feet towered above us as we went in very close in order to get our anchor down, as the water is very deep to quite a short distance from the shore. West Bay was our selection, and so clear was the water that we could see the anchor at the bottom in 15 fathoms. A number of sharks and other fish appeared at once and several birds. Evans wanted to explore, so Oates, Rennick, Atkinson and myself went away with him—pulling the boat. We examined the various landings and found them all rocky and dangerous. There was a slight surf although the sea looked like a mill-pond. We finally decided on a previously unused place, which was a little inlet among the rocks.

"There was nothing but rock, but there was a little nook where we decided to try and land. We returned to breakfast and found that Wilson and Cherry-Garrard had shot several Frigate and other birds from the ship, the little Norwegian boat—called a Pram—being used to pick them up. By way of explanation I may say that Wilson is a specialist in birds and is making a collection for the British Museum.

"We all landed as soon as possible. Wilson and Garrard with their guns for birds: Oates with the dogs, and Atkinson with a small rifle: Lillie after plants and geological specimens: Nelson and Simpson along the shore after sea beasts, etc.: and last but not least came the entomological party, under yours truly, with Wright and, later, Evans, as assistants. Pennell joined up with Wilson, so altogether we were ready to 'do' the island. I have taken over the collection of insects for the expedition, as the other scientists all have so much to do that they were only too glad to shove the small beasts on me. Atkinson is a specialist in parasites: it is called 'Helminthology.' I never heard that name before. He turns out the interior of every beast that is killed, and being also a surgeon, I suppose the subject must be interesting. White terns abounded on the island. They were ghost-like and so tame that they would sit on one's hat. They laid their eggs on pinnacles of rock without a vestige of nest, and singly. They looked just like stones. I suppose this was a protection from the land-crabs, about which you will have heard. The land-crabs of Trinidad are a byword and they certainly deserve the name, as they abound from sea-level to the top of the island. The higher up the bigger they were. The surface of the hills and valleys was covered with loose boulders, and the whole island being of volcanic origin, coarse grass is everywhere, and at about 1500 feet is an area of tree ferns and subtropical vegetation, extending up to nearly the highest parts. The withered trees of a former forest are everywhere and their existence unexplained, though Lillie had many ingenious theories. The island has been in our hands, the Germans', and is now Brazilian. Nobody has been able to settle there permanently, owing to the land-crabs. These also exclude mammal life. Captain Kidd made a treasure depôt there, and some five years ago a chap named Knight lived on the island for six months with a party of Newcastle miners—trying to get at it. He had the place all right, but a huge landslide has covered up three-quarters of a million of the pirate's gold. The land-crabs are little short of a nightmare. They peep out at you from every nook and boulder. Their dead staring eyes follow your every step as if to say, 'If only you will drop down we will do the rest.' To lie down and sleep on any part of the island would be suicidal. Of course, Knight had a specially cleared place with all sorts of precautions, otherwise he would never have survived these beasts, which even tried to nibble your boots as you stood—staring hard at you the whole time. One feature that would soon send a lonely man off his chump is that no matter how many are in sight they are all looking at you, and they follow step by step with a sickly deliberation. They are all yellow and pink, and next to spiders seem the most loathsome creatures on God's earth. Talking about spiders [Bowers always had the greatest horror of spiders]—I have to collect them as well as insects. Needless to say I caught them with a butterfly net, and never touched one. Only five species were known before, and I found fifteen or more—at any rate I have fifteen for certain. Others helped me to catch them, of course. Another interesting item to science is the fact that I caught a moth hitherto unknown to exist on the island, also various flies, ants, etc. Altogether it was a most successful day. Wilson got dozens of birds, and Lillie plants, etc. On our return to the landing-place we found to our horror that a southerly swell was rolling in, and great breakers were bursting on the beach. About five P.M. we all collected and looked at the whaler and pram on one side of the rollers and ourselves on the other. First it was impossible to take off the guns and specimens, so we made them all up to leave for the morrow. Second, a sick man had come ashore for exercise, and he could not be got off: finally, Atkinson stayed ashore with him. The breakers made the most awe-inspiring cauldron in our little nook, and it meant a tough swim for all of us. Three of us swam out first and took a line to the pram, and finally we got a good rope from the whaler, which had anchored well out, to the shore. I then manœuvred the pram, and everybody plunged into the surf and hauled himself out with the rope. All well, but minus our belongings, and got back to the ship; very wet and ravenous was a mild way to put it. During my 12 to 4 watch that night the surf roared like thunder, and the ship herself was rolling like anything, and looked horribly close to the shore. Of course she was quite safe really. It transpired that Atkinson and the seaman had a horrible night with salt water soaked food, and the crabs and white terns which sat and watched them all night, squawking in chorus whenever they moved. It must have been horrible, though I would like to have stayed, and had I known anybody was staying would have volunteered. This with the noise of the surf and the cold made it pretty rotten for them. In the morning, Evans, Rennick, Oates and I, with two seamen and Gran, took the whaler and pram in to rescue the maroons. At first we thought we would do it by a rocket line to the end of the sheer cliff. The impossibility of such an idea was at once evident, so Gran and I went in close in the pram, and hove them lines to get off the gear first. I found the spoon-shaped pram a wonderful boat to handle. You could go in to the very edge of the breaking surf, lifted like a cork on top of the waves, and as long as you kept head to sea and kept your own head, you need never have got on the rocks, as the tremendous back-swish took you out like a shot every time. It was quite exciting, however, as we would slip in close in a lull, and the chaps in the whaler would yell, 'Look out!' if a big wave passed them, in which case you would pull out for dear life. Our first lines carried away, and then, with others, Rennick and I this time took the pram while Atkinson got as near the edge as safe to throw us the gear. I was pulling, and by watching our chances we rescued the cameras and glasses, once being carried over 12 feet above the rocks and only escaping by the back-swish. Then the luckiest incident of the day occurred, when in a lull we got our sick man down, and I jumped out, and he in, as I steadied the boat's stern. The next minute the boat flew out on the back-wash with the seaman absolutely dry, and I was of course enveloped in foam and blackness two seconds later by a following wave. Twice the day before this had happened, but this time for a moment I thought, 'Where will my head strike?' as I was like a feather in a breeze in that swirl. When I banked it was about 15 feet above, and, very scratched and winded, I clung on with my nails and scrambled up higher. The next wave, a bigger one, nearly had me, but I was just too high to be sucked back. Atkinson and I then started getting the gear down, Evans having taken my place in the pram. By running down between waves we hove some items into the boat, including the guns and rifles, which I went right down to throw. These were caught and put into the boat, but Evans was too keen to save a bunch of boots that Atkinson threw down, and the next minute the pram passed over my head and landed high and dry, like a bridge, over the rocks between which I was wedged. I then scrambled out as the next wave washed her still higher, right over and over, with Evans and Rennick just out in time. The next wave—a huge one—picked her up, and out she bumped over the rocks and out to sea she went, water-logged, with the guns, fortunately, jammed under the thwarts. She was rescued by the whaler, baled out, and then Gran and one of the seamen manned her battered remains again, and we, unable to save the gear otherwise, lashed it to life-buoys, threw it into the sea and let it drift out with the back-wash to be picked up by the pram.

"Clothes, watches and ancient guns, rifles, ammunition, birds (dead) and all specimens were, with the basket of crockery and food, soaked with salt water. However, the choice was between that or leaving them altogether, as anybody would have said had they seen the huge rollers breaking among the rocks and washing 30 to 40 feet up with the spray; in fact, we were often knocked over and submerged for a time, clinging hard to some rock or one of the ropes for dear life. Evans swam off first. Then I was about half an hour trying to rescue a hawser and some lines entangled among the rocks. It was an amusing job. I would wait for a lull, run down and haul away, staying under for smaller waves and running up the rocks like a hare when the warning came from the boat that a series of big ones were coming in. I finally rescued most of it—had to cut off some and got it to the place opposite the boat, and with Rennick secured it and sent it out to sea to be picked up. My pair of brown tennis shoes (old ones) had been washed off my feet in one of the scrambles, so I was wearing a pair of sea-boots—Nelson's, I found—which, fortunately for him, was one of the few pairs saved. The pram came in, and waiting for a back-wash Rennick swam off. I ran down after the following wave, and securing my green hat, which by the bye is a most useful asset, struck out through the boiling, and grabbed the pram safely as we were lifted on the crest of an immense roller. However, we were just beyond its breaking-point, so all was well, and we arrived aboard after eight hours' wash and wetness, and none the worse, except for a few scratches, and yours truly in high spirits. We stayed there that night, and the following, Thursday, morning left. Winds are not too favourable so far, as we dropped the S.E. Trades almost immediately, and these are the variables between the Trades and the Westerlies. Still 2500 miles off our destination. Evans has therefore decided to steer straight for Simon's Town and miss out the other islands. It is a pity, but as it is winter down here, and the worst month of the year for storms at Tristan Da Cunha, it is perhaps just as well. I am longing to get to the Cape to have your letters and hear all about you. Except for the absence of news, life aboard is much to be desired. I simply love it, and enjoy every day of my existence here. Time flies like anything, and though it must have been long to you, to us it goes like the wind—so different to that fortnight on the passage home from India."[35]

---

[35] Bowers' letter.

After the return of the boat's crew we left South Trinidad, and the zoologists had a busy time trying to save as many as possible of the bird skins which had been procured. They skinned on all through the following night, and, considering that the birds had been lying out in the tropics for twenty-four hours soaked with sea-water and had been finally capsized in the overturned boat, the result was not so disappointing as was expected. But the eggs and many other articles were lost. Since the black-breasted and white-breasted petrels were seen flying and nesting paired together, it is reasonable to suppose that their former classification as two separate species will have to be revised.

Soon after leaving South Trinidad we picked up our first big long swell, logged at 8, and began to learn that the Terra Nova can roll as few ships can. This was followed by a stiff gale on our port beam, and we took over our first green seas. Bowers wrote home as follows:

August 7th, Sunday.

"All chances of going to Tristan are over, and we are at last booming along with strong Westerlies with the enormous Southern rollers lifting us like a cork on their crests. We have had a stiff gale and a very high sea, which is now over, though it is still blowing a moderate gale, and the usual crowd of Albatross, Mollymawks, Cape Hens, Cape Pigeons, etc., are following us. These will be our companions down to the South. Wilson's idea is that, as the prevailing winds round the forties are Westerlies, these birds simply fly round and round the world—via Cape Horn, New Zealand and the Cape of Good Hope. We have had a really good opportunity now of testing the ship's behaviour, having been becalmed with a huge beam swell rolling 35° each way, and having stood out a heavy gale with a high sea. In both she has turned up trumps, and really I think a better little sea boat never floated. Compared to the Loch Torridon—which was always awash in bad weather—we are as dry as a cork, and never once shipped a really heavy sea. Of course a wooden ship has some buoyancy of herself, and we are no exception. We are certainly an exception for general seaworthiness—if not for speed—and a safer, sounder ship there could not be. The weather is now cool too—cold, some people call it. I am still comfortable in cotton shirts and whites, while some are wearing Shetland gear. Nearly everybody is provided with Shetland things. I am glad you have marked mine, as they are all so much alike. I am certainly as well provided with private gear as anybody, and far better than most, so, being as well a generator of heat in myself, I should be O.K. in any temperature. By the bye Evans and Wilson are very keen on my being in the Western Party, while Campbell wants me with him in the Eastern Party. I have not asked to go ashore, but am keen on anything and am ready to do anything. In fact there is so much going on that I feel I should like to be in all three places at once—East, West and Ship."

CHAPTER II

MAKING OUR EASTING DOWN

"Ten minutes to four, sir!"

It is an oilskinned and dripping seaman, and the officer of the watch, or his so-called snotty, as the case may be, wakes sufficiently to ask:

"What's it like?"

"Two hoops, sir!" answers the seaman, and makes his way out.

The sleepy man who has been wakened wedges himself more securely into his six foot by two—which is all his private room on the ship—and collects his thoughts, amid the general hubbub of engines, screw and the roll of articles which have worked loose, to consider how he will best prevent being hurled out of his bunk in climbing down, and just where he left his oilskins and sea-boots.

If, as is possible, he sleeps in the Nursery, his task may not be so simple as it may seem, for this cabin, which proclaims on one of the beams that it is designed to accommodate four seamen, will house six scientists or pseudo-scientists, in addition to a pianola. Since these scientists are the youngest in the expedition their cabin is named the Nursery.

Incidentally it forms also the gangway from the wardroom to the engine-room, from which it is divided only by a wooden door, which has a bad habit of swinging open and shutting with the roll of the ship and the weight of the oilskins hung upon it, and as it does so, wave upon wave, the clatter of the engines advances and recedes.

If, however, it is the officer of the watch he will be in a smaller cabin farther aft which he shares with one other man only, and his troubles are simplified.

Owing to the fact that the seams in the deck above have travelled many voyages, and have been strained in addition by the boat davits and deck-houses built on the poop, a good deal of water from this part of the deck, which is always awash in bad weather, finds its way below, that is into the upper bunks of our cabins. In order that only a minimum of this may find its way into our blankets a series of shoots, invented and carefully tended by the occupants of these bunks, are arranged to catch this water as it falls and carry it over our heads on to the deck of the cabin.

Thus it is that when this sleepy officer or scientist clambers down on to the deck he will, if he is lucky, find the water there, instead of leaving it in his bunk.

He searches round for his sea-boots, gets into his oilskins, curses if the strings of his sou'wester break as he tries to tie them extra firmly round his neck, and pushes along to the open door into the wardroom. It is still quite dark, for the sun does not rise for another hour and a half, but the diminished light from the swinging oil-lamp which hangs there shows him a desolate early morning scene which he comes to hate—especially if he is inclined to be sick.

As likely as not more than one sea has partially found its way down during the night, and a small stream runs over the floor each time the ship rolls. The white oilcloth has slipped off the table, and various oddments, dirty cocoa cups, ash-trays, and other litter from the night are rolling about too. The tin cups and plates and crockery in the pantry forrard of the wardroom come together with a sickening crash.

The screw keeps up a ceaseless chonk-chonk-chonk (pause), chonk-chonk-chonk (pause), chonk-chonk-chonk.

Watching his opportunity he slides down across the wet linoleum to the star-board side, whence the gangway runs up to the chart-house and so out on to the deck. Having glanced at the barograph slung up in the chart-room, and using all his strength to force the door out enough to squeeze through, he scrambles out into blackness.

The wind is howling through the rigging, the decks are awash. It is hard to say whether it is raining, for the spray cut off by the wind makes rain a somewhat insignificant event. As he makes his way up on to the bridge, not a very lofty climb, he looks to see what sail is set, and judges so far as he can the force of the wind.

Campbell, for he is the officer of the morning watch (4 A.M.-8 A.M.) has a talk with the officer he is relieving, Bowers. He is given the course, the last hour's read-ing on the Cherub patent log trailing out over the stern, and the experiences of the middle watch of the wind, whether rising or falling or squalling, and its effect on the sails and the ship. "If you keep her on her present course, she's all right, but if you try and bring her up any more she begins to shake. And, by the way, Pe-nelope wants to be called at 4.30." Bowers' 'snotty,' who is Oates, probably makes some ribald remarks, such as no midshipman should to a full lieutenant, and they both disappear below. Campbell's snotty, myself, appears about five minutes af-terwards trying to look as though some important duty and not bed had kept him from making an earlier appearance. Meanwhile the leading hand musters the watch on deck and reports them all present.

"How about that cocoa?" says Campbell. Cocoa is a useful thing in the morn-ing watch, and Gran, who used to be Campbell's snotty, and whose English was not then perfect, said he was glad of a change because he "did not like being turned into a drumstick" (he meant a domestic).

So cocoa is the word and the snotty starts on an adventurous voyage over the deck to the galley which is forrard; if he is unlucky he gets a sea over him on the way. Here he finds the hands of the watch, smoking and keeping warm, and he forages round for some hot water, which he gets safely back to the pantry down in the wardroom. Here he mixes the cocoa and collects sufficient clean mugs (if he can find them), spoons, sugar and biscuits to go round. These he carefully "chocks off" while he goes and calls Wilson and gives him his share—for Wilson gets up at 4.30 every morning to sketch the sunrise, work at his scientific paintings and watch the sea-birds flying round the ship. Then back to the bridge, and woe betide him if he falls on the way, for then it all has to be done over again.

Pennell, who sleeps under the chart table on the bridge, is also fed and inquires anxiously whether there are any stars showing. If there are he is up immediately to get an observation, and then retires below to work it out and to tabulate the endless masses of figures which go to make up the results of his magnetic observations—dip, horizontal force and total force of the magnetic needle.

A squall strikes the ship. Two blasts of the whistle fetches the watch out, and "Stand by topsail halyards," "In inner jib," sends one hand to one halyard, the midshipman of the watch to the other, and the rest on to foc'stle and to the jib downhaul. Down comes the jib and the man standing by the fore topsail halyard, which is on the weather side of the galley, is drenched by the crests of two big seas which come over the rail.

But he has little time to worry about things like this, for the wind is increasing and "Let go topsail halyards" comes through the megaphone from the bridge, and he wants all his wits to let go the halyard from the belaying-pins and jump clear of the rope tearing through the block as the topsail yard comes sliding down the mast.

"Clew up" is the next order, and then "All hands furl fore and main upper topsails," and up we go out on to the yard. Luckily the dawn is just turning the sea grey and the ratlines begin to show up in relief. It is far harder for the first and middle watches, who have to go aloft in complete darkness. Once on the yard you are flattened against it by the wind. The order to take in sail always fetches Pennell out of his chart-house to come and take a hand.

The two sodden sails safely furled—luckily they are small ones—the men reach the deck to find that the wind has shifted a little farther aft and they are to brace round. This finished, it is broad daylight, and the men set to work to coil up preparatory to washing decks—not that this would seem very necessary. Certainly there is no hose wanted this morning, and a general kind of tidying up and coiling down ropes is more what is done.

The two stewards, Hooper, who is to land with the Main Party, and Neale, who will remain with the Ship's Party, turn out at six and rouse the afterguard for the pumps, a daily evolution, and soon an unholy din may be heard coming up from the wardroom. "Rouse and shine, rouse and shine: show a leg, show a leg" (a relic of the old days when seamen took their wives to sea). "Come on, Mr. Nelson, it's seven o'clock. All hands on the pumps!"

From first to last these pumps were a source of much exercise and hearty curses. A wooden ship always leaks a little, but the amount of water taken in by the Terra Nova even in calm weather was extraordinary, and could not be traced until the ship was dry-docked in Lyttelton, New Zealand, and the forepart was flooded.

In the meantime the ship had to be kept as dry as possible, a process which was not facilitated by forty gallons of oil which got loose during the rough weather after leaving South Trinidad, and found its way into the bilges. As we found later, some never-to-be-sufficiently-cursed stevedore had left one of the bottom boards only half-fitted into its neighbours. In consequence the coal dust and small pieces of coal, which was stowed in this hold, found their way into the bilges. Forty gallons of oil completed the havoc and the pumps would gradually get more and more blocked until it was necessary to send for Davies, the carpenter, to take parts of them to pieces and clear out the oily coal balls which had stopped them. This pumping would sometimes take till nearly eight, and then would always have to be repeated again in the evening, and sometimes every watch had to take a turn. At any rate it was good for our muscles.

The pumps were placed amidships, just abaft the main mast, and ran down a shaft adjoining the after hatch, which led into the holds which were generally used for coal and patent fuel. The spout of the pump opened about a foot above the deck, and the plungers were worked by means of two horizontal handles, much as a bucket is wound up on the drum of a cottage well. Unfortunately, this part of the main deck, which is just forward of the break of the poop, is more subject to seas breaking inboard than any other part of the ship, so when the ship was labouring the task of those on the pump was not an enviable one. During the big gale going South the water was up to the men's waists as they tried to turn the handles, and the pumps themselves were feet under water.

From England to Cape Town these small handles were a great inconvenience. There was very much pumping to be done and there were plenty of men to do it, but the handles were not long enough to allow more than four men to each handle. Also they gave no secure purchase when the ship was rolling heavily, and when a big roll came there was nothing to do but practically stop pumping and hold on, or you found yourself in the scuppers.

At Cape Town a great improvement was made by extending the crank handles right across the decks, the outside end turning in a socket under the rail. Fourteen men could then get a good purchase on the handles and pumping became a more pleasant exercise and less of a nuisance.

Periodically the well was sounded by an iron rod being lowered on the end of a rope, by which the part that came up wet showed the depth of water left in the bilge. When this had been reduced to about a foot in the well, the ship was practically dry, and the afterguard free to bathe and go to breakfast.

Meanwhile the hands of the watch had been employed on ropes and sails as the wind made necessary, and, when running under steam as well as sail, hoisting ashes up the two shoots from the ash-pits of the furnaces to the deck, whence they went into the ditch.

It is eight bells (8 o'clock) and the two stewards are hurrying along the decks, hoping to get the breakfast safely from galley to wardroom. A few naked officers are pouring sea-water over their heads on deck, for we are under sail alone and there is no steam to work the hose. The watch keepers and their snotties of the night before are tumbling out of their bunks, and a great noise of conversation is coming from the wardroom, among which some such remarks as: "Give the jam a wind, Marie"; "After you with the coffee"; "Push along the butter" are frequent. There are few cobwebs that have not been blown away by breakfast-time.

Rennick is busy breakfasting preparatory to relieving Campbell on the bridge. Meanwhile, the hourly and four-hourly ship's log is being made up—force of the wind, state of the sea, height of the barometer, and all the details which a log has to carry—including a reading of the distance run as shown by the patent log line— (many is the time I have forgotten to take it just at the hour and have put down what I thought it ought to be, and not what it was).

The morning watch is finished.

Suddenly there is a yell from somewhere amidships—"Steady"—a stranger might have thought there was something wrong, but it is a familiar sound, answered by a "Steady It Is, Sir," from the man at the wheel, and an anything but respectful, "One—two—three—Steady," from everybody having breakfast. It is Pennell who has caused this uproar. And the origin is as follows:

Pennell is the navigator, and the standard compass, owing to its remoteness from iron in this position, is placed on the top of the ice-house. The steersman, however, steers by a binnacle compass placed aft in front of his wheel. But these two compasses for various reasons do not read alike at a given moment, while the standard is the truer of the two.

At intervals, then, Pennell or the officer of the watch orders the steersman to "Stand by for a steady," and goes up to the standard compass, and watches the needle. Suppose the course laid down is S. 40 E. A liner would steer almost true to this course unless there was a big wind or sea. But not so the old Terra Nova. Even with a good steersman the needle swings a good many degrees either side of the S. 40 E. But as it steadies momentarily on the exact course Pennell shouts his "Steady," the steersman reads just where the needle is pointing on the compass card before him, say S. 47 E., and knows that this is the course which is to be steered by the binnacle compass.

Pennell's yells were so frequent and ear-piercing that he became famous for them, and many times in working on the ropes in rough seas and big winds, we have been cheered by this unmusical noise over our heads.

We left Simon's Bay on Friday, September 2, 'to make our Easting down' from the Cape of Good Hope to New Zealand, that famous passage in the Roaring Forties which can give so much discomfort or worse to sailing ships on their way.

South Africa had been hospitable. The Admiral Commanding the Station, the Naval Dockyard, and H.M.S. Mutine and H.M.S. Pandora, had been more than kind. They had done many repairs and fittings for us and had sent fatigue parties to do it, thus releasing men for a certain amount of freedom on shore, which was appreciated after some nine weeks at sea. I can remember my first long bath now.

Scott, who was up country when we arrived, joined the ship here, and Wilson travelled ahead of us to Melbourne to carry out some expedition work, chiefly dealing with the Australian members who were to join us in New Zealand.

One or two of us went out to Wynberg, which Oates knew well, having been invalided there in the South African War with a broken leg, the result of a fight against big odds when, his whole party wounded, he refused to surrender. He told me later how he had thought he would bleed to death, and the man who lay next to him was convinced he had a bullet in the middle of his brain—he could feel it wobbling about there! Just now his recollections only went so far as to tell of a badly wounded Boer who lay in the next bed to him when he was convalescent, and how the Boer insisted on getting up to open the door for him every time he left the ward, much to his own discomfort.

Otherwise the recollections which survive of South Africa are an excellent speech made on the expedition by John Xavier Merriman, and the remark of a seaman who came out to dinner concerning one John, the waiter, that "he moved about as quick as a piece of sticking-plaster!"

Leaving Simon's Town at daybreak we did magnetic work all day, sailing out from False Bay with a biggish swell in the evening. We ran southerly in good weather until Sunday morning, when the swell was logged at 8 and the glass was falling fast. By the middle watch it was blowing a full gale and for some thirty hours we ran under reefed foresail, lower topsails and occasionally reefed upper topsails, and many of us were sick.

Then after two days of comparative calm we had a most extraordinary gale from the east, a thing almost unheard of in these latitudes (38° S. to 39° S.). All that we could do was to put the engines at dead slow and sail northerly as close to the wind as possible. Friday night, September 9, it blew force 10 in the night, and the morning watch was very lively with the lee rail under water.

Directly after breakfast on Saturday, September 10, we wore ship, and directly afterwards the gale broke and it was raining, with little wind, during the day.

The morning watch had a merry time on Tuesday, September 13, when a fresh gale struck them while they were squaring yards. So unexpected was it that the main yards were squared and the fore were still round, but it did not last long and was followed by two splendid days—fine weather with sun, a good fair wind and the swell astern.

THE ROARING FORTIES—E. A. WILSON, DEL.

The big swell which so often prevails in these latitudes is a most inspiring sight, and must be seen from a comparatively small ship like the Terra Nova for its magnitude to be truly appreciated. As the ship rose on the crest of one great hill of water the next big ridge was nearly a mile away, with a sloping valley between. At times these seas are rounded in giant slopes as smooth as glass; at others they curl over, leaving a milk-white foam, and their slopes are marbled with a beautiful spumy tracery. Very wonderful are these mottled waves: with a following sea, at one moment it seems impossible that the great mountain which is overtaking the ship will not overwhelm her, at another it appears inevitable that the ship will fall into the space over which she seems to be suspended and crash into the gulf which lies below.

But the seas are so long that they are neither dangerous nor uncomfortable—though the Terra Nova rolled to an extraordinary extent, quite constantly over 50° each way, and sometimes 55°.

The cooks, however, had a bad time trying to cook for some fifty hands in the little galley on the open deck. Poor Archer's efforts to make bread sometimes ended in the scuppers, and the occasional jangle of the ship's bell gave rise to the saying that "a moderate roll rings the bell, and a big roll brings out the cook."

Noon on Sunday, September 18, found us in latitude 39° 20′ S. and longitude 66° 9′ E., after a very good run, for the Terra Nova, of 200 miles in the last twenty-four hours. This made us about two days' run from St. Paul, an uninhabited island formed by the remains of an old volcano, the crater of which, surrounded as it were by a horse-shoe of land, forms an almost landlocked harbour. It was hoped to make a landing here for scientific work, but it is a difficult harbour to make. We ran another two hundred miles on Monday, and on Tuesday all preparations were made for the landing, with suitable equipment, and we were not a little excited at the opportunity.

At 4.30 A.M. the next morning all hands were turned out to take in sail preparatory to rounding St. Paul which was just visible. The weather was squally, but not bad. By 5 A.M., however, it was blowing a moderate gale, and by the time we had taken in all sail we had to give up hopes of a landing. We were thoroughly sick of sails by the time we finally reefed the foresail and ran before the wind under this and lower topsails.

We passed quite close to the island and could see into the crater, and the cliffs beyond which rose from it, covered with greenish grass. There were no trees, and of birds we only saw those which frequent these seas. We had hoped to find penguins and albatross nesting on the island at this time of the year, and this failure to land was most disappointing. The island is 860 feet high, and, for its size, precipitous. It extends some two miles in length and one mile in breadth.

The following day all the afterguard were turned on to shift coal. It should be explained that up to this time the bunkers, which lay one on the port and the other on the starboard side of the furnaces, had been entirely filled as required by two or more officers who volunteered from day to day.

We took on board 450 tons of Crown Patent Fuel at Cardiff in June 1910. This coal is in the form of bricks, and is most handy since it can be thrown by hand from the holds through the bunker doors in the boiler-room bulkhead which after a time was left higher than the sinking level of the coal. The coal to be landed was this patent fuel, and it was now decided to shift farther aft all the patent fuel which was left, and stack it against the boiler-room bulkhead, the coal which was originally there having been fed to the furnaces. Thus the dust which was finding its way through the floorboards, and choking the pumps, could be swept up, and a good stow could be made preparatory to the final fit-out in New Zealand, while the coal which was to be taken on board at Lyttelton could be loaded through the main hatch.

In the meantime the gale which had sprung up six days before and prevented us landing had died down. After leaving St. Paul we had let the fires out and run under sail alone, and the following two days we ran 119 and 141 miles respectively, being practically becalmed at times on the following day, and only running 66 miles.

By Tuesday night, September 27, we had finished the coaling, and we celebrated the occasion by a champagne dinner. At the same time we raised steam. Scott was anxious to push on, and so indeed was everybody else. But the wind was not disposed to help us, and headed us a good deal during the next few days, and it was not until October 2 that we were able to set all plain sail in the morning watch.

This absence of westerly winds in a region in which they are usually too strong for comfort was explained by Pennell by a theory that we were travelling in an anticyclone, which itself was travelling in front of a cyclone behind us. We were probably moving under steam about the same pace as the disturbance, which would average some 150 miles a day.

From this may be explained many of the reports of continual bad weather met by sailing ships and steamers in these latitudes. If we had been a sailing ship without auxiliary steam the cyclone would have caught us up, and we should have been travelling with it, and consequently in continual bad weather. On the other hand, a steamer pure and simple would have steamed through good and bad alike. But we, with our auxiliary steam, only made much the same headway as the disturbance travelling in our wake, and so remained in the anticyclone.

Physical observations were made on the outward voyage by Simpson and Wright[36] into the atmospheric electricity over the ocean, one set of which consisted of an inquiry into the potential gradient, and observations were undertaken at Melbourne for the determination of the absolute value of the potential gradient over the sea.[37] Numerous observations were also made on the radium content of the atmosphere over the ocean, to be compared afterwards with observations in the Antarctic air. The variations in radium content were not large. Results were also obtained on the voyage of the Terra Nova to New Zealand upon the subject of natural ionization in closed vessels.

In addition to the work of the ship and the physical work above mentioned, work in vertebrate zoology, marine biology and magnetism, together with four-hourly observations of the salinity and temperature of the sea, was carried out during the whole voyage.

In vertebrate zoology Wilson kept an accurate record of birds, and he and Lillie another record of whales and dolphins. All the birds which could be caught, both at sea and on South Trinidad Island, were skinned and made up into museum specimens. They were also examined for external and internal parasites by Wilson, Atkinson and myself, as were also such fish and other animals as could be caught, including flying fish, a shark, and last but not least, whales in New Zealand.

The method of catching these birds may be worth describing. A bent nail was tied to a line, the other end of which was made fast to the halyards over the stern. Sufficient length of line was allowed either to cause the nail to just trail in the sea in the wake of the ship or for the line to just clear the sea. Thus when the halyard was hoisted to some thirty or forty feet above the deck, the line would be covering a considerable distance of sea.

The birds flying round the ship congregate for the main part in the wake, for here they find the scraps thrown overboard on which they feed. I have seen six albatross all together trying to eat up an empty treacle tin.

As they fly to and fro their wings are liable to touch the line which is spread out over the sea. Sometimes they will hit the line with the tips of their wings, and then there is no resulting capture, but sooner or later a bird will touch the line with the part of the wing above the elbow-joint (humerus). It seems that on feeling the contact the bird suddenly wheels in the air, thereby causing a loop in the line which tightens round the bone. At any rate the next thing that happens is that the

[36] Vide *Scott's Last Expedition,* vol. ii. pp. 454-456.

[37] "Atmospheric Electricity over Ocean," by G. C. Simpson and C. S. Wright, *Pro. Roy. Soc.* A, vol. 85, 1911.

bird is struggling on the line and may be hauled on board.

The difficulty is to get a line which is light enough to fly in the air, but yet strong enough to hold the large birds, such as albatross, without breaking. We tried fishing line with no success, but eventually managed to buy some 5-ply extra strong cobbler's thread, which is excellent for the purpose. But we wanted not only specimens, but also observations of the species, the numbers which appeared, and their habits, for little is known as yet of these sea birds. And so we enlisted the help of all who were interested, and it may be said that all the officers and many of the seamen had a hand in producing the log of sea birds, to which additions were made almost hourly throughout the daylight hours. Most officers and men knew the more common sea birds in the open ocean, and certainly of those in the pack and fringes of the Antarctic continent, which, with rare exceptions, is the southern limit of bird life.

A number of observations of whales, illustrated by Wilson, were made, but the results so far as the seas from England to the Cape and New Zealand are concerned, are not of great importance, partly because close views were seldom obtained, and partly because the whales inhabiting these seas are fairly well known. On October 3, 1910, in latitude 42° 17′ S. and longitude 111° 18′ E., two adults of Balaenoptera borealis (Northern Rorqual) were following the ship close under the counter, length 50 feet, with a light-coloured calf some 18-20 feet long swimming with them. It was established by this and by a later observation in New Zealand, when Lillie helped to cut up a similar whale at the Norwegian Whaling Station at the Bay of Islands, that this Rorqual which frequents the sub-Antarctic seas is identical with our Northern Rorqual;[38] but this was the only close observation of any whales obtained before we left New Zealand.

General information with regard to such animals is useful, however, as showing the relative abundance of plankton on which the whales feed in the ocean. There are, for instance, more whales in the Antarctic than in warmer seas; and some whales at any rate (e.g. Humpback whales) probably come north into warmer waters in the winter rather for breeding purposes than to get food.[39]

With regard to dolphins four species were observed beyond question. The rarest dolphin seen was Tersio peronii, the peculiarity of which is that it has no dorsal fin. This was seen on October 20, 1910, in latitude 42° 51′ S. and longitude 153° 56′ E.

Reports of whales and dolphins which are not based upon carcases and skeletons must be accepted with caution. It is most difficult to place species with scientific accuracy which can only be observed swimming in the water, and of which more often than not only blows and the dorsal fins can be observed. The nomenclature of dolphins especially leaves much to be desired, and it is to be hoped that some expedition in the future will carry a Norwegian harpooner, who could do other work as well since they are very good sailors. Wilson was strongly of this opinion and tried hard to get a harpooner, but they are expensive people so long

[38] *See* B.A.E., 1910, Nat. Hist. Report, vol. i. No. 3, p. 117.
[39] *Ibid.* p. 111.

as the present boom in whaling lasts, and perhaps it was on the score of expense that the idea was regretfully abandoned. We carried whaling gear formerly taken on the Discovery Expedition, and kindly lent for this expedition by the Royal Geographical Society of London. A few shots were tried, but an unskilled harpooner stands very little chance. If you go whaling you must have had experience.

The ship was not slowed down to enable marine biological observations to be taken on this part of the expedition, but something like forty samples of plankton were taken with a full-speed net. We were unable to trawl on the bottom until we reached Melbourne, when a trawl was made in Port Phillip Harbour to try the gear and accustom men to its use. It was not a purpose of the expedition to spend time in deep-sea work until it reached Antarctic seas.

For four days the wind, such as there was of it, was dead ahead; it is not very often in the Forties that a ship cannot make progress for want of wind. But having set all plain sail on October 2 with a falling glass we got a certain amount of wind on the port beam, and did 158 miles in the next twenty-four hours. Sunday being quiet Scott read service while the officers and men grouped round the wheel. We seldom had service on deck; for Sundays became proverbial days for a blow on the way out, and service, if held at all, was generally in the ward-room. On one famous occasion we tried to play the pianola to accompany the hymns, but, since the rolls were scored rather for musical effect than for church services, the pianola was suddenly found to be playing something quite different from what was being sung. All through the expedition the want of some one who could play the piano was felt, and such a man is certainly a great asset in a life so far removed from all the pleasures of civilization. As Scott wrote in The Voyage of the Discovery, where one of the officers used to play each evening: "This hour of music has become an institution which none of us would willingly forgo. I don't know what thoughts it brings to others, though I can readily guess; but of such things one does not care to write. I can well believe, however, that our music smooths over many a ruffle and brings us to dinner each night in that excellent humour, where all seem good-tempered, though 'cleared for action' and ready for fresh argument."

The wind freshened to our joy; Scott was impatient; there was much to be done and the time for doing it was not too long, for it had been decided to leave New Zealand at an earlier date than had been attempted by any previous expedition, in order to penetrate the pack sooner and make an early start on the depôt journey. The faintest glow of the Aurora Australis which was to become so familiar to us was seen at this time, but what aroused still more interest was the capture of several albatross on the lines flowing out over the stern.

The first was a 'sooty' (cornicoides). We put him down on the deck, where he strutted about in the proudest way, his feet going flop—flop—flop as he walked. He was a most beautiful bird, sooty black body, a great black head with a line of white over each eye and a gorgeous violet line running along his black beak. He treated us with the greatest contempt, which, from such a beautiful creature, we had every appearance of deserving. Another day a little later we caught a wandering albatross, a black-browed albatross, and a sooty albatross all together, and set them on the deck tethered to the ventilators while their photographs were taken.

They were such beautiful birds that we were loath to kill them, but their value as scientific specimens outweighed the wish to set them free, and we gave them ether so that they did not suffer.

The Southern Ocean is the home of these and many species of birds, but among them the albatross is pre-eminent. It has been mentioned that Wilson believed that the albatross, at any rate, fly round and round the world over these stormy seas before the westerly winds, landing but once a year on such islands as Kerguelen, St. Paul, the Auckland Islands and others to breed. If so, the rest that they can obtain upon the big breaking rollers which prevail in these latitudes must be unsatisfactory judged by the standard of more civilized birds. I have watched sea birds elsewhere of which the same individuals appeared to follow the ship day after day for many thousands of miles, but on this voyage I came to the conclusion that a different set of birds appeared each morning, and that they were hungry when they arrived. Certainly they flew astern and nearer to the ship in the morning, feeding on the scraps thrown overboard. As the day went on and the birds' hunger was satisfied, they scattered, and such of them as continued to fly astern of the ship were a long way off. Hence we caught the birds in the early morning, and only one bird was caught after mid-day.

The wind continued favourable and was soon blowing quite hard. On Friday, October 7, we were doing 7.8 knots under sail alone, which was very good for the old Terra Push, as she was familiarly called: and we were then just 1000 miles from Melbourne. By Saturday night we were standing by topgallant halyards. Campbell took over the watch at 4 A.M. on Sunday morning. It was blowing hard and squally, but the ship still carried topgallants. There was a big following sea.

At 6.30 A.M. there occurred one of those incidents of sea life which are interesting though not important. Quite suddenly the first really big squall we had experienced on the voyage struck us. Topgallant halyards were let go, and the fore topgallant yard came down, but the main topgallant yard jammed when only half down. It transpired afterwards that a gasket which had been blown over the yard had fouled the block of the sheet of the main upper topsail. The topgallant yard was all tilted to starboard and swaying from side to side, the sail seemed as though it might blow out at any moment, and was making a noise like big guns, and the mast was shaking badly.

It was expected that the topgallant mast would go, but nothing could be done while the full fury of the wind lasted. Campbell paced quietly up and down the bridge with a smile on his face. The watch was grouped round the ratlines ready to go aloft, and Crean volunteered to go up alone and try and free the yard, but permission was refused. It was touch and go with the mast and there was nothing to be done.

The squall passed, the sail was freed and furled, and the next big squall found us ready to lower upper topsails and all was well. Finally the damage was a split sail and a strained mast.

The next morning a new topgallant sail was bent, but quite the biggest hailstorm I have ever seen came on in the middle of the operation. Much of the hail must have been inches in circumference, and hurt even through thick clothes and oilskins. At the same time there were several waterspouts formed. The men on the topgallant yard had a beastly time. Below on deck men made hail-balls and pretended they were snow.

From now onwards we ran on our course before a gale. By the early morning of October 12 Cape Otway light was in sight. Working double tides in the engine-room, and with every stitch of sail set, we just failed to reach Port Phillip Heads by mid-day, when the tide turned, and it was impossible to get through. We went up Melbourne Harbour that evening, very dark and blowing hard.

A telegram was waiting for Scott:

"Madeira. Am going South. AMUNDSEN."

This telegram was dramatically important, as will appear when we come to the last act of the tragedy. Captain Roald Amundsen was one of the most notable of living explorers, and was in the prime of life—forty-one, two years younger than Scott. He had been in the Antarctic before Scott, with the Belgica Expedition in 1897-99, and therefore did not consider the South Pole in any sense our property. Since then he had realized the dream of centuries of exploration by passing through the North-West Passage, and actually doing so in a 60-ton schooner in 1905. The last we had heard of him was that he had equipped Nansen's old ship, the Fram, for further exploration in the Arctic. This was only a feint. Once at sea, he had told his men that he was going south instead of north; and when he reached Madeira he sent this brief telegram, which meant, "I shall be at the South Pole before you." It also meant, though we did not appreciate it at the time, that we were up against a very big man.

The Admiral Commanding the Australian Station came on board. The event of the inspection was Nigger, the black ship's cat, distinguished by a white whisker on the port side of his face, who made one adventurous voyage to the Antarctic and came to an untimely end during the second. The seamen made a hammock for him with blanket and pillow, and slung it forward among their own bedding. Nigger had turned in, not feeling very well, owing to the number of moths he had eaten, the ship being full of them. When awakened by the Admiral, Nigger had no idea of the importance of the occasion, but stretched himself, yawned in the most natural manner, turned over and went to sleep again.

This cat became a well-known and much photographed member of the crew of the Terra Nova. He is said to have imitated the Romans of old, being a greedy beast, by having eaten as much seal blubber as he could hold, made himself sick, and gone back and resumed his meal. He had most beautiful fur. When the ship was returning from the Antarctic in 1911 Nigger was frightened by something on deck and jumped into the sea, which was running fairly rough. However, the ship was hove to, a boat lowered, and Nigger was rescued. He spent another happy year on board, but disappeared one dark night when the ship was returning from her second journey to the South in 1912, during a big gale. He often went aloft with the men, of his own accord. This night he was seen on the main lower topsail yard, higher than which he never would go. He disappeared in a big squall, probably because the yard was covered with ice.

Wilson rejoined the ship at Melbourne; and Scott left her, to arrange further business matters, and to rejoin in New Zealand. When he landed I think he had seen enough of the personnel of the expedition to be able to pass a fair judgment upon them. I cannot but think that he was pleased. Such enthusiasm and comradeship as prevailed on board could bear only good fruit. It would certainly have been possible to find a body of men who could work a sailing ship with greater skill, but not men who were more willing, and that in the midst of considerable discomfort, to work hard at distasteful jobs and be always cheerful. And it must have been clear that with all the energy which was being freely expended, the expedition came first, and the individual nowhere. It is to the honour of all concerned that from the time it left London to the time it returned to New Zealand after three years, this spirit always prevailed.

Among the executive officers Scott was putting more and more trust in Campbell, who was to lead the Northern Party. He was showing those characteristics which enabled him to bring his small party safely through one of the hardest winters that men have ever survived. Bowers also had shown seamanlike qualities which are an excellent test by which to judge the Antarctic traveller; a good seaman in sail will probably make a useful sledger: but at this time Scott can hardly have foreseen that Bowers was to prove "the hardest traveller that ever undertook a Polar journey, as well as one of the most undaunted." But he had already proved himself a first-rate sailor. Among the junior scientific staff too, several were showing qualities as seamen which were a good sign for the future. Altogether I think it must have been with a cheerful mind that Scott landed in Australia.

When we left Melbourne for New Zealand we were all a bit stale, which was not altogether surprising, and a run ashore was to do us a world of good after five months of solid grind, crowded up in a ship which thought nothing of rolling 50° each way. Also, though everything had been done that could be done to provide them, the want of fresh meat and vegetables was being felt, and it was an excellent thing that a body of men, for whom every precaution against scurvy that modern science could suggest was being taken, should have a good course of antiscorbutic food and an equally beneficial change of life before leaving civilization.

And so it was with some anticipation that on Monday morning, October 24, we could smell the land—New Zealand, that home of so many Antarctic expeditions, where we knew that we should be welcomed. Scott's Discovery, Shackleton's Nimrod, and now again Scott's Terra Nova have all in turn been berthed at the same quay in Lyttelton, for aught I know at the same No. 5 Shed, into which they have spilled out their holds, and from which they have been restowed with the addition of all that New Zealand, scorning payment, could give. And from there they have sailed, and thither their relief ships have returned year after year. Scott's words of the Discovery apply just as much to the Terra Nova. Not only did New Zealand do all in her power to help the expedition in an official capacity, but the New Zealanders welcomed both officers and men with open arms, and "gave them to understand that although already separated by many thousands of miles from their native land, here in this new land they would find a second home, and those who would equally think of them in their absence, and welcome them on their return."

But we had to sail round the southern coast of New Zealand and northwards up the eastern coast before we could arrive at our last port of call. The wind went ahead, and it was not until the morning of October 28 that we sailed through Lyttelton Heads. The word had gone forth that we should sail away on November 27, and there was much to be done in the brief month that lay ahead.

There followed four weeks of strenuous work into which was sandwiched a considerable amount of play. The ship was unloaded, when, as usual, men and officers acted alike as stevedores, and she was docked, that an examination for the source of the leak might be made by Mr. H. J. Miller of Lyttelton, who has performed a like service for more than one Antarctic ship. But the different layers of sheathing protecting a ship which is destined to fight against ice are so complicated that it is a very difficult matter to find the origin of a leak. All that can be said with any certainty is that the point where the water appears inside the skin of the ship is almost certainly not the locality in which it has penetrated the outside sheathing. "Our good friend Miller," wrote Scott, "attacked the leak and traced it to the stern. We found the false stern split, and in one case a hole bored for a long-stern through-bolt which was much too large for the bolt.... The ship still leaks but the water can now be kept under with the hand pump by two daily efforts of a quarter of an hour to twenty minutes." This in Lyttelton; but in a not far distant future every pump was choked, and we were baling with three buckets, literally for our lives.

Bowers' feat of sorting and restowing not only the stores we had but the cheese, butter, tinned foods, bacon, hams and numerous other products which are grown in New Zealand, and which any expedition leaving that country should always buy there in preference to carrying them through the tropics, was a master-stroke of clear-headedness and organization. These stores were all relisted before stowing and the green-banded or Northern Party and red-banded or Main Party stores were not only easily distinguishable, but also stowed in such a way that they were forthcoming without difficulty at the right time and in their due order.

The two huts which were to form the homes of our two parties down South had been brought out in the ship and were now erected on a piece of waste ground near, by the same men who would be given the work to do in the South.

The gear peculiar to the various kinds of scientific work which it was the object of the expedition to carry out was also stowed with great care. The more bulky objects included a petrol engine and small dynamo, a very delicate instrument for making pendulum observations to test the gravity of the earth, meteorological screens, and a Dines anemometer. There was also a special hut for magnetic observations, of which only the framework was finally taken, with the necessary but bulky magnetic instruments. The biological and photographic gear was also of considerable size.

For the interior of the huts there were beds with spring mattresses—a real luxury but one well worth the space and money,—tables, chairs, cooking ranges and piping, and a complete acetylene gas plant for both parties. There were also extensive ventilators which were not a great success. The problem of ventilation in polar regions still remains to be solved.

Food can be packed into a comparatively small space, but not so fuel, and this is one of the greatest difficulties which confront the polar traveller. It must be conceded that in this respect Norway, with her wonderful petrol-driven Fram, is far ahead of us. The Terra Nova depended on coal, and the length of the ship's stay in the South, and the amount of exploration she could do after landing the shore parties, depended almost entirely upon how much coal she could be persuaded to hold after all the necessaries of modern scientific exploration had been wedged tightly into her.

The Terra Nova sailed from New Zealand with 425 tons of coal in her holds and bunkers, and 30 tons on deck in sacks. We were to hear more of those sacks.

Meanwhile stalls were being built under the forecastle for fifteen ponies, and, since room could not be found below for the remaining four, stalls were built on the port side of the fore hatch; the decks were caulked, and deck houses and other fittings which might carry away in the stormy seas of the South were further secured.

As the time of departure drew near, and each day of civilization appeared to be more and more desirable, the scene in Lyttelton became animated and congested. Here is a scientist trying to force just one more case into his small laboratory, or decanting a mass of clothing, just issued, into the bottom of his bunk, to be slept on since there was no room for it on the deck of his cabin. On the main deck Bowers is trying to get one more frozen sheep into the ice-house, in the rigging working parties are overhauling the running gear. The engine-room staff are busy on the engine, and though the ship is crowded there is order everywhere, and it is clean.

But the scene on the morning of Saturday, November 26, baffles description. There is no deck visible: in addition to 30 tons of coal in sacks on deck there are 2½ tons of petrol, stowed in drums which in turn are cased in wood. On the top of sacks and cases, and on the roof of the ice-house are thirty-three dogs, chained far enough apart to keep them from following their first instinct—to fight the nearest animal they can see: the ship is a hubbub of howls. In the forecastle and in the four stalls on deck are the nineteen ponies, wedged tightly in their wooden stalls, and dwarfing everything are the three motor sledges in their huge crates, 16′ x 5′ x 4′, two of them on either side of the main hatch, the third across the break of the poop. They are covered with tarpaulins and secured in every possible way, but it is clear that in a big sea their weight will throw a great strain upon the deck. It is not altogether a cheerful sight. But all that care and skill can do has been done to ensure that the deck cargo will not shift, and that the animals may be as sheltered as possible from wind and seas. And it's no good worrying about what can't be helped.

CHAPTER III

SOUTHWARD

Open the bones, and you shall nothing find
In the best face but filth; when, Lord, in Thee
The beauty lies in the discovery.

GEORGE HERBERT.

Telegrams from all parts of the world, special trains, all ships dressed, crowds and waving hands, steamers out to the Heads and a general hullabaloo—these were the incidents of Saturday, November 26, 1910, when we slipped from the wharf at Lyttelton at 3 P.M. We were to call at Dunedin before leaving civilization, and arrived there on Sunday night. Here we took on the remainder of our coal. On Monday night we danced, in fantastic clothing for we had left our grand clothes behind, and sailed finally for the South the following afternoon amidst the greatest enthusiasm. The wives remained with us until we reached the open sea.

Amongst those who only left us at the last minute was Mr. Kinsey of Christchurch. He acted for Scott in New Zealand during the Discovery days, and for Shackleton in 1907. We all owe him a deep debt of gratitude for his help. "His interest in the expedition is wonderful, and such interest on the part of a thoroughly shrewd business man is an asset of which I have taken full advantage. Kinsey will act as my agent in Christchurch during my absence; I have given him an ordinary power of attorney, and I think have left him in possession of all the facts. His kindness to us was beyond words."[40]

"Evening.—Loom of land and Cape Saunders Light blinking."[41]

The ponies and dogs were the first consideration. Even in quite ordinary weather the dogs had a wretched time. "The seas continually break on the weather bulwarks and scatter clouds of heavy spray over the backs of all who must venture into the waist of the ship. The dogs sit with their tails to this invading water, their coats wet and dripping. It is a pathetic attitude deeply significant of cold and misery; occasionally some poor beast emits a long pathetic whine. The group forms a picture of wretched dejection; such a life is truly hard for these poor creatures."[42]

The ponies were better off. Four of them were on deck amidships and they were well boarded round. It is significant that these ponies had a much easier

---

[40] *Scott's Last Expedition*, vol. i. p. 6.
[41] *Scott's Last Expedition*, vol. i. p. 7.
[42] *Ibid.* p. 9.

time in rough weather than those in the bows of the ship. "Under the forecastle fifteen ponies close side by side, seven one side, eight the other, heads together, and groom between—swaying, swaying continually to the plunging, irregular motion."

"One takes a look through a hole in the bulkhead and sees a row of heads with sad, patient eyes come swinging up together from the starboard side, whilst those on the port swing back; then up come the port heads, while the starboard recede. It seems a terrible ordeal for these poor beasts to stand this day after day for weeks together, and indeed though they continue to feed well the strain quickly drags down their weight and condition; but nevertheless the trial cannot be gauged from human standards."[43]

The seas through which we had to pass to reach the pack-ice must be the most stormy in the world. Dante tells us that those who have committed carnal sin are tossed about ceaselessly by the most furious winds in the second circle of Hell. The corresponding hell on earth is found in the southern oceans, which encircle the world without break, tempest-tossed by the gales which follow one another round and round the world from West to East. You will find albatross there—great Wanderers, and Sooties, and Mollymawks—sailing as lightly before these furious winds as ever do Paolo and Francesca. Round the world they go. I doubt whether they land more than once a year, and then they come to the islands of these seas to breed.

There are many other beautiful sea-birds, but most beautiful of all are the Snowy petrels, which approach nearer to the fairies than anything else on earth. They are quite white, and seemingly transparent. They are the familiar spirits of the pack, which, except to nest, they seldom if ever leave, flying "here and there independently in a mazy fashion, glittering against the blue sky like so many white moths, or shining snowflakes."[44] And then there are the Giant petrels, whose coloration is a puzzle. Some are nearly white, others brown, and they exhibit every variation between the one and the other. And, on the whole, the white forms become more general the farther south you go. But the usual theory of protective coloration will not fit in, for there are no enemies against which this bird must protect itself. Is it something to do with radiation of heat from the body?

A ship which sets out upon this journey generally has a bad time, and for this reason the overladen state of the Terra Nova was a cause of anxiety. The Australasian meteorologists had done their best to forecast the weather we must expect. Everything which was not absolutely necessary had been ruthlessly scrapped. Yet there was not a square inch of the hold and between-decks which was not crammed almost to bursting, and there was as much on the deck as could be expected to stay there. Officers and men could hardly move in their living quarters when standing up, and certainly they could not all sit down. To say that we were heavy laden is a very moderate statement of the facts.

Thursday, December 1, we ran into a gale. We shortened sail in the afternoon

[43] *Ibid.* p. 8.
[44] Wilson in the *Discovery Natural History Reports.*

to lower topsails, jib and stay-sail. Both wind and sea rose with great rapidity, and before the night came our deck cargo had begun to work loose. "You know how carefully everything had been lashed, but no lashings could have withstood the onslaught of these coal sacks for long. There was nothing for it but to grapple with the evil, and nearly all hands were labouring for hours in the waist of the ship, heaving coal sacks overboard and re-lashing the petrol cases, etc., in the best manner possible under such difficult and dangerous circumstances. The seas were continually breaking over these people and now and again they would be completely submerged. At such times they had to cling for dear life to some fixture to prevent themselves being washed overboard, and with coal bags and loose cases washing about, there was every risk of such hold being torn away.

"No sooner was some semblance of order restored than some exceptionally heavy wave would tear away the lashing, and the work had to be done all over again."[45]

The conditions became much worse during the night and things were complicated for some of us by sea-sickness. I have lively recollections of being aloft for two hours in the morning watch on Friday and being sick at intervals all the time. For sheer downright misery give me a hurricane, not too warm, the yard of a sailing ship, a wet sail and a bout of sea-sickness.

It must have been about this time that orders were given to clew up the jib and then to furl it. Bowers and four others went out on the bowsprit, being buried deep in the enormous seas every time the ship plunged her nose into them with great force. It was an education to see him lead those men out into that roaring inferno. He has left his own vivid impression of this gale in a letter home. His tendency was always to underestimate difficulties, whether the force of wind in a blizzard, or the troubles of a polar traveller. This should be remembered when reading the vivid accounts which his mother has so kindly given me permission to use:

"We got through the forties with splendid speed and were just over the fifties when one of those tremendous gales got us. Our Lat. was about 52° S., a part of the world absolutely unfrequented by shipping of any sort, and as we had already been blown off Campbell Island we had nothing but a clear sweep to Cape Horn to leeward. One realized then how in the Nimrod—in spite of the weather—they always had the security of a big steamer to look to if things came to the worst. We were indeed alone, by many hundreds of miles, and never having felt anxious about a ship before, the old whaler was to give me a new experience.

"In the afternoon of the beginning of the gale I helped make fast the T.G. sails, upper topsails and foresail, and was horrified on arrival on deck to find that the heavy water we continued to ship, was starting the coal bags floating in places. These, acting as battering-rams, tore adrift some of my carefully stowed petrol cases and endangered the lot. I had started to make sail fast at 3 P.M. and it was 9.30 P.M. when I had finished putting on additional lashings to everything I could. So rapidly did the sea get up that one was continually afloat and swimming about. I turned in for 2 hours and lay awake hearing the crash of the seas and thinking

[45] *Scott's Last Expedition*, vol. i. pp. 11-12.

how long those cases would stand it, till my watch came at midnight as a relief. We were under 2 lower topsails and hove to, the engines going dead slow to assist keeping head to wind. At another time I should have been easy in my mind; now the water that came aboard was simply fearful, and the wrenching on the old ship was enough to worry any sailor called upon to fill his decks with garbage fore and aft. Still 'Risk nothing and do nothing,' if funds could not supply another ship, we simply had to overload the one we had, or suffer worse things down south. The watch was eventful as the shaking up got the fine coal into the bilges, and this mixing with the oil from the engines formed balls of coal and grease which, ordinarily, went up the pumps easily; now however with the great strains, and hundreds of tons on deck, as she continually filled, the water started to come in too fast for the half-clogged pumps to cope with. An alternative was offered to me in going faster so as to shake up the big pump on the main engines, and this I did—in spite of myself—and in defiance of the first principles of seamanship. Of course, we shipped water more and more, and only to save a clean breach of the decks did I slow down again and let the water gain. My next card was to get the watch on the hand-pumps as well, and these were choked, too, or nearly so.

"Anyhow with every pump,—hand and steam,—going, the water continued to rise in the stokehold. At 4 A.M. all hands took in the fore lower topsail, leaving us under a minimum of sail. The gale increased to storm force (force 11 out of 12) and such a sea got up as only the Southern Fifties can produce. All the afterguard turned out and the pumps were vigorously shaken up,—sickening work as only a dribble came out. We had to throw some coal overboard to clear the after deck round the pumps, and I set to work to rescue cases of petrol which were smashed adrift. I broke away a plank or two of the lee bulwarks to give the seas some outlet as they were right over the level of the rail, and one was constantly on the verge of floating clean over the side with the cataract force of the backwash. I had all the swimming I wanted that day. Every case I rescued was put on the weather side of the poop to help get us on a more even keel. She sagged horribly and the unfortunate ponies,—though under cover,—were so jerked about that the weather ones could not keep their feet in their stalls, so great was the slope and strain on their forelegs. Oates and Atkinson worked among them like Trojans, but morning saw the death of one, and the loss of one dog overboard. The dogs, made fast on deck, were washed to and fro, chained by the neck, and often submerged for a considerable time. Though we did everything in our power to get them up as high as possible, the sea went everywhere. The wardroom was a swamp and so were our bunks with all our nice clothing, books, etc. However, of this we cared little, when the water had crept up to the furnaces and put the fires out, and we realized for the first time that the ship had met her match and was slowly filling. Without a pump to suck we started the forlorn hope of buckets and began to bale her out. Had we been able to open a hatch we could have cleared the main pump well at once, but with those appalling seas literally covering her, it would have meant less than 10 minutes to float, had we uncovered a hatch.

"The Chief Engineer (Williams) and carpenter (Davies), after we had all put our heads together, started cutting a hole in the engine room bulkhead, to enable us to get into the pump-well from the engine room; it was iron and, therefore, at least a 12 hours job. Captain Scott was simply splendid, he might have been at Cowes, and to do him and Teddy Evans credit, at our worst strait none of our landsmen who were working so hard knew how serious things were. Capt. Scott said to me quietly—'I am afraid it's a bad business for us—What do you think?' I said we were by no means dead yet, though at that moment, Oates, at peril of his life, got aft to report another horse dead; and more down. And then an awful sea swept away our lee bulwarks clean, between the fore and main riggings,—only our chain lashings saved the lee motor sledge then, and I was soon diving after petrol cases. Captain Scott calmly told me that they 'did not matter'—This was our great project for getting to the Pole—the much advertised motors that 'did not matter'; our dogs looked finished, and horses were finishing, and I went to bale with a strenuous prayer in my heart, and 'Yip-i-addy' on my lips, and so we pulled through that day. We sang and re-sang every silly song we ever knew, and then everybody in the ship later on was put on 2-hour reliefs to bale, as it was impossible for flesh to keep heart with no food or rest. Even the fresh-water pump had gone wrong so we drank neat lime juice, or anything that came along, and sat in our saturated state awaiting our next spell. My dressing gown was my great comfort as it was not very wet, and it is a lovely warm thing.

"To make a long yarn short, we found later in the day that the storm was easing a bit and that though there was a terrible lot of water in the ship, which, try as we could, we could not reduce, it certainly had ceased to rise to any great extent. We had reason to hope then that we might keep her afloat till the pump wells could be cleared. Had the storm lasted another day, God knows what our state would have been, if we had been above water at all. You cannot imagine how utterly helpless we felt in such a sea with a tiny ship,—the great expedition with all its hopes thrown aside for its life. God had shown us the weakness of man's hand and it was enough for the best of us,—the people who had been made such a lot of lately—the whole scene was one of pathos really. However, at 11 P.M. Evans and I with the carpenter were able to crawl through a tiny hole in the bulkhead, burrow over the coal to the pump-well cofferdam, where, another hole having been easily made in the wood, we got down below with Davy lamps and set to work. The water was so deep that you had to continually dive to get your hand on to the suction. After 2 hours or so it was cleared for the time being and the pumps worked merrily. I went in again at 4.30 A.M. and had another lap at clearing it. Not till the afternoon of the following day, though, did we see the last of the water and the last of the great gale. During the time the pumps were working, we continued the baling till the water got below the furnaces. As soon as we could light up, we did, and got the other pumps under weigh, and, once the ship was empty, clearing away the suction was a simple matter. I was pleased to find that after all I had only lost about 100 gallons of the petrol and bad as things had been they might have been worse....

"You will ask where all the water came from seeing our forward leak had been stopped. Thank God we did not have that to cope with as well. The water came chiefly through the deck where the tremendous strain,—not only of the deck load, but of the smashing seas,—was beyond conception. She was caught at a tremendous disadvantage and we were dependent for our lives on each plank standing its own strain. Had one gone we would all have gone, and the great anxiety was not so much the existing water as what was going to open up if the storm continued. We might have dumped the deck cargo, a difficult job at best, but were too busy baling to do anything else....

"That Captain Scott's account will be moderate you may be sure. Still, take my word for it, he is one of the best, and behaved up to our best traditions at a time when his own outlook must have been the blackness of darkness...."

Characteristically Bowers ends his account:

"Under its worst conditions this earth is a good place to live in."

Priestley wrote in his diary:

"If Dante had seen our ship as she was at her worst, I fancy he would have got a good idea for another Circle of Hell, though he would have been at a loss to account for such a cheerful and ribald lot of Souls."

The situation narrowed down to a fight between the incoming water and the men who were trying to keep it in check by baling her out. The Terra Nova will never be more full of water, nearly up to the furnaces, than she was that Friday morning, when we were told to go and do our damndest with three iron buckets. The constructors had not allowed for baling, only for the passage of one man at a time up and down the two iron ladders which connected the engine-room floor plates with the deck. If we used more than three buckets the business of passing them rapidly up, emptying them out of the hatchway, and returning them empty, became unprofitable. We were divided into two gangs, and all Friday and Friday night we worked two hours on and two hours off, like fiends.

Wilson's Journal describes the scene:

"It was a weird night's work with the howling gale and the darkness and the immense seas running over the ship every few minutes and no engines and no sail, and we all in the engine-room oil and bilge water, singing chanties as we passed up slopping buckets full of bilge, each man above slopping a little over the heads of all below him; wet through to the skin, so much so that some of the party worked altogether naked like Chinese coolies; and the rush of the wave backwards and forwards at the bottom grew hourly less in the dim light of a couple of engine-room oil lamps whose light just made the darkness visible, the ship all the time rolling like a sodden lifeless log, her lee gunwale under water every time."

"There was one thrilling moment in the midst of the worst hour on Friday when we were realizing that the fires must be drawn, and when every pump had failed to act, and when the bulwarks began to go to pieces and the petrol cases were all afloat and going overboard, and the word was suddenly passed in a shout from the hands at work in the waist of the ship trying to save petrol cases that smoke was coming up through the seams in the afterhold. As this was full of coal and patent fuel and was next the engine-room, and as it had not been opened for the airing it required to get rid of gas, on account of the flood of water on deck making it impossible to open the hatchway, the possibility of a fire there was patent to every one, and it could not possibly have been dealt with in any way short of opening the hatches and flooding the ship, when she must have foundered. It was therefore a thrilling moment or two until it was discovered that the smoke was really steam, arising from the bilge at the bottom having risen to the heated coal."[46]

Meanwhile men were working for all our lives to cut through two bulkheads which cut off all communication with the suction of the hand-pumps. One bulkhead was iron, the other wood.

Scott wrote at this time:

"We are not out of the wood, but hope dawns, as indeed it should for me, when I find myself so wonderfully served. Officers and men are singing chanties over their arduous work. Williams is working in sweltering heat behind the boiler to get the door made in the bulkhead. Not a single one has lost his good spirits. A dog was drowned last night, one pony is dead and two others in a bad condition— probably they too will go. Occasionally a heavy sea would bear one of them away, and he was only saved by his chain. Meares with some helpers had constantly to be rescuing these wretched creatures from hanging, and trying to find them better shelter, an almost hopeless task. One poor beast was found hanging when dead; one was washed away with such force that his chain broke and he disappeared overboard; the next wave miraculously washed him on board again and he is fit and well. [I believe the dog was Osman.] The gale has exacted heavy toll, but I feel all will be well if we can only cope with the water. Another dog has just been washed overboard—alas! Thank God the gale is abating. The sea is still mountainously high but the ship is not labouring so heavily as she was."[47]

The highest waves of which I can find any record were 36 feet high. These were observed by Sir James C. Ross in the North Atlantic.[48]

On December 2 the waves were logged, probably by Pennell, who was extremely careful in his measurements, as being 'thirty-five feet high (estimated).' At one time I saw Scott, standing on the weather rail of the poop, buried to his waist in green sea. The reader can then imagine the condition of things in the waist of the ship, "over and over again the rail, from the fore-rigging to the main, was covered by a solid sheet of curling water which swept aft and high on the poop."[49] At another time Bowers and Campbell were standing upon the bridge, and the ship rolled sluggishly over until the lee combings of the main hatch were under the sea. They watched anxiously, and slowly she righted herself, but "she won't do that often," said Bowers. As a rule if a ship gets that far over she goes down.

Our journey was uneventful for a time, but of course it was not by any means smooth. "I was much disturbed last night by the motion; the ship was pitching and twisting with short sharp movements on a confused sea, and with every plunge my thoughts flew to our poor ponies. This afternoon they are fairly well, but one

[46] Wilson's Journal.
[47] *Scott's Last Expedition*, vol. i. pp. 14-15.
[48] Raper, *Practice of Navigation*, article 547.
[49] *Scott's Last Expedition*, vol. i. p. 13.

knows that they must be getting weaker as time goes on, and one longs to give them a good sound rest with a ship on an even keel. Poor patient beasts! One wonders how far the memory of such fearful discomfort will remain with them—animals so often remember places and conditions where they have encountered difficulties or hurt. Do they only recollect circumstances which are deeply impressed by some shock of fear or sudden pain, and does the remembrance of prolonged strain pass away? Who can tell? But it would seem strangely merciful if nature should blot out these weeks of slow but inevitable torture."[50]

On December 7, noon position 61° 22′ S., 179° 56′ W., one berg was sighted far away to the west, as it gleamed every now and then in the sun. Two more were seen the next day, and at 6.22 A.M. on December 9, noon position 65° 8′ S., 177° 41′ W., the pack was sighted ahead by Rennick. All that day we passed bergs and streams of ice. The air became dry and bracing, the sea was calm, and the sun shining on the islands of ice was more than beautiful. And then Bump! We had just charged the first big floe, and we were in the pack.

"The sky has been wonderful, with every form of cloud in every condition of light and shade; the sun has continually appeared through breaks in the cloudy heavens from time to time, brilliantly illuminating some field of pack, some steep-walled berg, or some patch of bluest sea. So sunlight and shadow have chased each other across our scene. To-night there is little or no swell—the ship is on an even keel, steady, save for the occasional shocks on striking ice.

"It is difficult to express the sense of relief this steadiness gives after our storm-tossed passage. One can only imagine the relief and comfort afforded to the ponies, but the dogs are visibly cheered and the human element is full of gaiety. The voyage seems full of promise in spite of the imminence of delay."[51]

We had met the pack farther north than any other ship.

What is pack? Speaking very generally indeed, in this region it is the sea-ice which forms over the Ross Sea area during the winter, and is blown northwards by the southerly blizzards. But as we shall see, the ice which forms over this area is of infinite variety. As a rule great sheets spread over the seas which fringe the Antarctic continent in the autumn, grow thicker and thicker during the winter and spring, and break up when the temperatures of sea and air rise in summer. Such is the ice which forms in normal seasons round the shores of McMurdo Sound, and up the coast of the western mountains of Victoria Land. In sheltered bays this ice will sometimes remain in for two years or even more, growing all the time, until some phenomenal break-up releases it. We found an example of this in the sea-ice which formed between Hut Point and the Barrier. But there are great waters which can never freeze for very long. Cape Crozier, for instance, where the Emperor penguins nest in winter, is one of the windiest places in the world. In July it was completely frozen over as far as we could see in the darkness from a height of 900 feet. Within a few days a hurricane had blown it all away, and the sea was black.

I believe, and we had experiences to prove me right, that there is a critical peri-

[50] *Scott's Last Expedition*, vol. i. pp. 21-22.
[51] *Ibid.* pp. 24-25.

od early in the winter, and that if sea-ice has not frozen thick enough to remain fast by that time, it is probable that the sea will remain open for the rest of the year. But this does not mean that no ice will form. So great is the wish of the sea to freeze, and so cold is the air, that the wind has only to lull for one instant and the surface is covered with a thin film of ice, as though by magic. But the next blizzard tears it out by force or a spring tide coaxes it out by stealth, whether it be a foot thick or only a fraction of an inch. Such an example we had at our very doors during our last winter, and the untamed winds which blew as a result were atrocious.

Thus it is that floes from a few inches to twenty feet thick go voyaging out to join the belt of ice which is known as the pack. Scott seems to have thought that the whole Ross Sea freezes over.[52] I myself think this doubtful, and I am, I believe, the only person living who has seen the Ross Sea open in mid-winter. This was on the Winter Journey undertaken by Wilson, Bowers and myself in pursuit of Emperor penguin eggs—but of that later.

It is clear that winds and currents are, broadly speaking, the governing factors of the density of pack-ice. By experience we know that clear water may be found in the autumn where great tracts of ice barred the way in summer. The tendency of the pack is northwards, where the ice melts into the warmer waters. But the bergs remain when all traces of the pack have disappeared, and, drifting northwards still, form the menace to shipping so well known to sailors rounding the Horn. It is not hard to imagine that one monster ice island of twenty miles in length, such as do haunt these seas, drifting into navigated waters and calving into hundreds of great bergs as it goes, will in itself produce what seamen call a bad year for ice. And the last stages of these, when the bergs have degenerated into 'growlers,' are even worse, for then the sharpest eye can hardly distinguish them as they float nearly submerged though they have lost but little of their powers of evil.

There are two main types of Antarctic berg. The first and most common is the tabular form. Bergs of this shape cruise about in thousands and thousands. A less common form is known as the pinnacled berg, and in almost every case this is a tabular berg which has been weathered or has capsized. The number of bergs which calve direct from a mountain glacier into the sea is probably not very great. Whence then do they come?

The origin of the tabular bergs was debated until a few years ago. They have been recorded up to forty and even fifty miles in length, and they have been called floe bergs, because it was supposed that they froze first as ordinary sea-ice and increased by subsequent additions from below. But now we know that these bergs calve off from the Antarctic Barriers, the largest of which is known as the Great Ice Barrier, which forms the southern boundary of the Ross Sea. We were to become very familiar with this vast field of ice. We know that its northern face is afloat, we guess that it may all be afloat. At any rate the open sea now washes against its face at least forty miles south of where it ran in the days of Ross. Though this Barrier may be the largest in the world, it is one of many. The most modern review of this mystery, Scott's article on The Great Ice Barrier, must serve until the next first-hand examination by some future explorer.

[52] *Scott's Last Expedition*, vol. i. p. 2.

A berg shows only about one-eighth of its total mass above water, and a berg two hundred feet high will therefore reach approximately fourteen hundred feet below the surface of the sea. Winds and currents have far more influence upon them than they have upon the pack, through which these bergs plough their way with a total disregard for such flimsy obstacles, and cause much chaos as they go. For the rest woe betide the ship which is so fixed into the pack that she cannot move if one of these monsters bears down upon her.

Words cannot tell the beauty of the scenes through which we were to pass during the next three weeks. I suppose the pack in winter must be a terrible place enough: a place of darkness and desolation hardly to be found elsewhere. But forms which under different conditions can only betoken horror now conveyed to us impressions of the utmost peace and beauty, for the sun had kissed them all.

"We have had a marvellous day. The morning watch was cloudy, but it gradually cleared until the sky was a brilliant blue, fading on the horizon into green and pink. The floes were pink, floating in a deep blue sea, and all the shadows were mauve. We passed right under a monster berg, and all day have been threading lake after lake and lead after lead. 'There is Regent Street,' said somebody, and for some time we drove through great streets of perpendicular walls of ice. Many a time they were so straight that one imagined they had been cut off with a ruler some hundreds of yards in length."[53]

MIDNIGHT — E. A. WILSON, DEL.

On another occasion:

"Stayed on deck till midnight. The sun just dipped below the southern hori-

---

[53] My own diary.

zon. The scene was incomparable. The northern sky was gloriously rosy and reflected in the calm sea between the ice, which varied from burnished copper to salmon pink; bergs and pack to the north had a pale greenish hue with deep purple shadows, the sky shaded to saffron and pale green. We gazed long at these beautiful effects."[54]

But this was not always so. There was one day with rain, there were days of snow and hail and cold wet slush, and fog. "The position to-night is very cheerless. All hope that this easterly wind will open the pack seems to have vanished. We are surrounded with compacted floes of immense area. Openings appear between these floes and we slide crab-like from one to another with long delays between. It is difficult to keep hope alive. There are streaks of water sky over open leads to the north, but everywhere to the south we have the uniform white sky. The day has been overcast and the wind force 3 to 5 from the E.N.E.—snow has fallen from time to time. There could scarcely be a more dreary prospect for the eye to rest upon."[55]

With the open water we left behind the albatross and the Cape pigeon which had accompanied us lately for many months. In their place we found the Antarctic petrel, "a richly piebald bird that appeared to be almost black and white against the ice floes,"[56] and the Snowy petrel, of which I have already spoken.

No one of us whose privilege it was to be there will forget our first sight of the penguins, our first meal of seal meat, or that first big berg along which we coasted close in order that London might see it on the film. Hardly had we reached the thick pack, which prevailed after the suburbs had been passed, when we saw the little Adélie penguins hurrying to meet us. Great Scott, they seemed to say, what's this, and soon we could hear the cry which we shall never forget. "Aark, aark," they said, and full of wonder and curiosity, and perhaps a little out of breath, they stopped every now and then to express their feelings, "and to gaze and cry in wonder to their companions; now walking along the edge of a floe in search of a narrow spot to jump and so avoid the water, and with head down and much hesitation judging the width of the narrow gap, to give a little standing jump across as would a child, and running on the faster to make up for its delay. Again, coming to a wider lead of water necessitating a plunge, our inquisitive visitor would be lost for a moment, to reappear like a jack-in-the-box on a nearer floe, where wagging his tail, he immediately resumed his race towards the ship. Being now but a hundred yards or so from us he pokes his head constantly forward on this side and on that, to try and make out something of the new strange sight, crying aloud to his friends in his amazement, and exhibiting the most amusing indecision between his desire for further investigation and doubt as to the wisdom and propriety of closer contact with so huge a beast."[57]

They are extraordinarily like children, these little people of the Antarctic

[54] *Scott's Last Expedition*, vol. i. p. 25.

[55] *Ibid.* p. 60.

[56] Wilson.

[57] Wilson, *Discovery Natural History Report*, vol. ii. part ii. p. 38.

world, either like children, or like old men, full of their own importance and late for dinner, in their black tail-coats and white shirt-fronts—and rather portly withal. We used to sing to them, as they to us, and you might often see "a group of explorers on the poop, singing 'She has rings on her fingers and bells on her toes, and she shall have music wherever she goes,' and so on at the top of their voices to an admiring group of Adélie penguins."[58]

Meares used to sing to them what he called 'God save,' and declared that it would always send them headlong into the water. He sang flat: perhaps that was why.

Two or more penguins will combine to push a third in front of them against a skua gull, which is one of their enemies, for he eats their eggs or their young if he gets the chance. They will refuse to dive off an ice-foot until they have persuaded one of their companions to take the first jump, for fear of the sea-leopard which may be waiting in the water below, ready to seize them and play with them much as a cat will play with a mouse. As Levick describes in his book about the penguins at Cape Adare: "At the place where they most often went in, a long terrace of ice about six feet in height ran for some hundreds of yards along the edge of the water, and here, just as on the sea-ice, crowds would stand near the brink. When they had succeeded in pushing one of their number over, all would crane their necks over the edge, and when they saw the pioneer safe in the water, the rest followed."[59]

It is clear then that the Adélie penguin will show a certain spirit of selfishness in tackling his hereditary enemies. But when it comes to the danger of which he is ignorant his courage betrays want of caution. Meares and Dimitri exercised the dog-teams out upon the larger floes when we were held up for any length of time. One day a team was tethered by the side of the ship, and a penguin sighted them and hurried from afar off. The dogs became frantic with excitement as he neared them: he supposed it was a greeting, and the louder they barked and the more they strained at their ropes, the faster he bustled to meet them. He was extremely angry with a man who went and saved him from a very sudden end, clinging to his trousers with his beak, and furiously beating his shins with his flippers. It was not an uncommon sight to see a little Adélie penguin standing within a few inches of the nose of a dog which was almost frantic with desire and passion.

The pack-ice is the home of the immature penguins, both Emperor and Adélie. But we did not see any large numbers of immature Emperors during this voyage.

We soon became acquainted with the sea-leopard, which waits under the ice-foot for the little penguins; he is a brute, but sinuous and graceful as the seal world goes. He preys especially upon the Adélie penguin, and Levick found no less than eighteen penguins, together with the remains of many others, in the stomach of one sea-leopard. In the water the leopard seems "a trifle faster than the Adélies, as one of them occasionally would catch up with one of the fugitives, who then, realizing that speed alone would not avail him, started dodging from side to side, and sometimes swam rapidly round and round in a circle of about twelve feet

---

[58] Wilson's Journal.
[59] Levick, *Antarctic Penguins*, p. 83.

diameter for a full minute or more, doubtless knowing that he was quicker in turning than his great heavy pursuer, but exhaustion would overtake him in the end, and we could see the head and jaws of the great sea-leopard rise to the surface as he grabbed his victim. The sight of a panic-stricken little Adélie tearing round and round in this manner was sadly common late in the season."[60]

Fish and small seal have also been found in its stomach. With long powerful head and neck and a sinuous body, it is equipped with most formidable teeth with which it tears strips out of the still living birds, and flippers which are adapted entirely for speed in the water. It is a solitary animal with a large range of distribution. It has been supposed to bring forth its young in the pack, but nothing definite is known on this subject. One day we saw a big sea-leopard swimming along with the ship. He dived under the floes and reappeared from floe to floe as we went, and for a time we thought he was interested in us. But soon we sighted another lying away on a floe, and our friend in the water began to rear his head up perpendicularly, and seemed to be trying to wind his mate, as we supposed. He was down wind from her, and appeared to find her at a distance of 150 to 200 yards, and the last we saw of him he was heading up the side of the floe where she lay.

There are four kinds of seal in the Antarctic; of one of these, the sea-leopard, I have already spoken. Another is called the Ross seal, for Sir James Ross discovered it in 1840. It seems to be a solitary beast, living in the pack, and is peculiar for its "pug-like expression of countenance."[61] It has always been rare, and no single specimen was seen on this expedition, though the Terra Nova must have passed through more pack than most whalers see in a life-time. It looks as if the Ross seal is more rare than was supposed.

A SEA LEOPARD

A WEDDELL SEAL

[60] Levick, *Antarctic Penguins*, p. 85.
[61] Wilson in the *Discovery Natural History Report, Zoology*, vol. ii. part i. p. 44.

The very common seal of the Antarctic is the Weddell, which seldom lives in the pack but spends its life catching fish close to the shores of the continent, and digesting them, when caught, lying sluggishly upon the ice-foot. We came to know them later in their hundreds in McMurdo Sound, for the Weddell is a land-loving seal and is only found in large numbers near the coast. Just at this time it was the crab-eating seal which we saw very fairly often, generally several of them together, but never in large numbers.

Wilson has pointed out in his article upon seals in the Discovery Report[62] that the Weddell and the crab-eater seal, which are the two commoner of the Antarctic seals, have agreed to differ both in habit and in diet, and therefore they share the field successfully. He shows that "the two penguins which share the same area have differentiated in a somewhat similar manner." The Weddell seal and the Emperor penguin "have the following points in common, namely, a littoral distribution, a fish diet and residential non-migratory habit, remaining as far south the whole year round as open water will allow; whereas the other two (the crab-eating seal and the Adélie penguin) have in common a more pelagic habit, a crustacean diet, and a distribution definitely migratory in the case of the penguin, and although not so definitely migratory in the case of the seal, yet checked from coming so far south as Weddell's seal in winter by a strong tendency to keep in touch with pelagic ice."[63] Wilson considers that the advantage lies in each case with the "non-migratory and more southern species," i.e. the Weddell seal and the Emperor penguin. I doubt whether he would confirm this now. The Emperor penguin, weighing six stones and more, seems to me to have a very much harder fight for life than the little Adélie.

Before the Discovery started from England in 1901 an 'Antarctic Manual' was produced by the Royal Geographical Society, giving a summary of the information which existed up to that date about this part of the world. It is interesting reading, and to the Antarctic student it proves how little was known in some branches of science at that date, and what strides were made during the next few years. To read what was known of the birds and beasts of the Antarctic and then to read Wilson's Zoological Report of the Discovery Expedition is an education in what one man can still do in an out-of-the-way part of the world to elucidate the problems which await him.

The teeth of a crab-eating seal "are surmounted by perhaps the most complicated arrangement of cusps found in any living mammal."[64] The mouth is so arranged that the teeth of the upper jaw fit into those of the lower, and "the cusps form a perfect sieve ... a hitherto unparalleled function for the teeth of a mammal."[65] The food of this seal consists mainly of Euphausiae, animals much like shrimps, which it doubtless keeps in its mouth while it expels the water through its teeth, like those whales which sift their food through their baleen plates." This development of cusps in the teeth of the [crab-eating seal] is probably a more

[62] *Discovery Natural History Report, Zoology*, vol. ii. part i. Wilson, pp. 32, 33.
[63] *Ibid.* p. 33.
[64] *Antarctic Manual: Seals*, by Barrett-Hamilton, p. 216.
[65] *Ibid.* p. 217.

perfect adaptation to this purpose than in any other mammal, and has been produced at the cost of all usefulness in the teeth as grinders. The grit, however, which
forms a fairly constant part of the contents of the stomach and intestines, serves,
no doubt, to grind up the shells of the crustaceans, and in this way the necessity
for grinders is completely obviated."[66]

The sea-leopard has a very formidable set of teeth suitable for his carnivorous
diet. The Weddell, living on fish, has a more simple group, but these are liable
to become very worn in old age, due to his habit of gnawing out holes in the ice
for himself, so graphically displayed on Ponting's cinematograph. When he feels
death approaching, the crab-eating seal, never inclined to live in the company of
more than a few of his kind, becomes still more solitary. The Weddell seal will
travel far up the glaciers of South Victoria Land, and there we have found them
lying dead. But the crab-eating seal will wander even farther. He leaves the pack.
"Thirty miles from the sea-shore and 3000 feet above sea-level, their carcases were
found on quite a number of occasions, and it is hard to account for such vagaries
on other grounds than that a sick animal will go any distance to get away from its
companions"[67] (and perhaps it should be added from its enemies).

Often the under sides of the floes were coloured a peculiar yellow. This coloration is caused by minute unicellular plants called diatoms. The floating life of
the Antarctic is most dense. "Diatoms were so abundant in parts of the Ross Sea,
that a large plankton net (18 meshes to an inch) became choked in a few minutes
with them and other members of the Phytoplankton. It is extremely probable that
in such localities whales feed upon the plants as well as the animals of the plankton."[68] I do not know to what extent these open waters are frequented by whales
during the winter, but in the summer months they are full of them, right down
to the fringe of the continent. Most common of all is the kind of sea-wolf known
as the Killer Whale, who measures 30 feet long. He hunts in packs up to at least a
hundred strong, and as we now know, he does not confine his attacks to seal and
other whales, but will also hunt man, though perhaps he mistakes him for a seal.
This whale is a toothed beast and a flesh-eater, and is more properly a dolphin.
But it seems that there are at least five or six other kinds of whales, some of which
do not penetrate south of the pack, while others cruise in large numbers right up
to the edge of the fast ice. They feed upon the minute surface life of these seas, and
large numbers of them were seen not only by the Terra Nova on her various cruis-
es, but also by the shore parties in the waters of McMurdo Sound. In both Wilson
and Lillie we had skilled whale observers, and their work has gone far to elucidate
the still obscure questions of whale distribution in the South.

The pack-ice offers excellent opportunities for the identification of whales,
because their movements are more restricted than in the open ocean. In order to
identify, the observer generally has only the blow, and then the shape of the back
and fin as the whale goes down, to guide him. In the pack he sometimes gets
more, as in the case of Balaenoptera acutorostrata (Piked whale) on March 3, 1911.

[66] *Discovery Natural History Report, Zoology*, vol. ii. part i. by E. A. Wilson, p. 36.
[67] *Discovery Natural History Report, Zoology*, vol. ii. part i. by E. A. Wilson.
[68] *Terra Nova Natural History Report, Cetacea*, vol. i. No. 3, p. 111, by Lillie.

The ship "was ploughing her way through thick pack-ice, in which the water was freezing between the floes, so that the only open spaces for miles around were those made by the slow movement of the ship. We saw several of these whales during the day, making use of the holes in the ice near the ship for the purpose of blowing. There was scarcely room between the floes for the whales to come up to blow in their usual manner, which consists in rising almost horizontally, and breaking the surface of the water with their backs. On this occasion they pushed their snouts obliquely out of the water, nearly as far as the eye, and after blowing, withdrew them below the water again. Commander Pennell noted that several times one rested its head on a floe not twenty feet from the ship, with its nostrils just on the water-line; raising itself a few inches, it would blow and then subside again for a few minutes to its original position with its snout resting on the floe. They took no notice of pieces of coal which were thrown at them by the men on board the ship."[69]

But no whale which we saw in the pack, and we often saw it elsewhere also, was so imposing as the great Blue whale, some of which were possibly more than 100 feet long. "We used to watch this huge whale come to the surface again and again to blow, at intervals of thirty to forty seconds, and from the fact that at each of four or five appearances no vestige of a dorsal fin was visible, we began to wonder whether we had not found the Right whale that was once reported to be so abundant in Ross Sea. Again and again the spout went up into the cold air, a white twelve-foot column of condensed moisture, followed by a smooth broad back, and yet no fin. For some time we remained uncertain as to its identity, till at last in sounding for a longer disappearance and a greater depth than usual, the hinder third of the enormous beast appeared above the surface for the first time with its little angular dorsal fin, at once dispelling any doubts we might have had."[70]

It is supposed to be the largest mammal that has ever existed.[71] As it comes up to blow, "one sees first a small dark hump appear and then immediately a jet of grey fog squirted upwards fifteen to eighteen feet, gradually spreading as it rises vertically into the frosty air. I have been nearly in these blows once or twice and had the moisture in my face with a sickening smell of shrimpy oil. Then the hump elongates and up rolls an immense blue-grey or blackish-grey round back with a faint ridge along the top, on which presently appears a small hook-like dorsal fin, and then the whole sinks and disappears."[72]

To the biologist the pack is of absorbing interest. If you want to see life, naked and unashamed, study the struggles of this ice-world, from the diatom in the ice-floe to the big killer whale; each stage essential to the life of the stage above, and living on the stage below:

THE PROTOPLASMIC CYCLE

[69] *Terra Nova Natural History Report, Zoology*, vol. i. No. 3, *Cetacea*, by D. G. Lillie, p. 114.

[70] *Discovery Natural History Report, Zoology*, vol. ii. part i. pp. 3-4, by E. A. Wilson.

[71] *Scott's Last Expedition*, vol. i. p. 22.

[72] Wilson's Journal, *Scott's Last Expedition*, vol. i. p. 613.

Big floes have little floes all around about 'em,
And all the yellow diatoms[73] couldn't do without 'em.
Forty million shrimplets feed upon the latter,
And *they* make the penguin and the seals and whales
Much fatter.

Along comes the Orca[74] and kills these down below,
While up above the Afterguard[75] attack them on the floe:
And if a sailor tumbles in and stoves the mushy pack in,
He's crumpled up between the floes, and so they get
Their whack in.

Then there's no doubt he soon becomes a Patent Fertilizer,
Invigorating diatoms, although they're none the wiser,
So the protoplasm passes on its never-ceasing round,
Like a huge recurring decimal ... to which no
End is found.[76]

We were early on the scene compared with previous expeditions, but I do not suppose this alone can explain the extremely heavy ice conditions we met. Possibly we were too far east. Our progress was very slow, and often we were hung up for days at a time, motionless and immovable, the pack all close about us. Patience and always more patience! "From the masthead one can see a few patches of open water in different directions, but the main outlook is the same scene of desolate hummocky pack."[77] And again: "We have scarcely moved all day, but bergs which have become quite old friends are on the move, and one has approached and almost circled us."[78]

And then without warning and reason, as far as we could see, it would open out again, and broad black leads and lakes would appear where there had been only white snow and ice before, and we would make just a few more miles, and sometimes we would raise steam only to suffer further disappointment. Generally speaking, a dark black sky means open water, and this is known as an open-water sky; high lights in the sky mean ice, and this is known as ice-blink.

The changes were as sudden as they were unexpected. Thus early in the morning of Christmas Eve, about a fortnight after we had entered the pack, "we have come into a region of where the open water exceeds the ice; the former lies in great irregular pools three or four miles or more across and connecting with many leads. The latter—and the fact is puzzling—still contain floes of enormous dimensions; we have just passed one which is at least two miles in diameter...." And then, "Alas! alas! at 7 A.M. this morning we were brought up with a solid sheet of pack

---

[73] Minute plants.
[74] Killer whale.
[75] Officers' mess on the Terra Nova.
[76] Griffith Taylor in *South Polar Times*.
[77] *Scott's Last Expedition*, vol. i. p. 35.
[78] *Ibid.* p. 39.

extending in all directions, save that from which we had come."[79]

Delay was always irksome to Scott. As time went on this waiting in the pack became almost intolerable. He began to think we might have to winter in the pack. And all the time our scanty supply of coal was being eaten up, until it was said that Campbell's party would never be taken to King Edward VII.'s Land. Scott found decisions to bank fires, to raise steam or to let fires out, most difficult at this time. "If one lets fires out it means a dead loss of over two tons, when the boiler has to be heated again. But this two tons would only cover a day under banked fires, so that for anything longer than twenty-four hours it is economy to put the fires out. At each stoppage one is called upon to decide whether it is to be for more or less than twenty-four hours."[80] Certainly England should have an oil-driven ship for polar work.

The Terra Nova proved a wonderfully fine ice ship. Bowers' middle watch especially became famous for the way in which he put the ship at the ice, and more than once Scott was alarmed by the great shock and collisions which were the result: I have seen him hurry up from his cabin to put a stop to it! But Bowers never hurt the ship, and she gallantly responded to the calls made upon her. Sometimes it was a matter of forcing two floes apart, at others of charging and breaking one. Often we went again and again at some stubborn bit, backing and charging alternately, as well as the space behind us would allow. If sufficient momentum was gained the ship rode upon the thicker floes, rising up upon it and pressing it down beneath her, until suddenly, perhaps when its nearest edge was almost amidships, the weight became too great and the ice split beneath us. At other times a tiny crack, no larger than a vein, would run shivering from our bows, which widened and widened until the whole ship passed through without difficulty. Always when below one heard the grumbling of the ice as it passed along the side. But it was slow work, and hard on the engines. There were days when we never moved at all.

"I can imagine few things more trying to the patience than the long wasted days of waiting. Exasperating as it is to see the tons of coal melting away with the smallest mileage to our credit, one has at least the satisfaction of active fighting and the hope of better fortune. To wait idly is the worst of conditions. You can imagine how often and how restlessly we climbed to the crow's nest and studied the outlook. And strangely enough there was generally some change to note. A water lead would mysteriously open up a few miles away, or the place where it had been would as mysteriously close. Huge icebergs crept silently towards or past us, and continually we were observing these formidable objects with range finder and compass to determine the relative movement, sometimes with misgivings as to our ability to clear them. Under steam the change of conditions was even more marked. Sometimes we would enter a lead of open water and proceed for a mile or two without hindrance; sometimes we would come to big sheets of thin ice which broke easily as our iron-shod prow struck them, and sometimes even a thin sheet would resist all our attempts to break it; sometimes we would push big floes

[79] *Ibid.* pp. 54, 55.
[80] *Scott's Last Expedition*, vol. i. p. 56.

with comparative ease and sometimes a small floe would bar our passage with such obstinacy that one would almost believe it possessed of an evil spirit; sometimes we passed through acres of sludgy sodden ice which hissed as it swept along the side, and sometimes the hissing ceased seemingly without rhyme or reason, and we found our screw churning the sea without any effect.

"Thus the steaming days passed away in an ever-changing environment and are remembered as an unceasing struggle.

"The ship behaved splendidly—no other ship, not even the Discovery, would have come through so well. Certainly the Nimrod would never have reached the south water had she been caught in such pack. As a result I have grown strangely attached to the Terra Nova. As she bumped the floes with mighty shocks, crushing and grinding a way through some, twisting and turning to avoid others, she seemed like a living thing fighting a great fight. If only she had more economical engines she would be suitable in all respects.

TERRA NOVA

"Once or twice we got among floes which stood 7 or 8 feet above water, with hummocks and pinnacles as high as 25 feet. The ship could have stood no chance had such floes pressed against her, and at first we were a little alarmed in such situations. But familiarity breeds contempt; there never was any pressure in the heavy ice, and I'm inclined to think there never would be.

"The weather changed frequently during our journey through the pack. The wind blew strong from the west and from the east; the sky was often darkly overcast; we had snowstorms, flaky snow, and even light rain. In all such circumstances we were better placed in the pack than outside of it. The foulest weather could do us little harm. During quite a large percentage of days, however, we had bright sunshine, which, even with the temperature well below freezing, made everything look bright and cheerful. The sun also brought us wonderful cloud effects, marvellously delicate tints of sky, cloud and ice, such effects as one might travel far to see. In spite of our impatience we would not willingly have missed many of the beautiful scenes which our sojourn in the pack afforded us. Ponting and Wilson have been busy catching these effects, but no art can reproduce such colours as the deep blue of the icebergs."[81]

As a rule the officer of the watch conned from the crow's nest, shouting his orders to the steersman direct, and to the engine-room through the midshipman of the watch, who stood upon the bridge. It is thrilling work to the officer in charge, who not only has to face the immediate problem of what floes he dare and what he dare not charge, but also to puzzle out the best course for the future,—but I expect he soon gets sick of it.

About this time Bowers made a fancy sketch of the Terra Nova hitting an enormous piece of ice. The masts are all whipped forward, and from the crow's nest is shot first the officer of the watch, followed by cigarette ends and empty cocoa mugs, and lastly the hay with which the floor was covered. Upon the forecastle stands Farmer Hayseed (Oates) chewing a straw with the greatest composure, and waiting until the hay shall fall at his feet, at which time he will feed it to his ponies. This crow's nest, which was a barrel lashed to the top of the mainmast, to which entrance was gained by a hinged trap-door, shielded the occupant from most of the wind. I am not sure that the steersman did not have the most uninviting job, but hot cocoa is a most comforting drink and there was always plenty to be had.

Rennick was busy sounding. The depths varied from 1804 to at least 3890 fathoms, and the bottom generally showed volcanic deposits. Our line of soundings showed the transition from the ocean depths to the continental shelf. A series of temperatures was gained by Nelson by means of reversible thermometers down to 3891 metres.

The winch upon which the sounding line was wound was worked by hand on this cruise. It was worked mechanically afterwards, and of course this ought always to be done if possible. Just now it was a wearisome business, especially when we lowered a water-sample bottle one day to 1800 metres, spent hours in winding it up and found it still open when it arrived at the surface! Water samples were also

---

[81] *Scott's Last Expedition*, vol. i. pp. 73-75.

obtained at the various depths. Lillie and Nelson were both busy tow-netting for plankton with full-speed, Apstein, Nansen, 24-and 180-mesh nets.

I don't think many at home had a more pleasant Christmas Day than we. It was beautifully calm with the pack all round. At 10 we had church with lots of Christmas hymns, and then decorated the ward-room with all our sledging flags. These flags are carried by officers on Arctic expeditions, and are formed of the St. George's Cross with a continuation ending in a swallow-tail in the heraldic colours to which the individual is entitled, and upon this is embroidered his crest. The men forrard had their Christmas dinner of fresh mutton at mid-day; there was plenty of penguin for them, but curiously enough they did not think it good enough for a Christmas dinner. The ward-room ate penguin in the evening, and after the toast of 'absent friends' we began to sing, and twice round the table everybody had to contribute a song. Ponting's banjo songs were a great success, also Oates's 'The Vly on the tu-urmuts.' Meares sang "a little song about our Expedition, and many of the members that Southward would go," of his own composition. The general result was that the watches were all over the place that night. At 4 A.M. Day whispered in my ear that there was nothing to do, and Pennell promised to call me if there was—so I remembered no more until past six.

And Crean's rabbit gave birth to seventeen little ones, and it was said that Crean had already given away twenty-two.

We had stopped and banked fires against an immense composite floe on the evening of Christmas Eve. How we watched the little changes in the ice and the wind, and scanned the horizon for those black patches which meant open water ahead. But always there was that same white sky to the south of us. And then one day there came the shadow of movement on the sea, the faintest crush on the brash ice, the whisper of great disturbances afar off. It settled again: our hopes were dashed to the ground. Then came the wind. It was so thick that we could not see far; but even in our restricted field changes were in progress.

"We commence to move between two floes, make 200 or 300 yards, and are then brought up bows on to a large lump. This may mean a wait of anything from ten minutes to half-an-hour, whilst the ship swings round, falls away, and drifts to leeward. When clear she forges ahead again and the operation is repeated. Occasionally when she can get a little way on she cracks the obstacle and slowly passes through it. There is a distinct swell—very long, very low. I counted the period as about nine seconds. Every one says the ice is breaking up."[82]

On December 28 the gale abated. The sky cleared, and showed signs of open water ahead. It was cold in the wind but the sun was wonderful, and we lay out on deck and basked in its warmth, a cheerful, careless crowd. After breakfast there was a consultation between Scott and Wilson in the crow's nest. It was decided to raise steam.

Meanwhile we sounded, and found a volcanic muddy bottom at 2035 fathoms. The last sounding showed 1400 fathoms; we had passed over a bank.

Steam came at 8 P.M. and we began to push forward. At first it was hard go-

[82] *Scott's Last Expedition*, vol. i. p. 62.

ing, but slowly we elbowed our way until the spaces of open water became more frequent. Soon we found one or two large pools, several miles in extent; then the floes became smaller. Later we could see no really big floes at all; "the sheets of thin ice are broken into comparatively regular figures, none more than thirty yards across," and "we are steaming amongst floes of small area evidently broken by swell, and with edges abraded by contact."[83]

We could not be far from the southern edge of the pack. Twenty-four hours after raising steam we were still making good progress, checking sometimes to carve our way through some obstacle. At last we were getting a return for the precious coal expended. The sky was overcast, the outlook from the masthead flat and dreary, but hour by hour it became more obvious that we neared the threshold of the open sea. At 1 A.M. on Friday, December 30 (lat. about 71½° S., noon observation 72° 17′ S., 177° 9′ E.) Bowers steered through the last ice stream. Behind was some 400 miles of ice. Cape Crozier was 334 miles (geog.) ahead.

---

[83] *Scott's Last Expedition,* vol. i. pp. 68, 69.

CHAPTER IV

LAND

Beyond this flood a frozen continent
Lies dark and wilde, beat with perpetual storms
Of whirlwind and dire hail, which on firm land
Thaws not, but gathers heap, and ruin seems
Of ancient pile; all else deep snow and ice....

MILTON, *Paradise Lost*, II.

"They say it's going to blow like hell. Go and look at the glass." Thus Titus Oates quietly to me a few hours before we left the pack.

I went and looked at the barograph and it made me feel sea-sick. Within a few hours I was sick, *very* sick; but we newcomers to the Antarctic had yet to learn that we knew nothing about its barometer. Nothing very terrible happened after all. When I got up to the bridge for the morning watch we were in open water and it was blowing fresh. It freshened all day, and by the evening it was blowing a southerly with a short choppy North Sea swell, and very warm. By 4 A.M. the next morning there was a big sea running and the dogs and ponies were having a bad time. Rennick had the morning watch these days, and I was his humble midshipman.

At 5.45 we sighted what we thought was a berg on the port bow. About three minutes later Rennick said, "There's a bit of pack," and I went below and reported to Evans. It was very thick with driving snow and also foggy, and before Evans got up to the bridge we were quite near the pack, and amongst bits which had floated from it, one of which must have been our berg. We took in the headsails as quickly as possible, these being the only sails set, and nosed along dead slow to leeward under steam alone. Gradually we could see either pack or the blink of it all along our port and starboard beam, while gradually we felt our way down a big patch of open water.

There was quite a meeting on the bridge, and it was decided to get well in, and lie in open water under lee of the pack till the gale blew itself out. "Under ordinary circumstances the safe course would have been to go about and stand to the east. But in our case we must risk trouble to get smoother water for the ponies. We passed a stream of ice over which the sea was breaking heavily, and one realized the danger of being amongst loose floes in such a sea. But soon we came to a compacter body of floes, and running behind this we were agreeably surprised to find comparatively smooth water. We ran on for a bit, then stopped and lay to."[84]

[84] *Scott's Last Expedition*, vol. i. p. 77.

All that day we lay behind that pack, steaming slowly to leeward every now and then, as the ice drifted down upon us. Towards night it began to clear. It was New Year's Eve.

I turned in, thinking to wake in 1911. But I had not been long asleep when I found Atkinson at my side. "Have you seen the land?" he said. "Wrap your blankets round you, and go and see." And when I got up on deck I could see nothing for a while. Then he said: "All the high lights are snow lit up by the sun." And there they were: the most glorious peaks appearing, as it were like satin, above the clouds, the only white in a dark horizon. The first glimpse of Antarctic land, Sabine and the great mountains of the Admiralty Range. They were 110 miles away. But

> Icy mountains high on mountains pil'd
> Seem to the shivering sailor from afar
> Shapeless and white, an atmosphere of cloud;[85]

and, truth to tell, I went back to my warm bunk. At midnight a rowdy mob, ringing the New Year in with the dinner-bell, burst into our Nursery. I expected to be hauled out, but got off with a dig in the ribs from Birdie Bowers.

In brilliant sunshine we coasted down Victoria Land. "To-night it is absolutely calm, with glorious bright sunshine. Several people were sunning themselves at 11 o'clock! Sitting on deck and reading."[86]

At 8.30 on Monday night, January 2, we sighted Erebus, 115 miles away. The next morning most of us were on the yards furling sail. We were heading for Cape Crozier, the northern face of Ross Island was open to our fascinated gaze, and away to the east stretched the Barrier face until it disappeared below the horizon. Adélie penguins and Killer whales were abundant in the water through which we steamed.

I have seen Fuji, the most dainty and graceful of all mountains; and also Kinchinjunga: only Michael Angelo among men could have conceived such grandeur. But give me Erebus for my friend. Whoever made Erebus knew all the charm of horizontal lines, and the lines of Erebus are for the most part nearer the horizontal than the vertical. And so he is the most restful mountain in the world, and I was glad when I knew that our hut would lie at his feet. And always there floated from his crater the lazy banner of his cloud of steam.

Now we had reached the Barrier face some five miles east of the point at which it joins the basalt cliffs of Cape Crozier. We could see the great pressure waves which had proved such an obstacle to travellers from the Discovery to the Emperor penguin rookery. The Knoll was clear, but the summit of Mount Terror was in the clouds. As for the Barrier we seemed to have known it all our lives, it was so exactly like what we had imagined it to be, and seen in the pictures and photographs.

Scott had a whaler launched, and we pulled in under the cliffs. There was a considerable swell.

---

[85] Thomson.
[86] *Scott's Last Expedition,* vol. i. p. 80.

"We were to examine the possibilities of landing, but the swell was so heavy in its break among the floating blocks of ice along the actual beach and ice foot that a landing was out of the question. We should have broken up the boat and have all been in the water together. But I assure you it was tantalizing to me, for there about six feet above us on a small dirty piece of the old bay ice about ten feet square one living Emperor penguin chick was standing disconsolately stranded, and close by stood one faithful old Emperor parent asleep. This young Emperor was still in the down, a most interesting fact in the bird's life history at which we had rightly guessed, but which no one had actually observed before. It was in a stage never yet seen or collected, for the wings were already quite clean of down and feathered as in the adult, also a line down the breast was shed of down and part of the head. This bird would have been a treasure to me, but we could not risk life for it, so it had to remain where it was. It was a curious fact that with as much clean ice to live on as they could have wished for, these destitute derelicts of a flourishing colony, now gone north to sea on floating bay ice, should have preferred to remain standing on the only piece of bay ice left, a piece about ten feet square and now pressed up six feet above water level, evidently wondering why it was so long in starting north with the general exodus which must have taken place just a month ago. The whole incident was most interesting and full of suggestion as to the slow working of the brain of these queer people. Another point was most weird to see, that on the *under* side of this very dirty piece of sea-ice, which was about two feet thick and which hung over the water as a sort of cave, we could see the legs and lower halves of dead Emperor chicks hanging through, and even in one place a dead adult. I hope to make a picture of the whole quaint incident, for it was a corner crammed full of Imperial history in the light of what we already knew, and it would otherwise have been about as unintelligible as any group of animate or inanimate nature could possibly have been. As it is, it throws more light on the life history of this strangely primitive bird....

"We were joking in the boat as we rowed under these cliffs and saying it would be a short-lived amusement to see the overhanging cliff part company and fall on us. So we were glad to find that we were rowing back to the ship and already 200 or 300 yards away from the place and in open water when there was a noise like crackling thunder and a huge plunge into the sea and a smother of rock dust like the smoke of an explosion, and we realized that the very thing had happened which we had just been talking about. Altogether it was a very exciting row, for before we got on board we had the pleasure of seeing the ship shoved in so close to these cliffs by a belt of heavy pack ice that to us it appeared a toss-up whether she got out again or got forced in against the rocks. She had no time or room to turn, and got clear by backing out through the belt of pack stern first, getting heavy bumps under the counter and on the rudder as she did so, for the ice was heavy and the swell considerable."[87]

Westward of Cape Crozier the sides of Mount Terror slope down to the sea, forming a possible landing-place in calm weather. Here there is a large Adélie penguin rookery in summer, and it was here that the Discovery left a record of her

---

[87] Wilson's Journal, *Scott's Last Expedition*, vol. i. pp. 613, 614.

movements tied to a post to guide the relieving ship the following year. It was the return of a sledge party which tried to reach this record from the Barrier that led to Vince's terrible death.[88] As we coasted along we could see this post quite plainly, looking as new as the day it was erected, and we know now that there is communication with the Barrier behind, while this rookery itself is free from the blizzards which sweep out to sea by Cape Crozier. It was therefore an excellent place to winter and it was a considerable disappointment to find that it was impossible to land.

This was the first sight we had of a rookery of the little Adélie penguin. Hundreds of thousands of birds dotted the shore, and there were many thousands in the sea round the ship. As we came to know these rookeries better we came to look upon these quaint creatures more as familiar friends than as casual acquaintances. Whatever a penguin does has individuality, and he lays bare his whole life for all to see. He cannot fly away. And because he is quaint in all that he does, but still more because he is fighting against bigger odds than any other bird, and fighting always with the most gallant pluck, he comes to be considered as something apart from the ordinary bird—sometimes solemn, sometimes humorous, enterprising, chivalrous, cheeky—and always (unless you are driving a dog-team) a welcome and, in some ways, an almost human friend.

The alternative landing-place to Cape Crozier was somewhere in McMurdo Sound, the essential thing being that we should have access to and from the Barrier, such communication having to be by sea-ice, since the land is for the most part impassable. As we steamed from Cape Crozier to Cape Bird, the N.W. extremity of Ross Island, we carried out a detailed running survey.

When we neared Cape Bird and Beaufort Island we could see that there was much pack in the mouth of the Strait. By keeping close in to the land we avoided the worst of the trouble, and "as we rounded Cape Bird we came in sight of the old well-remembered landmarks—Mount Discovery and the Western Mountains—seen dimly through a hazy atmosphere. It was good to see them again, and perhaps after all we are better this side of the Island. It gives one a homely feeling to see such a familiar scene."[89]

Right round from Cape Crozier to Cape Royds the coast is cold and forbidding, and for the most part heavily crevassed. West of Cape Bird are some small penguin rookeries, and high up on the ice slopes could be seen some grey granite boulders. These are erratics, brought by ice from the Western Mountains, and are evidence of a warmer past when the Barrier rose some two thousand feet higher than it does now, and stretched many hundreds of miles farther out to sea. But now the Antarctic is becoming colder, the deposition of snow is therefore farther north, and the formation of ice correspondingly less.

---

[88] See Introduction, p. xxxv.
[89] *Scott's Last Expedition*, vol. i. p. 87.

SOUNDING—E. A. WILSON, DEL.

KRISRAVITZA

Many watched all night, as this new world unfolded itself, cape by cape and mountain by mountain. We pushed through some heavy floes and "at 6 A.M. (on January 4) we came through the last of the Strait pack some three miles north of Cape Royds. We steered for the Cape, fully expecting to find the edge of the pack-ice ranging westward from it. To our astonishment we ran on past the Cape with clear water or thin sludge ice on all sides of us. Past Cape Royds, past Cape Barne, past the glacier on its south side, and finally round and past Inaccessible Island, a good two miles south of Cape Royds. The Cape itself was cut off from the south. We could have gone farther, but the last sludge ice seemed to be increasing in thickness, and there was no wintering spot to aim for but Cape Armitage.[90] I have never seen the ice of the Sound in such a condition or the land so free from snow. Taking these facts in conjunction with the exceptional warmth of the air, I came to the conclusion that it had been an exceptionally warm summer. At this point it was evident that we had a considerable choice of wintering spots. We could have gone to either of the small islands, to the mainland, the Glacier Tongue, or pretty well anywhere except Hut Point. My main wish was to choose a place that would not

[90] The extreme south point of the island, a dozen miles farther, on one of whose minor headlands, Hut Point, stood the Discovery hut.

be easily cut off from the Barrier, and my eye fell on a cape which we used to call the Skuary, a little behind us. It was separated from the old Discovery quarters by two deep bays on either side of the Glacier Tongue, and I thought that these bays would remain frozen until late in the season, and that when they froze over again the ice would soon become firm. I called a council and put these propositions. To push on to the Glacier Tongue and winter there; to push west to the 'tombstone' ice and to make our way to an inviting spot to the northward of the cape we used to call 'the Skuary.' I favoured the latter course, and on discussion we found it obviously the best, so we turned back close around Inaccessible Island and steered for the fast ice off the Cape at full speed. After piercing a small fringe of thin ice at the edge of the fast floe the ship's stem struck heavily on hard bay ice about a mile and a half from the shore. Here was a road to the Cape and a solid wharf[91]

Scott, Wilson and Evans walked away over the sea-ice, but were soon back. They reported an excellent site for a hut on a shelving beach on the northern side of the Cape before us, which was henceforward called Cape Evans, after our second in command. Landing was to begin forthwith.

First came the two big motor sledges which took up so much of our deck space. In spite of the hundreds of tons of sea-water which had washed over and about them they came out of their big crates looking "as fresh and clean as if they had been packed on the previous day."[92] They were running that same afternoon.

We had a horse-box for the ponies, which came next, but it wanted all Oates' skill and persuasion to get them into it. All seventeen of them were soon on the floe, rolling and kicking with joy, and thence they were led across to the beach where they were carefully picketed to a rope run over a snow slope where they could not eat sand. Shackleton lost four out of eight ponies within a month of his arrival. His ponies were picketed on rubbly ground at Cape Royds, and ate the sand for the salt flavour it possessed. The fourth pony died from eating shavings in which chemicals had been packed. This does not mean that they were hungry, merely that these Manchurian ponies eat the first thing that comes in their way, whether it be a bit of sugar or a bit of Erebus.

Meanwhile the dog-teams were running light loads between the ship and the shore. "The great trouble with them has been due to the fatuous conduct of the penguins. Groups of these have been constantly leaping on to our floe. From the moment of landing on their feet their whole attitude expressed devouring curiosity and a pig-headed disregard for their own safety. They waddle forward, poking their heads to and fro in their usually absurd way, in spite of a string of howling dogs straining to get at them. 'Hulloa!' they seem to say, 'here's a game—what do all you ridiculous things want?' And they come a few steps nearer. The dogs make a rush as far as their harness or leashes allow. The penguins are not daunted in the least, but their ruffs go up and they squawk with semblance of anger, for all the world as though they were rebutting a rude stranger—their attitude might be imagined to convey, 'Oh, that's the sort of animal you are; well, you've come to

[91] *Scott's Last Expedition*, vol. i. pp. 88-90.
[92] *Ibid.* p. 91.

the wrong place—we aren't going to be bluffed and bounced by you,' and then the final fatal steps forward are taken and they come within reach. There is a spring, a squawk, a horrid red patch on the snow, and the incident is closed."[93]

Everything had to be sledged nearly a mile and a half across the sea-ice, but at midnight, after seventeen hours' continuous work, the position was most satisfactory. The large amount of timber which went to make the hut was mostly landed. The ponies and dogs were sleeping in the sun on shore. A large green tent housed the hut builders, and the site for the hut was levelled.

"Such weather in such a place comes nearer to satisfying my ideal of perfection than any condition I have ever experienced. The warm glow of the sun with the keen invigorating cold of the air forms a combination which is inexpressibly health-giving and satisfying to me, whilst the golden light on this wonderful scene of mountain and ice satisfies every claim of scenic magnificence. No words of mine can convey the impressiveness of the wonderful panorama displayed to our eyes.... It's splendid to see at last the effect of all the months of preparation and organisation. There is much snoring about me as I write (2 A.M.) from men tired after a hard day's work and preparing for such another to-morrow. I also must sleep, for I have had none for 48 hours—but it should be to dream happily."[94]

Getting to bed about midnight and turning out at 5 A.M. we kept it up day after day. Petrol, paraffin, pony food, dog food, sledges and sledging gear, hut furniture, provisions of all kinds both for life at the hut and for sledging, coal, scientific instruments and gear, carbide, medical stores, clothing—I do not know how many times we sledged over that sea-ice, but I do know that we were landed as regards all essentials in six days. "Nothing like it has been done before; nothing so expeditious and complete."[95] ... and "Words cannot express the splendid way in which every one works."[96]

The two motors, the two dog-teams, man-hauling parties, and, as they were passed for work by Oates, the ponies; all took part in this transport. As usual Bowers knew just where everything was, and where it was to go, and he was most ably seconded on the ship by Rennick and Bruce. Both man-hauling parties and pony-leaders commonly did ten journeys a day, a distance of over thirty miles. The ponies themselves did one to three or four journeys as they were considered fit.

Generally speaking the transport seemed satisfactory, but it soon became clear that sea-ice was very hard on the motor sledge runners. "The motor sledges are working well, but not very well; the small difficulties will be got over, but I rather fear they will never draw the loads we expect of them. Still they promise to be a help, and they are a lively and attractive feature of our present scene as they drone along over the floe. At a little distance, without silencers, they sound exactly like threshing machines."[97]

[93] *Scott's Last Expedition*, vol. i. pp. 52-93.
[94] *Ibid.* pp. 92-94.
[95] *Scott's Last Expedition*, vol. i. p. 111.
[96] *Ibid.* p. 94.
[97] *Ibid.* p. 100.

The ponies were the real problem. It was to be expected that they would be helpless and exhausted after their long and trying voyage. Not a bit of it! They were soon rolling about, biting one another, kicking one another, and any one else, with the best will in the world. After two days' rest on shore, twelve of them were thought fit to do one journey, on which they pulled loads varying from 700 to 1000 lbs. with ease on the hard sea-ice surface. But it was soon clear that these ponies were an uneven lot. There were the steady workers like Punch and Nobby; there were one or two definitely weak ponies like Blossom, Blücher and Jehu; and there were one or two strong but rather impossible beasts. One of these was soon known as Weary Willie. His outward appearance belied him, for he looked like a pony. A brief acquaintance soon convinced me that he was without doubt a cross between a pig and a mule. He was obviously a strong beast and, since he always went as slowly as possible and stopped as often as possible it was most difficult to form any opinion as to what load he was really able to draw. Consequently I am afraid there is little doubt that he was generally overloaded until that grim day on the Barrier when he was set upon by a dog-team. It was his final collapse at the end of the Depôt journey which caused Scott to stay behind when we went out on the sea-ice. But of that I shall speak again.

Twice only have I ever seen Weary Willie trot. We were leading the ponies now as always with halters and without bits. Consequently our control was limited especially on ice, but doubtless the ponies' comfort was increased, especially in cold weather when a metal bit would have been difficult if not impossible. On this occasion he and I had just arrived at the ship after a trudge in which I seemed to be pulling both Weary and the sledge. Just then a motor back-fired, and we started back across that floe at a pace which surprised Weary even more than myself, for he fell over the sledge, himself and me, and for days I felt like a big black bruise. The second occasion on which he got a move on was during the Depôt journey when Gran on ski tried to lead him.

Christopher and Hackenschmidt were impossible ponies. Christopher, as we shall see, died on the Barrier a year after this, fighting almost to the last. Hackenschmidt, so called "from his vicious habit of using both fore and hind legs in attacking those who came near him,"[98] led an even more lurid life but had a more peaceful end. Whether Oates could have tamed him I do not know: he would have done it if it were possible, for his management of horses was wonderful. But in any case Hackenschmidt sickened at the hut while we were absent on the Depôt journey, for no cause which could be ascertained, gradually became too weak to stand, and was finally put out of his misery.

There was a breathless minute when Hackenschmidt, with a sledge attached to him, went galloping over the hills and boulders. Below him, all unconscious of his impending fate, was Ponting, adjusting a large camera with his usual accuracy. Both survived. There were runaways innumerable, and all kinds of falls. But these ponies could tumble about unharmed in a way which would cause an English horse to lie up for a week. "There is no doubt that the bumping of the sledges close

---

[98] *Scott's Last Expedition*, vol. i. p. 230.

at the heels of the animals is the root of the evil."[99]

There were two adventures during this first week of landing stores which might well have had a more disastrous conclusion. The first of these was the adventure of Ponting and the Killer whales.

"I was a little late on the scene this morning, and thereby witnessed a most extraordinary scene. Some six or seven killer whales, old and young, were skirting the fast floe edge ahead of the ship; they seemed excited and dived rapidly, almost touching the floe. As we watched, they suddenly appeared astern, raising their snouts out of water. I had heard weird stories of these beasts, but had never associated serious danger with them. Close to the water's edge lay the wire stern rope of the ship, and our two Esquimaux dogs were tethered to this. I did not think of connecting the movement of the whales with this fact, and seeing them so close I shouted to Ponting, who was standing abreast of the ship. He seized his camera and ran towards the floe edge to get a close picture of the beasts, which had momentarily disappeared. The next moment the whole floe under him and the dogs heaved up and split into fragments. One could hear the booming noise as the whales rose under the ice and struck it with their backs. Whale after whale rose under the ice, setting it rocking fiercely; luckily Ponting kept his feet and was able to fly to security. By an extraordinary chance also, the splits had been made around and between the dogs, so that neither of them fell into the water. Then it was clear that the whales shared our astonishment, for one after another their huge hideous heads shot vertically into the air through the cracks which they had made. As they reared them to a height of six or eight feet it was possible to see their tawny head markings, their small glistening eyes, and their terrible array of teeth—by far the largest and most terrifying in the world. There cannot be a doubt that they looked up to see what had happened to Ponting and the dogs.

"The latter were horribly frightened and strained to their chains, whining; the head of one killer must certainly have been within five feet of one of the dogs.

"After this, whether they thought the game insignificant, or whether they missed Ponting is uncertain, but the terrifying creatures passed on to other hunting grounds, and we were able to rescue the dogs, and what was even more important, our petrol—five or six tons of which was waiting on a piece of ice which was not split away from the main mass.

"Of course, we have known well that killer whales continually skirt the edge of the floes and that they would undoubtedly snap up any one who was unfortunate enough to fall into the water; but the facts that they could display such deliberate cunning, that they were able to break ice of such thickness (at least 2½ feet), and that they could act in unison, were a revelation to us. It is clear that they are endowed with singular intelligence, and in future we shall treat that intelligence with every respect."[100]

We were to be hunted by these Killer whales again.

The second adventure was the loss of the third motor sledge. It was Sunday

[99] *Scott's Last Expedition*, vol. i. pp. 113-114.
[100] *Scott's Last Expedition*, vol. i. pp. 94.-96.

morning, January 8, and Scott had given orders that this motor was to be hoisted out of the ship. "This was done first thing and the motor placed on firm ice. Later Campbell told me one of the men had dropped a leg through crossing a sludgy patch some 200 yards from the ship. I didn't consider it very serious, as I imagined the man had only gone through the surface crust. About 7 A.M. I started for the shore with a single man load, leaving Campbell looking about for the best crossing for the motor."[101]

I find a note in my own diary as to what happened after that: "Last night the ice was getting very soft in places, and I was a little doubtful about leading ponies over a spot on the route to the hut which is about a quarter of a mile from the ship. It has been thawing very fast the last few days, and has been very hot as Antarctic weather goes. This morning was the same, and Bailey went in up to his neck.

"Some half-hour after the motor was put on to the floe, we were told to tow it on to firm ice as that near the ship was breaking up. All hands started on a long tow line. We got on to the rotten piece, and somebody behind shouted 'You must run.' From that moment everything happened very quickly. Williamson fell right in through the ice; immediately afterwards we were all brought up with a jerk. Then the line began to pull us backwards; the stern of the motor had sunk through the ice, and the whole car began to sink. It slowly went right through and disappeared and then the tow line followed it. Everything possible was done to hang on to the rope, but in the end we had to let it go, each man keeping his hold until he was dragged to the lip of the hole. Then we made for the fast ice, leaving the rotten bit between us and the ship.

"Pennell and Priestley sounded their way back to the ship, and Day asked Priestley to bring his goggles when he returned. They came back with a life-line, Pennell leading. Suddenly the ice gave way under Priestley, who disappeared entirely and came up, so we learned afterwards, under the ice, there being a big current. In a moment Pennell was lying flat upon the floe on his chest, got his hand under Priestley's arm, and so pulled him out. All Priestley said was, 'Day, here are your goggles.' We all got back to the ship, but communication between the ship and the shore was interrupted for the rest of the day, when a solid road was found right up to the ship in another place."[102]

Meanwhile the hut was rising very quickly, and Davies, who was Chippy Chap, the carpenter, deserves much credit. He was a leading shipwright in the navy, always willing and bright, and with a very thorough knowledge of his job. I have seen him called up hour after hour, day and night, on the ship, when the pumps were choked by the coal balls which formed in the bilges, and he always arrived with a smile on his face. Altogether he was one of our most useful men. In this job of hut-building he was helped by two of our seamen, Keohane and Abbott, and others. Latterly I believe there were more people working than there were hammers!

A plan of this hut is given here. It was 50 feet long, by 25 feet wide, and 9 feet

[101] *Ibid.* p. 106.
[102] My own diary.

to the eaves. The insulation, which was very satisfactory, was seaweed, sewn up in the form of a quilt.

"The sides have double [match-] boarding inside and outside the frames, with a layer of our excellent quilted seaweed insulation between each pair of boardings. The roof has a single match-boarding inside, but on the outside is a match-boarding, then a layer of 2-ply ruberoid, then a layer of quilted seaweed, then a second match-boarding, and finally a cover of 3-ply ruberoid."[103]

The floor consisted of a wooden boarding next the frame, then a quilt of seaweed, then a layer of felt upon which was a second boarding and finally linoleum.

We thought we should be warm, and we were. In fact, during the winter, with twenty-five men living there, and the cooking range going, and perhaps also the stove at the other end, the hut not infrequently became fuggy, big though it was.

The entrance was through a door in a porch before you got to the main door. In the porch were the generators of the acetylene gas, which was fitted throughout by Day, who was also responsible for the fittings of the ventilator, cooking range, and stove, the chimney pipes from these running along through the middle of the hut before entering a common vent. Little heat was lost. The pipes were fitted with dampers, and air inlets which could be opened or shut at will to control the ventilation. Besides a big ventilator in the top of the hut there was an adjustable air inlet also at the base of the chamber which formed the junction of the two chimneys. The purpose of this was also ventilation, but it was not successful.

The bulkhead which separated the men's quarters, or mess deck, from the rest of the hut, was formed of such cases as contained goods in glass, including wine, which would have frozen and broken outside. The bulkhead did not go as high as the top of the hut. When the contents of a case were wanted, a side of the box was taken out, and the empty case then formed a shelf.

We started to live in the hut on January 18, beautifully warm, the gramophone going, and everybody happy. But for a long time before this most of the landing party had been living in tents on shore. It was very comfortable, far more so than might be supposed, judging only by the popular idea of a polar life. We were now almost landed, there were just a few things more to come over from the ship. "It was blowing a mild blizzard from the south, and I took a sledge over to the ship, which was quite blotted out in blinding snow at times. It was as hard to get an empty sledge over, as generally it is to drag a full one. Tea on the ship, which was very full of welcome, but also very full of the superiority of their own comforts over those of the land. Their own comforts were not so very obvious, since they had tried to get the stove in the wardroom going for the first time. They were all coughing in the smoke, and everything inside was covered with smuts."[104]

The hut itself was some twelve feet above the sea, and situated upon what was now an almost sandy beach of black lava. It was thought that this was high enough to be protected from any swell likely to arrive in such a sheltered place, but, as we

[103] *Scott's Last Expedition*, vol. i. p. 111.
[104] My own diary.

shall see, Scott was very anxious as to the fate of the hut, when, on the Depôt journey, a swell removed not only miles of sea-ice and a good deal of Barrier, but also the end of Glacier Tongue. We never saw this beach again, for the autumn gales covered it with thick drifts of snow, and the thaw was never enough to remove this for the two other summers we spent here. There is no doubt this was an exceptional year for thaw. We never again saw a little waterfall such as was now tumbling down the rocks from Skua Lake into the sea.

The little hill of 66 feet high behind us was soon named Wind Vane Hill, and there were other meteorological instruments there besides. A snow-drift or ice-drift always forms to leeward of any such projection, and that beneath this hill was large enough for us to drive into it two ice caves. The first of these was to contain our larder, notably the frozen mutton carcasses brought down by us from New Zealand in the ice-house on deck. These, however, showed signs of mildew, and we never ate very freely of them. Seal and penguin were our stock meat foods, and mutton was considered to be a luxury.

The second cave, 13 feet long by 5 feet wide, hollowed out by Simpson and Wright, was for the magnetic instruments. The temperature of these caves was found to be fairly constant. Unfortunately, this was the only drift into which we could tunnel, and we had no such mass of snow and ice as is afforded by the Barrier, which can be burrowed, and was burrowed extensively by Amundsen and his men.

The cases containing the bulk of our stores were placed in stacks arranged by Bowers up on the sloping ground to the west of the hut, beginning close to the entrance door. The sledges lay on the hill side above them. This arrangement was very satisfactory during the first winter, but the excessive blizzards of the second winter and the immense amount of snow which was gathering about the camp caused us to move everything up to the top of the ridge behind the hut where the wind kept them more clear. Amundsen found it advisable to put his cases in two long lines.[105]

The dogs were tethered to a long chain or rope. The ponies' stable was built against the northern side of the hut, and was thus sheltered from the blizzards which always blow here from the south. Against the south side of the hut Bowers built himself a store-room. "Every day he conceives or carries out some plan to benefit the camp."[106]

"Scott seems very cheery about things," I find in my diary about this time. And well he might be. A man could hardly be better served. We slaved until we were nearly dead-beat, and then we found something else to do until we were quite dead-beat. Ship's company and landing parties alike, not only now but all through this job, did their very utmost, and their utmost was very good. The way men worked was fierce.

"If you can picture our house nestling below this small hill on a long stretch of black sand, with many tons of provision cases ranged in neat blocks in front of it

[105] *The South Pole*, vol. i. p. 278.
[106] *Scott's Last Expedition*, vol. i. p. 128.

and the sea lapping the ice-foot below, you will have some idea of our immediate vicinity. As for our wider surroundings it would be difficult to describe their beauty in sufficiently glowing terms. Cape Evans is one of the many spurs of Erebus and the one that stands closest under the mountain, so that always towering above us we have the grand snowy peak with its smoking summit. North and south of us are deep bays, beyond which great glaciers come rippling over the lower slopes to thrust high blue-walled snouts into the sea. The sea is blue before us, dotted with shining bergs or ice floes, whilst far over the Sound, yet so bold and magnificent as to appear near, stand the beautiful Western Mountains with their numerous lofty peaks, their deep glacial valley and clear cut scarps, a vision of mountain scenery that can have few rivals."[107]

MT. EREBUS, THE RAMP AND THE HUT

"Before I left England people were always telling me the Antarctic must be

[107] *Ibid.* p. 129.

dull without much life. Now we are in ourselves a perfect farmyard. There are nineteen ponies fifty yards off and thirty dogs just behind, and they howl like the wolves they are at intervals, led by Dyk. The skuas are nesting all round and fighting over the remains of the seals which we have killed, and the penguins which the dogs have killed, whenever they have got the chance. The collie bitch which we have brought down for breeding purposes wanders about the camp. A penguin is standing outside my tent, presumably because he thinks he is going to moult here. A seal has just walked up into the horse lines—there are plenty of Weddell and penguins and whales. On board we have Nigger and a blue Persian kitten, with rabbits and squirrels. The whole place teems with life.

"Franky Drake is employed all day wandering round for ice for watering the ship. Yesterday he had made a pile out on the floe, and the men wanted to have a flag put on it, and have it photographed, and called 'Mr. Drake's Furthest South.'"[108]

January 25 was fixed as the day upon which twelve of us, with eight ponies and the two dog-teams, were to start south to lay a depôt upon the Barrier for the Polar Journey. Scott was of opinion that the bays between us and the Hut Point Peninsula would freeze over in March, probably early in March, and that we should most of us get back to Cape Evans then. At the same time the ponies could not come down over the cliffs of this tongue of land, and preparations had to be made for a lengthy stay at Hut Point for them and their keepers. For this purpose Scott meant to use the old Discovery hut at Hut Point.[109]

On January 15 he took Meares and one dog-team, and started for Hut Point, which was fifteen statute miles to the south of us. They crossed Glacier Tongue, finding upon it a depôt of compressed fodder and maize which had been left by Shackleton. The open water to the west nearly reached the Tongue.

On arrival at the hut Scott was shocked to find it full of snow and ice. This was serious, and, as we found afterwards the drifted snow had thawed down into ice the whole of the inside of this hut was a big ice block. In the middle of this ice was a pile of cases left by the Discovery as a depôt. They were, we knew, full of biscuit.

"There was something too depressing in finding the old hut in such a desolate condition. I had had so much interest in seeing all the old landmarks and the huts apparently intact. To camp outside and feel that all the old comforts and cheer had departed was dreadfully heartrending."[110]

That night "we slept badly till the morning and, therefore, late. After breakfast we went up the hills; there was a keen S.E. breeze, but the sun shone and my spirits revived. There was very much less snow everywhere than I had ever seen. The ski run was completely cut through in two places, the Gap and Observation Hill almost bare, a great bare slope on the side of Arrival Heights, and on top of Crater Heights an immense bare table-land. How delighted we should have been to see it like this in the old days! The pond was thawed and the confervae green in fresh

[108] My own diary.
[109] See Introduction, p. xxxiv.
[110] *Scott's Last Expedition*, vol. i. p. 122.

water. The hole which we had dug in the mound in the pond was still there, as Meares discovered by falling into it up to his waist, and getting very wet.

"On the south side we could see the pressure ridges beyond Pram Point as of old—Horseshoe Bay calm and unpressed—the sea-ice pressed on Pram Point and along the Gap ice front, and a new ridge running around C. Armitage about 2 miles off. We saw Ferrar's old thermometer tubes standing out of the snow slope as though they'd been placed yesterday. Vince's cross might have been placed yesterday—the paint was so fresh and the inscription so legible."[111]

We had two officers who had been with Shackleton in his 1908 Expedition—Priestley, who was in our Northern Party, and Day, who was in charge of our motors. Priestley with two others sledged over to Cape Royds and has left an account of the old hut there:

"After pitching tent Levick and I went over to the hut to forage. On the way I visited Derrick Point and took a large seven-pound tin of butter while Levick opened up the hut. It was very dark inside but I pulled the boarding down from the windows so that we could see all right. It was very funny to see everything lying about just as we had left it, in that last rush to get off in the lull of the blizzard. On Marston's bunk was a sixpenny copy of the Story of Bessie Costrell, which some one had evidently read and left open. Perhaps what brought the old times back again more than anything else was the fact that as I came out of the larder the sleeve of my wind clothes caught the tap of the copper and turned it on. When I heard the drip of the water I turned instinctively and turned the tap off, almost expecting to hear Bobs' raucous voice cursing me for my clumsiness. Perhaps what strikes one more forcibly than anything else is the fact that nothing has been disturbed. On the table was the remains of a batch of bread that Bobs had cooked for us and that was only partially consumed before the Nimrod called for us. Some of the rolls showed the impression of bites given to them in 1909. All round the bread were the sauces, pickles, pepper and salt of our usual standing lunch, and a half-opened tin of gingerbreads was a witness to the dryness of the climate for they were still crisp as the day they were opened.

"In the cubicle near the larder were the loose tins that poor Armytage and myself had collected from all round the hut before we left.

"On the shelves of my cubicle are still stacked the magazines and paper brought down by the relief ship. Nothing is changed at all except the company. It is almost dismal. I expect to see people come in through the door after a walk over the surrounding hills.

"We had not much time to look round us; for Campbell was cooking in the tent, so we slung a few tins of jam, a plum-pudding, some tea, and gingerbreads into a sack, and returned to camp. By this time it was snowing heavily and continued to do so after dinner so that we turned in immediately (1.30 p.m.) and went off to sleep. One thing worth mentioning is that on several of the drifts are well-defined hoof marks, some of them looking so new that we could have sworn that they had been made this year.

[111] *Ibid.* pp. 122-123.

"The Old Sport [Levick] gave us a start by suddenly announcing that he could see a ship quite close, and for some time we were on tenterhooks, but his ship proved to be the Terra Nova ice-anchored off the Skuary.

"The whole place is very eerie, there is such a feeling of life about it. Not only do I feel it but the others do also. Last night after I turned in I could have sworn that I heard people shouting to each other.

"I thought that I had only got an attack of nerves but Campbell asked me if I had heard any shouting, for he had certainly done so. It must have been the seals calling to each other, but it certainly did sound most human. We are getting so worked up that we should not be a bit surprised to see a settlement of Japanese or some other such people some day when we stroll round towards Blacksand Beach. The Old Sport created some amusement this evening by opening a tin of Nestlé's milk at both ends instead of making the two holes at one end. He informed us that he had got so used to using two whole tins of milk for cocoa for fourteen people at night that he always opened them that way.

"As a consequence we have to spend most of our spare time making bungs to keep the milk in the tin."[112]

Meanwhile, as was to be expected, the action of the, I suspect, abnormal summer sea temperature was showing its effect upon the sea-ice. Sea-ice thaws from below when the temperature of the water rises. The northern ice goes out first here, being next to the open water, but big thaw pools form at the same time wherever a current of water flows over shallows, as at the end of Cape Evans, Hut Point and Cape Armitage.

On January 17 the ice was breaking away between the point of Cape Evans and the ship, although a road still remained fast between the ship and the shore. The ship began to get up steam, but the fast ice broke away quickly that night. I believe they got steam in three hours, twelve hours being the time generally allowed: only just in time, however, for she broke adrift as it was reported. The next morning she made fast to the ice only 200 yards from the ice-foot of the Cape.

"For the present the position is extraordinarily comfortable. With a southerly blow she would simply bind on to the ice, receiving great shelter from the end of the Cape. With a northerly blow she might turn rather close to the shore, where the soundings run to three fathoms, but behind such a stretch of ice she could scarcely get a sea or swell without warning. It looks a wonderfully comfortable little nook, but of course one can be certain of nothing in this place; one knows from experience how deceptive the appearance of security may be."[113]

The ship's difficulties were largely due to the shortage of coal. Again on the night of January 20-21 we had an anxious time.

"Fearing a little trouble I went out of the hut in the middle of the night and saw at once that she was having a bad time—the ice was breaking with a northerly swell and the wind increasing, with the ship on dead lee shore; luckily the ice an-

---

[112] Priestley's diary.
[113] *Scott's Last Expedition*, vol. i. p. 127.

chors had been put well in on the floe and some still held. Pennell was getting up steam and his men struggling to replace the anchors.

"We got out the men and gave some help. At 6 steam was up, and I was right glad to see the ship back out to windward, leaving us to recover anchors and hawsers."[114]

A big berg drove in just after the ship had got away, and grounded where she had been lying. The ship returned in the afternoon, and it seems that she was searching round for an anchorage, and trying to look behind this berg. There was a strongish northerly wind blowing. The currents and soundings round Cape Evans were then unknown. The current was setting strongly from the north through the strip of sea which divides Inaccessible Island from Cape Evans, a distance of some two-thirds of a mile. The engines were going astern, but the current and wind were too much for her, and the ship ran aground, being fast for some considerable distance aft—some said as far as the mainmast.

"Visions of the ship failing to return to New Zealand and of sixty people waiting here arose in my mind with sickening pertinacity, and the only consolation I could draw from such imaginations was the determination that the southern work should go on as before—meanwhile the least ill possible seemed to be an extensive lightening of the ship with boats as the tide was evidently high when she struck—a terribly depressing prospect.

"Some three or four of us watched it gloomily from the shore whilst all was bustle on board, the men shifting cargo aft. Pennell tells me they shifted 10 tons in a very short time.

"The first ray of hope came when by careful watching one could see that the ship was turning very slowly, then one saw the men running from side to side and knew that an attempt was being made to roll her off. The rolling produced a more rapid turning movement at first, and then she seemed to hang again. But only for a short time; the engines had been going astern all the time and presently a slight movement became apparent. But we only knew she was getting clear when we heard cheers on board, and more cheers from the whaler.

"Then she gathered stern way and was clear. The relief was enormous."[115]

All this took some time, and Scott himself came back into the hut with us and went on bagging provisions for the Depôt journey. At such times of real disaster he was a very philosophical man. We were not yet ready to go sledging, but on January 23 the ice in North Bay all went out, and that in South Bay began to follow it. Because this was our road to the Barrier, it was suddenly decided that we must start on the Depôt journey the following day or perhaps not at all. Already it was impossible to get sledges south off the Cape: but there was a way to walk the ponies along the land until they could be scrambled down a steep rubbly slope on to sea-ice which still remained. Would it float away before we got there? It was touch and go. "One breathes a prayer that the Road holds for the few remaining hours.

[114] *Ibid.* p. 134.
[115] *Scott's Last Expedition*, vol. i. p. 136.

It goes in one place between a berg in open water and a large pool of the Glacier face—it may be weak in that part, and at any moment the narrow isthmus may break away. We are doing it on a very narrow margin."[116]

---

[116] *Scott's Last Expedition,* vol. i. p. 138

CHAPTER V

THE DEPÔT JOURNEY

The dropping of the daylight in the west.

Robert Browning.

January to March 1911

Scott	Meares	Crean
Wilson	Atkinson	Forde
Lieut. Evans	Cherry-Garrard	Dimitri
Bowers	Gran	
Oates	Keohane	

Imaginative friends of the thirteen men who started from Cape Evans on January 24, 1911, may have thought of them as athletes, trained for some weeks or months to endure the strains which they were to face, sleeping a good nine hours a night, eating carefully regulated meals and doing an allotted task each day under scientific control.

They would be far from the mark. For weeks we had turned in at midnight too tired to take off our clothes, and had been lucky if we were allowed to sleep until 5 A.M. We had eaten our meals when we could, and we had worked in the meantime just as hard as it was physically possible to do. If we sat down on a packing-case we went to sleep.

And we finally left the camp in a state of hurry bordering upon panic. Since the ice to the south of us, the road to the Barrier, was being nibbled away by thaw, winds and tides, it was impossible to lead the ponies down from the Cape on to the sea-ice. The open sea was before us and on our right front. It was necessary to lead them up among the lava blocks which lay on the escarpment of Erebus, south-eastwards towards Land's End, and thence to slide them down a steep but rubbly slope to the ice which still remained. As a matter of fact that ice went out the very next day.

During the last two days provisions had been bagged with the utmost despatch; sledges packed; letters scribbled; clothing sorted and rough alterations to it made. Scott was busy, with Bowers' help, making such arrangements as could be suggested for a further year's stay, for which the ship was to order the necessaries. Oates was busy weighing out the pony food for the journey, sorting harness, and generally managing a most unruly mob of ponies. Many were the arguments as to the relative value of a pair of socks or their equivalent weight in tobacco, for we were allowed 12 lbs. of private gear apiece, to consist of everything which we did not habitually wear on our bodies. This included such things as:

- Sleeping-boots.
- Sleeping-socks.
- Extra pair of day socks.
- A shirt.
- Tobacco and pipe.
- Notebook for diary and pencil.
- Extra balaclava helmet.
- Extra woollen mitts.
- Housewife containing buttons, needles, darning needles, thread and wool.
- Extra pair of finnesko.
- Big safety-pins with which to hang up our socks.
- And perhaps one small book.

My most vivid recollection of the day we started is the sight of Bowers, out of breath, very hot, and in great pain from a bad knock which he had given his knee against a rock, being led forward by his big pony Uncle Bill, over whom temporarily he had but little control. He had been left behind in the camp, giving last instructions about the storage of cases and management of provisions, and had practically lost himself in trying to follow us over what was then unknown ground. He was wearing all the clothing which was not included in his personal gear, for he did not think it fair to give the pony the extra weight. He had bruised his leg in an ugly way, and for many days he came to me to bandage it. He was afraid that if he let the doctors see it they would forbid him to go forward. He had had no sleep for seventy-two hours.

That first night (January 24) we pitched our inexperienced camp not far from Hut Point. But our first taste of sledging was not without incident. Starting with the ponies only we walked them to Glacier Tongue, where the ice and open water joined, and as we went we watched the ship pass us out in the Strait and moor up to the end of the Tongue. Getting the ponies across the Tongue with its shallow but numerous crevasses and holes was ticklish work, but we tethered them safely off the Terra Nova, which meanwhile was landing dogs, sledges and gear. There we got some lunch on board. A large lead in the sea-ice to the south of the Tongue necessitated some hours' work in man-hauling all sledges along the back of the Tongue until a way could be found down on to safe ice. We then followed with the ponies. "If a pony falls into one of these holes I shall sit down and cry," said Oates. Within three minutes my pony was wallowing, with only his head and forelegs visible, in a mess of brash and snow, which had concealed a crack in the sea-ice which was obviously not going to remain much longer in its present position. We got lashings round him and hauled him out. Poor Guts! He was fated to drown: but in an hour he appeared to have forgotten all about his mishap, and was pulling his first load towards Hut Point as gallantly as always.

The next day we took further stores from the ship to the camp which had formed. Some of these loads were to be left on the edge of the Barrier when we got there, but for the present we had to relay, that is, take one load forward and come back for another.

On the 26th we sledged back to the ship for our last load, and said good-bye on the sea-ice to those men with whom we had already worked so long, to Campbell and his five companions who were to suffer so much, to cheery Pennell and his ship's company.

Before we left, Scott thanked Pennell and his men "for their splendid work. They have behaved like bricks, and a finer lot of men never sailed in a ship.... It was a little sad to say farewell to all these good fellows and Campbell and his men. I do most heartily trust that all will be successful in their ventures, for indeed their unselfishness and their generous high spirit deserve reward. God bless them."

Four of that Depôt party were never to see these men again, and Pennell, Commander of the Queen Mary, went down with his ship in the battle of Jutland.

Two days later, January 28, we sledged our first loads on to the Barrier. By that day we had done nearly ninety miles of relay work, first from the ship at Glacier Tongue to our camp off Hut Point, and then onwards. Those first days of sledging were wonderful! What memories they must have brought to Scott and Wilson when to us, who had never seen them before, these much-discussed landmarks were almost like old friends. As we made our way over the frozen sea every seal-hole was of interest, and every type of wind-swept snow a novelty. The peak of Terror opened out behind the crater of Erebus, and we walked under Castle Rock and Danger Slope until, rounding the promontory, we saw the little jagged Hut Point, and on it the cross placed there to Vince's memory, all unchanged. There was the old Discovery hut and the Bay in which the Discovery lay, and from which she was almost miraculously freed at the last moment, only to be flung upon the shoal which runs out from the Point, where some tins of the old Discovery days lie on the bottom still and glint in the evening sun. And round about the Bay were the Heights of which we had read, Observation Hill, and Crater Hill separated from it by The Gap—through which the wind was streaming; of course it was, for this must be the famous Hut Point wind.

A few hundred more blizzards had swept over it since those days, but it was all just the same, even to Ferrar's little stakes placed across the glacierets to mark their movement, more, even to the footsteps still plainly visible on the slopes.

The ponies were dragging up to 900 lbs. each these days, and though they did not seem to be unduly distressed, two of them soon showed signs of lameness. This caused some anxiety, but the trouble was mended by rest. On the whole, though the surface was hard, I think we were giving them too much weight.

The sea-ice off Hut Point and Observation Hill was already very dangerous, and had we then had the experience and knowledge of sea-ice with which we can now look back, it is probable that we should not have slept so easily upon its surface. Parties travelling to Hut Point and beyond in summer must keep well out from the Point and Cape Armitage. But all haste was being made to transport the necessary stores on to the Barrier surface, where a big home depôt could be made, so far as we could judge, in safety. The pressure ridges in the sea-ice between Cape Armitage and Pram Point, which are formed by the movement of the Barrier, were large, and in some of the hollows countless seals were playing in the water. Judging by the size of these ridges and by the thickness of this ice when it broke up, the ice south of Hut Point was at least two years old.

I well remember the day we took the first of our loads on to the Barrier. I expect we were all a little excited, for to walk upon the Barrier for the first time was indeed an adventure: what kind of surface was it, and how about these beastly crevasses of which we had read so much? Scott was ahead, and so far as we could see there was nothing but the same level of ice all round — when suddenly he was above us, walking up the sloping and quite invisible drift. A minute after and our ponies and sledges were up and over the tide crack, and beneath us soft and yielding snow, very different from the hard wind-swept surface of the frozen sea, which we had just left. Really it was rather prosaic and a tame entrance. But the Barrier is a tricky place, and it takes years to get to know her.

On our outward journey this day Oates did his best to kill a seal. My own tent was promised some kidneys if we were good, and our mouths watered with the prospect of the hoosh before us. The seal had been left for dead, and when on our homeward way we neared the place of his demise Titus went off to carve our dinner from him. The next thing we saw was the seal lolloping straight for his hole, while Oates did his best to stab him. The quarry made off safely not much hurt, for, as we discovered later, a clasp-knife is quite useless to kill a seal. Oates returned with a bad cut, as his hand had slipped down the knife; and it was a long time before he was allowed to forget it.

This Barrier, which we were to know so well, was soft, too soft for the ponies, and apparently flat. Only to our left, some hundreds of yards distant, there were two little snowy mounds. We got out the telescope which we carried, but could make nothing of them. While we held our ponies Scott walked towards them, and soon we saw him brushing away snow and uncovering something dark beneath. They were tents, obviously left by Shackleton or his men when the Nimrod was embarking his Southern party from the Barrier. They were snowed up outside, and iced up inside almost to the caps. Afterwards we dug them out, a good evening's work. The fabric was absolutely rotten, we just tore it down with our hands, but the bamboos and caps were as sound as ever. When we had dug down to the floor-cloth we found everything intact as when it was left. The cooker was there and a primus — Scott lighted it and cooked a meal; we often used it afterwards. And there were Rowntree's cocoa, Bovril, Brand's extract of beef, sheep's tongues, cheese and biscuits — all open to the snow and all quite good. We ate them for several days. There is something impressive in these first meals off food which has been exposed for years.

It was on a Saturday, January 28, that we took our first load a short half-mile on to the Barrier and left it at a place afterwards known as the Fodder Depôt. Two days later we moved our camp 1 mile 1200 yards farther on to the Barrier and here was erected the main depôt, known as Safety Camp. 'Safety' because it was supposed that even if a phenomenal break-up of sea-ice should occur, and take with it part of the Barrier, this place would remain. Subsequent events proved the supposition well founded. This short bit of Barrier sledging gave all of us food for thought, for the surface was appallingly soft, and the poor ponies were sinking deep. It was obvious that no animals could last long under such conditions. But somehow Shackleton had got his four a long way.

There was now no hurry, for there was plenty of food. It was only when we went on from here that we must economize food and travel fast. It was determined to give the ponies a rest while we made the depôt and rearranged sledges, which we did on the following day. We had with us one pair of pony snow-shoes, a circle of wire as a foundation, hooped round with bamboo, and with beckets of the same material. The surface suggested their trial, which was completely successful. The question of snow-shoes had been long and anxiously considered, and shoes for all the ponies were at Cape Evans; but as we had so lately landed from the ship the ponies had not been trained in their use, and they had not been brought.

Scott immediately sent Wilson and Meares with a dog-team to see whether the sea-ice would allow them to reach Cape Evans and bring back shoes for the other ponies. Meanwhile the next morning saw us trying to accustom the animals to wearing snow-shoes by exercising them in the one pair we possessed. But it seemed no use continuing to do this after the dog party came in. They had found the sea-ice gone between Glacier Tongue and Winter Quarters and so were empty-handed. They reported that a crevasse at the edge of the Tongue had opened under the sledge, which had tilted back into the crevasse but had run over it. These Glacier Tongue crevasses are shallow things; Gran fell into one later and walked out of the side of the Tongue on to the sea-ice beyond!

It was determined to start on the following day with five weeks' provisions for men and animals; to go forward for about fourteen days, depôt two weeks' provisions and return. Most unfortunately Atkinson would have to be left behind with Crean to look after him. He had chafed his foot, and the chafe had suppurated. To his great disappointment there was no alternative but to lie up. Luckily we had another tent, and there was the cooker and primus we had dug out of Shackleton's tent. Poor Crean was to spend his spare time in bringing up loads from the Fodder Depôt to Safety Camp and, worse still from his point of view, dig a hole downwards into the Barrier for scientific observations!

We left the following morning, February 2, and marched on a patchy surface for five miles (Camp 4). The temperature was above zero and Scott decided to see whether the surface was not better at night. On the whole, it is problematical whether this is the case—we came to the conclusion later that the ideal surface for pulling a sledge on ski was found at a temperature of about +16°. But there is no doubt whatever that ponies should do their work at night, when the temperature is colder, and rest and sleep when the sun has its greatest altitude and power. And so we camped and turned in to our sleeping-bags at 4 P.M. and marched again soon after midnight, doing five miles before and five miles after lunch: lunch, if you please, being about 1 A.M., and a very good time, for just then the daylight seemed to be thin and bleak and one always felt the cold.

Our road lay eastwards through the Strait, some twenty-five miles in width, which runs between the low, rather uninteresting scarp of White Island to the south, and the beautiful slopes of Erebus and Terror to the north. This part of the Barrier is stagnant, but the main stream in front of us, unchecked by land, flows uninterruptedly northwards towards the Ross Sea. Only where the stream presses against the Bluff, White Island and, most important of all, Cape Crozier, and rubs itself against the nearly stationary ice upon which we were travelling, pressures and rendings take place, forming some nasty crevasses. It was intended to steer nearly east until this line was crossed some distance north of White Island, and then steer due south.

It is most difficult on a large snow surface to say whether it is flat. Certainly there are plenty of big crevasses for several miles in this neighbourhood, though they are generally well covered, and we found only very small ones on this out-ward journey. I am inclined to think there are also some considerable pressure waves. As we came up to Camp 5 we floundered into a pocket of soft snow in which one pony after another plunged deeper and deeper until they were buried up to their bellies and could move no more. I suppose it was an old crevasse filled with soft snow, or perhaps one of the pressure-ridge hollows which had been re-cently drifted up. My own pony somehow got through with his sledge to the other side, and every moment I expected the ground to fall below us and a chasm to swallow us up. The others had to be unharnessed and led out. The only set of snow-shoes was then put on to Bowers' big pony and he went back and drew the stranded sledges out. Beyond we pitched our camp.

On February 3-4 we marched for ten miles to Camp 6. In the last five miles we crossed several crevasses, our first; and I heard Oates ask some one what they looked like. "Black as hell," he said, but we saw no more just now, for this march carried us beyond the line of pressure which runs between White Island and Cape Crozier. This halt was called Corner Camp, as we turned here and marched due south. Corner Camp will be heard of again and again in this story: it is thirty miles from Hut Point.

By 4 P.M. it was blowing our first Barrier blizzard. We were to find out after-wards that a Corner Camp blizzard blows nearly as often as a Hut Point wind. The Bluff seems to be the breeding-place for these disturbances, which pour out towards the sea by way of Cape Crozier. Corner Camp is in the direct line between the two.

One summer blizzard is much like another. The temperature, never very low, rises, and you are not cold in the tent. Sometimes a blizzard is a very welcome rest: after weeks of hard pulling, dragging yourself awake each morning, feeling as though you had only just gone to sleep, with the mental strain perhaps which work among crevasses entails, it is most pleasant to be put to bed for two or three days. You may sleep dreamlessly nearly all the time, rousing out for meals, or waking occasionally to hear from the soft warmth of your reindeer bag the deep boom of the tent flapping in the wind, or drowsily you may visit other parts of the world, while the drifting snow purrs against the green tent at your head.

But outside there is raging chaos. It is blowing a full gale: the air is full of falling snow, and the wind drives this along and adds to it the loose snow which is lying on the surface of the Barrier. Fight your way a few steps away from the tent, and it will be gone. Lose your sense of direction and there is nothing to guide you back. Expose your face and hands to the wind, and they will very soon be frost-bitten. And this at midsummer. Imagine the added cold of spring and autumn: the cold and darkness of winter.

The animals suffer most, and during this first blizzard all our ponies were weakened, and two of them became practically useless. It must be remembered that they had stood for five weeks upon a heaving deck; they had been through one very bad gale: the time during which we were unloading the ship was limited, and since that time they had dragged heavy loads the greater part of 200 miles. Nothing was left undone for them which we could manage, but necessarily the Antarctic is a grim place for ponies. I think Scott felt the sufferings of the ponies more than the animals themselves. It was different for the dogs. These fairly warm blizzards were only a rest for them. Snugly curled up in a hole in the snow they allowed themselves to be drifted over. Bieleglas and Vaida, two half brothers who pulled side by side, always insisted upon sharing one hole, and for greater warmth one would lie on the top of the other. At intervals of two hours or so they fraternally changed places.

This blizzard lasted three days.

We now marched nearly due south, the open Barrier in front, Mount Terror and the sea behind, for five days, covering fifty-four miles, when, being now level with the southern extremity of the Bluff, we laid the Bluff Depôt. The bearings of Bluff Depôt, as well as those of Corner Camp, are given in Scott's Last Expedition.

The characteristics of these days were the collapse of two of the ponies, Blücher and Blossom, and the partial collapse of a third, Jimmy Pigg, although the surface hardened, becoming a marbled series of wind-swept ridges and domes in this region. For the rest the new hands were finding out how to keep warm on the Barrier, how to pitch a tent and cook a meal in twenty minutes, and the thousand and one little tips which only experience can teach. But all the care in the world could do little for the poor ponies.

It must be confessed at once that some of these ponies were very poor material, and it must be conceded that Oates who was in charge of them started with a very great handicap. From first to last it was Oates' consummate management, seconded by the care and kindness of the ponies' leaders, which obtained results which often exceeded the most sanguine hopes.

One evening we watched Scott digging crumbly blocks of snow out of the Barrier and building a rough wall, something like a grouse butt, to the south of his pony. In our inmost hearts I fear we viewed these proceedings with distrust, and

saw in it but little usefulness,—one little bit of leaky wall in a great plain of snow
But a very little wind (which you must understand comes almost invariably from
the south) convinced us from personal experience what a boon these walls could
be. Henceforward every night on camping each pony leader built a wall behind
his pony while his pemmican was cooking, and came out after supper to finish this
wall before he turned in to his sleeping-bag—no small thing when you consider
that the warmth of your hours of rest depends largely upon getting into your bag
immediately you have eaten your hoosh and cocoa. And not seldom you might
hear a voice in your dreams: "Bill! Nobby's kicked his wall down"; and out Bill
would go to build it up again.

DOGSKIN 'MITTS'

SLEDGING SPOON, CUP AND PANNIKIN

Oates wished to take certain of the ponies as far south as possible on the Depôt journey, and then to kill them and leave the meat there as a depôt of dog food for the Polar Journey. Scott was against this plan. Here at Bluff Depôt he decided to send back the three weakest ponies (Blossom, Blücher and Jimmy Pigg, with their leaders, Lieutenant Evans, Forde and Keohane). They started back the next morning (February 13) while the remainder of the party went forward over a surface which gradually became softer as we left behind the windy region of the Bluff. We now had with us the two teams of dogs, driven by Meares and Wilson, and five ponies.

- Scott with 'Nobby.'
- Oates with 'Punch.'
- Bowers with 'Uncle Bill.'
- Gran with 'Weary Willie.'
- Cherry-Garrard with 'Guts.'

Scott, Wilson, Meares and myself inhabited one tent, Bowers, Oates and Gran the other. Scott was evolving in his mind means by which ponies should follow one another in a string, the second pony with his leading rein fastened to the back of the sledge of the first and so on, the cavalcade to be managed by two or three men only, instead of one man to lead each pony.

Sunday night (February 12) we started from Bluff Depôt and did seven miles before lunch against a considerable drift and wind. It was pretty cold, and ten minutes after we left our lunch camp with the ponies it was blowing a full blizzard. The dog party had not started, so we camped and slept five in the four-man tent, and it was by no means uncomfortable. Probably this was the time when Scott first thought of taking a five-man party to the Pole. By Monday evening the blizzard was over, the dogs came up, and we did 6½ miles of very heavy going. Gran's pony, Weary Willie, a sluggish and obstinate animal, was far behind, as usual, when we halted our ponies at the camping place. Farther off the dog-teams were coming up. What happened never became clear. Poor Weary, it seems, was in difficulties in a snow-drift: the dogs of one team being very hungry took charge of their sledge and in a moment were on the horse, to all purposes a pack of ravenous wolves. Gran and Weary made a good fight and the dogs were driven off, but Weary came into camp without his sledge, covered with blood and looking very sick.

We halted after doing only ¾ mile more after lunch; for the pony was done, and little wonder. The following day we did 7½ miles with difficulty, both Uncle Bill and Weary Willie going very slowly and stopping frequently. The going was very deep. The ponies were fast giving out, and it was evident that we had much to learn as to their use on the Barrier; they were thin and very hungry; their rations were unsatisfactory; and the autumn temperatures and winds were beyond their strength. We went on one more day in a minus twenty temperature and light airs, and then in latitude 79° 29′ S. it was determined to lay the depôt, which was afterwards known as One Ton, and return. In view of subsequent events it should be realized that this depôt was just a cairn of snow in which were buried food and oil, and over which a flag waved on a bamboo. There is no land visible from One Ton except on a very clear day and it is 130 geographical miles from Hut Point.

We spent a day making up the mound which contained about a ton of provisions, oil, compressed fodder, oats and other necessaries for the forthcoming Polar Journey. Scott was satisfied with the result, and indeed this depôt ensured that we could start southwards for the Pole fully laden from this point.

Here the party was again split into two for the return. Scott was anxious to get such news about the landing of Campbell's party on King Edward VII.'s Land as the ship should have left at Hut Point on her return journey. He decided to take the two dog-teams, the first with himself and Meares, the second with Wilson and myself, and make a quick return, leaving Bowers with Oates and Gran to help him to bring back the five ponies, driving them one behind the other.

THE RETURN OF THE PONY PARTY FROM ONE TON DE-PÔT

(From a Letter written by Bowers)

As our loads were so light Titus thought it would be better for the ponies to do their full march in one stretch and so have a longer rest. We, therefore, decided to forgo lunch and have a good meal on camping. The recent trails were fresh enough to follow and so saved us steering by compass, which is very difficult as the needle will only come to rest after you have been standing still for about a minute. That march was extraordinary, the snowy mist hid all distant objects and made all close ones look gigantic. Although we were walking on a flat undulating plain, one could not get away from the impression that the ground was hilly—quite steep in places with deep hollows by the wayside. Suddenly a herd of apparent cattle would appear in the distance, then you would think, 'No, it's a team of dogs broken loose and rushing towards you.' In another moment one would be walking over the black dots of some old horse droppings which had been the cause of the hallucinations. Since then I have often been completely taken in by appearances under certain conditions of light, and the novelty has worn off. Sastrugi are the hard waves formed by wind on a snow surface; these are seldom more than a foot or so in height, and often so obscured as to be imperceptible irregularities. On this occasion they often appeared like immense ridges until you walked over them. After going about 10 miles we spotted a tiny black triangle in the dead white void ahead, it was over a mile away and was the lunch camp of the dogs. We were fairly close before they broke camp and hurriedly packed up. I thought they looked rather sheepish at having been caught up, like the hare and the tortoise again. Still we had been marching very quickly and Scott was delighted to see Weary Willie going so well. They then dashed off, and after completing just over 12 miles we reached Pagoda Cairn where a bale of fodder had been left.

Here we camped and threw up our walls as quickly as possible to shelter the beasts from the cold wind. Weary was the most annoying, he would deliberately back into his wall and knock the whole structure down. In the case of my own pony, I had to put the wall out of his reach as his aim in life was to eat it, generally beginning at the bottom. He would diligently dislodge a block, and bring down the whole fabric. One cannot be angry with the silly beggars—Titus says a horse has practically no reasoning power, the thing to do is simply to throw up another wall and keep on at it.

The weather cleared during the night, and the next day, February 19, we started off under ideal conditions, the sun was already dipping pretty low, marks easy to pick up, and on this occasion we could plainly see a cairn over seven miles away, raised by the mirage; the only trouble about seeing things so far off is that they take such an awful time to reach. Mirage is a great feature down here and one of the most common of optical phenomena on the Barrier; it is often difficult to persuade oneself that open water does not lie ahead. We passed the scene of Weary Willie's fight with the dogs during the march and also had an amusing argument as to a dark object on the snow ahead. At first we thought it was the dog camp again, but it turned out to be an empty biscuit tin, such is the deceptive nature of the light. Later we sighted our old blizzard camp and decided to utilize the walls again. Weary Willie was decidedly worse and had to be literally jumped along by the pony to which he was attached. Within half a mile of the walls Weary refused to go farther, and after wasting some time in vain efforts to urge him on we had to camp where we were, having only done 10½ miles. This was very sad, but I took hope from the fact that Titus, who is usually pretty pessimistic, had not yet given up hopes of getting him back alive. He had an extra whack of oats at the expense of the other ponies, and my big beast made up for his shortage by hauling the sledge towards him with his tethered leg, and forcing his nose into our precious biscuit tank, out of which he helped himself liberally at our expense. The sledges were now too light to anchor the animals, so we had to peg them down with anything we could and bank them up with snow.

Weary was better the next day (February 20) but we decided at the outset to go no farther than the Bluff Camp where we had left some fodder. This was barely 10 miles off, yet my old animal showed signs of lassitude before the end; there was nothing alarming, however, and we saw the depôt over five miles off which interested the beasts, who see these things and somehow connect them, in the backs of their silly old heads, with food and rest. Weary Willie made a decided improvement, so we camped in high spirits. Captain Scott had asked me if possible to take some theodolite observations for the determination of the position of Bluff Camp. Ours is much farther off and farther beyond the Bluff than the old Discovery Depôt A, which was practically the same position Shackleton used. In both cases, Scott and Shackleton were keeping nearer the coast; now, however, that the Beardmore has been discovered we can aim straight for that, which takes one farther east by at least 15 miles off the Bluff. This is rather an advantage, I think, as close in to this remarkable headland the onward movement of the Barrier arrested by the immovable hills causes a terrific chaos of crevasses off the cliffs at the end. These extend many miles and include some chasms big enough to take the Terra Nova all standing. Needless to remark, one is well clear of this sort of scenery with ponies—hence our course. I was unable to get any observations, unfortunately, as it clouded over almost at once and later in the day started to snow without wind. This often happens before a bliz, and as we were anxious about the ponies to say nothing of our own shortage of biscuit we felt a trifle apprehensive. It was very gloomy when we left camp at midnight, as the midnight sun was already cartwheeling the southern horizon, the first sign of autumn, also the season had undoubtedly broken up, and the sky was covered with low stratus clouds as thick as a hedge. We lost sight of the cairn almost at once and followed the remains of old tracks for a little while till the snowy gloom made it impossible to see them. You will remember that it was at the Bluff Camp that Teddy Evans returned with the three weak ponies, so there were plenty of traces of our march now. Just on four miles from the start I saw a small mound some distance to the west, and struck over there: it was a small cairn without the signs of a camp and rather puzzled me at the time. As I shall mention it later I will call it X for convenience. We then pushed on and I found steering most difficult. In the fuzzy nothingness ahead one could see no point on which to fix the eye, and the compass required standing still to look at it every time. Our sledging compasses are spirit ones, and as steady as a small hand compass could possibly be. You will understand, however, that owing to the proximity of the Magnetic Pole the pull on the needle is chiefly downwards. It is forced into a horizontal position by a balancing weight on the N. side, so it is obvious that its direction power is greatly reduced. On the ship, owing to the vibration of the engines and the motors, we were absolutely unable to steer by the compass at all when off the region of the Magnetic Pole.

On this occasion (February 21) we zig-zagged all over the place—first I went ahead, and Oates said I zig-zagged, then he went ahead, and I understood at once, as it was impossible to walk straight for two consecutive minutes. However, we plodded along with frequent stoppages till the wind came away, and then having determined the direction of that, steered by keeping the snow on our backs. The wind was not strong enough to be unpleasant, and all was well. We legged it into the void for nearly seven miles beyond X Cairn when I suddenly found myself only a few yards away from another cairn. This shows that somehow, without the use of tracks or landmarks, we had marched seven miles without being able to see thirty yards, and had yet hit off the direct track to a T; of course, it was only coincidence, though some people might credit themselves with superlative navigating powers on such evidence. The wind increased, and with the knowledge I now have of blizzards I would camp at once. Then I thought it better to shove on, as the ponies were marching splendidly. The danger lay in the fact that though it is easy enough for you to march with the wind behind, you can't march for ever and you will probably get tired before the wind does. Camping in a stiff breeze is always difficult, to say nothing of a gale; and for three men with five ponies to manage would be wellnigh impossible. Fortunately for us this was not really a blizzard, though it was quite near enough to one. The sky broke later and showed the Bluff and White Island, and then the scurrying clouds of drift would encircle us to break again and come on again.

After having done seventeen miles we got a lull and stopped to camp right away. We were pretty quick about it, and fortunately got the ponies picketed, and tent pitched, before the wind came down on us again. We were pretty hungry by the time the walls were erected. Still we were quite happy, ate everything we could get, except the three lumps of sugar I always kept for old Uncle Bill out of my whack. The little blow blew itself out towards evening and in perfect calm and sunshine I got a splendid set of observations. Erebus and Terror were showing up as clear as a bell and I got a large number of angles for Evans' survey. We started out as usual, and had the most pleasant, as well as the longest, of our return marches on the last day of summer, February 22. We did eighteen miles right off the reel, the sun was brilliant from midnight onwards. He now half immersed himself below the horizon for a short interval once in 24 hours. All old cairns were visible a tremendous distance, six or seven miles at least for big ones. Mount Terror lay straight ahead and looked so clear that it seemed impossible to imagine it 70 miles away. At the end of our march we saw a small cairn beyond our 8th outward camp mound. Nobody would have rigged up another cairn so close without an object, so the thought of a dead horse flashed through my mind at once. Titus was so sure that Blücher would never get back, that he had bet Gran a biscuit on it. I saw the cairn had a fodder bale on the top, and later saw a note made fast to the wire. It was in Teddy Evans' handwriting and to our surprise recorded Blossom's death. Titus was so sure that Blossom would survive Blücher that we started to think back and thus the mystery of X Cairn was clear to me. I was quite certain now that both the ancient ponies had died and that Jimmy Pigg had returned alone. The following day (February 23) was a good marching day also, but a bit cloudy latterly. We did fourteen miles as this evidence of pony failure made us all the more anxious about ours, though really they were going very well. About eight miles on we came to one of Evans' camps and the solitary pony wall told its own tale of the death of the other two. He must have had a miserable return. At eleven miles there were two bales of fodder depôted, we were only 50 miles odd from our destination off Cape Armitage, and had one meal over three days' food. If, therefore, we could average 15 miles a day that would suffice. It was a silly risk in view of blizzards and other possibilities, chiefly our own inexperience. As it was

I took it and left the fodder there for next year.

February 24 was another march into impenetrable gloom. Fortunately Corner Camp, though dark enough, was not shaded in mist. I examined it for notes and evidence and found some. The sun set properly now, and had we been farther from home I should have changed to day marching. I have seldom seen such a scene of utter desolation as Corner Camp presented on that gloomy day. The fog then settled down and like people of the mist, we struck off blindly to the N.W. At 3.15 A.M. a light S. breeze came away; I dreaded a blizzard with so little pony food and already regretted my folly in leaving the fodder. After doing twelve miles we had to camp, as it was impossible even to march straight in the white haze. We made five colossal walls and turned in, hoping for the best. Fortune favours the reckless, as well as the brave, at times, and it did this time, as the blizzard still held off. The signs of one impending were unmistakable notwithstanding. Weary Willie did less well on February 25, and as the surface became heavier, we had to camp after only doing eleven miles.

I thought best in view of the threatening appearance of the weather to have a six hours' rest, and march into Safety Camp the same day, a distance of eight miles. We found to our horror that Gran had dropped the top cap of our primus at the last camp. Cold food stared us in face!

However, we did manage to melt some snow for a cheering drink by cutting a piece of tin as near the shape of the cap as possible. Our biscuit was finished owing to the ravages of my pony. Before turning in I saw some specks to the N. and skipping my theodolite on its tripod, looked through the telescope and saw two tents and a number of ski stuck up. [This was Scott's man-hauling party together with Jimmy Pigg, going out to Corner Camp.] This we concluded was either a man-hauling, or man and beast party bound for Corner Camp. We overslept and so did not get away till the afternoon. It was still very cloudy and threatening. I found that I had steered considerably to the southward of the right direction in the fog, and it is lucky we met with no crevasses off White Island. Safety Camp at last appeared, and the last four miles seemed interminable. We had given the animals their last feed before starting, not a particle remained, but they stuck it. The surface was very heavy. Once, however, that they had seen the camp they never stopped. I suppose they knew they were nearly home. We marched in about 9.30 P.M. I said 'Thank God' when I looked at the weather, and the empty sledges. The dogs were in camp, also the dome tent [we had some tents shaped like a dome in addition to those we used for sledging], out of which Uncle Bill (the real 'Uncle Bill Wilson') and Meares emerged. We soon had the ponies behind walls and well fed, borrowed their primus for ourselves, and had a square meal of pemmican and biscuit with fids of seal liver in it.

(End of Bowers' Account.)

THE RETURN OF THE DOG PARTY

The history of the dog-teams was eventful. We travelled fast, doing nearly 78 miles in the first three days, by which time we were approaching Corner Camp

The dogs were thin and hungry and we were pushing them each day just so long as they could pull, running ourselves for the most part. Scott determined to cut the corner, that is to miss Corner Camp and cut diagonally across our outward track. It was not expected that this would bring us across any badly crevassed area.

We started on the evening of February 20 in a very bad light. It was coldish, with no wind. After going about three miles I saw a drop in the level of the Barrier which the sledge was just going to run over. I shouted to Wilson to look out, but he had already jumped on to the sledge (for he was running) having seen Stareek put his paws through. It was a nasty crevasse, about twenty feet across with blue holes on both sides. The sledge ran over and immediately on the opposite side was brought up by a large 'haystack' of pressure which we had not seen owing to the light. Meares' team, on our left, never saw any sign of pressure. The light was so bad that we never saw this cairn of ice until we ran into it.

We ran level for another two miles, Meares and Scott on our left. We were evidently crossing many crevasses. Quite suddenly we saw the dogs of their team disappearing, following one another, just like dogs going down a hole after some animal.

"In a moment," wrote Scott, "the whole team were sinking—two by two we lost sight of them, each pair struggling for foothold. Osman the leader exerted all his strength and kept a foothold—it was wonderful to see him. The sledge stopped and we leapt aside. The situation was clear in another moment. We had been actually travelling along the bridge [or snow covering] of a crevasse, the sledge had stopped on it, whilst the dogs hung in their harness in the abyss, suspended between the sledge and the leading dog. Why the sledge and ourselves didn't follow the dogs we shall never know."

We of the other sledge stopped hurriedly, tethered our team and went to their assistance with the Alpine rope. Osman, the big leader, was in great difficulties. He crouched resisting with all his enormous strength the pull of the rope upon which the team hung in their harness in mid air. It was clear that if Osman gave way the sledge and dogs would probably all be lost down the crevasse.

First we pulled the sledge off the crevasse, and drove the tethering peg and driving stick through the cross pieces to hold it firm. Scott and Meares then tried to pull up the rope from Osman's end, while we hung on to the sledge to prevent it slipping down the crevasse. They could not move it an inch. We then put the strain as much as possible on to a peg. Meanwhile two dogs had fallen out of their harness into the crevasse and could be seen lying on a snow-ledge some 65 feet down. Later they curled up and went to sleep. Another dog as he hung managed to get some purchase for his feet on the side of the crevasse, and a free fight took place among several more of them, as they dangled, those that hung highest using the backs of those under them to get a purchase.

"It takes one a little time," wrote Scott, "to make plans under such sudden circumstances, and for some minutes our efforts were rather futile. We could not get an inch on the main trace of the sledge or on the leading rope, which was binding Osman to the snow with a throttling pressure. Then thought became clearer. We unloaded our sledge, putting in safety our sleeping-bags with the tent and cooker. Choking sounds from Osman made it clear that the pressure on him must soon be relieved. I seized the lashing off Meares' sleeping-bag, passed the tent poles across the crevasse, and with Meares managed to get a few inches on the leading line; this freed Osman, whose harness was immediately cut.

"Then securing the Alpine rope to the main trace we tried to haul up together. One dog came up and was unlashed, but by this time the rope had cut so far back at the edge that it was useless to attempt to get more of it. But we could now unbend the sledge, and do that for which we should have aimed from the first, namely, run the sledge across the gap and work from it. We managed to do this, our fingers constantly numbed. Wilson held on to the anchored trace whilst the rest of us laboured at the leader end. The leading rope was very small and I was fearful of its breaking, so Meares was lowered down a foot or two to secure the Alpine rope to the leading end of the trace; this done, the work of rescue proceeded in better order. Two by two we hauled the animals up to the sledge and one by one cut them out of their harness. Strangely the last dogs were the most difficult, as they were close under the lip of the gap, bound in by the snow-covered rope. Finally, with a gasp we got the last poor creature on to firm snow. We had recovered eleven of the thirteen."[117]

The dogs had been dangling for over an hour, and some of them showed signs of internal injuries. Meanwhile the two remaining dogs were lying down the crevasse on a snow-ledge. Scott proposed going down on the Alpine rope to get them; all his instincts of kindness were aroused, as well as the thought of the loss of two of the team. Wilson thought it was a mad idea and very dangerous, and said so, asking however whether he might not go down instead of Scott if anybody had to go. Scott insisted, and we paid down the 90-foot Alpine rope to test the distance. The ledge was about 65 feet below. We lowered Scott, who stood on the ledge while we hauled up the two dogs in turn. They were glad to see him, and little wonder!

But the rescued dogs which were necessarily running about loose on the Barrier, in their mangled harnesses, chose this moment to start a free fight with the other team. With a hurried shout down the crevasse we had to rush off to separate them. Nougis I. had been considerably mauled before this was done—also, incidentally, my heel! But at last we separated them, and hauled Scott to the surface. It was all three of us could do and our fingers were frost-bitten towards the end.

Scott's interest in the incident, apart from the recovery of the dogs, was scientific. Since we were running across the line of cleavage when the dogs went down, it was to be expected that we should be crossing the crevasses at right angles, and not be travelling, as actually happened, parallel to, or along them. While we were getting him up the sixty odd feet to which we had lowered him he kept muttering: "I wonder why this is running the way it is—you expect to find them at right angles," and when down the crevasse he wanted to go off exploring, but we managed to persuade him that the snow-ledge upon which he was standing was utterly unsafe, and indeed we could see the nothingness below through the blue

[117] *Scott's Last Expedition*, vol. i. pp. 180-81.

holes in the shelf. Another regret was that we had no thermometer: the temperature of the inside of the Barrier is of great interest and a fairly reliable record of the average temperature throughout the year might have been obtained when so far down into it. Altogether we could congratulate ourselves on a fortunate ending to a nasty business. We expected several more miles of crevasses, and the wind was getting up, driving the surface drift like smoke over the ground, with a very black sky to the south. We pitched the tent, had a good meal and mended the dog harness which had been ruthlessly cut in clearing the dogs. Luckily we found no more crevasses for it was now blowing hard, and rescue work would have been difficult, and we pushed on as far as possible that night, doing eleven miles after lunch, and sixteen for the day. It had been strenuous, for we had been working in or over the crevasse for 2½ hours, and dogs and men were tired out. It cleared and became quite warm as we camped. There was a pleasant air of friendship in the tent that night, rather more than usual. That is generally the result of this kind of business.

We reached Safety Camp next day (February 22) anxious for news of the ship's doings, the landing of Campbell's party, and of the ponies which had been sent back from the Bluff Depôt. Lieutenant Evans, Forde and Keohane, the pony leaders, were there, but only one pony. The other two had died of exhaustion soon after they left us and we had passed the cairns which marked their graves without knowledge. Their story was grim, and they had had a mournful journey back. First Blossom, and then Blücher collapsed, their ends being hastened by the blizzard of February 1.

This crevasse incident, followed by the news of the loss of the ponies, was a blow to Scott, and his mind was also uneasy about Atkinson and Crean, whom we had left here, and who had disappeared leaving no record. Nor was the report from the Terra Nova here, so we judged that the missing men and the report must be at Hut Point. After three or four hours' sleep, and a cup of tea and a biscuit, we started man-hauling with cooker and sleeping-bags: the former because we were to have our good meal at the hut, the latter in case we were hung up. Travelling over the sea-ice as far as the Gap, from which we saw that the open sea reached to Hut Point, we made our way into the hut, and there was a mystery. The accumulations of ice which we found in it were dug away: there was a notice outside dated February 8 saying, "mail for Captain Scott is in bag inside south door." We hunted everywhere, but there was no Atkinson nor Crean, nor mail, nor the things which the ship was to have brought. All kinds of wild theories were advanced. By the presence of a fresh onion and some bread it was clear that the ship's party had been there, but the rest was utterly vague. It was then suggested that we were expected back about this time, and that the missing men had been sledging to Safety Camp round Cape Armitage on the very shaky sea-ice while we passed them as we came through the Gap. Sledge tracks were found leading on to the sea-ice: we started back in doubt. Scott was terribly anxious, we were all tired, and the depôt never seemed to come nearer. It was not until we were some two hundred yards from it that we saw the extra tent. "Thank God!" I heard Scott mutter under his breath, and "I believe you were even more anxious than I was, Bill."

Atkinson had the ship's mail, signed by Campbell. "Every incident of the day," Scott wrote, "pales before the startling contents of the mail-bag which At-kinson gave me—a letter from Campbell setting out his doings and the finding of Amundsen established in the Bay of Whales."

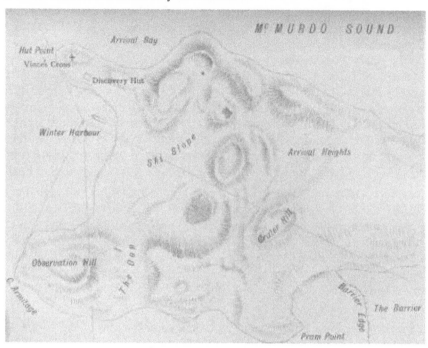

HUT POINT—E. A. WILSON, DEL.

Strongly as Scott tries to word this, it quite fails to convey how he felt, and how we all felt more or less, in spite of the warning conveyed in the telegram from Madeira to Melbourne. For an hour or so we were furiously angry, and were possessed with an insane sense that we must go straight to the Bay of Whales and have it out with Amundsen and his men in some undefined fashion or other there and then. Such a mood could not and did not bear a moment's reflection; but it was natural enough. We had just paid the first instalment of the heart-breaking la-bour of making a path to the Pole; and we felt, however unreasonably, that we had earned the first right of way. Our sense of co-operation and solidarity had been wrought up to an extraordinary pitch; and we had so completely forgotten the spirit of competition that its sudden intrusion jarred frightfully. I do not defend our burst of rage—for such it was—I simply record it as an integral human part of my narrative. It passed harmlessly; and Scott's account proceeds as follows:

"One thing only fixes itself definitely in my mind. The proper, as well as the wiser, course for us is to proceed exactly as though this had not happened. To go forward and do our best for the honour of the country without fear or panic. There is no doubt that Amundsen's plan is a very serious menace to ours. He has a short-er distance to the Pole by 60 miles—I never thought he could have got so many dogs safely to the ice. His plan of running them seems excellent. But, above and beyond all, he can start his journey early in the season—an impossible condition with ponies."[118]

We read that on leaving McMurdo Sound the Terra Nova coasted eastward along the Barrier face, with Campbell and his men who were to be landed on King Edward VII.'s Land if possible. She surveyed the face of the Barrier as she went from Cape Crozier to longitude 170° W., whence she shaped a course direct for Cape Colbeck, which Priestley states in his diary "is only 200 feet high according to our measurement and looks uncommonly like common or garden Barrier."

Here they met heavy pack, and were forced to return without finding any place where the cliff was low enough to allow Campbell and his five men to land. They coasted back, making for an inlet known as Balloon Bight. Priestley tells the story:

"February 1, 1911. Our trip has not been without outcome after all, and all our doubts about wintering here or in South Victoria Land have been settled in a startling fashion. About ten o'clock we steamed into a deep bay in the Barrier which proved to be Shackleton's Bay of Whales, and our observations in the last expedition [Shackleton's] have been wonderfully upheld. Our present sights and angles Pennell tells me are almost a duplicate of those that we got. Every one has always been doubtful about the Bay of Whales we reported, but now the matter has been set at rest finally. There is no doubt now that Balloon Bight and the neighbouring bay marked on the Discovery's chart have become merged into one, and further, that since that period the resulting bight has broken back considerably more: indeed it seems to have altered a good deal on its western border since our visit to it in 1908. Otherwise it is the same, the same deceptive caves and shadows having from a distance the appearance of rock exposures, the same pressure-ridged cliffs, the same undulations behind, the same expanse of sea-ice and even the same crowds of whales. I hope that before we leave we shall find it possible to survey the bight, but that depends on the weather. It was satisfactory to find all our observations coming right and everybody backing up Shackleton, and I turned in last night feeling quite cheerful and believing that there would be a really good chance of the Eastern Party finding a home on the Barrier here—our last chance of surveying King Edward's Land.

"However, man proposes but God disposes, and I was waked up by Lillie at one o'clock this morning by the astounding news that there was a ship in the bay at anchor to the sea-ice. All was confusion on board for a few minutes, everybody rushing up on deck with cameras and clothes.

"It was no false alarm, there she was within a few yards of us, and what is more, those of us who had read Nansen's books recognized the Fram.

"She is rigged with fore and aft sails and as she has petrol engines she has no funnel. Soon afterwards the men forward declared that they sighted a hut on the Barrier, and the more excited declared that there was a party coming out to meet

---

[118] *Scott's Last Expedition*, vol. i. pp. 187-188. Scott started for the Pole on November 1, 1911. Amundsen started on September 8, 1911, but had to turn back owing to low temperatures; he started again on October 19.

us. Campbell, Levick, and myself were therefore lowered over the side of the ship while she was being made fast, and set off on ski towards the dark spot we could see. This proved to be only an abandoned depôt and we returned to the ship where Campbell, who in his anxiety to be the first to meet them had left us beginners far behind, had opened up conversation with the night watchman.

"He informed us that there were only three men on board and that the remainder of them were settling Amundsen in winter quarters about as far from the depôt as the depôt was from the ship. Amundsen is coming to visit the Fram to-morrow, and we are staying long enough to allow Pennell and Campbell to interview him. They reached the pack about January 6 and were through it by the 12th, so they did not have as bad a time as we did. They inform us that Amundsen does not intend to make his descent on the Pole until next year. This is encouraging as it means a fair race for the next summer, though the news we are bringing to them will keep the Western [Main] Party on tenterhooks of excitement all the winter.

"Our plans have of course been decided for us. We cannot according to etiquette trench on their winter quarters, but must return to McMurdo Sound and then go off towards Robertson Bay and settle ourselves as best we can. While we are waiting events we have not been by any means idle. Rennick got a sounding, 180 fathoms, and the crew have killed three seals, including one beautiful silver crab-eater, Lillie has secured water samples at 50, 100, 150, and 170 fathoms and has had a haul with the plankton net, and Williams is endeavouring to fit up the trawl for a haul to-morrow if we get time and appropriate weather. I got a roll of films and gave the roll to Drake to take home and get developed in Christchurch. There are photographs of the Fram, of the Fram and Terra Nova together, of their depôt, and of the ice-cliffs and the sea-ice which is decidedly overcut, the thick snow having been removed in places by the swell until a ledge several yards wide is lying just submerged.

"It has been calm all the night with the snow falling at intervals.

"February 4, 1911. I was waked at seven o'clock this morning by Levick demanding the loan of my camera. It appears that Amundsen, Johansen and six men had arrived at the Fram this morning at about 6.30 A.M., and had come over to interview Campbell and Pennell. Campbell, Pennell and Levick then went back to breakfast with them and stayed until nearly noon when they returned telling us to expect Amundsen, Nilsen, the first lieutenant of the Fram who is taking her back after landing the party, and a young lieutenant whose name none of us caught, to lunch. After lunch a party of officers and men went to see the rest of the Norwegians, see over the ship, and say good-bye. I did not go and was able to show Lieut Jensen over the ship in the meantime. About three o'clock we let go the ice anchor and parted from the Fram, steaming along the ice very slowly in order to dredge from 190 to 300 fathoms. The haul was successful, about two bucketsful of the muddy bottom being secured, and a still more valuable catch from the biological point of view were two long crinoids, about a couple of feet in length and in fairly perfect condition, which had become attached to the outside of the net.

"We are now standing along the Barrier continuing our survey to the bight we first struck, after which we sail to Cape Evans, stay a day there and then make up North to try and effect a lodgment on the coast beyond Cape Adare.

"During the morning Browning and I examined the ice-face forming the eastern face of the bight. We found it to be made of clear ice of grain from a quarter to three-eighths of an inch in size and full of bubbles.

"On the way there I took a couple of photographs of some of Amundsen's dogs, and when we were there I got a few of crevasses and caves in the Barrier face.

"Well! we have left the Norwegians and our thoughts are full, too full, of them at present. The impression they have left with me is that of a set of men of distinctive personality, hard, and evidently inured to hardship, good goers and pleasant and good-humoured. All these qualities combine to make them very dangerous rivals, but even did one want not to, one cannot help liking them individually in spite of the rivalry.

"One thing I have particularly noticed is the way in which they are refraining from getting information from us which might be useful to them. We have news which will make the Western Party as uneasy as ourselves and the world will watch with interest a race for the Pole next year, a race which may go any way, and may be decided by luck or by dogged energy and perseverance on either side.

"The Norwegians are in dangerous winter quarters, for the ice is breaking out rapidly from the Bay of Whales which they believe to be Borchgrevink's Bight, and they are camped directly in front of a distinct line of weakness. On the other hand if they get through the winter safely (and they are aware of their danger), they have unlimited dogs, the energy of a nation as northern as ourselves, and experience with snow-travelling that could be beaten by no collection of men in the world.

"There remains the Beardmore Glacier. Can their dogs face it, and if so, who will get there first. One thing I feel and that is that our Southern Party will go far before they permit themselves to be beaten by any one, and I think that two parties are very likely to reach the Pole next year, but God only knows which will get there first.

"A few of the things we learnt about the Norwegians are as follows:

"The engines of the Fram occupy only half the size of our wardroom, the petrol tanks have not needed replenishment since they left Norway, and their propeller can be lifted by three men. They kept fresh potatoes from Norway to the Barrier. (Some of them must surely be renegade Irishmen.) They have each a separate cabin 'tween-decks in the Fram, and are very comfortable. They are using for transporting their stores to the hut, eight teams of five dogs each, working every alternate day.

"They intend to use for the Polar Journey teams of ten dogs, each team working one day out of two. Their dogs stop at a whistle, and if they make a break they can be stopped by overturning the sledge, empty or full as the case may be. They are nine in the shore party and ten in the ship. Their ship is going back to Buenos Ayres with Nilsen in charge and during the winter is to encircle the world, sounding all the way.

"They are not starting on the dash South this year and do not yet know wheth-er they will lay depôts this year. They have 116 dogs and ten of these are bitches, so that they can rear pups, and have done so very successfully on the way out. The Fram acts like a cork in the sea; she rolls tremendously but does not ship water, and during the voyage they have had the dogs running loose about the decks. There is a lot more miscellaneous information, but I may remember it more co-herently a little later when the main impressions of the rencontre are a little more faint."[119]

It will be seen that Priestley missed three points. First, he was left with a con-ventional but very erroneous impression of Amundsen as a blunt Norwegian sail-or, not in the least an intellectual. Second, he thought Amundsen had camped on the ice and not on terra firma. Third, he thought Amundsen was going to the Pole by the old route over the Beardmore. The truth was that Amundsen was an explor-er of the markedly intellectual type, rather Jewish than Scandinavian, who had proved his sagacity by discovering solid footing for the winter by pure judgment. For the moment, let it be confessed, we all underrated Amundsen, and could not shake off the feeling that he had stolen a march on us.

Back to McMurdo Sound, and the news left at Hut Point. Then the two ponies which had been allotted to Campbell were swum ashore at Cape Evans, since he thought that now they would be of more use to Scott than to himself. Subsequent events proved the extreme usefulness of this unselfish act. The Terra Nova would steam north and try and land Campbell's party on the extreme northern shores of Queen Victoria Land. At the same time there was so little coal left that it might be necessary to go straight back to New Zealand. Campbell regretted not being able to see Scott, supposing that the altered circumstances caused Scott to wish to rearrange his parties, and also because Amundsen had asked Campbell to land his party at the Bay of Whales, giving him the area to the east to explore, and Camp-bell did not wish to accept before getting Scott's permission.

As we know now coal ran so short that it came to an alternative of dumping Campbell, his men and gear hastily on the beach at Cape Adare, or taking them back to New Zealand. As one member of the crew said: "Exploring is all very well in its way, but it is a thing which can be very easily overdone." The ship was as ready to get rid of them as they were to get rid of the ship. They were landed, working to their waists in the surf, and the ship got safely back to New Zealand.

Scott decided that the period of waiting until the pony party arrived from One Ton should be employed in sledging stores out to Corner Camp. But the dog-teams were done, "the dogs are thin as rakes; they are ravenous and very tired. I feel this should not be, and that it is evident that they are underfed. The ration must be increased next year and we must have some properly-thought-out diet. The biscuit alone is not good enough."[120] In addition, several dogs were feeling the effects of injuries due to the crevasse incident. There remained the men and the

[119] Priestley's diary.
[120] *Scott's Last Expedition*, vol. i. p. 185.

one pony which had survived out of the three sent back from Bluff Depôt, namely Jimmy Pigg.

The party started on Friday, February 24, marching by day. It consisted of Scott, Crean and myself with one sledge and tent, Lieutenant Evans, Atkinson and Forde with a second sledge and tent, and Keohane leading James Pigg. On the second night out we saw the pony party pass us in the distance on their way to Safety Camp.[121] At Corner Camp Scott decided to leave Lieutenant Evans' party to come in with the pony more slowly, and himself to push on with Crean and myself at top speed for Safety Camp. We made a forced march well into the night, doing twenty-six miles for the day, and camped some ten miles from Safety Camp, where the pony party must by this time have arrived.

The events which followed were disastrous, and the steps which led to a catastrophe which entailed the loss of much of our best transport, and only by a miracle did not lead to the loss of several lives, were complicated. At this moment, the night of February 26, there were three parties on the Barrier. Behind Scott was Lieutenant Evans' party and the pony, James Pigg. Scott himself was camped within easy marching distance of Safety Camp with Crean and myself. At Safety Camp were the two dog-teams with Wilson and Meares, while the pony party from One Ton Depôt had just arrived with five ponies which were for the most part thin, hungry and worn. Between Safety Camp and Hut Point lay the frozen sea, which might or might not break up this year, but we knew from our observations a few days before that the ice was in a shaky condition. At that time the ice sheet extended some seven miles to the north of Hut Point. The season was fast closing in: temperatures of fifty or sixty degrees of frost had been common for the last fortnight, and this was bad for the ponies. We had been unfortunate in having several severe blizzards, and it was already clear that it was these autumn blizzards more than cold temperatures and soft surfaces which the ponies could not endure. Scott was most anxious to get the animals into such shelter as we could make for them at Hut Point.

The next morning, February 27, we woke to a regular cold autumn blizzard—very thick, wind force 9 and temperature about minus twenty. This was disheartening, and indeed with our six worn ponies still on the Barrier the outlook for them was discouraging. The blizzard came to an end the next morning. Scott must take up the first part of that day's story:

"Packed up at 6 A.M. and marched into Safety Camp. Found every one very cold and depressed. Wilson and Meares had had continuous bad weather since we left, Bowers and Oates since their arrival. The blizzard had raged for two days. The animals looked in a sorry condition, but all were alive. The wind blew keen and cold from the east. There could be no advantage in waiting here, and soon all arrangements were made for a general shift to Hut Point. Packing took a long time. The snowfall had been prodigious, and parts of the sledges were 3 or 4 feet under drift. About 4 o'clock the two dog-teams got safely away. Then the pony party prepared to go. As the cloths were stript from the ponies the ravages of the <u>blizzard became</u> evident. The animals, without exception, were terribly emaciated,

[121] See p. 123.

and Weary Willie was in a pitiable condition.

"The plan was for the ponies to follow the dog tracks, our small party to start last and get in front of the ponies on the sea-ice. I was very anxious about the sea-ice passage owing to the spread of the water holes."[122]

The two dog-teams left with Meares and Wilson some time before the ponies, and for the moment they go out of this story.

Bowers' pony, Uncle Bill, was ready first, and he started with him. We got three more ponies harnessed, Punch, Nobby and Guts, and tried to harness Weary Willie, but when we attempted to lead him forward he immediately fell down.

Scott rapidly reorganized. He sent Crean and me forward with the three better ponies to join Bowers, now waiting a mile ahead. Oates and Gran he kept with himself, to try and help the sick pony. His diary tells how "we made desperate efforts to save the poor creature, got him once more on his legs, gave him a hot oat mash. Then, after a wait of an hour, Oates led him off, and we packed the sledge and followed on ski; 500 yards from the camp the poor creature fell again and I felt it was the last effort. We camped, built a snow wall round him, and did all we possibly could to get him on his feet. Every effort was fruitless, though the poor thing made pitiful struggles. Towards midnight we propped him up as comfortably as we could and went to bed.

"Wednesday, March 1. A.M. Our pony died in the night. It is hard to have got him back so far only for this. It is clear that these blizzards are terrible for the poor animals. Their coats are not good, but even with the best of coats it is certain they would lose condition badly if caught in one, and we cannot afford to lose condition at the beginning of a journey. It makes a late start necessary for next year.

"Well, we have done our best and bought our experience at a heavy cost. Now every effort must be bent on saving the remaining animals."[123]

A letter from Bowers home, which certainly does not overstate the adventures of himself and the two men sent forward to join him, is probably the best description of the incidents which followed. It will be remembered that Crean and I with three ponies were sent from Safety Camp to join him: he was already leading one pony. Night was beginning to fall, and the light was bad, but from the edge of the Barrier the two dog-teams could still be seen as black dots in the distance towards Cape Armitage.

"On the night of February 28 I led off with my pony and was surprised at the delay in the others leaving—knowing nothing of Weary's collapse. Over the edge of the Barrier I went, and at the bottom of the snow incline awaited the others. To my surprise Cherry and Crean appeared with Punch, Nobby and Guts in a string, and then I heard the reason for Oates and Scott not having come on. My orders were to push on to Hut Point over the sea-ice without delay, and to follow the dogs; previously I had been told to camp on the sea-ice only in case of the beasts being unable to go on. We had four pretty heavy sledges, as we were taking six

[122] *Scott's Last Expedition*, vol. i. pp. 190-191.
[123] *Scott's Last Expedition*, vol. i. pp. 191-192.

weeks' man food and oil to the hut, as well as a lot of gear from the depôt, and pony food, etc. Unfortunately the dogs misunderstood their orders and, instead of piloting us, dashed off on their own. We saw them like specks in the distance in the direction of the old seal crack. Having crossed this they wheeled to the right in the direction of Cape Armitage and disappeared into a black indefinite mist, which seemed to pervade everything in that direction. We heard afterwards that in a mile or two they came to some alarming signs and, turning, made for the Gap where they got up on to the land about midnight.

"I plugged on in their tracks, till we came to the seal crack which was an old pressure-ridge running many miles S.W. from Pram Point. We considered the ice behind this crack—over which we had just come—fast ice; it was older ice than that beyond, as it had undoubtedly frozen over first. Having crossed the crack we streaked on for Cape Armitage. The animals were going badly, owing to the effects of the blizzard, and frequent stoppages were necessary. On coming to some shaky ice we headed farther west as there were always some bad places off the cape, and I thought it better to make a good circuit. Crean, who had been over the ice recently, told me it was all right farther round. However, about a mile farther on I began to have misgivings; the cracks became too frequent to be pleasant, and although the ice was from five to ten feet thick, one does not like to see water squelching between them, as we did later. It spells motion, and motion on sea-ice means breakage. I shoved on in the hope of getting on better ice round the cape, but at last came a moving crack, and that decided me to turn back. We could see nothing owing to the black mist, everything looked solid as ever, but I knew enough to mistrust moving ice, however solid it seemed. It was a beastly march back: dark, gloomy and depressing. The beasts got more and more down in their spirits and stopped so frequently that I thought we would never reach the seal crack. I said to Cherry, however, that I would take no risks, and camp well over the other side on the old sound ice if we could get there. This we managed to do eventually. Here there was soft snow, whereas on the sea side of the crack it was hard: that is the reason we lost the dogs' tracks at once on crossing. Even over this crack I thought it best to march as far in as possible. We got well into the bay, as far as our exhausted ponies would drag, before I camped and threw up the walls, fed the beasts, and retired to feed ourselves. We had only the primus with the missing cap and it took over 1½ hours to heat up the water; however, we had a cup of pemmican. It was very dark, and I mistook a small bag of curry powder for the cocoa bag, and made cocoa with that, mixed with sugar; Crean drank his right down before discovering anything was wrong. It was 2 P.M. before we were ready to turn in. I went out and saw everything quiet: the mist still hung to the west, but you could see a good mile and all was still. The sky was very dark over the Strait though, the unmistakable sign of open water. I turned in. Two and a half hours later I awoke, hearing a noise. Both my companions were snoring, I thought it was that and was on the point of turning in again having seen that it was only 4.30, when I heard the noise again. I thought—'my pony is at the oats!' and went out.

"I cannot describe either the scene or my feelings. I must leave those to your imagination. We were in the middle of a floating pack of broken-up ice. The tops

of the hills were visible, but all below was thin mist and as far as the eye could
see there was nothing solid; it was all broken up, and heaving up and down with
the swell. Long black tongues of water were everywhere. The floe on which we
were had split right under our picketing line, and cut poor Guts' wall in half. Guts
himself had gone, and a dark streak of water alone showed the place where the ice
had opened under him. The two sledges securing the other end of the line were
on the next floe and had been pulled right to the edge. Our camp was on a floe no
more than 30 yards across. I shouted to Cherry and Crean, and rushed out in my
socks to save the two sledges; the two floes were touching farther on and I dragged
them to this place and got them on to our floe. At that moment our own floe split in
two, but we were all together on one piece. I then got my finnesko on, remarking
that we had been in a few tight places, but this was about the limit. I have been
told since that I was quixotic not to leave everything and make for safety. You will
understand, however, that I never for one moment considered the abandonment
of anything.

"We packed up camp and harnessed up our ponies in remarkably quick time.
When ready to move I had to decide which way to go. Obviously towards Cape
Armitage was impossible, and to the eastward also, as the wind was from that
direction, and we were already floating west towards the open sound. Our only
hope lay to the south, and thither I went. We found the ponies would jump the
intervals well. At least Punch would and the other two would follow him. My idea
was never to separate, but to get everything on to one floe at a time; and then wait
till it touched or nearly touched another in the right direction, and then jump the
ponies over and drag the four sledges across ourselves. In this way we made slow
but sure progress. While one was acting all was well, the waiting for a lead to close
was the worst trial. Sometimes it would take 10 minutes or more, but there was so
much motion in the ice that sooner or later bump you would go against another
piece, and then it was up and over. Sometimes they split, sometimes they bounced
back so quickly that only one horse could get over, and then we had to wait again.
We had to make frequent detours and were moving west all the time with the
pack, still we were getting south, too.

"Very little was said. Crean like most bluejackets behaved as if he had done
this sort of thing often before. Cherry, the practical, after an hour or two dug out
some chocolate and biscuit, during one of our enforced waits, and distributed it.
I felt at that time that food was the last thing on earth I wanted, and put it in my
pocket; in less than half an hour, though, I had eaten the lot. The ponies behaved
as well as my companions, and jumped the floes in great style. After getting them
on a new floe we simply left them, and there they stood chewing at each others'
head ropes or harness till we were over with the sledges and ready to take them on
again. Their implicit trust in us was touching to behold. A 12-feet sledge makes an
excellent bridge if an opening is too wide to jump. After some hours we saw fast
ice ahead, and thanked God for it. Meanwhile a further unpleasantness occurred
in the arrival of a host of the terrible 'killer' whales. These were reaping a harvest
of seal in the broken-up ice, and cruised among the floes with their immense black
fins sticking up, and blowing with a terrific roar. The Killer is scientifically known

as the Orca, and, though far smaller than the sperm and other large whales, is a much more dangerous animal. He is armed with a huge iron jaw and great blunt socket teeth. Killers act in concert, too, and, as you may remember, nearly got Ponting when we were unloading the ship, by pressing up the thin ice from beneath and splitting it in all directions.

"It took us over six hours to get close to the fast ice, which proved to be the Barrier, some immense chunks of which we actually saw break off and join the pack. Close in, the motion was less owing to the jambing up of the ice somewhere farther west. We had only just cleared the Strait in time though, as all the ice in the centre, released beyond Cape Armitage, headed off into the middle of the Strait, and thence to the Ross Sea. Our spirits rose as we neared the Barrier edge, and I made for a big sloping floe which I expected would be touching; at any rate I anticipated no difficulty. We rushed up the slope towards safety, and were little prepared for the scene that met our eyes at the top. All along the Barrier face a broad lane of water from thirty to forty feet wide extended. This was filled with smashed-up brash ice, which was heaving up and down to the swell like the contents of a cauldron. Killers were cruising there with fiendish activity, and the Barrier edge was a sheer cliff of ice on the other side fifteen to twenty feet high. It was a case of so near and yet so far. Suddenly our great sloping floe calved in two, so we beat a hasty retreat. I selected a sound-looking floe just clear of this turmoil, that was at least ten feet thick, and fairly rounded, with a flat surface. Here we collected everything and having done all that man could do, we fed the beasts and took counsel.

"Cherry and Crean both volunteered to do anything, in the spirit they had shown right through. It appeared of first necessity to communicate with Captain Scott. I guessed his anxiety on our behalf, and, as we could do nothing more, we wanted help of some sort. It occurred to me that a man working up to windward along the Barrier face might happen upon a floe touching [the Barrier]. It was obviously impossible to take ponies up there anywhere, but an active man might wait his opportunity. Going to windward, too, he could always retreat on to our floe, as the ice was being pushed together in our direction. The next consideration was, whom to send. To go myself was out of the question. The problem was whether to send one, or both, my companions. As my object was to save the animals and gear, it appeared to me that one man remaining would be helpless in the event of the floe splitting up, as he would be busy saving himself. I therefore decided to send one only. This would have to be Crean, as Cherry, who wears glasses, could not see so well. Both volunteered, but as I say, I thought out all the pros and cons and sent Crean, knowing that, at the worst, he could get back to us at any time. I sent a note to Captain Scott, and, stuffing Crean's pockets with food, we saw him depart.

"Practical Cherry suggested pitching the tent as a mark of our whereabouts, and having done this I mounted the theodolite to watch Crean through the telescope. The rise and fall of the floe made this difficult, especially as a number of Emperor penguins came up and looked just like men in the distance. Fortunately the sunlight cleared the frost smoke, and as it fell calm our westerly motion began to decrease. The swell started to go down. Outside us in the centre of the Strait all the ice had gone out, and open water remained. We were one of a line of loose floes floating near the Barrier edge. Crean was hours moving to and fro before I had the satisfaction of seeing him up on the Barrier. I said: 'Thank God one of us is out of the wood, anyhow.'

"It was not a pleasant day that Cherry and I spent all alone there, knowing as we did that it only wanted a zephyr from the south to send us irretrievably out to sea; still there is satisfaction in knowing that one has done one's utmost, and I felt that having been delivered so wonderfully so far, the same Hand would not forsake us at the last.

"We gave the ponies all they could eat that day. The Killers were too interested in us to be pleasant. They had a habit of bobbing up and down perpendicularly, so as to see over the edge of a floe, in looking for seals. The huge black and yellow heads with sickening pig eyes only a few yards from us at times, and always around us, are among the most disconcerting recollections I have of that day. The immense fins were bad enough, but when they started a perpendicular dodge they were positively beastly. As the day wore on skua gulls, looking upon us as certain carrion, settled down comfortably near us to await developments. The swell, however, was getting less and less and it resolved itself into a question of speed, as to whether the wind or Captain Scott would reach us first.

"Crean had got up into the Barrier at great risks to himself as I gathered afterwards from his very modest account. He had reached Captain Scott some time after his [Scott's] meeting with Wilson.[124] I heard that at the time Captain Scott was very angry with me for not abandoning everything and getting away safely myself. For my own part I must say that the abandoning of the ponies was the one thing that had never entered my head. It was a long way round, but at 7 P.M. he arrived at the edge of the Barrier opposite us with Oates and Crean. Everything was still, and Cherry and I could have got on safe ice at any time during the last half hour by using the sledge as a ladder. A big overturned fragment had jambed in the lane, between a high floe and the Barrier edge, and, there being no wind, it remained there. However, there was the consideration of the ponies, so we waited.

"Scott, instead of blowing me up, was too relieved at our safety to be anything but pleased. I said: 'What about the ponies and the sledges?' He said: 'I don't care a damn about the ponies and sledges. It's you I want, and I am going to see you safe here up on the Barrier before I do anything else.' Cherry and I had got everything ready, so, dragging up two sledges, we dumped the gear off them, and using them as ladders, one down from the berg on to the buffer piece of ice, and the other up to the top of the Barrier, we got up without difficulty. Captain Scott was so pleased, that I realized the feeling he must have had all day. He had been blaming himself for our deaths, and here we were very much alive. He said: 'My dear chaps, you can't think how glad I am to see you safe—Cherry likewise.'

"I was all for saving the beasts and sledges, however, so he let us go back and haul the sledges on to the nearest floe. We did this one by one and brought the

---

[124] Wilson camped with the two dog-teams on the land, and in the morning saw us floating on the ice-floes through his field-glasses. He made his way along the peninsula until he could descend on to the Barrier, where he joined Scott.

ponies along, while Titus dug down a slope from the Barrier edge in the hope of getting the ponies up it. Scott knew more about ice than any of us, and realizing the danger we didn't, still wanted to abandon things. I fought for my point tooth and nail, and got him to concede one article and then another, and still the ice did not move till we had thrown and hauled up every article on to the Barrier except the two ladders and the ponies.

"To my intense disappointment at this juncture the ice started to move again. Titus had been digging down a road in the Barrier edge, and I hoped to dig down a similar slope from the floe, the snow thus shovelled down would go over the blue ice chunk, cover up the slippery ice and level it up. It would have taken hours, but was the only chance of getting the animals up. We dug like fury until Captain Scott peremptorily ordered us up. I ran up on the floe and took the nosebags off the ponies before we got on to the Barrier, and hauled the sledges up. It was only just in time. There was the faintest south-easterly air, but, like a black snake, the lane of water stretched between the ponies and ourselves. It widened almost imperceptibly, 2 feet, 6 feet, 10 feet, 20 feet, and, sick as we were about the ponies, we were glad to be on the safe side of that.

"We dragged the sledges in a little way, and, leaving them, pitched the two tents half a mile farther in, for bits of the Barrier were continually calving. While supper (it was about 3 A.M.) was being cooked, Scott and I walked down again. The wind had gone to the east, and all the ice was under weigh. A lane 70 feet wide extended along the Barrier edge, and Killers were chasing up and down it like racehorses. Our three unfortunate beasts were some way out, sailing parallel to the Barrier. We returned, and if ever one could feel miserable I did then. My feelings were nothing to what poor Captain Scott had had to endure that day. I at once broached the hopeful side of the subject, remarking that, with the two Campbell had left, we had ten ponies at Winter quarters. He said, however, that he had no confidence whatever in the motors after the way their rollers had become messed up unloading the ship. He had had his confidence in the dogs much shaken on the return journey, and now he had lost the most solid asset—the best of his pony transport. He said: 'Of course we shall have a run for our money next season, but as far as the Pole is concerned I have but very little hope.' We had a mournful meal, but after the others turned in I went down again, and by striking across diagonally came abreast of the ponies' floe, over a mile away. They were moving west fast, but they saw me, and remained huddled together not the least disturbed, or doubting that we would bring them their breakfast nosebags as usual in the morning. Poor trustful creatures! If I could have done it then, I would gladly have killed them rather than picture them starving on that floe out on the Ross Sea, or eaten by the exultant Killers that cruised around.

"After breakfast Captain Scott sent me to bring up the sledges. It was dead calm again. Hope always springs, so I took his pair of glasses and looked west from the Barrier edge. Nearly all the ice had gone, but a medley of floes had been hurled up against a long point of Barrier much farther west. To my delight I saw three green specks on one of these—the pony rugs—and all four of us legged it back to the tent to tell Captain Scott. We were soon off over the Barrier. It was a long way, but we had a tent and some food. Crean had a bad day of snow-blindness, and could see absolutely nothing. So, on arrival at the place, we pitched the tent and left him there. The ponies were in a much worse place than the day before, but the ice was still there, and some floes actually touched the Barrier.

"After our recent experience Captain Scott would only let us go on condition that as soon as he gave the order we were to drop everything and run for the Barrier. I was in a feverish hurry, and with Titus and Cherry selected a possible route over about six floes, and some low brash ice. The hardest jump was the first one, but it was nothing to what they had done the day before, so we put Punch at it. Why he hung fire I cannot think,[125] but he did, at the very edge, and the next moment was in the water. I will draw a veil over our struggle to get the plucky little pony out. We could not manage it, and Titus had at last to put an end to his struggles with a pick.

"There was now my pony and Nobby. We abandoned that route, while Captain Scott looked out another and longer one by going right out on the sea-floes. This we decided on, if we could get the animals off their present floe, which necessitated a good jump on any side. Captain Scott said he would have no repetition of Punch's misfortune if he could help it. He would rather kill them on the floe. Anyhow, we rushed old Nobby at the jump, but he refused. It seemed no good, but I rushed him at it again and again. Scott was for killing them [it should be remembered that this ice, with the men on it, might drift away from the Barrier at any moment, and then there might be no further chance of saving the men] but I was not, and, pretending not to hear him, I rushed the old beast again. He cleared it beautifully, and Titus, seizing the opportunity, ran my pony at it with similar success. We then returned to the Barrier and worked along westward till a suitable place for getting up was found. There Scott and Cherry started digging a road, while Titus and I went out via the sea-ice to get the ponies. We had an empty sledge as a bridge or ladder, in case of emergency, and had to negotiate about forty floes to reach the animals. It was pretty easy going, though, and we brought them along with great success as far as the two nearest floes. At this place the ice was jambed.

"Nobby cleared the last jump splendidly, when suddenly in the open water pond on one side a school of over a dozen of the terrible whales arose. This must have flurried my horse just as he was jumping, as instead of going straight he jumped [sideways] and just missed the floe with his hind legs. It was another horrible situation, but Scott rushed Nobby up on the Barrier, while Titus, Cherry and I struggled with poor old Uncle Bill. Why the whales did not come under the ice and attack him I cannot say—perhaps they were full of seal, perhaps they were so engaged in looking at us on the top of the floe that they forgot to look below; anyhow, we got him safely as far as [the bottom of the Barrier cliff], pulling him through the thin ice towards a low patch of brash.

"Captain Scott was afraid of something happening to us with those devilish whales so close, and was for abandoning the horse right away. I had no eyes or ears for anything but the horse just then, and getting on to the thin brash ice got the

[125] I think he was stiff after standing so many hours.—A. C.-G.

Alpine rope fast to each of the pony's forefeet. Crean was too blind to do anything but hold the rescued horse on the Barrier, but the other four of us pulled might and main till we got the old horse out and lying on his side. The brash ice was so thin that, had a 'Killer' come up then he would have scattered it, and the lot of us into the water like chaff. I was sick with disappointment when I found that my horse could not rise. Titus said: 'He's done; we shall never get him up alive.' The cold water and shock on top of all his recent troubles, had been too much for the undefeated old sportsman. In vain I tried to get him to his feet; three times he tried and then fell over backwards into the water again. At that moment a new danger arose. The whole piece of Barrier itself started to subside.

"It had evidently been broken before, and the tide was doing the rest. We were ordered up and it certainly was all too necessary; still Titus and I hung over the old Uncle Bill's head. I said: 'I can't leave him to be eaten alive by those whales.' There was a pick lying up on the floe. Titus said: 'I shall be sick if I have to kill another horse like I did the last.' I had no intention that anybody should kill my own horse but myself, and getting the pick I struck where Titus told me. I made sure of my job before we ran up and jumped the opening in the Barrier, carrying a blood-stained pick-axe instead of leading the pony I had almost considered safe.

"We returned to our old camp that night (March 2) with Nobby, the only one saved of the five that left One Ton Depôt. I was fearfully cut up about my pony and Punch, but it was better than last night; we knew they would not have to starve and that all their troubles were now at an end. Before supper I went for a walk along the Barrier with Scott, and the next day we started back. We left one tent, two sledges and a lot of gear as Nobby could only pull two light sledges, and we could not pull an excessive weight on that bad surface. As it was we had over 800 lbs. on the sledge when we left. It was a glaring day with the surface soft and sandy, a combination of unpleasant circumstances. It took five hours to drag as far as the place we had originally gone down on to the sea-ice from the Barrier.

"Evans and his party should now have arrived from Corner Camp, and as Captain Scott wanted to see if they had left a note at Safety Camp, I walked up there while the tea was being brewed. It was about 1¼ miles away, and I found traces of the party in the snow, but no note. It fed me up to see the walls so recently occupied by our ponies, and I was glad to leave. The afternoon march was interminable; it seemed as if we would never reach the coast. At last we came to the Pram Point Pressure Ridges where the Barrier joins the peninsula to eastward of Cape Armitage. They are waves of ice up to 20 feet in height running along parallel to each other with a valley in between each, and are only crevassed badly at the outer end as far as we have seen, though there are smaller crevasses right along. We camped in one of these valleys about 9.30 P.M.; I was thoroughly tired, so I think was everybody else. We were about a mile from the ice edge; and the problem was where to get Nobby up the precipitous slopes. This was solved by the arrival of Evans, Atkinson, Forde and Keohane about midnight. They had seen us coming in from the heights, and had come down for news. Teddy Evans had arrived the day before, and, being warned off the Barrier edge by a note left by Captain Scott, had made for the land with his party, and one horse Jimmy Pigg. He had found a good way up a mile or so farther east, almost under Castle Rock. He had walked to Hut Point with Atkinson the next day and heard of the loss of Cherry, myself and the animals from Bill Wilson and Meares who had been left there to look after their teams. I hadn't seen Atkinson for quite a while when we met this time.

"The next day we relayed the sledges up the slope which was about 700 feet high rising from a small bay. It was so steep that the pony could only be led up and we had to put on crampons to grip the ice. These are merely a sole of leather with light metal plates for foot and heel containing spikes. [These were altered afterwards.] They have leather beckets and a lanyard rove off for making them fast over the finnesko. It took us all the morning to get everything up to the top and then it started to blow. The camp was wonderfully sheltered. Jimmy Pigg and Nobby were reunited after many weeks, and to show their friendliness the former bit the latter in the back of the neck as a first introduction. Atkinson had gone to Hut Point to reassure Uncle Bill as to our safety and arrived again with Gran just as we got the last load up. There was no sugar at the hut except what the dogs had brought in, so Gran, who was quite fresh, volunteered to get a couple of bags from the depôt at Safety Camp, which could plainly be seen out on the Barrier. We all went to the edge of the slope to see him go down it on ski. He did it splendidly and must have been going with the speed of an express train down the incline, and he was on the Barrier in an incredibly short time compared to the hours we had dragged up the same slope with the loads. Teddy, Titus and Keohane were left at the camp to be joined by Gran later. Scott started off for Hut Point with Crean and Cherry on his sledge, while I followed with Forde and Atkinson. The others helped us up several hundred feet of slope and left us under Castle Rock.

"It was here that they mistook their way in the blizzard and lost a man from the Discovery. Though it was fine below it was blowing like anything on the heights. I was too busily occupied to see much of the hills and snow-slopes which I got to know so well later. It was about three miles direct to the hut, but very up and down hill. At the last, however, you see the Bay in panorama with Cape Armitage on one side, and Hut Point on the other, where the Discovery lay two whole years. It is a magnificent view from the heights and for wild desolate grandeur would take some beating; the Western Mountains and the great dome of Mount Discovery across the black strait of water, covered with dark frost smoke, and here and there an iceberg driving fast towards the sea. About half a mile below us was the little hut and, on the left, the 800-feet pyramid of Observation Hill. It is a perfect chaos of hills and extinct craters just here.

"It was blowing like fun. We left one sledge on the top of ski-slope and just took what was necessary on the other, such as our bags, etc. It was my first experience of steep downhill sledging. Instead of anybody pulling forward we all had to hang back and guide the sledge down the slippery incline without letting it take charge or getting upset. It is great fun. On reaching the head of the Bay, however, we had quite a dangerous little bit to cross. Here it was swept of snow and there was nothing but glassy ice and the incline ended in a low ice-cliff with the water below it. Attached as we were to the sledge we should have been at a disadvantage had it come to swimming, which a slip might easily have brought about. We scratched carefully across this and then headed down on the snow, arriving at the hut all well. The old hut had changed tremendously since I last saw it, having been dug out and cleared of snow and ice. Two unrecognizable sweeps greeted us heartily, they were Bill and Meares; the dogs howled a chorus for our benefit; it was quite like coming home. Inside the hut, the cause of the blackness was apparent, they had a blubber fire going, an open one, with no chimney or uptake for the smoke. After such a long open-air life it fairly choked me, and for once I could not eat a square meal. We all slept in a row against the west wall of the hut with our feet inboard.

"The next morning Captain Scott, Bill, Cherry and I set out to walk to Castle Rock and meet the other party. It was fairly fizzing from the sea, but clear. Once up on the Heights, however, we seemed to get less wind. A couple of hours later we were at the great rock, Castle Rock, which is one of the best landmarks about here. The party in the Saddle Camp had relayed two of the sledges up the slope; these we hauled on to the top while the two ponies were harnessed and brought up. There were three sledges left to take on altogether, so the ponies took one each and we the other. Meanwhile Captain Scott walked over the shoulder under Castle Rock to see down the Strait and came back with the intelligence that he could hardly believe his eyes, but half the Glacier Tongue had broken off and disappeared. This great Tongue of ice had stood there on arrival of the Discovery, ten years before, and had remained ever since; it had a depôt of Shackleton's on it, and Campbell had depôted his fodder on it for us. On the eventful night of the break-up of the ice at least three miles of the Tongue which had been considered practically terra firma had gone, after having been there probably for centuries. We headed for the hut: Bill had looked out a route for the ponies, to avoid slippery places. It started to bliz, but was not too thick for us to see our bearings. At the top of Ski Slope the ponies were taken out of the sledges and led down a circuitous route over the rocks. The rest of us put everything we wanted on one sledge and leaving the others up there went down the slope as before. The two ponies arrived before us and were stabled in the verandah.

"That night for the first time since the establishment of Safety Camp the depôt party were all together again, minus six ponies. In concluding my report to Captain Scott on the 'floe' incident, which he asked me to set down long afterwards, I said, 'In reconsidering the foregoing I have come to the conclusion that I underestimated the danger signs on the sea-ice on February 28, and on the following day might have attached more importance to the safety of my companions. As it was, however, all circumstances seemed to conspire together to make the situation unavoidable.' I did not forget to mention the splendid behaviour of Cherry and Crean, and, for my own part, I have no regrets. I took the blame for my lack of experience, but knew that having done everything I could do, it did not concern me if anybody liked to criticize my action. My own opinion is that it just had to be, the circumstances leading to it were too devious for mere coincidence. Six hours earlier we could have walked to the hut on sound sea-ice. A few hours later we should have seen open water on arrival at the Barrier edge. The blizzard that knocked out the beasts, the death of Weary, the misunderstanding of the dogs, everything, fitted in to place us on the sea-ice during the only two hours of the whole year that we could possibly have been in such a position. Let those who believe in coincidence carry on believing. Nobody will ever convince me that there was not something more. Perhaps in the light of next year we shall see what was meant by such an apparent blow to our hopes. Certainly we shall start for the Pole with less of that foolish spirit of blatant boast and ridiculous blind self-assurance, that characterized some of us on leaving Cardiff.

"Poor Captain Scott had now a new anxiety thrust upon him. The Winter Station with ponies, stores and motors was all situated on a low beach not twenty yards from the water's edge, and now that the ice had gone out (and the hut was not six feet above sea-level at the floor) how had they fared in the storm? This was a problem we could not solve without going to see. Cape Evans, though dimly in sight, was as far off as New Zealand till the sea froze over. The idea of attempting the shoulder of Erebus did occur to Captain Scott, but it was so heavily crevassed as to make a journey from our side almost impossible. On the other side Professor David's party got up to the Summit without finding a crevasse. Captain Scott took his reverses like a brick. I often went out for a walk with him and sometimes he discussed his plans for next season. He took his losses very philosophically and never blamed any of us."

This is the end of that part of Bowers' letter which deals with the incident. Crean told me afterwards how he got on to the Barrier. He first made for the Gap, following the best path of the ice, but then had to retrace his steps and make for White Island jumping from floe to floe. But then "I was pretty lively," said he: and "there were lots of penguins and seals and killers knocking round that day."

Crean had one of the ski sticks and that "was a great help to me for getting over the floes. It was a sloping piece like what you were on and it was very near touching the Barrier, in one corner of it only. Well, I dug a hole with the ski stick in the side of the Barrier for a step for one foot, and when I finished the hole I straddled my legs and got one on the floe and one in the side of the Barrier. Then I got the stick and dug it in on top and I gave myself a bit of a spring and got my outside leg up top. It was a terrible place but I thought it was the only chance.

"I made straight for Safety Camp and they must have spotted me: for I think it was Gran that met me on skis. Then Scott and Wilson and Oates met me a long way out: I explained how it happened. He was worried-looking a bit, but he never said anything out of the way. He told Oates to go inside and light the primus and give me a meal."

A more detailed account of the behaviour of the hundreds of whales which infested the lanes of open water between the broken floes and calved bergs is of interest. Most of them at any rate were Killer whales (Orca gladiator), and they were cruising about in great numbers, snorting and blowing, while occasionally they would in some extraordinary way raise themselves and look about over the ice, resting the fore part of their enormous yellow and black bodies on the edge of the floes. They were undisguisedly interested in us and the ponies, and we felt that if we once got into the water our ends would be swift and bloody.

But I have a very distinct recollection that the whales were not all Killers, and that some, at any rate, were Bottle-nosed whales. This was impressed upon me by one of the most dramatic moments of that night and day.

We made our way very slowly, sometimes waiting twenty minutes for the floe on which we were to touch the next one in the direction we were trying to go, but before us in the distance was a region of sea-ice which appeared to slope gradually up on to the fast Barrier beyond. As we got nearer we saw a dark line appear at intervals between the two. This we considered was a crevasse at the edge of the Barrier which was opening and shutting with the very big swell which was running, and on which all the floes were bobbing up and down. We told one another that we could rush the ponies over this as it closed.

We approached the Barrier and began to rise up on the sloping floes which had edged the Barrier and so on to small bergs which had calved from the Barrier itself. Leaving Crean with the ponies, Bowers and I went forward to prospect, and rose on to a berg from which we hoped to reach the Barrier.

I can never forget the scene that met us. Between us and the Barrier was a lane of some fifty yards wide, a seething cauldron. Bergs were calving off as we watched: and capsizing: and hitting other bergs, splitting into two and falling apart. The Killers filled the whole place. Looking downwards into a hole between our berg and the next, a hole not bigger than a small room, we saw at least six whales. They were so crowded that they could only lie so as to get their snouts out of the water, and my memory is that their snouts were bottle-nosed. At this moment our berg split into two parts and we hastily retreated to the lower and safer floes.

Now in the Zoological Report of the Discovery Expedition Wilson states that the true identity of the Bottle-nosed whale (Hyperoodon rostrata) in Antarctic Seas has not been conclusively established. But that inasmuch as it certainly frequents seas so far as 48° S. latitude it is probable that certain whales which he and other members of that expedition saw frequenting the edge of the ice were, as they appeared to be, Bottle-nosed whales. For my part, without great knowledge of whales, I am convinced that these whales which lay but twenty feet below us were whales of this species.

After our rescue by Scott we pitched our tents, as has been described, at least half a mile from the fast edge of the Barrier. All night long, or as it really was, early morning, the Killers were snorting and blowing under the Barrier, and sometimes, it seemed, under our tents. Time and again some member of the party went out of the tent to see if the Barrier had not broken farther back, but there was no visible change, and it must have been that the apparently solid ice on which we were, was split up by crevasses by the big swell which had been running, and that round us, hidden by snow bridges, were leads of water in which whales were cruising in search of seal.

The next day most of the ice had gone out to sea, and I do not think the whales were so numerous. The most noticeable thing about them that day was the organization shown by the band of whales which appeared after Bowers' pony, Uncle

Bill, had fallen between two floes, and we were trying to get him towards the Barrier. "Good God, look at the whales," said some one, and there, in a pool of water behind the floe on which we were working, lay twelve great whales in perfect line, facing the floe. And out in front of them, like the captain of a company of soldiers, was another. As we turned they dived as one whale, led by the big fellow in front, and we certainly expected that they would attack the floe on which we stood. Whether they never did so, or whether they tried and failed, for the floes here were fifteen or sixteen feet thick, I do not know; we never saw them again.

One other incident of those days is worth recalling. "Cherry, Crean, we're floating out to sea," was the startling awakening from Bowers, standing in his socks outside the tent at 4.30 A.M. that Wednesday morning. And indeed at first sight on getting outside the tent it looked a quite hopeless situation. I thought it was madness to try and save the ponies and gear when, it seemed, the only chance at all of saving the men was an immediate rush for the Barrier, and I said so. "Well, I'm going to try," was Bowers' answer, and, quixotic or no, he largely succeeded. I never knew a man who treated difficulties with such scorn.

There must be some of my companions who look back upon Hut Point with a peculiar fondness, such as men get for places where they have experienced great joys and great trials. And Hut Point has an atmosphere of its own. I do not know what it is. Partly aesthetic, for the sea and great mountains, and the glorious colour effects which prevail in spring and autumn, would fascinate the least imaginative; partly mysterious, with the Great Barrier knocking at your door, and the smoke of Erebus by day and the curtain of Aurora by night; partly the associations of the place—the old hut, the old landmarks, so familiar to those who know the history of the Discovery Expedition, the stakes in the snow, the holes for which ice was dug to water the ship, Vince's Cross on the Point. Now there is another Cross, on Observation Hill.

And yet when we first arrived the hut was comfortless enough. Wilson and Meares and Gran had been there some days; they had found some old bricks and a grid, and there was an open blubber fire in the middle of the floor. There was no outlet for the smoke and smuts and it was impossible to see your neighbour, to speak without coughing, or to open your eyes long before they began to smart. Atkinson and Crean had cleared the floor of ice in our absence, but the space between the lower and upper roofs was solid with blue ice, and the lower roof sagged down in places in a dangerous way. The wind howled continuously and to say that the hut was cold is a very mild expression of the reality.

This hut was built by the Discovery Expedition, who themselves lived in the ship which lay off the shore frozen into the sea-ice, as a workroom and as a refuge in case of shipwreck. It was useful to them in some ways, but was too large to heat with the amount of coal available, and was rather a white elephant. Scott wrote of it that "on the whole our large hut has been and will be of use to us, but its uses are never likely to be of such importance as to render it indispensable, nor cause it to be said that circumstances have justified the outlay made on it, or the expenditure of space and trouble in bringing it to its final home. It is here now, however, and here it will stand for many a long year with such supplies as will afford the necessaries of life to any less fortunate party who may follow in our footsteps and be forced to search for food and shelter."[126]

Well! It was to be more useful to Scott in 1910 to 1913 than he imagined in 1902. We found the place with its verandah complete, the remains of the two magnetic huts and a rubbish heap. It was wonderful what that rubbish heap yielded up. Bricks to build a blubber stove, a sheet of iron to put over the top of it, a length of stove piping to form a chimney. Somehow somebody made cement, and built the bricks together, and one of the magnetic huts gave up its asbestos sheeting to insulate the chimney from the woodwork of the roofs. An old door made a cook's table, old cases turned upside down made seats. The provisions left by the Discovery were biscuits contained in some forty large packing cases. These we piled up across the middle of our house as a bulkhead and the old Discovery winter awning was dug out of the snow outside and fixed against the wall thus made to keep the warmth in. At night we cleared the floor space and spread our bags.

HUT POINT FROM OBSERVATION HILL

The two precious survivors of the eight ponies with which we started on our journey were housed in the verandah, which was made wind-proof and snow-proof. The more truculent dogs lay tethered outside, the more docile were allowed their freedom, but even so the dog fights were not infrequent. We had one poor little dog, Makaka by name. When unloading the ship this dog had been overrun by the sledge which he was helping to pull; he suffered again when the team of dogs fell down the crevasse, and was now partially paralysed. He was a wretched object, for the hair refused to grow on his hind quarters, but he was a real sportsman and had no idea of giving in. Meares and I went out one night when it was blowing hard, attracted by the cries of a dog. It was Makaka who had ventured to climb a steep slope and was now afraid to return. When the dogs finally returned to Cape Evans, Makaka was allowed to run by the side of the team; but when Cape

[126] Scott, *The Voyage of the Discovery*, vol. i. p. 350.

Evans was reached he was gone. Search failed to find him and, after some weeks hope of him was abandoned. But a month afterwards Gran and Debenham went over to Hut Point, and here at the entrance of the hut they found Makaka, pitifully weak but able to bark to them. He must have lived on seal, but how he did so in that condition is a mystery.

The reader may ask how it was that being so near our Winter Quarters at Cape Evans we were unable to reach them immediately. Cape Evans is fifteen miles across the sea from Hut Point, and though both huts are on the same island—Hut Point being at the end of a peninsula and Cape Evans on the remains of a flow of lava which juts out into the sea—the land which joins the two has never yet been crossed by a sledge party owing to the great ice falls which cover the slopes of Erebus. A glance at the map will show that although Hut Point is surrounded with sea, or sea-ice, on every side except that of Arrival Heights, the Barrier abuts upon the Hut Point Peninsula to the south beyond Pram Point. Thus there is always communication with the Barrier by a devious route by which indeed we had just arrived, but farther progress north is cut off until the cold temperature of the autumn and winter causes the open sea to freeze. We arrived at Hut Point on March 5 and Scott expected to be able to cross on the newly-frozen ice by about March 21. However, it was nearly a month after that when the first party could pass to Cape Evans, and then only the Bays were frozen and the Sound was still open water owing to the winds which swept the ice out to sea almost as soon as it was formed.

On the top of all the anxieties which had oppressed him lately Scott had a great fear that a swell so phenomenal as to break up Glacier Tongue, a landmark which had probably been there for centuries, might have swept away our hut at Cape Evans. He was so alarmed about it that he told Wilson and myself to prepare to form a sledging party with him to penetrate the Erebus icefalls and reach Cape Evans. "Went yesterday to Castle Rock with Wilson to see what chance there might be of getting to Cape Evans. The day was bright and it was quite warm walking in the sun. There is no doubt the route to Cape Evans lies over the worst corner of Erebus. From this distance (some 7 or 8 miles at least) the whole mountain side looks a mass of crevasses, but a route might be found at a level of 3000 or 4000 feet."[127] After some days the project was abandoned as being hopeless.

On March 8 Bowers led a party to bring in the gear and provisions which had been left at Disaster Camp, the material, that is, which had been rescued from the sea-ice. They were away three days and found the pulling very hard. "At the corner of the bay the Barrier was buckled into round ridges which took a couple of hours to cross. We marched for some time alongside an enormous crevasse, which lay like a street near us. I examined it at one point which must have been 15 feet wide, and though it was impossible to see the bottom for snow cornices it was undoubtedly open as I could hear a seal blowing below."[128]

Bowers' letter describes them dragging their heavy load up the slope to Castle Rock: "It took us all the morning to reach Saddle Camp with the loads in two

[127] *Scott's Last Expedition*, vol. i. p. 201.
[128] Bowers.

journeys. I found a steady plod up a steep hill without spells is better and less exhausting than a rush and a number of rests. This theory I put into practice with great success. I don't know whether everybody saw eye to eye with me over the idea of getting to the top without a spell. After the second sledge was up Atkinson said: 'I don't mind you as a rule, but there are times when I positively hate you.'"

Defoe could have written another Robinson Crusoe with Hut Point instead of San Juan Fernandez. Our sledging supplies were mostly exhausted and we depended upon the seals we could kill for food, fuel and light. We were smutty as sweeps from the blubber we burned; and a more blackguard-looking crew would have been hard to find. We spent our fine days killing, cutting up and carrying in seal when we could find them, or climbing the various interesting hills and craters which abound here, and our evenings in long discussions which seldom settled anything. Some looked after dogs, and others after ponies; some made geological collections; others sketched the wonderful sunsets; but before and above all we ate and slept. We must have spent a good twelve hours asleep in our bags every day after our six weeks' sledging. And we rested. Perhaps this is not everybody's notion of a very good time, but it was good enough for us.

The Weddell seal which frequents the seas which fringe the Antarctic continent was a standby for most of our wants; for he can at a pinch provide not only meat to eat, fuel for your fire and oil for your lamp, but also leather for your finnesko and an antidote to scurvy. As he lies out on the sea-ice, a great ungainly shape, nothing short of an actual prod will persuade him to take much notice of an Antarctic explorer. Even then he is as likely as not to yawn in your face and go to sleep again. His instincts are all to avoid the water when alarmed, for he knows his enemies the killer whales live there: but if you drive him into the water he is transformed in the twinkling of an eye into a thing of beauty and grace, which can travel and turn with extreme celerity and which can successfully chase the fish on which he feeds.

We were lucky now in that a small bay of sea-ice, about an acre in extent, still remained within two miles of us at a corner where Barrier, sea, and land meet, called Pram Point by Scott in the Discovery days.

Now Pram Point during the summer months is one of the most populous seal nurseries in McMurdo Sound. In this neighbourhood the Barrier, moving slowly towards the Peninsula, buckles the sea-ice into pressure ridges. As the trough of each ridge is forced downwards, so in summer pools of sea water are formed in which the seal make their holes and among these ridges they lie and bask in the sun: the males fight their battles, the females bring forth their young: the children play and chase their tails just like kittens. Now that the sea-ice had broken up, many seal were to be found in this sheltered corner under the green and blue ice-cliffs of Crater Hill.

If you go seal killing you want a big stick, a bayonet, a flensing knife and a steel. Any big stick will do, so long as it will hit the seal a heavy blow on the nose: this stuns him and afterwards mercifully he feels no more. The bayonet knife (which should be fitted into a handle with a cross-piece to prevent the slipping of the hand down on to the blade) should be at least 14 inches long without the handle; this is used to reach the seal's heart. Our flensing knives were one foot long including the handle, the blades were seven inches long by 1¼ inches broad: some were pointed and others round and I do not know which was best. The handles should be of wood as being warmer to hold.

Killing and cutting up seals is a gruesome but very necessary business, and the provision of suitable implements is humane as well as economic in time and labour. The skin is first cut off with the blubber attached: the meat is then cut from the skeleton, the entrails cleaned out, the liver carefully excised. The whole is then left to freeze in pieces on the snow, which are afterwards collected as rock-like lumps. The carcass can be cut up with an axe when needed and fed to the dogs. Nothing except entrails was wasted.

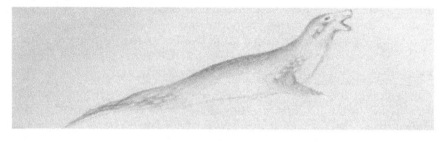

SEALS

SEALS

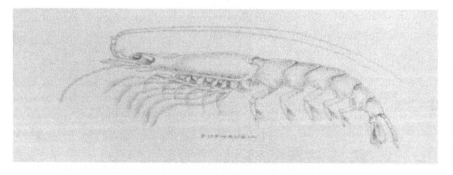

FROM THE SEA—E. A. WILSON, DEL.

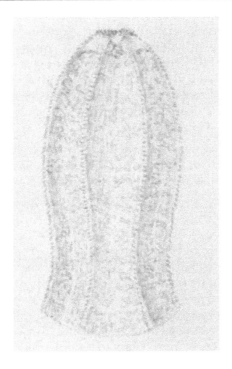

FROM THE SEA — E. A. WILSON, DEL.

Lighting was literally a burning question. I do not know that any lamp was better than a tin matchbox fed with blubber, with strands of lamp wick sticking up in it, but all kinds of patterns big and small were made by proud inventors; they generally gave some light, though not a brilliant one. There were more ambitious attempts than blubber. The worst of these perhaps was produced by Oates. Somebody found some carbide and Oates immediately schemed to light the hut with acetylene. I think he was the only person who did not view the preparation with ill-concealed nervousness. However, Wilson took the situation into his tactful hands. For several days Oates and Wilson were deep in the acetylene plant scheme and then, apparently without reason, it was found that it could not be done. It was a successful piece of strategy which no woman could have bettered.

Bowers, Wilson, Atkinson and I were on Crater Hill one morning when we espied a sledge party approaching from the direction of Castle Rock. As we expected, this was the Geological party, consisting of Griffith Taylor, Wright, Debenham and Seaman Evans, home from the Western Mountains. They entirely failed to recognize in our black faces the men whom they had last seen from the ship at Glacier Tongue. I hope their story will be told by Debenham. For days their doings were the topic of conversation. Both numerically and intellectually they were an addition to our party, which now numbered sixteen. Taylor especially is seldom at a loss for conversation and his remarks are generally original, if sometimes crude. Most of us were glad to listen when the discussions in which he was a leading figure raged round the blubber stove. Scott and Wilson were always in the thick of it, and the others chimed in as their interest, knowledge and experience led. Rash statements on questions of fact were always dangerous, for our small community contained so many specialists that errors were soon exposed. At the same time there were few parts of the world that one or other of us had not visited at least once. Later, when we came to our own limited quarters, books of reference were constantly in demand to settle disputes. Such books as the Times Atlas, a good encyclopaedia and even a Latin Dictionary are invaluable to such expeditions for this purpose. To them I would add Who's Who.

From odd corners we unearthed some Contemporary Reviews, the Girls' Own Paper and the Family Herald, all of ten years ago! We also found encased in ice an incomplete copy of Stanley Weyman's My Lady Rotha; it was carefully thawed out and read by everybody, and the excitement was increased by the fact that the end of the book was missing.

"Who's going to cook?" was one of the last queries each night, and two men would volunteer. It is not great fun lighting an ordinary coal fire on a cold winter's morning, but lighting the blubber fire at Hut Point when the metal frosted your fingers and the frozen blubber had to be induced to drip was a far more arduous task. The water was converted from its icy state and, by that time, the stove was getting hot, in inverse proportion to your temper. Seal liver fry and cocoa with unlimited Discovery Cabin biscuits were the standard dish for breakfast, and when it was ready a sustained cry of 'hoosh' brought the sleepers from their bags, wiping reindeer hairs from their eyes. I think I was responsible for the greatest breakfast failure when I fried some biscuits and sardines (we only had one tin). Leaving the biscuits in the frying pan, the lid of a cooker, after taking it from the fire, they went on cooking and became as charcoal. This meal was known as 'the burnt-offering.' On April 1 Bowers prepared to make a fool of two of us by putting chaff in our pannikins and covering the top only with seal meat. The plan turned back upon the maker, for he had not enough left to make up the deficiency, and, as I found out many weeks afterwards, surreptitiously gave up his own hoosh to the April fools and went without himself. Of such are the small incidents which afforded real amusement and even live in the memory as outstanding features of our existence.

Breakfast done, there was a general clean-up. One seized the apology for a broom which existed: day foot-gear, finnesko, hair socks, ordinary socks and puttees, took the place of fleecy sleeping-socks and fur-lined sleeping-boots: lunch cooks began to make their preparations: ice was fetched for water: a frozen chunk of red seal meat or liver was levered and chopped with an ice axe from the general store of seal meat: fids of sealskin, with the blubber attached, a good three inches of it perhaps, were brought in and placed by the stove, much as we bring in a scuttle of coal. Gradually the community scattered as duty or inclination led, leaving some members to dig away the snow-drifts which had accumulated round the door and windows during the night.

By lunch time every one had some new item of interest. Wright had found a new form of ice crystal: Scott had tested the ice off the Point and found it five inches thick: Wilson had found new seal holes off Cape Armitage, and we had hopes of finding our food and fuel nearer home: Atkinson had killed an Emperor penguin which weighed over ninety pounds, a record: and the assistant zoologist felt he would have to skin it, and did not want to do so: Meares had found an excellent place to roll stones down Arrival Heights into the sea: Debenham had a new theory to account for the Great Boulder, as a mammoth block different in structure from the surrounding geological features was called: Bowers had a scheme for returning from the Pole by the Plateau instead of the Barrier: Oates might be heard saying that he thought he could do with another chupattie. A favourite pastime was the making of knots. Could you make a clove hitch with one hand?

The afternoon was like the morning, save that the sun was now sinking behind the Western Mountains. These autumn effects were among the most beautiful sights of the world, and it was now that Wilson made the sketches for many of the water-colours which he afterwards painted at Winter Quarters. The majority were taken from the summit of Observation Hill, crouching under the lee of the rocks into which, nearly two years after, we built the Cross which now stands to commemorate his death and that of his companions. He sketched quickly with bare fingers and mittened hands, jotting down the outlines of hills and clouds, and pencilling in the colours by name. After a minute, more or less, the fingers become too cold for such work, and they must be put back into the wool and fur mitts until they are again warm enough to continue. Pencil and sketch book, a Winsor and Newton, were carried in a little blubber-stained wallet on his belt. Scott carried his sledge diaries in similar books in a similar wallet made of green Willesden canvas and fastened with a lanyard.

There was a good fug in the hut by dinner time: this was a mixed blessing. It was good for our gear: sleeping-bags, finnesko, mitts, socks were all hung up and dried, most necessary after sledging, and most important for the preservation of the skins; but it also started the most infernal drip-drip from the roof. I have spoken of the double roof of the old Discovery hut. This was still full of solid ice; indeed some time afterwards a large portion of it fell, but luckily the inhabitants were outside. The immediate problem was to prevent the leaks falling on ourselves, our food or our clothing and bags. And so every tin was brought into use and hung from leaky spots, while water chutes came into their own. As the stove cooled so did the drip cease, and in no prehistoric cavern did more stalactites and stalagmites grow apace.

On March 16 the last sledge party to the Barrier that season started for Corner Camp with provisions to increase the existing depôt there. The party was in charge of Lieutenant Evans, and consisted of Bowers, Oates, Atkinson, Wright, and myself, with two seamen, Crean and Forde. The journey out and back took eight days and was uneventful as sledge journeys go. Thick weather prevailed for several days, and after running down our distance to Corner Camp we waited for it to clear. We found ourselves six miles from the depôt and among crevasses, which goes to show how easy it is to steer off the course under such conditions, and how creditable the navigation is when a course is kept correctly, sometimes more by instinct than by skill.

But we got our first experience of cold weather sledging which was useful. The minus thirties and forties are not very cold as we were to understand cold afterwards, but quite cold enough to start with; cold enough to teach you how to look after your footgear, handle metal and not to waste time. However, the sun was still well up during the day, and this makes all the difference, since any sun does more drying of clothes and gear than none at all. At the same time we began to realize the difficulties which attend upon spring journeys, though we could only imagine what might be the trials on a journey in mid-winter, such as we intended to essay

It is easy to be wise after the event, but, in looking back upon the expedition as a whole, and the tragedy which was to come, mainly from the unforeseen cold of the autumn on the Barrier (such as minus forties in February) it seems that we might have grasped that these temperatures were lower than might have been expected in the middle of March quite near the open sea. Even if this had occurred to any one, and I do not think that it did, I doubt whether the next step of reasoning would have followed, namely, the possibility that the interior of the Barrier would, as actually happened, prove to be much colder than was expected at this date. On the contrary I several times heard Scott mention the possibility of the Polar Party not returning until April. At the same time it must be realized that pony transport to the foot of the Beardmore Glacier made a late start inevitable, for the blizzards our ponies had already suffered proved that spring weather on the Barrier would be intolerable to them. As a matter of fact, Scott says in his Message to the Public, "no one in the world would have expected the temperature and surfaces which we encountered at this time of the year."

We returned to find everything at Hut Point, including the hut, covered with frozen spray. This was the result of a blizzard of which we only felt the tail end on the Barrier. Scott wrote: "The sea was breaking constantly and heavily on the ice foot. The spray carried right over the Point—covering all things and raining on the roof of the hut. Poor Vince's cross, some 30 feet above the water, was enveloped in it. Of course the dogs had a very poor time, and we went and released two or three, getting covered in spray during the operation—our wind clothes very wet. This is the third gale from the South since our arrival here (i.e. in 2½ weeks). Any one of these would have rendered the Bay impossible for a ship, and, therefore, it is extraordinary that we should have entirely escaped such a blow when the Discovery was in it in 1902."[129]

It is difficult to see long distances across open water at this time of year because the comparatively warm water throws up into the air a fog, known as frost-smoke. If there is a wind this smoke is carried over the surface of the sea, but if calm the smoke rises and forms a dense curtain. Standing on Arrival Heights, which form the nail of the finger-like Peninsula on which we now lived, we could see the four islands which lie near Cape Evans, and a black smudge in the face of the glaciers which descend from Erebus, which we knew to be the face of the steep slope above Cape Evans, afterwards named The Ramp. But, for the present, our comfortable hut might have been thousands of miles away for all the good it was to us. As soon as the wind fell calm the sea was covered by a thin layer of ice, in twenty-four hours it might be four or five inches thick, but as yet it never proved

[129] *Scott's Last Expedition*, vol. i. p. 207.

strong enough to resist the next blizzard. In March the ice to the south was safe; there was appearance of ice in the two bays at the foot of Erebus' slopes in the beginning of April.

We treated newly formed ice with far too little respect. It was on April 7 that Scott asked whether any of us would like to walk northwards over the newly formed ice towards Castle Rock. We had walked about two miles, the ice heaving up and down as we went, dodging the open pools and leads to the best of our ability, when Taylor went right in. Luckily he could lever himself out without help, and returned to the hut with all speed. We prepared to cross this ice to Cape Evans the next day, but the whole of it went out in the night. On another occasion we were prepared to set out the following morning, but the ice on which we were to cross went out on the turn of the tide some five hours before we timed ourselves to start.

Scott was of opinion that the ice in the two Bays under Erebus was firm, and prepared to essay this route. The first of these bays is formed by the junction of the Hut Point Peninsula with Erebus to the south, and by Glacier Tongue to the north. Crossing Glacier Tongue a party can descend on to the second bay beyond, the northern boundary of which is Cape Evans. The Dellbridge Islands, of which Great Razorback is in direct line between Glacier Tongue and Cape Evans, help to hold in any ice which forms here. The route had never been attempted before, but it was hoped that a way down from the Peninsula on to the frozen sea might be found at the Hutton Cliffs, an outcrop of lava rock in the irregular ice face.

"A party consisting of Scott, Bowers, Taylor, and Seaman Evans with one tent, and Lieutenant Evans, Wright, Debenham, Gran and Crean with another, started for Hut Point. It was dark to the south and snowing by the time they reached the top of Ski Slope. We helped them past Third Crater. The ice from Hut Point to Glacier Tongue was impossible, and so they went on past Castle Rock and were to try and get down somewhere by the Hutton Cliffs on to some fast sea-ice which seemed to have held there some time, and so across Glacier Tongue on to sea-ice which also seemed to be fast as far as Cape Evans.

"After lunch Wilson and I started about 4 P.M. in half a blizzard. It was much better on the Heights and fairly clear towards Erebus, but we could not see any traces of the party on the ice.

"April 12. This morning as it was beginning to get light a blizzard started, and it is blowing very hard now. The large amount of snow which has fallen will make it very thick. We are all anxious about the returning party, for Scott talked of camping on the sea-ice. The ice in Arrival Bay (just north of Hut Point) has gone out. They have sleeping-bags, food for two meals, and a full primus for each tent.

"April 13. We were very anxious about the returning party, especially when all the ice north of Hut Point went out. The blizzard blew itself out this morning, and it was a great change to see White Island and The Bluff once more. Atkinson came in before lunch and told me that, looking from the Heights, the ice from Glacier Tongue to Cape Evans appeared to have gone out. This sobered our lunch. We all made our way to Second Crater afterwards, and found the ice from the Hutton

Cliffs to Glacier Tongue and thence to Cape Evans was still in.

"Before leaving, Scott arranged to give Véry Lights at 10 P.M. from Cape Evans on the first clear night of the next three. To-night is the third, and the first clear night. We were out punctually, and then as we watched a flare blazed up, followed by quite a firework display. We all went wild with excitement—knowing that all was well. Meares ran in and soaked some awning with paraffin, and we lifted it as an answering flare and threw it into the air again and again, until it was burning in little bits all over the snow. The relief was great."[130]

Bowers must tell the story of the returning party:

"We topped the ridges and headed for Erebus beyond Castle Rock. It looked a little threatening at first, but cleared a bit as we got on. It was quite interesting to be breaking new ground. Scott is a fine stepper in a sledge, and he set a fast and easy swing all the time. It was snowing and misty when we got beyond the Hutton Cliffs, but we pitched the tents for lunch before going down the slope. There was no doubt that a blizzard was coming up. It cleared during lunch, which we finished about 3.30 P.M., as it had been a long morning march.

"It was just as well for us that the mist cleared, for the slope was not only crevassed in one direction, but it ended in a high ice-cliff. By working along we found a lowish place about thirty feet down from top to bottom. Over this we lowered men and sledges. It had started to blow and the drift was flying off the cliff in clouds. We put in a couple of strong male bamboos to lower the last man away, leaving the Alpine rope there to facilitate ascent (*i.e.* for any party returning to Hut Point with food). We then repacked the sledges and headed across the bay towards the Glacier Tongue, where we arrived after dark about 6 P.M. The young sea-ice was covered in a salt deposit which made it like pulling a sledge over treacle instead of ice, and it was very heavy going after the snow uplands. The Tongue was mostly hard blue ice, which is slipperiness itself, and crevassed every few yards. Most of these were bridged, but you were continually pushing a foot, or sometimes two, into nothingness, in the semi-darkness. None of us, however, went down to the extent of our harness.

"Arrived on the other side we struck a sheltered dip, where we decided to camp for something to eat. It was after 8 P.M. and I was for camping there for the night, as it seemed to me folly to venture upon a piece of untried newly frozen sea-ice in inky darkness, with a blizzard coming up behind us. Against this of course we were only five miles from Cape Evans, and though we had hardly any grub with us, not having anticipated the cliff or the saltness of the sea-ice, and having to set out to do the journey in one day, I thought hunger in a sleeping-bag better than lying out in a blizzard on less than one foot of young ice.

"After a meal we started off at 9.30 P.M. in a snowy mist in which we could literally see nothing. It had fallen calm though, and at last we could see the outline of the nearest of the Dellbridge Islands called the Great Razorback; our course lay for a smaller island ahead called the Little Razorback. As we neared the Little Razorback Island the snow hid everything; in fact we could hardly see the island itself

[130] My own diary.

when we were right under it. It was impossible to go wandering on, so we had after all to camp on the sea-ice. There was scarcely any snow to put on the valances of the tents, and the wet salt soaked the bags, and you knew that there was only about six or ten inches of precarious ice between you and the black waters beneath. Altogether I decided that I for one would lie awake in such an insecure camp.

"As expected the blizzard overtook us shortly after midnight, and the shrieking of the wind among the rocks above might have been pretty unpleasant had it not assured me that we were still close to the island and not moving seaward. Needless to say, I said that I was sure the camp was as safe as a church. At daylight Taylor dived out and in until the wind from the door blew out the ice valance and the next moment the tent closed on us like an umbrella. We would never have spread it again had not some of the drift settled round us, and so we were able to secure it after an hour or two. The air was full of thick drift, and to work off some of Taylor's energy I said we might climb the island and look for Cape Evans.

"The island rose up straight from the sea at a sharp angle all round, and we climbed it with difficulty. On the top we saw the reason of its name, as it was absolutely so sharp right along that you could bestride the top as though sitting in a saddle. It was too windy sitting up there to be pleasant, so we descended, having seen nothing but clouds of flying snow, and the peak of Inaccessible Island. At the bottom of the weather side we found a small ledge perfectly flat and just big enough to take two tents pitched close together. At this place the island made a wind buffer and it was practically calm though the blizzard yelled all round. I urged Captain Scott to camp on this ledge and Taylor fizzled for making for Cape Evans, so Scott decided to ensure Taylor's safety, as he put it, and we made for the ledge. Once there we had an ideal camp on good hard ground and no wind, and had we had food the blizzard might have lasted a week for aught I cared.

THE HUT, EREBUS AND WHALE-BACK CLOUDS

"We were two nights there and on the morning of the 13th it took off enough for us to head for home. We saw Sunny Jim's [Simpson's] Observatory on the Hill, but still did not know how the hut had fared till we got round the cape into North Bay. There was the Winter Station all intact, however, and though North Bay had only just frozen in, it was strong enough to bear us safely. Somebody saw us and in another moment the hut poured out her little party, consisting of Sunny Jim, Ponting, Nelson, Day, Lashly, Hooper, Clissold, Dimitri and Anton. Ponting's face was a study as he ran up; he failed to recognize any of us and stopped dead with a blank look—as he admitted afterwards, he thought it was the Norwegian expedition for the space of a moment; and then we were all being greeted as heartily as if we had really done something to be proud of.

"The motors had had to be shifted, and a lot of gear placed higher up the beach, but the water had never reached near the hut, so all was well. Inside it looked tremendous, and we looked at our grimy selves in a glass for the first time for three months; no wonder Ponting did not recognize the ruffians. He photographed a group of us, which will amuse you some day, when it is permissible to send photos. We ate heartily and had hot baths and generally civilized ourselves. I have since concluded that the hut is the finest place in the southern hemisphere, but then I could not shake down to it at once. I hankered for a sleeping-bag out on the snow, or for the blubbery atmosphere of Hut Point. I expect the truth of the matter was that all my special pals, Bill, Cherry, Titus, and Atch, had been left behind.

"We found eight ponies at Winter Quarters in the stable, Hackenschmidt having died. These with our two at Hut Point left us with ten to start the winter with. I at once looked out the other big Siberian horse that had been a pair with my late lamented (they were the only Siberian ponies, all the rest being Manchurians) and singled him out for myself, should 'the powers that be' be willing.

"A party had to return to Hut Point with some provision in a day or two, so I asked to go. Captain Scott had decided to go himself, but said he would be very pleased if I would go too; so it being a fine day we left the following Monday. The two teams consisted of Captain Scott, Lashly, Day and Dimitri with one tent and sledge, and Crean, Hooper, Nelson and myself with the other. We had it fine as far as the Glacier Tongue; and then along came the cheery old south wind in our faces; we crossed the Tongue and struggled against this till we could camp under the Hutton Cliffs where we got some shelter. All of us had our faces frost-bitten, the washing and shaving having made mine quite tender. It was a bit of a job getting up the cliff: we had to stand on top of a pile of fallen ice and hoist a 10-feet sledge on to our shoulders, at least on to the shoulders of the tall ones; this just touched the overhanging cornice. A cornice of snow is caused by continual drift over a sharp edge: it takes all sorts of fantastic shapes, but usually hangs over like this. Looking edgeways it looks as if it must fall down, but as a matter of fact is usually very tough indeed. In this case steps were cut in it with an ice axe from our extemporary ladder, and Captain Scott and I got up first. With the aid of a rope and the ladder we got the light ones up first, and hauled up the gear last of all; hanging the sledge from the top with one rope enabled the last two to struggle up it assisted by a rope round them from above. It was a cold job and more frost-bites occurred in two of our novices, one on a foot and the other on a finger.

"We faced the blast again, but got it partially behind us on reaching the Heights. We camped for the night under Castle Rock on an inclined slope. It calmed down to a glorious night with a low temperature. Crean and I lay head down hill to make Nelson and Hooper—who had never sledged before—more comfortable. As a result Crean slipped half out of the tent and let in a cold stream of air under the valance, for which I was at a loss to account until the morning disclosed him thus, fast asleep of course. It takes a lot to worry Captain Scott's coxswain.

"We arrived at Hut Point and had a great reception there, chiefly on account of the food we brought, particularly the sugar. We had been living on some paraffin sugar when I left before, and even this was finished. The next day we stayed there to kill seals. Cherry and I skinned one and then went for a walk round Cape Armitage. It was blowing big guns off the cape, fairly fizzing in fact. We went as far as Pram Point and then turned, coming in with it behind us. I only had a thin balaclava and my ears were nearly nipped."[131]

Meanwhile those of us who had been left at Hut Point with the ponies and dogs journeyed out one afternoon to Safety Camp to get some more bales of compressed fodder. Easter Sunday we spent in a howling blizzard, which cleared in the afternoon sufficiently to see a golden sun sinking into a sea of purple frost-smoke and drift.

I have it on record that we had tinned haddock this day for breakfast, made by Oates with great care, a biscuit and cheese hoosh for lunch, and a pemmican fry this evening, followed by cocoa with a tin of sweetened Nestlé's milk in it, truly a great luxury. For the rest we mended our finnesko, and read Bleak House. Meares told us how the Chinese who were going to war with the Lolos (who are one of the Eighteen tribes on the borders of Thibet and China) tied the Lolo hostage to a bench, and, having cut his throat, caught the blood which dripped from it. Into this they dipped their flag, and then cut out the heart and liver, which the officers ate, while the men ate the rest!

The relief party arrived on April 18: "We had spent such a happy week, just the seven of us, at the Discovery hut that I think, glad as we were to see the men, we would most of us have rather been left undisturbed, and I expected that it would mean that we should have to move homewards, as it turned out.

"Meares is to be left in charge of the party which remains, namely Forde and Keohane of the old stagers, and Nelson, Day, Lashly and Dimitri of the new-comers. He is very amusing with the stores and is evidently afraid that the food which has just been brought in (sugar, self-raising flour, chocolate, etc.) will all be eaten up by those who have brought it. So we have dampers without butter, and a minimum of chocolate.

"Tuesday and Tuesday night was one of our few still, cold days, nearly minus thirty. The sea northwards from Hut Point, whence the ice had previously all gone out, froze nearly five inches by Wednesday mid-day, when we got three more seal.

[131] Bowers.

Scott was evidently thinking that on Thursday, when we were to start, we might go by the sea-ice all the way—when suddenly with no warning it silently floated out to sea."[132]

A CORNICE OF SNOW

The following two teams travelled to Cape Evans via the Hutton Cliffs on April 21: 1st team Scott, Wilson, Atkinson, Crean; 2nd team Bowers, Oates, Cherry-Garrard, Hooper. It was blowing hard, as usual, at the Hutton Cliffs, and we got rather frost-bitten when lowering the sledges on to the sea-ice. The sun was leaving us for the next four months, but luckily the light just lasted for this operation though not for the subsequent meal which we hastily ate under the cliffs, nor for the crossing of Glacier Tongue. Bowers wrote home:

"I had the lighter team and, knowing what a flier Captain Scott is I took care to have the new sledge myself. Our weights were nothing and the difference was only in the sledge runners, but it made all the difference to us that day. Scott fairly legged it, as I expected, and we came along gaily behind him. He could not understand it when the pace began to tell more on his heavy team than on us. After lowering down the sledges over the cliffs we recovered the rope we had left in the first place, and then struck out over the sea-ice. Then our good runners told so much that I owned up to mine being the better sledge, and offered to give them one of my team. This was declined, but after we crossed the Tongue Captain Scott said he would like to change sledges at the Little Razorback. At any time over this stretch we could have run away from his team, and once they got our sledge they started that game on us. We expected it, and never had I stepped out so hard before. We had been marching hard for nearly 12 hours and now we had two miles' spurt to do, and we should have stuck it, bad runners and all, had we had smooth ice. As

[132] My own diary.

it was we struck a belt of rough ice, and in the dark we all stumbled and I went down a whack, that nearly knocked me out. This was not noticed fortunately, and still we hung on to the end of their sledge while I turned hot and cold and sick and went through the various symptoms before I got my equilibrium back, which I fortunately did while legging it at full speed. They started to go ahead soon after that though, and we could not hold our own, although we were close to the cape. I had the same thing happen again after another fall but we stuck it round the cape and arrived only about 50 yards behind. I have never felt so done, and so was my team. Of course we need not have raced, but we did, and I would do the same thing every time. Titus produced a mug of brandy he had sharked from the ship and we all lapped it up with avidity. The other team were just about laid out, too, so I don't think there was much to be said either way."[133]

Two days later the sun appeared for the last time for four months.

Looking back I realized two things. That sledging, at any rate in summer and autumn, was a much less terrible ordeal than my imagination had painted it, and that those Hut Point days would prove some of the happiest in my life. Just enough to eat and keep us warm, no more—no frills nor trimmings: there is many a worse and more elaborate life. The necessaries of civilization were luxuries to us: and as Priestley found under circumstances compared to which our life at Hut Point was a Sunday School treat, the luxuries of civilization satisfy only those wants which they themselves create.

---

[133] Bowers' letter.

CHAPTER VI

THE FIRST WINTER

The highest object that human beings can set before themselves is not the pur
suit of any such chimera as the annihilation of the unknown; it is simply the un
wearied endeavour to remove its boundaries a little further from our little sphere
of action.—HUXLEY.

And so we came back to our comfortable hut. Whatever merit there may be
in going to the Antarctic, once there you must not credit yourself for being there
To spend a year in the hut at Cape Evans because you explore is no more laudable
than to spend a month at Davos because you have consumption, or to spend an
English winter at the Berkeley Hotel. It is just the most comfortable thing and the
easiest thing to do under the circumstances.

In our case the best thing was not at all bad, for the hut, as Arctic huts go
was as palatial as is the Ritz, as hotels go. Whatever the conditions of darkness
cold and wind, might be outside, there was comfort and warmth and good cheer
within.

And there was a mass of work to be done, as well as at least two journeys of
the first magnitude ahead.

When Scott first sat down at his little table at Winter Quarters to start working
out a most complicated scheme of weights and averages for the Southern Journey
his thoughts were gloomy, I know. "This is the end of the Pole," he said to me
when he pulled us off the bergs after the sea-ice had broken up; the loss of six po
nies out of the eight with which we started the Depôt Journey, the increasing ema
ciation and weakness of the pony transport as we travelled farther on the Barrier
the arrival of the dogs after their rapid journey home, starved rakes which looked
as though they were absolutely done—these were not cheerful recollections with
which to start to plan a journey of eighteen hundred miles.

On the other hand, we had ten ponies left, though two or three of them were
of more than doubtful quality; and it was obvious that considerable improvement
could and must be made in the feeding of both ponies and dogs. With regard to
the dogs the remedy was plain; their ration was too small. With regard to the po
nies the question was not so simple. One of the main foods for the ponies which
we had brought was compressed fodder in the shape of bales. Theoretically this
fodder was excellent food value, and was made of wheat which was cut green and
pressed. Whether it was really wheat or not I do not know, but there could be no
two opinions about its nourishing qualities for our ponies. When fed upon it they

lost weight until they were just skin and bone. Poor beasts! It was pitiful to see them.

In Oates we had a man who had forgotten as much as most men know about horses. It was no fault of his that this fodder was inadequate, nor that we had lost so many of the best ponies which we had. Oates had always been for taking the worst ponies out on the Depôt Journey: travelling as far on to the Barrier as they could go, and there killing them and depôting their flesh. Now Oates took the ten remaining ponies into his capable hands. Some of them were scarecrows, especially poor Jehu, who was never expected to start at all, and ended by gallantly pulling his somewhat diminished load eight marches beyond One Ton Camp, a distance of 238 miles. Another, Christopher, was a man-killer if ever a horse was; he had to be thrown in order to attach him to the sledge; to the end he would lay out any man who was rash enough to give him the chance; once started, and it took four men to achieve this, it was impossible to halt him during the day's march, and so Oates and his three tent mates and their ponies had to go without any lunch meal for 130 miles of the Southern Journey.

Oates trained them and fed them as though they were to run in the Derby. They were exercised whenever possible throughout the winter and spring by those who were to lead them on the actual journey. Fresh and good food was found in the shape of oilcake and oats, a limited quantity of each of which had been brought and was saved for the actual Polar Journey, and everything which care and foresight could devise was done to save them discomfort. It is a grim life for animals, but in the end we were to know that up to the time of that bad blizzard almost at the Glacier Gateway, which was the finishing post of these plucky animals, they had fed all they needed, slept as well and lived as well as any, and better than most horses in ordinary life at home. "I congratulate you, Titus," said Wilson, as we stood under the shadow of Mount Hope, with the ponies' task accomplished, and "I thank you," said Scott.

Titus grunted and was pleased.

Transport difficulties for the Polar Journey were considerable, but in every other direction the outlook was bright. The men who were to do the sledging had been away from Winter Quarters for three months. They had had plenty of sledging experience, some of it none too soft. The sledges, clothing, man-food, and outfit generally were excellent, although some changes were suggested and could be put into effect. There was no obvious means, however, of effecting the improvement most desired, a satisfactory snow-shoe for the ponies.

The work already accomplished was enormous. On the Polar Journey the ponies and dogs could now travel light for the first hundred and thirty geographical miles, when, at One Ton Camp, they would for the first time take their full loads: the advantage of being able to start again with full loads when so far on your way is obvious when it is considered that the distance travelled depends upon the weight of food that can be carried. During the geological journey on the western side of the Sound, Taylor and his party had carried out much useful geological work in Dry Valley and on the Ferrar and Koettlitz Glaciers, which had been accurately plotted for the charts, and had been examined for the first time by an expert physiographer and ice specialist. The ordinary routine of scientific and meteorological observations usual with all Scott's sledging parties was observed.

Further, at Cape Evans there had been running for more than three months a scientific station, which rivalled in thoroughness and exactitude any other such station in the world. I hope that later a more detailed account may be given of this continuous series of observations, some of them demanding the most complex mechanism, and all of them watched over by enthusiastic experts. It must here suffice to say that we who on our return saw for the first time the hut and its annexes completely equipped were amazed; though perhaps the gadget which appealed most to us at first was the electric apparatus by which the cook, whose invention it was, controlled the rising of his excellent bread.

Glad as we were to find it all and to enjoy the food, bath and comfort which it offered, we had no illusions about Cape Evans itself. It is uninteresting, as only a low-lying spit of black lava covered for the most part with snow, and swept constantly by high winds and drift, can be uninteresting. The kenyte lava of which it is formed is a remarkable rock, and is found in few parts of the world: but when you have seen one bit of kenyte you have seen all. Unlike the spacious and lofty Hut Point Peninsula, thirteen miles to the south, it has no outstanding hills and craters; no landmarks such as Castle Rock. Unlike the broad folds of Cape Royds, six miles to the north, it has none of the rambling walks and varied lakes, in which is found most of the limited plant life which exists in these latitudes, and though a few McCormick skuas meet here, there is no nursery of penguins such as that which makes Cape Royds so attractive in summer. Nor has the Great Ice Sheet, which reached up Erebus and spread over the Ross Sea in the past, spilled over Cape Evans in its retreat a wealth of foreign granites, dolerites, porphyrys and sandstone such as cover the otherwise dull surface round Shackleton's old Winter Quarters.

Cape Evans is a low lava flow jutting out some three thousand feet from the face of the glaciers which clothe the slopes of Erebus. It is roughly an equilateral triangle in shape, at its base some three thousand feet (9/16th mile) across. This base-line, which divides the cape from the slopes of Erebus and the crevassed glaciers and giant ice-falls which clothe them, consists of a ramp with a slope of thirty degrees, and a varying height of some 100 to 150 feet. From our hut, four hundred yards away, it looks like a great embankment behind which rises the majestic volcano Erebus, with its plume of steam and smoke.

The cape itself does not rise on the average more than thirty feet, and somewhat resembles the back of a hog with several backbones. The hollows between the ridges are for the most part filled with snow and ice, while in one or two places where the accumulation of snow is great enough there are little glacierets which do not travel far before they ignominiously peter out. There are two small lakes, called Skua Lake and Island Lake respectively. There is only one hill which is almost behind the hut, and is called Wind Vane Hill, for on it were placed one of our wind vanes and certain other meteorological instruments. Into the glacieret which flowed down in the lee of this hill we drove two caves, which gave both an even low temperature and excellent insulation. One of them was therefore used or our magnetic observations, and the other as an ice-house for the mutton we had brought from New Zealand.

The north side, upon which we had built our hut, slopes down by way of a rubbly beach to the sea in North Bay. We knew there was a beach for we landed upon it, but we never saw it again even in the height of summer, for the winter blizzards formed an ice foot several feet thick. The other side of the cape ends abruptly in black bastions and baby cliffs some thirty feet high. The apex of the triangle which forms as it were the cape proper is a similar kenyte bluff. The whole makes a tricky place on which to walk in the dark, for the surface is strewn with boulders of all sizes and furrowed and channelled by drifts of hard and icy snow, and quite suddenly you may find yourself prostrate upon a surface of slippery blue ice. It may be easily imagined that it is no seemly place to exercise skittish ponies or mules in a cold wind, but there is no other place when the sea-ice is unsafe.

Come and stand outside the hut door. All round you, except where the cape joins the mountain, is the sea. You are facing north with your back to the Great Ice Barrier and the Pole, with your eyes looking out of the mouth of McMurdo Sound over the Ross Sea towards New Zealand, two thousand miles of open water, pack and bergs. Look over the sea to your left. It is mid-day, and though the sun will not appear above the horizon he is still near enough to throw a soft yellow light over the Western Mountains. These form the coast-line thirty miles across the Sound, and as they disappear northwards are miraged up into the air and float, black islands in a lemon sky. Straight ahead of you there is nothing to be seen but black open sea, with a high light over the horizon, which you know betokens pack; this is ice blink. But as you watch there appears and disappears a little dark smudge. This puzzles you for some time, and then you realize that this is the mirage of some far mountain or of Beaufort Island, which guards the mouth of McMurdo Sound against such traffic as ever comes that way, by piling up the ice floes across the entrance.

As you still look north, in the middle distance, jutting out into the sea, is a low black line of land, with one excrescence. This is Cape Royds, with Shackleton's old hut upon it; the excrescence is High Peak, and this line marks the first land upon the eastern side of McMurdo Sound which you can see, and indeed is actually the most eastern point of Ross Island. It disappears abruptly behind a high wall, and if you let your eyes travel round towards your right front you see that the wall is a perpendicular cliff two hundred feet high of pure green and blue ice, which falls sheer into the sea, and forms, with Cape Evans, on which we stand, the bay which lies in front of our hut, and which we called North Bay. This great ice-cliff with its crevasses, towers, bastions and cornices, was a never-ending source of delight to us; it forms the snout of one of the many glaciers which slide down the slopes of Erebus: in smooth slopes and contours where the mountain underneath is of regular shape: in impassable icefalls where the underlying surface is steep or broken. This particular ice stream is called the Barne Glacier, and is about two miles across. The whole background from our right front to our right rear, that is from N.E. to S.E., is occupied by our massive and volcanic neighbour, Erebus. He stands 13,500 feet high. We live beneath his shadow and have both admiration and

friendship for him, sometimes perhaps tinged with respect. However, there ar
no signs of dangerous eruptive disturbances in modern times, and we feel prett
safe, despite the fact that the smoke which issues from his crater sometimes rise
in dense clouds for many thousands of feet, and at others the trail of his plume ca
be measured for at least a hundred miles.

If you are not too cold standing about (it does not pay to stand about at Cap
Evans) let us make our way behind the hut and up Wind Vane Hill. This is onl
some sixty-five feet high, yet it dominates the rest of the cape and is steep enoug
to require a scramble, even now when the wind is calm. Look out that you do no
step on the electric wires which connect the wind-vane cups on the hill with th
recording dial in the hut. These cups revolve in the wind, the revolutions bein
registered electrically: every four miles a signal was sent to the hut, and a pe
working upon a chronograph registered one more step. There is also a meteorc
logical screen on the summit, which has to be visited at eight o'clock each mornin
in all weathers.

**PLATE I.—A SUMMER VIEW OVER CAPE EVANS AND MCMUR-
DO SOUND FROM THE RAMP—EMERY WALKER LIMITED, COL
LOTYPERS.**

Arrived on the top you will now be facing south, that is in the opposite di
rection to which you were facing before. The first thing that will strike you is tha
the sea, now frozen in the bays though still unfrozen in the open sound, flow
in nearly to your feet. The second, that though the sea stretches back for nearl
twenty miles, yet the horizon shows land or ice in every direction. For a ship th
is a cul-de-sac, as Ross found seventy years ago. But as soon as you have graspe
these two facts your whole attention will be riveted to the amazing sight on you
left. Here are the southern slopes of Erebus; but how different from those whicl
you have lately seen. Northwards they fell in broad calm lines to a beautiful statel
cliff which edged the sea. But here—all the epithets and all the adjectives whicl
denote chaotic immensity could not adequately tell of them. Visualize a torren
ten miles long and twenty miles broad; imagine it falling over mountainous rock
and tumbling over itself in giant waves; imagine it arrested in the twinkling of a
eye, frozen and white. Countless blizzards have swept their drifts over it, but hav
failed to hide it. And it continues to move. As you stand in the still cold air yo
may sometimes hear the silence broken by the sharp reports as the cold contract
it or its own weight splits it. Nature is tearing up that ice as human beings tea
paper.

The sea-cliff is not so high here, and is more broken up by crevasses and caves, and more covered with snow. Some five miles along the coast the white line is broken by a bluff and black outcrop of rock; this is Turk's Head, and beyond it is the low white line of Glacier Tongue, jutting out for miles into the sea. We know, for we have already crossed it, that there is a small frozen bay of sea-ice beyond, but all we can see from Cape Evans is the base of the Hut Point Peninsula, with a rock outcrop just showing where the Hutton Cliffs lie. The Peninsula prevents us from seeing the Barrier, though the Barrier wind is constantly flowing over it, as the clouds of drift now smoking over the Cliffs bear witness. Farther to the right still, the land is clear: Castle Rock stands up like a sentinel, and beyond are Arrival Heights and the old craters we have got to know so well during our stay at Hut Point. The Discovery hut, which would, in any case, be invisible at fifteen miles, is round that steep rocky corner which ends the Peninsula, due south from where we stand.

There remains undescribed the quadrant which stretches to our right front from south to west. Just as we have previously seen the line of the Western Mountains disappearing to the north miraged up in the light of the mid-day sun, so now we see the same line of mountains running south, with many miles of sea or Barrier between us and them. On the far southern horizon, almost in transit with Hut Point, stands Minna Bluff, some ninety miles away, beyond which we have laid the One Ton Depôt, and from this point, as our eyes move round to the right, we see peak after peak of these great mountain ranges—Discovery, Morning, Lister, Hooker, and the glaciers which divide them one from another. They rise almost without a break to a height of thirteen thousand feet. Between us and them is the Barrier to the south, and the sea to the north. Unless a blizzard is impending or blowing, they are clearly visible, a gigantic wall of snow and ice and rock, which bounds our view to the west, constantly varied by the ever-changing colour of the Antarctic. Beyond is the plateau.

We have not yet mentioned four islands which lie within a radius of about three miles from where we stand. The most important is a mile from the end of Cape Evans and is called Inaccessible Island, owing to the inhospitality of its steep lava side, even when the sea is frozen; we found a way up, but it is not a very interesting place. Tent Island lies farther out and to the south-west. The remaining two, which are more islets than islands, rise in front of us in South Bay. They are called Great and Little Razorback, being ribs of rock with a sharp divide in the centre. The latter of these is the refuge upon which Scott's party returning to Cape Evans pitched their camp when overtaken by a blizzard some weeks ago. All these islands are of volcanic origin and black in general colour, but I believe there is evidence to show that the lava stream which created them flowed from McMurdo Sound rather than from the more obvious craters of Erebus. Their importance in this story is the indirect help they gave in holding in sea-ice against southerly blizzards, and in forming landmarks which proved useful more than once to men who had lost their bearings in darkness and thick weather. In this respect also several icebergs which sailed in from the Ross Sea and grounded on the shallows which run between Inaccessible Island and the cape, as well as in South Bay, were most useful as well as being interesting and beautiful. For two years we watched the weathering of these great towers and bastions of ice by sea and sun and wind, and left them still lying in the same positions, but mere tumbled ruins of their former selves.

Many places in the panorama we have examined show black rock, and the cape on which we stand exposes at times more black than white. This fact alway puzzles those who naturally conclude that all the Antarctic is covered with ice and snow. The explanation is simple, that winds of the great velocity which prevails in this region will not only prevent snow resting to windward of out-cropping rocks and cliffs, but will even wear away the rocks themselves. The fact that these winds always blow from the south, or southerly, causes a tendency for this aspect of any projecting rock to be blown free from snow, while the north or lee side is drifted up by a marbled and extremely hard tongue of snow, which disappears into a point at a distance which depends upon the size of the rock.

Of course for the most part the land is covered to such a depth by glaciers and snow that no wind will do more than pack the snow or expose the ice beneath. At the same time, to visualize the Antarctic as a white land is a mistake, for, not only is there much rock projecting wherever mountains or rocky capes and islands rise but the snow seldom looks white, and if carefully looked at will be found to be shaded with many colours, but chiefly with cobalt blue or rose-madder, and all the gradations of lilac and mauve which the mixture of these colours will produce. A White Day is so rare that I have recollections of going out from the hut or the tent and being impressed by the fact that the snow really looked white. When to the beautiful tints in the sky and the delicate shading on the snow are added perhaps the deep colours of the open sea, with reflections from the ice foot and ice-cliffs in it, all brilliant blues and emerald greens, then indeed a man may realize how beautiful this world can be, and how clean.

Though I may struggle with inadequate expression to show the reader that this pure Land of the South has many gifts to squander upon those who woo her chiefest of these gifts is that of her beauty. Next, perhaps, is that of grandeur and immensity, of giant mountains and limitless spaces, which must awe the most casual, and may well terrify the least imaginative of mortals. And there is one other gift which she gives with both hands, more prosaic, but almost more desirable That is the gift of sleep. Perhaps it is true of others as is certainly the case with me that the more horrible the conditions in which we sleep, the more soothing and wonderful are the dreams which visit us. Some of us have slept in a hurricane of wind and a hell of drifting snow and darkness, with no roof above our heads, with no tent to help us home, with no conceivable chance that we should ever see our friends again, with no food that we could eat, and only the snow which drifted into our sleeping-bags which we could drink day after day and night after night We slept not only soundly the greater part of these days and nights, but with a certain numbed pleasure. We wanted something sweet to eat: for preference tinned peaches in syrup! Well! That is the kind of sleep the Antarctic offers you at her worst, or nearly at her worst. And if the worst, or best, happens, and Death comes for you in the snow, he comes disguised as Sleep, and you greet him rather as a welcome friend than as a gruesome foe. She treats you thus when you are in the extremity of peril and hardship; perhaps then you can imagine what draughts of deep and healthy slumber she will give a tired sledger at the end of a long day's march in summer, when after a nice hot supper he tucks his soft dry warm furry bag round him with the light beating in through the green silk tent, the homely smell of tobacco in the air, and the only noise that of the ponies tethered outside, munching their supper in the sun.

And so it came about that during our sojourn at Cape Evans, in our comfortable warm roomy home, we took our full allotted span of sleep. Most were in their bunks by 10 P.M., sometimes with a candle and a book, not rarely with a piece of chocolate. The acetylene was turned off at 10.30, for we had a limited quantity of carbide, and soon the room was in complete darkness, save for the glow of the galley stove and where a splash of light showed the night watchman preparing his supper. Some snored loudly, but none so loud as Bowers; others talked in their sleep, the more so when some nasty experience had lately set their nerves on edge. There was always the ticking of many instruments, and sometimes the ring of a little bell: to this day I do not know what most of them meant. On a calm night no sound penetrated except, perhaps, the whine of a dog, or the occasional kick of a pony in the stable outside. Any disturbance was the night watchman's job. But on a bad blizzard night the wind, as it tore seawards over the hut, roared and howled in the ventilator let into the roof: in the more furious gusts the whole hut shook, and the pebbles picked up by the hurricane scattered themselves noisily against the woodwork of the southern wall. We did not get many nights like these the first winter; during the second we seemed to get nothing else. One ghastly blizzard blew for six weeks.

The night watchman took his last hourly observation at 7 A.M., and was free to turn in after waking the cook and making up the fire. Frequently, however, he had so much work to do that he preferred to forgo his sleep and remain up. For instance, if the weather looked threatening, he would take his pony out for exercise as soon as possible in the morning, or those lists of stores were not finished, or that fish trap had to be looked after: all kinds of things.

A sizzling on the fire and a smell of porridge and fried seal liver heralded breakfast, which was at 8 A.M. in theory and a good deal later in practice. A sleepy eye might see the meteorologist stumping out (Simpson always stumped) to change the records in his magnetic cave and visit his instruments on the Hill. Twenty minutes later he would be back, as often as not covered with drift and his wind helmet all iced up. Meanwhile, the more hardy ones were washing: that is, they rubbed themselves, all shivering, with snow, of a minus temperature, and pretended they liked it. Perhaps they were right, but we told them it was swank. I'm not sure that it wasn't! It should be explained that water was seldom possible in a land where ice is more abundant than coal.

One great danger threatened all our meals in this hut, namely that of a Cag. A Cag is an argument, sometimes well informed and always heated, upon any subject under the sun, or temporarily in our case, the moon. They ranged from the Pole to the Equator, from the Barrier to Portsmouth Hard and Plymouth Hoe.

They began on the smallest of excuses, they continued through the widest field, they never ended; they were left in mid air, perhaps to be caught up again and twisted and tortured months after. What caused the cones on the Ramp; the formation of ice crystals; the names and order of the public-houses if you left the Main Gate of Portsmouth Dockyard and walked to the Unicorn Gate (if you ever reached so far); the best kinds of crampons in the Antarctic, and the best place in London for oysters; the ideal pony rug; would the wine steward at the Ritz look surprised if you asked him for a pint of bitter? Though the Times Atlas does not rise to public-houses nor Chambers's Encyclopaedia sink to behaviour at our more expensive hotels, yet they settled more of these disputes than anything else.

On the day we are discussing, though mutterings can still be heard from Nelson's cubicle, the long table has been cleared and every one is busy by 9.30. From now until supper at 7 work is done by all in some form or other, except for a short luncheon interval. I do not mean for a minute that we all sit down, as a man may do in an office at home, and solidly grind away for upwards of nine hours or more. Not a bit of it. We have much work out of doors, and exercise is a consideration of the utmost importance. But when we go out, each individual quite naturally takes the opportunity to carry out such work as concerns him, whether it deals with ice or rocks, dogs or horses, meteorology or biology, tide-gauges or balloons.

When blizzards allowed, the ponies were exercised by their respective leaders between breakfast and mid-day, when they were fed. This exercising of animals might be a pleasant business, on the other hand it could be the deuce and all: it depended on the pony and the weather. A blubber fire was kept burning in the snug stable, which was built against the lee wall of the hut: the ponies were, therefore, quite warm, and found it chilly directly they were led outside, even if there was no wind.

The difficulties of exercising them in the dark were so great that with the best intentions in the world it was difficult to give them sufficient work for the good feeding they received. Add to this the fact that one at any rate of these variable animals was really savage, and that most of them were keen to break away if possible, and the hour of exercise was not without its thrills even on the calmest and most moonlight days. The worst days were those when it was difficult to say whether the ponies should be taken out on the sea-ice or not. It was thick weather that was to be feared, for then, if the leader once lost his bearings, it was most difficult for him to return. An overcast sky, light falling snow, perhaps a light northerly wind generally meant a blizzard, but the blizzard might not break for twenty-four hours, it might be upon you in four seconds. It was difficult to say whether the pony should miss his exercise, whether the fish trap should be raised, whether to put off your intended trip to Cape Royds. Generally the risks were taken, for, on the whole, it is better to be a little over-bold than a little over-cautious, while always there was a something inside urging you to do it just because there was a certain risk, and you hardly liked not to do it. It is so easy to be afraid of being afraid!

Let me give one instance: it must be typical of many. It was thick as it could be, no moon, no stars, light falling snow, and not even a light breeze to keep in your face to give direction. Bowers and I decided to take our ponies out, and once over the tide crack, where the working sea-ice joins the fast land-ice, we kept close under the tall cliffs of the Barne Glacier. So far all was well, and also when we struck along a small crack into the middle of the bay, where there was a thermometer screen. This we read with some difficulty by the light of a match and started back towards the hut. In about a quarter of an hour we knew we were quite lost until an iceberg which we recognized showed us that we had been walking at right angles to our course, and got us safe home.

On a clear crisp day, with the full moon to show you the ridges and cracks and sastrugi, it was most pleasant to put on your ski and wander forth with no object but that of healthy pleasure. Perhaps you would make your way round the bluff end of the cape and strike southwards. Here you may visit Nelson working with his thermometers and current meters and other instruments over a circular hole in the ice, which he keeps open from day to day by breaking out the 'biscuit' of newly formed ice. He has connected himself with the hut by telephone, and built round himself an igloo of drifted snow and the aforesaid 'biscuits,' which effectually shelter him from the wind. Or you may meet Meares and Dimitri returning with the dog-teams from a visit to Hut Point. A little farther on the silence is complete. But now your ear catches the metallic scratch of ski sticks on hard ice; there is some one else ski-ing over there, it may be many miles away, for sound travels in an amazing way. Every now and then there comes a sharp crack like a pistol shot; it is the ice contracting in the glaciers of Erebus, and you know that it is getting colder. Your breath smokes, forming white rime over your face, and ice in your beard; if it is very cold you may actually hear it crackle as it freezes in mid air!

These were the days which remain visibly in the mind as the most enjoyable during this first winter season. It was all so novel, these much-dreaded, and amongst us much-derided, terrors of the Long Winter Night. The atmosphere is very clear when it is not filled with snow or ice crystals, and the moonlight lay upon the land so that we could see the main outlines of the Hut Point Peninsula, and even Minna Bluff out on the Barrier ninety miles away. The ice-cliffs of Erebus showed as great dark walls, but above them the blue ice of the glaciers gleamed silvery, and the steam flowed lazily from the crater carried away in a long line, showing us that the northerly breezes prevailed up there, and were storing up trouble in the south. Sometimes a shooting star would seem to fall right into the mountain, and for the most part the Aurora flitted uneasily about in the sky.

The importance of plenty of out-door exercise was generally recognized, and our experience showed us that the happiest and healthiest members of our party during this first year were those who spent the longest period in the fresh air. As a rule we walked and worked and ski-ed alone, not I feel sure because of any individual distaste for the company of our fellows but rather because of a general inclination to spend a short period of the day without company. At least this is certainly true of the officers: I am not so sure about the men. Under the circumstances, the only time in the year that a man could be alone was in his walks abroad from Winter Quarters, for the hut, of course, was always occupied, and when sledging this sardine-like existence was continuous night and day.

There was one regular exception to this rule. Every possible evening, that is to

say if it was not blowing a full blizzard, Wilson and Bowers went up the Ramp to
gether 'to read Bertram.' Now this phrase will convey little meaning without some
explanation. I have already spoken of the Ramp as the steep rubbly slope partly
covered by snow and partly by ice which divided the cape on which we lived from
the glaciated slopes of Erebus. After a breathless scramble up this embankment
one came upon a belt of rough boulder-strewn ground from which arose at inter
vals conical mounds, the origin of which puzzled us for many months. At length
by the obvious means of cutting a section through one of them, it was proved
that there was a solid kenyte lava block in the centre of this cone, proving that the
whole was formed by the weathering of a single rock. Threading your way for
some hundreds of yards through this terrain, a scramble attended by many slips
and falls on a dark night, you reached the first signs of glaciation. A little farther
isolated in the ice stream, is another group of debris cones, and on the largest of
these we placed meteorological Screen "B," commonly called Bertram. This screen
together with "A" (Algernon) and "C" (Clarence), which were in North and South
Bays respectively, were erected by Bowers, who thought, rightly, that they would
form an object to which men could guide their walks, and that at the same time the
observations of maximum, minimum and present temperatures would be a useful
check to the meteorologist when he came to compare them with those taken at
the hut. As a matter of fact the book in which we used to enter these observations
shows that the air temperatures out on the sea-ice vary considerably from those
on the cape, and that the temperatures several hundred feet up on the slopes of
Erebus are often several degrees higher than those taken at sea-level. I believe that
much of the weather in this part of the world is an intensely local affair, and these
screens produced useful data.

Wilson and Bowers would go up the Ramp when it was blowing and drifting
fairly hard, so that although the rocks and landmarks immediately round them
were visible, all beyond was blotted out. It is quite possible to walk thus among
landmarks which you know at a time when it is most unwise to go out on to the
sea-ice where there are no fixed points to act as a guide.

It was Wilson's pleasant conceit to keep his balaclava rolled up, so that his face
was bare, on such occasions, being somewhat proud of the fact that he had not,
as yet, been frost-bitten. Imagine our joy when he entered the hut one cold windy
evening with two white spots on his cheeks which he vainly tried to hide behind
his dogskin mitts.

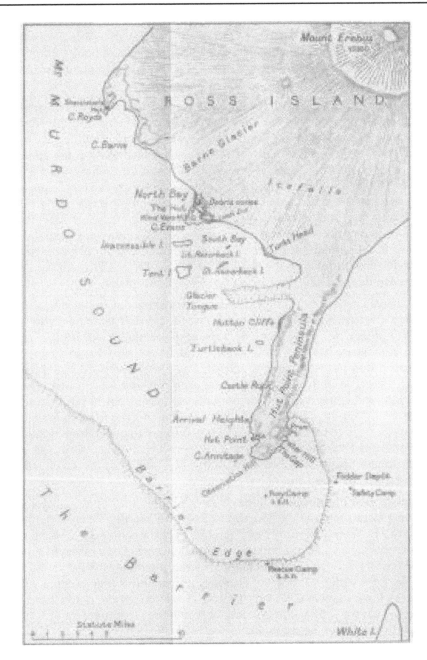

MCMURDO SOUND—APSLEY CHERRY-GARRARD, DEL.—EMERY WALKER LTD., COLLOTYPERS.

The ponies' lunch came at mid-day, when they were given snow to drink and compressed fodder with oats or oil-cake on alternate days to eat, the proportion of which was arranged according to the work they were able to do in the present,

or expected to do in the future. Our own lunch was soon after one, and a few
minutes before that time Hooper's voice would be heard: "Table please, Mr. Debenham," and all writing materials, charts, instruments and books would have to
be removed. On Sunday, this table displayed a dark blue cloth, but for meals and
at all other times it was covered with white oilcloth.

Lunch itself was a pleasant meatless meal, consisting of limited bread and butter with plenty of jam or cheese, tea or cocoa, the latter being undoubtedly a most
useful drink in a cold country. Many controversies raged over the rival merits of
tea and cocoa. Some of us made for ourselves buttered toast at the galley fire;
must myself confess to a weakness for Welsh Rarebit, and others followed my example on cheese days in making messes of which we were not a little proud. Scott
sat at the head of the table, that is at the east end, but otherwise we all took our
places haphazard from meal to meal as our conversation, or want of it, merited, or
as our arrival found a vacant chair. Thus if you felt talkative you might always find
a listener in Debenham; if inclined to listen yourself it was only necessary to sit
near Taylor or Nelson; if, on the other hand, you just wanted to be quiet, Atkinson
or Oates would, probably, give you a congenial atmosphere.

There was never any want of conversation, largely due to the fact that no conversation was expected: we most of us know the horrible blankness which comes
over our minds when we realize that because we are eating we are also supposed
to talk, whether we have anything to say or not. It was also due to the more primitive reason that in a company of specialists, whose travels extended over most
parts of the earth, and whose subjects overlapped and interlocked at so many
points, topics of conversation were not only numerous but full of possibilities of
expansion. Add to this that from the nature of our work we were probably people of an inquisitive turn of mind and wanted to get to the bottom of the subjects
which presented themselves, and you may expect to find, as was in fact the case,
an atmosphere of pleasant and quite interesting conversation which sometimes
degenerated into heated and noisy argument.

The business of eating over, pipes were lit without further formality. I mention
pipes only because while we had a most bountiful supply of tobacco, the kindly
present of Mr. Wills, our supply of cigarettes from the same source was purposely
limited and only a small quantity were landed, allowing of a ration to such members who wished. Consequently cigarettes were an article of some value, and in a
land where the ordinary forms of currency are valueless they became a frequent
stake to venture when making bets. Indeed, "I bet you ten cigarettes," or "I bet you
a dinner when we get back to London," became the most frequent bids of the ar-
gumentative gambler, occasionally varied when the bettor was more than usually
certain of the issue by the offer of a pair of socks.

By two o'clock we were dispersed once more to our various works and duties.
If it was bearable outside, the hut would soon be empty save for the cook and a
couple of seamen washing up the plates; otherwise every one went out to make
the most of any glimmering of daylight which still came to us from the sun below
the northern horizon. And here it may be explained that whereas in England the
sun rises more or less in the east, is due south at mid-day, and sets in the west, this

is not the case in the Antarctic regions. In the latitude in which we now lived the sun is at his highest at mid-day in the north, at his lowest at midnight in the south. As is generally known he remains entirely above the horizon for four months of the summer (October-February) and entirely below the horizon for four months in the winter (April 21-August 21). About February 27, the end of summer, he begins to set and rise due south at midnight; the next day he sets a little earlier and dips a little deeper. During March and April he is going deeper and deeper every day, until, by the middle of April, he is set all the time except for just a peep over the northern horizon at mid-day, which is his last farewell before he goes away.

The reverse process takes place from August 21 onwards. On this date the sun just peeped above the sea to the north of our hut. The next day he rose a little higher and longer, and in a few weeks he was rising well in the east and sinking behind the Western Mountains. But he did not stop there. Soon he was rising in the S.E. until in the latter days of September he never rose, for he never set; but circled round us by day and night. On Midsummer Day (December 21) at the South Pole the sun circles round for twenty-four hours without changing his altitude for one minute of a degree, but elsewhere he is always rising in the sky until mid-day in the north and falling from that time until midnight in the south.

Often, far too often, it was blizzing, and it was impossible to go out except into the camp to take the observations, to care for the dogs, to get ice for water or to bring in stores. Even a short excursion of a few yards had to be made with great care under such circumstances, and certainly no one went outside more than was necessary, if only because one was obliged to dig the accumulated drift from the door before it was possible to proceed. Blizzard or no blizzard, most men were back in the hut soon after four, and from then until 6.30 worked steadily at their jobs. As supper time approached some kindly-disposed person would sit down and play on the Broadwood pianola which was one of our blessings, and so it was that we came to supper with good tempers as well as keen appetites.

Soup, in which the flavour of tomatoes occurred all too frequently, followed by seal or penguin, and twice a week by New Zealand mutton, with tinned vegetables, formed the basis of our meal, and this was followed by a pudding. We drank lime juice and water which sometimes included a suspicious penguin flavour derived from the ice slopes from which our water was quarried.

During our passage out to New Zealand in the ship (or as Meares always insisted on calling her, the steamer) it was our pleasant custom to have a glass of port or a liqueur after dinner. Alas, we had this no longer: after leaving New Zealand space allowed of little wine being carried in the Terra Nova, even if the general medical opinion of the expedition had not considered its presence undesirable. We had, however, a few cases for special festivals, as well as some excellent liqueur brandy which was carried as medical comforts on our sledge journeys. Any officer who allowed the distribution of this luxury on nearing the end of a journey became extremely popular.

Lack of wine probably led to the suspension of a custom which had prevailed on the Terra Nova, namely, the drinking of the old toast of Saturday night, "Sweethearts and wives; may our sweethearts become our wives, and our wives remain our sweethearts," and that more appropriate (in our case) toast of Sunday, namely, "absent friends." We had but few married officers, though I must say most survivors of the expedition hurried to remedy this single state of affairs when they returned to civilization. Only two of them are unmarried now. Most of them will probably make a success of it, for the good Arctic explorer has most of the defects and qualities of a good husband.

On the top of the pianola, close to the head of the table, lived the gramophone; and under the one looking-glass we possessed, which hung on the bulkhead of Scott's cubicle, was a home-made box with shelves on which lay our records. It was usual to start the gramophone after dinner, and its value may be imagined. It is necessary to be cut off from civilization and all that it means to enable you to realize fully the power music has to recall the past, or the depths of meaning in it to soothe the present and give hope for the future. We had also records of good classical music, and the kindly-disposed individual who played them had his reward in the pleasant atmosphere of homeliness which made itself felt. After dinner had been cleared away, some men sat on at the table occupied with books and games. Others dispersed to various jobs. In the matter of games it was noticeable that one would have its vogue and yield place to another without any apparent reason. For a few weeks it might be chess, which would then yield its place to draughts and backgammon, and again come into favour. It is a remarkable fact that, though we had playing cards with us none of our company appeared desirous to use them. In fact I cannot remember seeing a game of cards played except in the ship on the voyage from England.

THE SEA'S FRINGE OF ICE

With regard to books we were moderately well provided with good modern iction, and very well provided with such authors as Thackeray, Charlotte Brontë, Bulwer-Lytton and Dickens. With all respect to the kind givers of these books, I would suggest that the literature most acceptable to us in the circumstances under which we did most of our reading, that is in Winter Quarters, was the best of the more recent novels, such as Barrie, Kipling, Merriman and Maurice Hewlett. We certainly should have taken with us as much of Shaw, Barker, Ibsen and Wells as we could lay our hands on, for the train of ideas started by these works and the discussions to which they would have given rise would have been a godsend to us in our isolated circumstances. The one type of book in which we were rich was Arctic and Antarctic travel. We had a library of these given to us by Sir Lewis Beaumont and Sir Albert Markham which was very complete. They were extremely popular, though it is probably true that these are books which you want rather to read on your return than when you are actually experiencing a similar life. They were used extensively in discussions or lectures on such polar subjects as clothing, food rations, and the building of igloos, while we were constantly referring to them on specific points and getting useful hints, such as the use of an inner lining to our tents, and the mechanism of a blubber stove.

I have already spoken of the importance of maps and books of reference, and these should include a good encyclopaedia and dictionaries, English, Latin and Greek. Oates was generally deep in Napier's History of the Peninsular War, and some of us found Herbert Paul's History of Modern England a great stand-by. Most of us managed to find room in our personal gear when sledging for some book which did not weigh much and yet would last. Scott took some Browning on the Polar Journey, though I only saw him reading it once; Wilson took Maud and In Memoriam; Bowers always had so many weights to tally and observations to record on reaching camp that I feel sure he took no reading matter. Bleak House was the most successful book I ever took away sledging, though a volume of poetry was useful, because it gave one something to learn by heart and repeat during the blank hours of the daily march, when the idle mind is all too apt to think of food in times of hunger, or possibly of purely imaginary grievances, which may become distorted into real foundations of discord under the abnormal strain of living for months in the unrelieved company of three other men. If your companions have much the same tastes as yourself it is best to pool your allowance of weights and take one book which will offer a wide field of thought and discussion. I have heard Scott and Wilson bless the thought which led them to take Darwin's Origin of Species on their first Southern Journey. Such is the object of your sledging book, but you often want the book which you read for half an hour before you go to sleep at Winter Quarters to take you into the frivolous fripperies of modern social life which you may not know and may never wish to know, but which it is often pleasant to read about, and never so much so as when its charms are so remote as to be entirely tantalizing.

Scott, who always amazed me by the amount of work he got through without any apparent effort, was essentially the driving force of the expedition: in the hut quietly organizing, working out masses of figures, taking the greatest interest in the scientific work of the station, and perhaps turning out, quite by the way, an

elaborate paper on an abstruse problem in the neighbourhood; fond of his pip
and a good book, Browning, Hardy (Tess was one of his favourites), Galsworthy
Barrie was one of his greatest friends.

He was eager to accept suggestions if they were workable, and always kee
to sift even the most unlikely theories if by any means they could be shaped t
the desired end: a quick and modern brain which he applied with thoroughnes
to any question of practice or theory. Essentially an attractive personality, wit
strong likes and dislikes, he excelled in making his followers his friends by a fe
words of sympathy or praise: I have never known anybody, man or woman, wh
could be so attractive when he chose.

Sledging he went harder than any man of whom I have ever heard. Men neve
realized Scott until they had gone sledging with him. On our way up the Bearc
more Glacier we were going at top pressure some seventeen hours out of the twer
ty-four, and when we turned out in the morning we felt as though we had only ju:
turned in. By lunch time we felt that it was impossible to get through in the afte
noon a similar amount of work to that which we had done in the morning. A cu
of tea and two biscuits worked wonders, and the first two hours of the afternoon'
march went pretty well, indeed they were the best hours' marching of the day; bu
by the time we had been going some 4½ or 5 hours we were watching Scott for tha
glance to right and left which betokened the search for a good camping site. "Spe
oh!" Scott would cry, and then "How's the enemy, Titus?" to Oates, who woul
hopefully reply that it was, say, seven o'clock. "Oh, well, I think we'll go on a littl
bit more," Scott would say. "Come along!" It might be an hour or more before w
halted and made our camp: sometimes a blizzard had its silver lining. Scott coul
not wait. However welcome a blizzard could be to tired bodies (I speak only c
summer sledging), to Scott himself any delay was intolerable. And it is hard t
realize how difficult waiting may be to one in a responsible position. It was ou
simple job to follow, to get up when we were roused, to pull our hardest, to d
our special work as thoroughly and quickly as possible; it was Scott who had t
organize distances and weights and food, as well as do the same physical work a
ourselves. In sledging responsibility and physical work are combined to an exter
seldom if ever found elsewhere.

His was a subtle character, full of lights and shades.

England knows Scott as a hero; she has little idea of him as a man. He was ce
tainly the most dominating character in our not uninteresting community: indeec
there is no doubt that he would carry weight in any gathering of human being:
But few who knew him realized how shy and reserved the man was, and it wa
partly for this reason that he so often laid himself open to misunderstanding.

Add to this that he was sensitive, femininely sensitive, to a degree whic
might be considered a fault, and it will be clear that leadership to such a man ma
be almost a martyrdom, and that the confidence so necessary between leader an
followers, which must of necessity be based upon mutual knowledge and trus
becomes in itself more difficult. It wanted an understanding man to appreciat
Scott quickly; to others knowledge came with experience.

He was not a *very* strong man physically, and was in his youth a weakly child, at one time not expected to live. But he was well proportioned, with broad shoulders and a good chest, a stronger man than Wilson, weaker than Bowers or Seaman Evans. He suffered from indigestion, and told me at the top of the Beardmore that he never expected to go on during the first stage of the ascent.

Temperamentally he was a weak man, and might very easily have been an irritable autocrat. As it was he had moods and depressions which might last for weeks, and of these there is ample evidence in his diary. The man with the nerves gets things done, but sometimes he has a terrible time in doing them. He cried more easily than any man I have ever known.

What pulled Scott through was character, sheer good grain, which ran over and under and through his weaker self and clamped it together. It would be stupid to say he had all the virtues: he had, for instance, little sense of humour, and he was a bad judge of men. But you have only to read one page of what he wrote towards the end to see something of his sense of justice. For him justice was God. Indeed I think you must read all those pages; and if you have read them once, you will probably read them again. You will not need much imagination to see what manner of man he was.

And notwithstanding the immense fits of depression which attacked him, Scott was the strongest combination of a strong mind in a strong body that I have ever known. And this because he was so weak! Naturally so peevish, highly strung, irritable, depressed and moody. Practically such a conquest of himself, such vitality, such push and determination, and withal in himself such personal and magnetic charm. He was naturally an idle man, he has told us so;[134] he had been a poor man, and he had a horror of leaving those dependent upon him in difficulties. You may read it over and over again in his last letters and messages.[135]

He will go down to history as the Englishman who conquered the South Pole and who died as fine a death as any man has had the honour to die. His triumphs are many—but the Pole was not by any means the greatest of them. Surely the greatest was that by which he conquered his weaker self, and became the strong leader whom we went to follow and came to love.

Scott had under him this first year in his Main Party a total of 15 officers and 9 men. These officers may be divided into three executive officers and twelve scientific staff, but the distinction is very rough, inasmuch as a scientist such as Wilson was every bit as executive as anybody else, and the executive officers also did much scientific work. I will try here briefly to give the reader some idea of the personality and activities of these men as they work any ordinary day in the hut. It should be noticed that not all the men we had with us were brought to do sledging work. Some were chosen rather for their scientific knowledge than for their physical or other fitness for sledging. The regular sledgers in this party of officers were Scott, Wilson, Evans, Bowers, Oates (ponies), Meares (dogs), Atkinson (surgeon), Wright (physicist), Taylor (physiographer), Debenham (geologist),

---

[134] *Scott's Last Expedition*, vol. i. p. 604.
[135] *Scott's Last Expedition*, vol. i. pp. 599, 602, 607.

Gran and myself, while Day was to drive his motors as far as they would go on the Polar Journey. This leaves Simpson, who was the meteorologist and whose observations had of necessity to be continuous; Nelson, whose observations into marine biology, temperatures of sea, salinity, currents and tides came under the same heading; and Ponting, whose job was photography, and whose success in this art everybody recognizes.

However much of good I may write of Wilson, his many friends in England those who served with him on the ship or in the hut, and most of all those who had the good fortune to sledge with him (for it is sledging which is far the greatest test) will all be dissatisfied, for I know that I cannot do justice to his value. If you knew him you could not like him: you simply had to love him. Bill was of the salt of the earth. If I were asked what quality it was before others that made him so useful, and so lovable, I think I should answer that it was because he never for one moment thought of himself. In this respect also Bowers, of whom I will speak in a moment, was most extraordinary, and in passing may I be allowed to say that this is a most necessary characteristic of a good Antarctic traveller? We had many such officers and seamen, and the success of the expedition was in no small measure due to the general and unselfish way in which personal likes and dislikes, wishes or tastes were ungrudgingly subordinated to the common weal. Wilson and Pennell set an example of expedition first and the rest nowhere which others followed ungrudgingly: it pulled us through more than one difficulty which might have led to friction.

Wilson was a man of many parts. He was Scott's right-hand man, he was the expedition's Chief of the Scientific Staff: he was a doctor of St. George's Hospital and a zoologist specializing in vertebrates. His published work on whales, penguins and seals contained in the Scientific Report of the Discovery Expedition is still the best available, and makes excellent reading even to the non-scientist. On the outward journey of the Terra Nova he was still writing up his work for the Royal Commission on Grouse Disease, the published report of which he never lived to see. But those who knew him best will probably remember Wilson by his water-colour paintings rather than by any other form of his many-sided work.

As a boy his father sent him away on rambling holidays, the only condition being that he should return with a certain number of drawings. I have spoken of the drawings which he made when sledging or when otherwise engaged away from painting facilities, as at Hut Point. He brought back to Winter Quarters a note-book filled with such sketches of outlines and colours: of sunsets behind the Western Mountains: of lights reflected in the freezing sea or in the glass houses of the ice foot: of the steam clouds on Erebus by day and of the Aurora Australis by night. Next door to Scott he rigged up for himself a table, consisting of two venesta cases on end supporting a large drawing-board some four feet square. On this he set to work systematically to paint the effects which he had seen and noted. He painted with his paper wet, and necessarily therefore, he worked quickly. An admirer of Ruskin, he wished to paint what he saw as truly as possible. If he failed to catch the effect he wished, he tore up the picture however beautiful the result he had obtained. There is no doubt as to the faithfulness of his colouring: the picture recalled then and will still recall now in intimate detail the effects which we saw together. As to the accuracy of his drawing it is sufficient to say that in the Discovery Expedition Scott wrote on his Southern Journey:

"Wilson is the most indefatigable person. When it is fine and clear, at the end of our fatiguing days he will spend two or three hours seated in the door of the tent, sketching each detail of the splendid mountainous coast-scene to the west. His sketches are most astonishingly accurate; I have tested his proportions by actual angular measurement and found them correct."[136]

In addition to the drawings of land, pack, icebergs and Barrier, the primary object of which was scientific and geographical, Wilson has left a number of paintings of atmospheric phenomena which are not only scientifically accurate but are also exceedingly beautiful. Of such are the records of auroral displays, parhelions, paraselene, lunar halos, fog bows, irridescent clouds, refracted images of mountains and mirage generally. If you look at a picture of a parhelion by Wilson not only can you be sure that the mock suns, circles and shafts appeared in the sky as they are shown on paper, but you can also rest assured that the number of degrees between, say, the sun and the outer ring of light were in fact such as he has represented them. You can also be certain in looking at his pictures that if cirrus cloud is shown, then cirrus and not stratus cloud was in the sky: if it is not shown, then the sky was clear. It is accuracy such as this which gives an exceptional value to work viewed from a scientific standpoint. Mention should also be made of the paintings and drawings made constantly by Wilson for the various specialists on the expedition whenever they wished for colour records of their specimens; in this connection the paintings of fish and various parasites are especially valuable.

I am not specially qualified to judge Wilson from the artistic point of view. But if you want accuracy of drawing, truth of colour, and a reproduction of the soft and delicate atmospheric effects which obtain in this part of the world, then you have them here. Whatever may be said of the painting as such, it is undeniable that an artist of this type is of inestimable value to an expedition which is doing scientific and geographical work in a little-known part of the earth.

Wilson himself set a low value on his artistic capacity. We used to discuss what Turner would have produced in a land which offered colour effects of such beauty. If we urged him to try and paint some peculiar effect and he felt that to do so was beyond his powers he made no scruple of saying so. His colour is clear, his brush-work clean: and he handled sledging subjects with the vigour of a professional who knew all there was to be known about a sledging life.

---

[136] Scott, *Voyage of the Discovery*, vol. ii. p. 53.

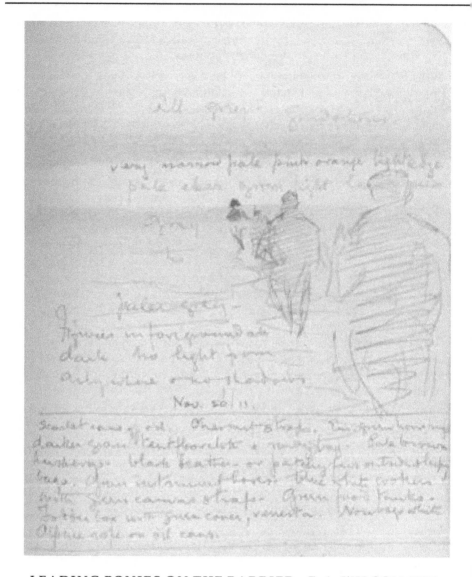

LEADING PONIES ON THE BARRIER—E. A. WILSON, DEL.

Scott and Wilson worked hand in hand to further the scientific objects of the expedition. For Scott, though no specialist in any one branch, had a most genuine love of science. "Science—the rock foundation of all effort," he wrote; and whether discussing ice problems with Wright, meteorology with Simpson, or geology with Taylor, he showed not only a mind which was receptive and keen to learn, but a knowledge which was quick to offer valuable suggestions. I remember Pennell condemning anything but scientific learning in dealing with the problems round us; 'no guesswork' was his argument. But he emphatically made an exception of Scott, who had an uncanny knack of hitting upon a solution. Over and over again in his diary we can read of the interest he took in pure and applied science, and it is oubtful whether this side of an expedition in high northern or southern latitudes as ever been more fortunate in their leader.

Wilson's own share in the scientific results is more obvious because he was the director of the work. But no published reports will give an adequate idea of the bility he showed in co-ordinating the various interests of a varied community, or of the tact he displayed in dealing with the difficulties which arose. Above all is judgment was excellent, and Scott as well as the rest of us relied upon him to very great extent. The value of judgment in a land where a wrong decision may mean disaster as well as loss of life is beyond all price; weather in which changes re most sudden is a case in point, also the state of sea-ice, the direction to be followed in difficult country when sledging, the best way of taking crevassed areas when they must be crossed, and all the ways by which the maximum of result may be combined with the minimum of danger in a land where Nature is sometimes almost too big an enemy to fight: all this wants judgment, and if possible experience. Wilson could supply both, for his experience was as wide as that of Scott, and I have constantly known Scott change his mind after a talk with Bill. For the rest I give quotations from Scott's diary:

"He has had a hand in almost every lecture given, and has been consulted in almost every effort which has been made towards the solution of the practical or theoretical problems of our Polar world."[137]

Again:

"Words must always fail me when I talk of Bill Wilson. I believe he really is the finest character I ever met—the closer one gets to him the more there is to admire. Every quality is so solid and dependable; cannot you imagine how that counts down here? Whatever the matter, one knows Bill will be sound, shrewdly practical, intensely loyal and quite unselfish. Add to this a wider knowledge of persons and things than is at first guessable, a quiet vein of humour and really consummate tact, and you have some idea of his values. I think he is the most popular member of the party, and that is saying much."[138]

And at the end, when Scott himself lay dying, he wrote to Mrs. Wilson:

"I can do no more to comfort you, than to tell you that he died as he lived, a brave, true man—the best of comrades and staunchest of friends."[139]

Physically Scott had been a delicate boy but developed into a strong man, 5 feet 9 inches in height, 11 stone 6 lbs. in weight, with a chest measurement of 39¼ inches. Wilson was not a particularly strong man. On leaving with the Discovery he was but lately cured of consumption, yet he went with Scott to his farthest South, and helped to get Shackleton back alive. Shackleton owed his life to those two. Wilson was of a slimmer, more athletic build, a great walker, 5 feet 10½ inches in height, 11 stones in weight, with a chest measurement of 36 inches. He was an ideal example of my contention, which I believe can be proved many times over

---

[137] *Scott's Last Expedition,* vol. i. p. 295.
[138] *Scott's Last Expedition,* vol. i. pp. 432-433.
[139] *Ibid.* p. 597.

to be a fact, that it is not strength of body but rather strength of will which carrie
a man farthest where mind and body are taxed at the same time to their utmo:
limit. Scott was 43 years of age at his death, and Wilson 39.

Bowers was of a very different build. Aged 28, he was only 5 feet 4 inche
in height while his chest measurement (which I give more as a general guide t
his physique than for any other reason) was 40 inches, and his weight 12 stone
He was recommended to Scott by Sir Clements Markham, who was dining or
day with Captain Wilson-Barker on the Worcester, on which ship Bowers wa
trained. Bowers was then home from India, and the talk turned to the Antarcti
Wilson-Barker turned to Sir Clements in the course of conversation and alludin
to Bowers said: "Here is a man who will be leading one of those expeditions som
day."

He lived a rough life after passing from the Worcester into the merchant se:
vice, sailing five times round the world in the Loch Torridon. Thence he passe
into the service of the Royal Indian Marine, commanded a river gunboat on th
Irrawaddy, and afterwards served on H.M.S. Fox, where he had considerable e:
perience, often in open boats, preventing the gun-running which was carried o
by the Afghans in the Persian Gulf.

Thence he came to us.

It is at any rate a curious fact, and it may be a significant one, that Bower
who enjoyed a greater resistance to cold than any man on this expedition, joine
it direct from one of the hottest places on the globe. My knowledge is insufficier
to say whether it is possible that any trace can be found here of cause and effec
especially since the opposite seems to be the more common experience, in tha
such people as return from India to England generally find the English winte
trying. I give the fact for what it may be worth, remarking only that the cold of a
English winter is generally damp, while that of the Antarctic is dry, so far at an
rate as the atmosphere is concerned. Bowers himself always professed the greate:
indifference not only to cold, but also to heat, and his indifference was not that c
a 'poseur,' as many experiences will show.

At the same time he was temperamentally one who refused to admit difficu
ties. Indeed, if he did not actually welcome them he greeted them with scorn, an
in scorning went far to master them. Scott believed that difficulties were made t
be overcome: Bowers certainly believed that he was the man to overcome then
This self-confidence was based on a very deep and broad religious feeling, an
carried conviction with it. The men swore by him both on the ship and ashor
"He's all right," was their judgment of his seamanship, which was admirable. "
like being with Birdie, because I always know where I am," was the remark mad
to me by an officer one evening as we pitched the tent. We had just been spendin
some time in picking up a depôt which a less able man might well have missed.

As he was one of the two or three greatest friends of my life I find it hard t
give the reader a mental picture of Birdie Bowers which will not appear extrava
gant. There were times when his optimism appeared forced and formal though
believe it was not really so: there were times when I have almost hated him for hi

infernal cheerfulness. To those accustomed to judge men by the standards of their fashionable and corseted drawing-rooms Bowers appeared crude. "You couldn't kill that man if you took a pole-axe to him," was the comment of a New Zealander at a dance at Christchurch. Such men may be at a discount in conventional life; but give me a snowy ice-floe waving about on the top of a black swell, a ship thrown aback, a sledge-party almost shattered, or one that has just upset their supper on to the floorcloth of the tent (which is much the same thing), and I will lie down and cry for Bowers to come and lead me to food and safety.

Those whom the gods love die young. The gods loved him, if indeed it be benevolent to show your favourites a clear, straight, shining path of life, with plenty of discomfort and not a little pain, but with few doubts and no fears. Browning might well have had Bowers in mind when he wrote of

One who never turned his back, but marched breast forward;
Never doubted clouds would break;
Never dreamed, though right were worsted, wrong would triumph;
Held we fall to rise, are baffled to fight better,
Sleep to wake.

There was nothing subtle about him. He was transparently simple, straightforward and unselfish. His capacity for work was prodigious, and when his own work happened to take less than his full time he characteristically found activity in serving a scientist or exercising an animal. So he used to help to send up balloons with self-recording instruments attached to them, and track the threads which led to them when detached. He was responsible for putting up the three outlying meteorological screens and read them more often than anybody else. At times he looked after some of the dogs because at the moment there was nobody else whose proper job it happened to be, and he took a particular fancy to one of our strongest huskies called Krisravitza, which is the Russian (so I'm told) for 'most beautiful.' This fancy originated in the fact that to Kris, as the most truculent of our untamed devils, fell a large share of well-deserved punishment. A living thing in trouble be it dog or man was something to be helped. Being the smallest man in the party he schemed to have allotted to him the largest pony available both for the Depôt and Polar Journeys. Their exercise, when he succeeded, was a matter for experiment, for his knowledge of horses was as limited as his love of animals was intense. He started to exercise his second pony (for the first was lost on the floe) by riding him. "I'll soon get used to him," he said one day when Victor had just deposited him in the tide-crack, "to say nothing of his getting used to me," he added in a more subdued voice.

This was open-air work, and as such more congenial than that which had to be done inside the hut. But his most important work was indoors, and he brought to it just the same restless enthusiasm which allowed no leisure for reading or relaxation.

He joined as one of the ship's officers in London. Given charge of the stores, the way in which he stowed the ship aroused the admiration of even the stevedores, especially when he fell down the main hatch one morning on to the pig-iron below, recovered consciousness in about half a minute, and continued work for the rest of the day as though nothing had happened.

As the voyage out proceeded it became obvious that his knowledge of the stores and undefeatable personality would be of great value to the shore party, and it was decided that he should land, to his great delight. He was personally responsible for all food supplies, whether for home consumption or for sledging, for all sledging stores and the distribution of weights, the loading of sledges, the consumption of coal, the issue of clothing, bosun's stores, and carpenter's stores. Incidentally the keeper of stores wanted a very exact knowledge of the cases which contained them, for the drifts of snow soon buried them as they lay in the camp outside.

As time proved his capacity Scott left one thing after another in Bowers' hands. Scott was a leader of men, and it is a good quality in such to delegate work from themselves on to those who prove their power to shoulder the burden. Undoubtedly Bowers saved Scott a great deal of work, and gave him time which he might not otherwise have been able to spare to interest himself in the scientific work of the station, greatly to its benefit, and do a good deal of useful writing. The two ways in which Bowers helped Scott most this winter were in the preparation of the plans and the working out of the weights of the Southern Journey, which shall be discussed later, and in the routine work of the station, for which he was largely responsible, and which ran so smoothly that I am unable to tell the reader how the stores were issued, or the dinner settled, by what rule the working parties for fetching ice for water and other kindred jobs about the camp were ordered. They just happened, and I don't know how. I only know that Bowers had the bunk above mine in the hut, and that when I was going to sleep he was generally standing on a chair and using his own bunk as a desk, and I conclude from the numerous lists of stores and weights which are now in my hands that these were being produced. Anyway the job was done, and the fact that we knew nothing about it goes far to prove how efficiently it was carried through.

For him difficulties simply did not exist. I have never known a more buoyant virile nature. Scott's writings abound in references to the extraordinary value he placed upon his help, and after the share which he took in the Depôt and Winter Journeys it was clear that he would probably be taken in the Polar Party, as indeed proved to be the case. No man of that party better deserved his place. "I believe he is the hardest traveller that ever undertook a Polar Journey, as well as one of the most undaunted."[140]

The standard is high.

---

[140] *Scott's Last Expedition*, vol. i. p. 362.

FROZEN SEA AND CLIFFS OF ICE

Bowers gave us two of our best lectures, the first on the Evolution of Sledge Foods, at the end of which he discussed our own rations on the Depôt Journey, and made suggestions which he had worked out scientifically for those of the Polar Journey. His arguments were sound enough to disarm the hostility if not to convert to his opinions at least one scientist who had come to hear him strongly of opinion that an untrained man should not discuss so complex a subject. The second lecture, on the Evolution of Polar Clothing, was also the fruit of much work. The general conclusion come to (and this was after the Winter Journey) was that our own clothing and equipment could not be bettered in any important respect, though it must be always understood that the expedition wore wind-proof clothing and not furs, except for hands and feet. When man-hauling, wind-proof, I am convinced, cannot be improved upon, but for dog-driving in cold weather I suspect that furs may be better.

The table was cleared after supper and we sat round it for these lectures three times a week. There was no compulsion about them, and the seamen only turned up for those which especially interested them, such as Meares' vivid account of his journeyings on the Eastern or Chinese borderland of Thibet. This land is inhabited by the 'Eighteen Tribes,' the original inhabitants of Thibet who were driven out by the present inhabitants, and Meares told us chiefly of the Lolos who killed his companion Brook after having persuaded him that they were friendly and anxious to help him. "He had no pictures and very makeshift maps, yet he held us really entranced for nearly two hours by the sheer interest of his adventures. The spirit of the wanderer is in Meares' blood: he has no happiness but in the wild places of the earth. I have never met so extreme a type. Even now he is looking forward to getting away by himself to Hut Point, tired already of our scant measure of civilization."[141]

Three lectures a week were too many in the opinion of the majority. The second winter with our very reduced company we had two a week, and I feel sure that this was an improvement. No officer nor seaman, however, could have had too many of Ponting's lectures, which gave us glimpses into many lands illustrated by his own inimitable slides. Thus we lived every now and then for a short hour in Burmah, India or Japan, in scenes of trees and flowers and feminine charm which were the very antithesis of our present situation, and we were all the better for it. Ponting also illustrated the subjects of other lectures with home-made slides of photographs taken during the autumn or from printed books. But for the most part the lecturers were perforce content with designs and plans, drawn on paper and pinned one on the top of the other upon a large drawing-board propped up on the table and torn off sheet by sheet.

From the practical point of view the most interesting evening to us was that on which Scott produced the Plan of the Southern Journey. The reader may ask why this was not really prepared until the winter previous to the journey itself, and the answer clearly is that it was impossible to arrange more than a rough idea until the autumn sledging had taught its lesson in food, equipment, relative reliability of dogs, ponies and men, and until the changes and chances of our life showed exactly what transport would be available for the following sledging season. Thus it was with lively anticipation that we sat down on May 8, an advisory committee as it were, to hear and give our suggestions on the scheme which Scott had evolved in the early weeks of the winter after the adventures of the Depôt Journey and the loss of six ponies.

[141] *Scott's Last Expedition*, vol. i. p. 396.

It was on just such a winter night, too, that Scott read his interesting paper n the Ice Barrier and Inland Ice which will probably form the basis for all future ʋork on these subjects. The Barrier, he maintained, is probably afloat, and covers t least five times the extent of the North Sea with an average thickness of some 00 feet, though it has only been possible to get the very roughest of levels. Acording to the movement of a depôt laid in the Discovery days the Barrier moved 08 yards towards the open Ross Sea in 13½ months. It must be admitted that the inclination of the ice-sheet is not sufficient to cause this, and the old idea that the lacier streams flowing down from Inland Plateau provide the necessary impetus s imperfect. It was Simpson's suggestion that "the deposition of snow on the Barier leads to an expansion due to the increase of weight." Some admittedly vague ideas as to the extent and character of the inland ice-sheet ended a clever and conincing paper which contained a lot of good reasoning.

Simpson proved an excellent lecturer, and in meteorology and in the explaiation of the many instruments with which his corner of the hut was full he posessed subjects which interested and concerned everybody. Nelson on Biological ʾroblems and Taylor on Physiography were always interesting. "Taylor, I dreamt ·f your lecture last night. How could I live so long in the world and not know omething of so fascinating a subject!" Thus Scott on the morning following one of hese lectures.[142] Wright on Ice Problems, Radium, and the Origin of Matter had iighly technical subjects which left many of us somewhat befogged. But Atkinson ·n Scurvy had an audience each member of which felt that he had a personal interst in the subject under discussion. Indeed one of his hearers was to suffer the adanced stage of this dread disease within six months. Atkinson inclined to Almroth Vright's theory that scurvy is due to an acid intoxication of the blood caused by ·acteria. He described the litmus-paper test which was practised on us monthly, nd before and after sledge journeys. In this the blood of each individual is drawn nd various strengths of dilute sulphuric acid are added to it until it is neutralized, he healthy man showing normal 30 to 50, while the man with scorbutic signs will ·e normal 50 to 90 according to the stage to which he has reached. The only thing ʋhich is certain to stop scurvy is fresh vegetables: fresh meat when life is otherʋise under extreme conditions will not do so, an instance being the Siege of Paris ʋhen they had plenty of horse meat. In 1795 voyages were being ruined by scurvy nd Anson lost 300 out of 500 men, but in that year the first discoveries were made nd lime-juice was introduced by Blaine. From this time scurvy practically disapʾeared from the Navy, and there was little scurvy in Nelson's days; but the reason s not clear, since, according to modern research, lime-juice only helps to prevent t. It continued in the Merchant Service, and in a decade from about 1865 some 400 ases were admitted into the Dreadnought Hospital, whereas in the decade 1887 to 896 there were only 38 cases. We had, at Cape Evans, a salt of sodium to be used ·o alkalize the blood as an experiment, if necessity arose. Darkness, cold, and hard ʋork are in Atkinson's opinion important causes of scurvy.

Nansen was an advocate of variety of diet as being anti-scorbutic, and Scott ecalled a story told him by Nansen which he had never understood. It appeared

---

[142] *With Scott: The Silver Lining*, Taylor, p. 240.

that some men had eaten tins of tainted food. Some of it was slightly tainted, som
of it was really bad. They rejected the really bad ones, and ate those only whic
were slightly tainted. "And of course," said Nansen, "they should have eaten th
worst."

I have since asked Nansen about this story. He tells me that he must hav
been referring to the crew of the Windward, the ship of the Jackson-Harmswort
Expedition to Franz Josef Land in 1894-97. The crew of this ship, which was trav
elling to and from civilization, got scurvy, though the land party kept healthy. C
this Jackson writes: "In the case of the crew of the Windward I fear that there wa
considerable carelessness in the use of tinned meats that were not free from tain
although tins quite gone were rejected.... We [on shore] largely used fresh bear
meat, and the crew of the Windward were also allowed as much as they could b
induced to eat. They, however, preferred tinned meat several days a week to
diet of bear's meat alone; and some of the crew had such a prejudice against bear
meat as to refuse to eat it at all."[143]

Of course tainted food should not have been eaten at all, but if it had to b
eaten, then, according to Nansen, the ptomaines which cause scurvy in the earli
stages of decomposition are destroyed by the ferment which forms in the late
stages. They should therefore have taken the worst tins, if any at all.

Wilson was strongly of opinion that fresh meat alone would stop scurvy: o
the Discovery seal meat cured it. As to scurvy on Scott's Discovery Southern Jour
ney, he made light of it: however, during the Winter Journey I remember Wilso
stating that Shackleton several times fell in a faint as he got outside the tent, an
he seems to have been seriously ill: Wilson knew that he himself had scurvy som
time before the others knew it, because the discoloration of his gums did not shov
in front for some time. He did not think their dogs on that journey had scurvy
but ptomaine poisoning from fish which had travelled through the tropics. H
was of opinion that on returning from sledge journeys on the Discovery they ha
wrongly attributed to scurvy such symptoms as rash on the body, swollen leg
and ankles, which were rather the result of excessive fatigue. I may add that w
had these signs on our return from the Winter Journey.

Then there were lectures on Geology by Debenham, on birds and beasts an
also on Sketching by Wilson, on Surveying by Evans: but perhaps no lecture re
mains more vividly in my memory than that given by Oates on what *we* calle
'The Mismanagement of Horses.' Of course to all of us who were relying upo
the ponies for the first stage of the Southern Journey the subject was of interest a
well as utility, but the greater share of interest centred upon the lecturer, for it wa
certainly supposed that taciturn Titus could not have concealed about his perso
the gift of the gab, and it was as certain as it could be that the whole business wa
most distasteful to him. Imagine our delight when he proved to have an elaborat
discourse with full notes of which no one had seen the preparation. "I have bee
fortunate in securing another night," he mentioned amidst mirth, and proceede
to give us the most interesting and able account of the minds and bodies of horse
in general and ours in particular. He ended with a story of a dinner-party at whic

[143] F. G. Jackson, *A Thousand Days in the Arctic*, vol. ii. pp. 380-381.

ιe was a guest, probably against his will. A young lady was so late that the party ;at down to dinner without waiting longer. Soon she arrived covered with blushes ιnd confusion. "I'm so sorry," she said, "but that horse was the limit, he ..." "Perιaps it was a jibber," suggested her hostess to help her out. "No, he was a — —. I ιeard the cabby tell him so several times."

Titus Oates was the most cheerful and lovable old pessimist that you could ιmagine. Often, after tethering and feeding our ponies at a night camp on the Barιier, we would watch the dog-teams coming up into camp. "I'll give these dogs ιen days more," he would murmur in a voice such as some people used when ιhey heard of a British victory. I am acquainted with so few dragoons that I do not ιnow their general characteristics. Few of them, I imagine, would have gone about νith the slouch which characterized his method of locomotion, nor would many οf them have dined in a hat so shabby that it was picked off the peg and passed ιound as a curiosity.

He came to look after the horses, and as an officer in the Inniskillings he, no ιoubt, had excellent training. But his skill went far deeper than that. There was ιittle he didn't know about horses, and the pity is that he did not choose our ponies ιor us in Siberia: we should have had a very different lot. In addition to his general ιharge of them all, Oates took as his own pony the aforesaid devil Christopher ιor the Southern Journey and for previous training. We shall hear much more of Christopher, who appeared to have come down to the Antarctic to initiate the νell-behaved inhabitants into all the vices of civilization, but from beginning to ɛnd Oates' management of this animal might have proved a model to any goverιor of a lunatic asylum. His tact, patience and courage, for Christopher was a very ιangerous beast, remain some of the most vivid recollections of a very gallant ξentleman.

In this connection let me add that no animals could have had more considɛrate and often self-sacrificing treatment than these ponies of ours. Granted that ιhey must be used at all (and I do not mean to enter into that question) they were ιed, trained, and even clothed as friends and companions rather than as beasts οf burden. They were never hit, a condition to which they were clearly unaccusιomed. They lived far better than they had before, and all this was done for them ιn spite of the conditions under which we ourselves lived. We became very fond of ɔur beasts but we could not be blind to their faults. The mind of a horse is a very ιimited concern, relying almost entirely upon memory. He rivals our politicians ιn that he has little real intellect. Consequently, when the pony was faced with ɔonditions different from those to which he was accustomed, he showed but little ιdaptability; and when you add to this frozen harness and rugs, with all their ιtraps and buckles and lashings, an incredible facility for eating anything within ιeach including his own tethering ropes and the headstalls, fringes and whatnots οf his companions, together with our own scanty provisions and a general wish ιo do anything except the job of the moment, it must be admitted that the pony ιeader's lot was full of occasions for bad temper. Nevertheless leaders and ponies νere on the best of terms (excepting always Christopher), which is really not surρrising when you come to think that most of the leaders were sailors whose love of animals is profound.

A lean-to roof was built against the northern side of the hut, and the ends an open side were boarded up. This building when buttressed by the bricks of coa which formed our fuel, and drifted up with snow by the blizzards, formed a extremely sheltered and even warm stable. The ponies stood in stalls with thei heads towards the hut and divided from it by a corridor; the bars which kept ther in carried also their food boxes. They lay down very little, the ground was too colc and Oates was of opinion that litter would not have benefited them if we had ha space in the ship to bring it. The floor of their stall was formed of the gravel o which the hut was built. On any future occasion it might be worth consideratio whether a flooring of wood might add to their comfort. As you walked down thi narrow passage you passed a line of heads, many of which would have a nip a you in the semi-darkness, and at the far end Oates had rigged up for himself blubber stove, more elaborate than the one we had made with the odds and end at Hut Point, but in principle the same, in that the fids of sealskin with the blubbe attached to them were placed on a grid, and the heat generated caused them t drop their oil on to ashes below which formed the fire. This fire not only warme the stable, but melted the snow to water the ponies and heated their bran mashe I do not wonder that this warm companionable home appealed to their mind when they were exercising in the cold, dark, windy sea-ice: they were always try ing to get rid of their leader, and if successful generally went straight back to th hut. Here they would dodge their pursuers until such time as they were sick c the game, when they quietly walked into the stable of their own accord to be wel comed with triumphant squeals and kickings by their companions.

I have already spoken of their exercise. Their ration during the winter was a follows:

- 8 A.M. Chaff.
- 12 NOON. Snow. Chaff and oats or oil-cake alternate days.
- 5 P.M. Snow. Hot bran mash with oil-cake, or boiled oats and chaff;
- finally a small quantity of hay.

In the spring they were got into condition on hard food all cold, and by a care fully increased scale of exercise during the latter part of which they drew sledge with very light loads.

Unfortunately I have no record as to what changes of feeding stuffs Oate would have made if it had been possible. Certainly we should not have brough the bales of compressed fodder, which as I have already explained,[144] was the oretically green wheat cut young, but practically no manner of use as a food though of some use perhaps as bulk. Probably he would have used hay for thi purpose at Winter Quarters had our stock of it not been very limited, for hay take up too much room on a ship when every square inch of stowage space is of val ue. The original weights of fodder with which we left New Zealand were: com

---

[144] See p. 179.

pressed chaff, 30 tons; hay, 5 tons; oil-cake, 5-6 tons; bran, 4-5 tons; and two kinds of oats, of which the white was better than the black. We wanted more bran than we had.[145] This does not exhaust our list of feeding stuffs, for one of our ponies called Snippets would eat blubber, and so far as I know it agreed with him.

We left New Zealand with nineteen ponies, seventeen of which were destined for the Main Party and two for the help of Campbell in the exploration of King Edward VII.'s Land. Two of these died in the big gale at sea, and we landed fifteen ponies at Cape Evans in January. Of these we lost six on the Depôt Journey, while Hackenschmidt, who was a vicious beast, sickened and wasted away in our absence, for no particular reason that we could discover, until there was nothing to do but shoot him. Thus eight only out of the original seventeen Main Party ponies which started from New Zealand were left by the beginning of the winter.

I have told[146] how, during our absence on the Depôt Journey, the ship had tried to land Campbell with his two ponies on King Edward VII.'s Land, but had been prevented from reaching it by pack ice. Coasting back in search of a landing place they found Amundsen in the Bay of Whales. Under the circumstances Campbell decided not to land his party there but to try and land on the north coast of South Victoria Land, in which he was finally successful. In the interval the ship returned to Cape Evans with the news, and since he was of opinion that his animals would be useless to him in that region he took the opportunity to swim the two ponies ashore, a distance of half a mile, for the ship could get no nearer and the sea-ice had gone. Thus we started the winter with Campbell's two ponies (Jehu and Chinaman), two ponies which had survived the Depôt Journey (Nobby and James Pigg), and six ponies which had been left at Cape Evans (Snatcher, Snippets, Bones, Victor, Michael and Christopher) a total of ten.

Of these ten Christopher was the only real devil with vice, but he was a strong pony, and it was clear that he would be useful if he could be managed. Bones, Snatcher, Victor and Snippets were all useful ponies. Michael was a highly-strung nice beast, but his value was doubtful; Chinaman was more doubtful still, and it was questionable sometimes whether Jehu would be able to pull anything at all. This leaves Nobby and Jimmy Pigg, both of which were with us on the Depôt Journey. Nobby was the best of the two; he was the only survivor from the sea-ice disaster, and I am not sure that his rescue did not save the situation with regard to the Pole. Jimmy Pigg was wending his way slowly back from Corner Camp at this time and so was also saved. He was a weak pony but did extremely well on the Polar Journey. It may be coincidence that these two ponies, the only ponies which had gained previous sledging experience, did better according to their strength than any of the others, but I am inclined to believe that their familiarity with the conditions on the Barrier was of great value to them, doing away with much useless worry and exhaustion.

And so it will be understood with what feelings of anxiety any cases of injury or illness to our ponies were regarded. The cases of injury were few and of small

[145] *Scott's Last Expedition*, vol. i. p. 4.
[146] See pp. 130-134.

importance, thanks to the care with which they were exercised in the dark on ice which was by no means free from inequalities. Let me explain in passing that this ice is almost always covered by at least a thin layer of drifted snow and for the most part is not slippery. Every now and then there would be a great banging and crashing heard through the walls of the hut in the middle of the night. The watchman would run out, Oates put on his boots, Scott be audibly uneasy. It was generally Bones or Chinaman kicking their stalls, perhaps to keep themselves warm, but by the time the watchman had reached the stable he would be met by a line of sleepy faces blinking at him in the light of the electric torch, each saying plainly that he could not possibly have been responsible for a breach of the peace!

But antics might easily lead to accidents, and more than once a pony was found twisted up in some way in his stall, or even to have fallen to the ground. Their heads were tied on either side to the stanchions of the stall, and so if they tried to lie down complications might arise. More alarming was the one serious case of illness, preceded by a slighter case of a similar nature in another pony. Jimmy Pigg had a slight attack of colic in the middle of June, but he was feeding all right again during the evening of the same day. It was at noon, July 14, that Bones went off his feed. This was followed by spasms of acute pain. "Every now and again he attempted to lie down, and Oates eventually thought it was wiser to allow him to do so. Once down, his head gradually drooped until he lay at length, every now and then twitching very horribly with the pain, and from time to time raising his head and even scrambling to his legs when it grew intense. I don't think I ever realized before how pathetic a horse could be under such conditions; no sound escapes him, his misery can only be indicated by those distressing spasms and by dumb movement of the head with a patient expression always suggestive of appeal."[147] Towards midnight it seemed that we were to lose him, and, apart from other considerations, we knew that unless we could keep all the surviving animals alive the risks of failure in the coming journey were much increased.

"It was shortly after midnight when I [Scott] was told that the animal seemed a little easier. At 2.30 I was again in the stable and found the improvement had been maintained; the horse still lay on its side with outstretched head, but the spasms had ceased, its eye looked less distressed, and its ears pricked to occasional noises. As I stood looking it suddenly raised its head and rose without effort to its legs; then in a moment, as though some bad dream had passed, it began to nose at some hay and at its neighbour. Within three minutes it had drunk a bucket of water and had started to feed."[148]

The immediate cause of the trouble was indicated by "a small ball of semi-fermented hay covered with mucus and containing tape-worms; so far not very serious, but unfortunately attached to this mass was a strip of the lining of the intestine."[149]

The recovery of Bones was uninterrupted. Two day later another pony went

[147] *Scott's Last Expedition,* vol. i. p. 352.
[148] *Ibid.* p. 353.
[149] *Scott's Last Expedition,* vol. i. p. 353.

ff his feed and lay down, but was soon well again.

Considerable speculation as to the original cause of this illness never found a satisfactory answer. Some traced it to a want of ventilation, and it is necessary to say that both the ponies who were ill stood next to the blubber stove; at any rate big ventilator was fitted and more fresh air let in. Others traced it to the want f water, supposing that the animals would not eat as much snow as they would ave drunk water; the easy remedy for this was to give them water instead of now. We also gave them more salt than they had had before. Whatever the cause ay have been we had no more of this colic, and the improvement in their condi- on until we started sledging was uninterrupted.

All the ponies were treated for worms; it was also found that they had lice, which were eradicated after some time and difficulty by a wash of tobacco and water. I know that Oates wished that he had clipped the ponies at the beginning of ne winter, believing that they would have grown far better coats if this had been one. He also would have wished for a loose box for each pony.

No account of the ponies would be complete without mention of our Russian ony boy, Anton. He was small in height, but he was exceedingly strong and had chest measurement of 40 inches.

EREBUS AND LANDS END

EREBUS BEHIND GREAT RAZORBACK

I believe both Anton and Dimitri, the Russian dog driver, were brought orig
nally to look after the ponies and dogs on their way from Siberia to New Zealan
But they proved such good fellows and so useful that we were very glad to tal
them on the strength of the landing party. I fear that Anton, at any rate, did n
realize what he was in for. When we arrived at Cape Crozier in the ship on ou
voyage south, and he saw the two great peaks of Ross Island in front and the Barr
er Cliff disappearing in an unbroken wall below the eastern horizon, he imagine
that he reached the South Pole, and was suitably elated. When the darkness of th
winter closed down upon us, this apparently unnatural order of things so preye
upon his superstitious mind that he became seriously alarmed. Where the sea-ic
joined the land in front of the hut was of course a working crack, caused by the ris
and fall of the tide. Sometimes the sea-water found its way up, and Anton was cor
vinced that the weird phosphorescent lights which danced up out of the sea we
devils. In propitiation we found that he had sacrificed to them his most cherishe
luxury, his scanty allowance of cigarettes, which he had literally cast upon the wa
ters in the darkness. It was natural that his thoughts should turn to the comfor
of his Siberian home, and the one-legged wife whom he was going to marry ther
and when it became clear that a another year would be spent in the South his min
was troubled. And so he went to Oates and asked him, "If I go away at the end o
this year, will Captain Scott disinherit me?" In order to try and express his ide
for he knew little English, he had some days before been asking "what we called
when a father died and left his son nothing." Poor Anton!

He looked long and anxiously for the ship, and with his kit-bag on his shou der was amongst the first to trek across the ice to meet her. Having asked for and obtained a job of work there was no happier man on board: he never left her until she reached New Zealand. Nevertheless he was always cheerful, always working, and a most useful addition to our small community.

It is still usual to talk of people living in complete married happiness when we really mean, so Mr. Bernard Shaw tells me, that they confine their quarrels to Thursday nights. If then I say that we lived this life for nearly three years, from the day when we left England until the day we returned to New Zealand, without any friction of any kind, I shall be supposed to be making a formal statement of somewhat limited truth. May I say that there is really no formality about it, and nothing but the truth. To be absolutely accurate I must admit to having seen a man in a very 'prickly' state on one occasion. That was all. It didn't last and may have been well justified for aught I know: I have forgotten what it was all about. Why we should have been more fortunate than polar travellers in general it is hard to say, but undoubtedly a very powerful reason was that we had no idle hours: there was no time to quarrel.

Before we went South people were always saying, "You will get fed up with one another. What will you do all the dark winter?" As a matter of fact the difficulty was to get through with the work. Often after working all through a long night-watch officers carried on as a matter of course through the following day in order to clear off arrears. There was little reading or general relaxation during the day: certainly not before supper, if at all. And while no fixed hours for work were laid down, the custom was general that all hours between breakfast and supper should be so used.

Our small company was desperately keen to obtain results. The youngest and most cynical pessimist must have had cause for wonder to see a body of healthy and not unintellectual men striving thus single-mindedly to add their small quota of scientific and geographical knowledge to the sum total of the world — with no immediate prospect of its practical utility. Laymen and scientists alike were determined to attain the objects to gain which they had set forth.

And I believe that in a vague intangible way there was an ideal in front of and behind this work. It is really not desirable for men who do not believe that knowledge is of value for its own sake to take up this kind of life. The question constantly put to us in civilization was and still is: "What is the use? Is there gold? or Is there coal?" The commercial spirit of the present day can see no good in pure science: the English manufacturer is not interested in research which will not give him a financial return within one year: the city man sees in it only so much energy wasted on unproductive work: truly they are bound to the wheel of conventional life.

Now unless a man believes that such a view is wrong he has no business to be 'down South.' Our magnetic and meteorological work may, I suppose, have a fairly immediate bearing upon commerce and shipping: otherwise I cannot imagine any branch of our labours which will do more at present than swell the central pool of unapplied knowledge. The members of this expedition believed that it was worth while to discover new land and new life, to reach the Southern Pole of the

earth, to make elaborate meteorological and magnetic observations and extend
ed geological surveys with all the other branches of research for which we were
equipped. They were prepared to suffer great hardship; and some of them died
for their beliefs. Without such ideals the spirit which certainly existed in our small
community would have been impossible.

But if the reasons for this happy state of our domestic life were due largely to
the adaptability and keenness of the members of our small community, I doubt
whether the frictions which have caused other expeditions to be less comfortable
than they might have been, would have been avoided in our case, had it not been
for the qualities in some of our men which set a fashion of hard work without any
thought of personal gain.

With all its troubles it is a good life. We came back from the Barrier, telling
one another we loathed the place and nothing on earth should make us return.
But now the Barrier comes back to us, with its clean, open life, and the smell of the
cooker, and its soft sound sleep. So much of the trouble of this world is caused by
memories, for we only remember half.

We have forgotten — or nearly forgotten — how the loss of a biscuit crumb left
a sense of injury which lasted for a week; how the greatest friends were so much
on one another's nerves that they did not speak for days for fear of quarrelling;
how angry we felt when the cook ran short on the weekly bag; how sick we were
after the first meals when we could eat as much as we liked; how anxious we were
when a man fell ill many hundreds of miles from home, and we had a fortnight of
thick weather and had to find our depôts or starve. We remember the cry of *Camp
Ho!* which preceded the cup of tea which gave us five more miles that evening; the
good fellowship which completed our supper after safely crossing a bad patch of
crevasses; the square inch of plum pudding which celebrated our Christmas Day;
the chanties we sang all over the Barrier as we marched our ponies along.

We travelled for Science. Those three small embryos from Cape Crozier, that
weight of fossils from Buckley Island, and that mass of material, less spectacular
but gathered just as carefully hour by hour in wind and drift, darkness and cold
were striven for in order that the world may have a little more knowledge, that it
may build on what it knows instead of on what it thinks.

Some of our men were ambitious: some wanted money, others a name; some
a help up the scientific ladder, others an F.R.S. Why not? But we had men who did
not care a rap for money or fame. I do not believe it mattered to Wilson when he
found that Amundsen had reached the Pole a few days before him — not much.
Pennell would have been very bored if you had given him a knighthood. Lillie
Bowers, Priestley, Debenham, Atkinson and many others were much the same.

But there is no love lost between the class of men who go out and do such
work and the authorities at home who deal with their collections. I remember a
conversation in the hut during the last bad winter. Men were arguing fiercely that
professionally they lost a lot by being down South, that they fell behindhand in
current work, got out of the running and so forth. There is a lot in that. And then
the talk went on to the publication of results, and the way in which they would

wish them done. A said he wasn't going to hand over his work to be mucked up by such and such a body at home; B said he wasn't going to have his buried in museum book-shelves never to be seen again; C said he would jolly well publish his own results in the scientific journals. And the ears of the armchair scientists who might deal with our hard-won specimens and observations should have been warm that night.

At the time I felt a little indignant. It seemed to me that these men ought to think themselves lucky to be down South at all: there were thousands who would have like to take their place. But now I understand quite a lot more than I did then. Science is a big thing if you can travel a Winter Journey in her cause and not regret it. I am not sure she is not bigger still if you can have dealings with scientists and continue to follow in her path.

CHAPTER VII

THE WINTER JOURNEY

Ah, but a man's reach should exceed his grasp,
Or what's a Heaven for?

R. Browning, *Andrea del Sarto.*

To me, and to every one who has remained here the result of this effort is the appeal it makes to our imagination, as one of the most gallant stories in Polar History. That men should wander forth in the depth of a Polar night to face the most dismal cold and the fiercest gales in darkness is something new; that they should have persisted in this effort in spite of every adversity for five full weeks is heroic. It makes a tale for our generation which I hope may not be lost in the telling.

Scott's Diary, at Cape Evans.

The following list of the Winter Journey sledge weights (for three men) is taken from the reckoning made by Bowers before we started:

Expendible Stores	lbs.	lbs.
'Antarctic' biscuit	135	
3 Cases for same	12	
Pemmican	110	
Butter	21	
Salt	3	
Tea	4	
Oil	60	
Spare parts for primus, and matches	2	
Toilet paper	2	
Candles	8	
Packing	5	
Spirit	8	370

Permanent Weights, etc.		
2 9-ft. Sledges, 41 lbs. each	82	
1 Cooker complete	13	

2 Primus filled with oil	8
1 Double tent complete	35
1 Sledging shovel	3.5
3 Reindeer sleeping-bags, 12 lbs. each	36
3 Eider-down sleeping-bag linings, 4 lbs. each	12
1 Alpine rope	5
1 Bosun's bag, containing repairing materials, and	
1 Bonsa outfit, containing repairing tools	5
3 Personal bags, each containing 15 lbs. spare clothing, etc.	45
Lamp box with knives, steel, etc., for seal and penguin	21
Medical and scientific box	40
2 Ice axes, 3 lbs. each	6
3 Man-harnesses	3
3 Portaging harnesses	3
Cloth for making roof and door for stone igloo	24
Instrument box	7
3 Pairs ski and sticks (discarded afterwards)	33
1 Pickaxe	11
3 Crampons, 2 lbs. 3 oz. each	6.5
2 Bamboos for measuring tide if possible, 14 feet each	4
2 Male bamboos	4
1 Plank to form top of door of igloo	2
1 Bag sennegrass	1
6 Small female bamboo ends and	
1 Knife for cutting snow block to make igloo	4
Packing	8	420
		790

The 'Lamp box' mentioned above contained the following:

- 1 Lamp for burning blubber.
- 1 Lamp for burning spirit.
- 1 Tent candle lamp.
- 1 Blubber cooker.
- 1 Blowpipe.

The party of three men set out with a total weight of 757 lbs. to draw, the ski and sticks in the above list being left behind at the last moment.

It was impossible to load the total bulk upon one 12-ft. sledge, and so two 9-sledges were taken, one toggled on behind the other. While this made the packin and handling of the gear much easier, it nearly doubled the friction surface again which the party had to pull.

June 22. Midwinter Nigl

A hard night: clear, with a blue sky so deep that it looks black: the stars a steel points: the glaciers burnished silver. The snow rings and thuds to your foc fall. The ice is cracking to the falling temperature and the tide crack groans as t water rises. And over all, wave upon wave, fold upon fold, there hangs the cu tain of the aurora. As you watch, it fades away, and then quite suddenly a gre beam flashes up and rushes to the zenith, an arch of palest green and orange, tail of flaming gold. Again it falls, fading away into great searchlight beams whi rise behind the smoking crater of Mount Erebus. And again the spiritual veil drawn—

Here at the roaring loom of Time I ply
And weave for God the garment thou seest him by.

Inside the hut are orgies. We are very merry—and indeed why not? The su turns to come back to us to-night, and such a day comes only once a year.

After dinner we had to make speeches, but instead of making a speech Bowe brought in a wonderful Christmas tree, made of split bamboos and a ski stic with feathers tied to the end of each branch; candles, sweets, preserved fruits, ar the most absurd toys of which Bill was the owner. Titus got three things whi pleased him immensely, a sponge, a whistle, and a pop-gun which went off whe he pressed in the butt. For the rest of the evening he went round asking wheth you were sweating. "No." "Yes, you are," he said, and wiped your face with t sponge. "If you want to please me very much you will fall down when I sho you," he said to me, and then he went round shooting everybody. At intervals blew the whistle.

He danced the Lancers with Anton, and Anton, whose dancing puts that the Russian Ballet into the shade, continually apologized for not being able to it well enough. Ponting gave a great lecture with slides which he had made sin we arrived, many of which Meares had coloured. When one of these came up or of us would shout, "Who coloured that," and another would cry, "Meares,"—the uproar. It was impossible for Ponting to speak. We had a milk punch, when Scc proposed the Eastern Party, and Clissold, the cook, proposed Good Old True Mil Titus blew away the ball of his gun. "I blew it into the cerulean—how doth Home have it?—cerulean azure—hence Erebus." As we turned in he said, "Cherry, a you responsible for your actions?" and when I said Yes, he blew loudly on h whistle, and the last thing I remembered was that he woke up Meares to ask hi whether he was fancy free.

It was a magnificent bust.

Five days later and three men, one of whom at any rate is feeling a little frigh

ened, stand panting and sweating out in McMurdo Sound. They have two sledges, one tied behind the other, and these sledges are piled high with sleeping-bags and camping equipment, six weeks' provisions, and a venesta case full of scientific gear for pickling and preserving. In addition there is a pickaxe, ice-axes, an Alpine rope, a large piece of green Willesden canvas and a bit of board. Scott's amazed remark when he saw our sledges two hours ago, "Bill, why are you taking all this oil?" pointing to the six cans lashed to the tray on the second sledge, had a bite in it. Our weights for such travelling are enormous—253 lbs. a man.

It is mid-day but it is pitchy dark, and it is not warm.

As we rested my mind went back to a dusty, dingy office in Victoria Street some fifteen months ago. "I want you to come," said Wilson to me, and then, "I want to go to Cape Crozier in the winter and work out the embryology of the Emperor penguins, but I'm not saying much about it—it might never come off." Well! this was better than Victoria Street, where the doctors had nearly refused to let me go because I could only see the people across the road as vague blobs walking. Then Bill went and had a talk with Scott about it, and they said I might come if I was prepared to take the additional risk. At that time I would have taken anything.

After the Depôt Journey, at Hut Point, walking over that beastly, slippery, sloping ice-foot which I always imagined would leave me some day in the sea, Bill asked me whether I would go with him—and who else for a third? There can have been little doubt whom we both wanted, and that evening Bowers had been asked. Of course he was mad to come. And here we were. "This winter travel is a new and bold venture," wrote Scott in the hut that night, "but the right men have gone to attempt it."

I don't know. There never could have been any doubt about Bill and Birdie. Probably Lashly would have made the best third, but Bill had a prejudice against seamen for a journey like this—"They don't take enough care of themselves, and they *will* not look after their clothes." But Lashly was wonderful—if Scott had only taken a four-man party and Lashly to the Pole!

What is this venture? Why is the embryo of the Emperor penguin so important to Science? And why should three sane and common-sense explorers be sledging away on a winter's night to a Cape which has only been visited before in daylight, and then with very great difficulty?

I have explained more fully in the Introduction to this book[150] the knowledge the world possessed at this time of the Emperor penguin, mainly due to Wilson. But it is because the Emperor is probably the most primitive bird in existence that the working out of his embryology is so important. The embryo shows remains of the development of an animal in former ages and former states; it recapitulates its former lives. The embryo of an Emperor may prove the missing link between birds and the reptiles from which birds have sprung.

Only one rookery of Emperor penguins had been found at this date, and this was on the sea-ice inside a little bay of the Barrier edge at Cape Crozier, which was guarded by miles of some of the biggest pressure in the Antarctic. Chicks had been

[150] See pp. xxxix-xlv.

found in September, and Wilson reckoned that the eggs must be laid in the beginning of July. And so we started just after midwinter on the weirdest bird's-nesting
expedition that has ever been or ever will be.

EMPERORS

But the sweat was freezing in our clothing and we moved on. All we could see
was a black patch away to our left which was Turk's Head: when this disappeared
we knew that we had passed Glacier Tongue which, unseen by us, eclipsed the
rocks behind. And then we camped for lunch.

That first camp only lives in my memory because it began our education of
camp work in the dark. Had we now struck the blighting temperature which we
were to meet....

There was just enough wind to make us want to hurry: down harness, each man to a strap on the sledge—quick with the floor-cloth—the bags to hold it down—now a good spread with the bamboos and the tent inner lining—hold them, Cherry, and over with the outer covering—snow on to the skirting and inside with the cook with his candle and a box of matches....

That is how we tied it: that is the way we were accustomed to do it, day after day and night after night when the sun was still high or at any rate only setting, sledging on the Barrier in spring and summer and autumn; pulling our hands from our mitts when necessary—plenty of time to warm up afterwards; in the days when we took pride in getting our tea boiling within twenty minutes of throwing off our harness: when the man who wanted to work in his fur mitts was thought a bit too slow.

But now it *didn't* work. "We shall have to go a bit slower," said Bill, and "we shall get more used to working in the dark." At this time, I remember, I was still trying to wear spectacles.

We spent that night on the sea-ice, finding that we were too far in towards Castle Rock; and it was not until the following afternoon that we reached and lunched at Hut Point. I speak of day and night, though they were much the same, and later on when we found that we could not get the work into a twenty-four-hour day, we decided to carry on as though such a convention did not exist; as in actual fact it did not. We had already realized that cooking under these conditions would be a bad job, and that the usual arrangement by which one man was cook for the week would be intolerable. We settled to be cook alternately day by day. For food we brought only pemmican and biscuit and butter; for drink we had tea, and we drank hot water to turn in on.

Pulling out from Hut Point that evening we brought along our heavy loads on the two nine-foot sledges with comparative ease; it was the first, and though we did not know it then, the only bit of good pulling we were to have. Good pulling to the sledge traveller means easy pulling. Away we went round Cape Armitage and eastwards. We knew that the Barrier edge was in front of us and also that the break-up of the sea-ice had left the face of it as a low perpendicular cliff. We had therefore to find a place where the snow had formed a drift. This we came right up against and met quite suddenly a very keen wind flowing, as it always does, from the cold Barrier down to the comparatively warm sea-ice. The temperature was -47° F., and I was a fool to take my hands out of my mitts to haul on the ropes to bring the sledges up. I started away from the Barrier edge with all ten fingers frost-bitten. They did not really come back until we were in the tent for our night meal, and within a few hours there were two or three large blisters, up to an inch long, on all of them. For many days those blisters hurt frightfully.

We were camped that night about half a mile in from the Barrier edge. The temperature was -56°. We had a baddish time, being very glad to get out of our shivering bags next morning (June 29). We began to suspect, as we knew only too well later, that the only good time of the twenty-four hours was breakfast, for then with reasonable luck we need not get into our sleeping-bags again for another seventeen hours.

PLATE II.—A PANORAMIC VIEW OF ROSS ISLAND FROM CRA-
TER HILL

The horror of the nineteen days it took us to travel from Cape Evans to Cape Crozier would have to be re-experienced to be appreciated; and any one would be a fool who went again: it is not possible to describe it. The weeks which followed them were comparative bliss, not because later our conditions were better—they were far worse—because we were callous. I for one had come to that point of suffering at which I did not really care if only I could die without much pain. They talk of the heroism of the dying—they little know—it would be so easy to die, a dose of morphia, a friendly crevasse, and blissful sleep. The trouble is to go on....

It was the darkness that did it. I don't believe minus seventy temperatures would be bad in daylight, not comparatively bad, when you could see where you were going, where you were stepping, where the sledge straps were, the cooker, the primus, the food; could see your footsteps lately trodden deep into the soft snow that you might find your way back to the rest of your load; could see the lashings of the food bags; could read a compass without striking three or four different boxes to find one dry match; could read your watch to see if the blissful moment of getting out of your bag was come without groping in the snow all about; when it would not take you five minutes to lash up the door of the tent, and five hours to get started in the morning....

But in these days we were never less than four hours from the moment when Bill cried "Time to get up" to the time when we got into our harness. It took two men to get one man into his harness, and was all they could do, for the canvas was frozen and our clothes were frozen until sometimes not even two men could bend them into the required shape.

The trouble is sweat and breath. I never knew before how much of the body's waste comes out through the pores of the skin. On the most bitter days, when we had to camp before we had done a four-hour march in order to nurse back our frozen feet, it seemed that we must be sweating. And all this sweat, instead of passing away through the porous wool of our clothing and gradually drying off us, froze and accumulated. It passed just away from our flesh and then became ice: we shook plenty of snow and ice down from inside our trousers every me we changed our foot-gear, and we could have shaken it from our vests and om between our vests and shirts, but of course we could not strip to this extent. ut when we got into our sleeping-bags, if we were fortunate, we became warm ough during the night to thaw this ice: part remained in our clothes, part passed to the skins of our sleeping-bags, and soon both were sheets of armour-plate.

As for our breath—in the daytime it did nothing worse than cover the lower arts of our faces with ice and solder our balaclavas tightly to our heads. It was no ood trying to get your balaclava off until you had had the primus going quite a ng time, and then you could throw your breath about if you wished. The trou- le really began in your sleeping-bag, for it was far too cold to keep a hole open rough which to breathe. So all night long our breath froze into the skins, and our spiration became quicker and quicker as the air in our bags got fouler and fouler: was never possible to make a match strike or burn inside our bags!

Of course we were not iced up all at once: it took several days of this kind of ing before we really got into big difficulties on this score. It was not until I got ut of the tent one morning fully ready to pack the sledge that I realized the possi- ilities ahead. We had had our breakfast, struggled into our foot-gear, and squared p inside the tent, which was comparatively warm. Once outside, I raised my head look round and found I could not move it back. My clothing had frozen hard as stood—perhaps fifteen seconds. For four hours I had to pull with my head stuck p, and from that time we all took care to bend down into a pulling position before eing frozen in.

By now we had realized that we must reverse the usual sledging routine and o everything slowly, wearing when possible the fur mitts which fitted over our oollen mitts, and always stopping whatever we were doing, directly we felt that ny part of us was getting frozen, until the circulation was restored. Henceforward was common for one or other of us to leave the other two to continue the camp ork while he stamped about in the snow, beat his arms, or nursed some exposed art. But we could not restore the circulation of our feet like this—the only way en was to camp and get some hot water into ourselves before we took our foot- ear off. The difficulty was to know whether our feet were frozen or not, for the nly thing we knew for certain was that we had lost all feeling in them. Wilson's nowledge as a doctor came in here: many a time he had to decide from our de- criptions of our feet whether to camp or to go on for another hour. A wrong deci- on meant disaster, for if one of us had been crippled the whole party would have een placed in great difficulties. Probably we should all have died.

On June 29 the temperature was -50° all day and there was sometimes a light reeze which was inclined to frost-bite our faces and hands. Owing to the weight f our two sledges and the bad surface our pace was not more than a slow and very eavy plod: at our lunch camp Wilson had the heel and sole of one foot frost-bit- n, and I had two big toes. Bowers was never worried by frost-bitten feet.

That night was very cold, the temperature falling to -66°, and it was -55° at reakfast on June 30. We had not shipped the eider-down linings to our sleep- g-bags, in order to keep them dry as long as possible. My own fur bag was too

big for me, and throughout this journey was more difficult to thaw out than th
other two: on the other hand, it never split, as did Bill's.

We were now getting into that cold bay which lies between the Hut Poir
Peninsula and Terror Point. It was known from old Discovery days that the Ba
rier winds are deflected from this area, pouring out into McMurdo Sound behin
us, and into the Ross Sea at Cape Crozier in front. In consequence of the lack (
high winds the surface of the snow is never swept and hardened and polished ;
elsewhere: it was now a mass of the hardest and smallest snow crystals, to pu
through which in cold temperatures was just like pulling through sand. I hav
spoken elsewhere of Barrier surfaces, and how, when the cold is very great, sledg
runners cannot melt the crystal points but only advance by rolling them over ar
over upon one another. That was the surface we met on this journey, and in so
snow the effect is accentuated. Our feet were sinking deep at every step.

And so when we tried to start on June 30 we found we could not move bot
sledges together. There was nothing for it but to take one on at a time and com
back for the other. This has often been done in daylight when the only risks ru
are those of blizzards which may spring up suddenly and obliterate tracks. No
in darkness it was more complicated. From 11 A.M. to 3 P.M. there was enough ligl
to see the big holes made by our feet, and we took on one sledge, trudged bac
in our tracks, and brought on the second. Bowers used to toggle and untogg
our harnesses when we changed sledges. Of course in this relay work we covere
three miles in distance for every one mile forward, and even the single sledge
were very hard pulling. When we lunched the temperature was -61°. After lunc
the little light had gone, and we carried a naked lighted candle back with us whe
we went to find our second sledge. It was the weirdest kind of procession, thre
frozen men and a little pool of light. Generally we steered by Jupiter, and I neve
see him now without recalling his friendship in those days.

We were very silent, it was not very easy to talk: but sledging is always
silent business. I remember a long discussion which began just now about col
snaps—was this the normal condition of the Barrier, or was it a cold snap?—wha
constituted a cold snap? The discussion lasted about a week. Do things slowly, a
ways slowly, that was the burden of Wilson's leadership: and every now and the
the question, Shall we go on? and the answer Yes. "I think we are all right as lor
as our appetites are good," said Bill. Always patient, self-possessed, unruffled, h
was the only man on earth, as I believe, who could have led this journey.

That day we made 3¼ miles, and travelled 10 miles to do it. The temperatur
was -66° when we camped, and we were already pretty badly iced up. That wa
the last night I lay (I had written slept) in my big reindeer bag without the linin
of eider-down which we each carried. For me it was a very bad night: a successio
of shivering fits which I was quite unable to stop, and which took possession c
my body for many minutes at a time until I thought my back would break, suc
was the strain placed upon it. They talk of chattering teeth: but when your bod
chatters you may call yourself cold. I can only compare the strain to that whic
I have been unfortunate enough to see in a case of lock-jaw. One of my big toe
was frost-bitten, but I do not know for how long. Wilson was fairly comfortable i

his smaller bag, and Bowers was snoring loudly. The minimum temperature that night as taken under the sledge was -69°; and as taken on the sledge was -75°. That is a hundred and seven degrees of frost.

We did the same relay work on July 1, but found the pulling still harder; and it was all that we could do to move the one sledge forward. From now onwards Wilson and I, but not to the same extent Bowers, experienced a curious optical delusion when returning in our tracks for the second sledge. I have said that we found our way back by the light of a candle, and we found it necessary to go back in our same footprints. These holes became to our tired brains not depressions but elevations: hummocks over which we stepped, raising our feet painfully and draggingly. And then we remembered, and said what fools we were, and for a while we compelled ourselves to walk through these phantom hills. But it was no lasting good, and as the days passed we realized that we must suffer this absurdity, for we could not do anything else. But of course it took it out of us.

During these days the blisters on my fingers were very painful. Long before my hands were frost-bitten, or indeed anything but cold, which was of course a normal thing, the matter inside these big blisters, which rose all down my fingers with only a skin between them, was frozen into ice. To handle the cooking gear or the food bags was agony; to start the primus was worse; and when, one day, I was able to prick six or seven of the blisters after supper and let the liquid matter out, the relief was very great. Every night after that I treated such others as were ready in the same way until they gradually disappeared. Sometimes it was difficult not to howl.

I *did* want to howl many times every hour of these days and nights, but I invented a formula instead, which I repeated to myself continually. Especially, I remember, it came in useful when at the end of the march with my feet frost-bitten, my heart beating slowly, my vitality at its lowest ebb, my body solid with cold, I used to seize the shovel and go on digging snow on to the tent skirting while the cook inside was trying to light the primus. "You've got it in the neck—stick it—stick it—you've got it in the neck," was the refrain, and I wanted every little bit of encouragement it would give me: then I would find myself repeating "Stick it—stick it—stick it—stick it," and then "You've got it in the neck." One of the joys of summer sledging is that you can let your mind wander thousands of miles away for weeks and weeks. Oates used to provision his little yacht (there was a pickled herring he was going to have): I invented the compactest little revolving bookcase which was going to hold not books, but pemmican and chocolate and biscuit and cocoa and sugar, and have a cooker on the top, and was going to stand always ready to quench my hunger when I got home: and we visited restaurants and theatres and grouse moors, and we thought of a pretty girl, or girls, and.... But now that was all impossible. Our conditions forced themselves upon us without pause: it was not possible to think of anything else. We got no respite. I found it best to refuse to let myself think of the past or the future—to live only for the job of the moment, and to compel myself to think only how to do it most efficiently. Once you let yourself imagine....

This day also (July 1) we were harassed by a nasty little wind which blew in our faces. The temperature was -66°, and in such temperatures the effect of even the lightest airs is blighting, and immediately freezes any exposed part. But we all fitted the bits of wind-proof lined with fur which we had made in the hut, across our balaclavas in front of our noses, and these were of the greatest comfort. They formed other places upon which our breath could freeze, and the lower parts of our faces were soon covered with solid sheets of ice, which was in itself an additional protection. This was a normal and not uncomfortable condition during the journey: the hair on our faces kept the ice away from the skin, and for myself would rather have the ice than be without it, until I want to get my balaclava off to drink my hoosh. We only made 2¼ miles, and it took 8 hours.

It blew force 3 that night with a temperature of -65.2°, and there was some drift. This was pretty bad, but luckily the wind dropped to a light breeze by the time we were ready to start the next morning (July 2). The temperature was then -60°, and continued so all day, falling lower in the evening. At 4 p.m. we watched a bank of fog form over the peninsula to our left and noticed at the same time that our frozen mitts thawed out on our hands, and the outlines of the land as shown by the stars became obscured. We made 2½ miles with the usual relaying, and camped at 8 p.m. with the temperature -65°. It really was a terrible march, and parts of both my feet were frozen at lunch. After supper I pricked six or seven of the worst blisters, and the relief was considerable.

I have met with amusement people who say, "Oh, we had minus fifty temperatures in Canada; they didn't worry *me*," or "I've been down to minus sixty something in Siberia." And then you find that they had nice dry clothing, a nice night's sleep in a nice aired bed, and had just walked out after lunch for a few minutes from a nice warm hut or an overheated train. And they look back upon it as an experience to be remembered. Well! of course as an experience of cold this can only be compared to eating a vanilla ice with hot chocolate cream after an excellent dinner at Claridge's. But in our present state we began to look upon minus fifties as a luxury which we did not often get.

That evening, for the first time, we discarded our naked candle in favour of the rising moon. We had started before the moon on purpose, but as we shall see she gave us little light. However, we owed our escape from a very sticky death to her on one occasion.

It was a little later on when we were among crevasses, with Terror above us but invisible, somewhere on our left, and the Barrier pressure on our right. We were quite lost in the darkness, and only knew that we were running downhill, the sledge almost catching our heels. There had been no light all day, clouds obscured the moon, we had not seen her since yesterday. And quite suddenly a little patch of clear sky drifted, as it were, over her face, and she showed us three paces ahead a great crevasse with just a shining icy lid not much thicker than glass. We should all have walked into it, and the sledge would certainly have followed us down. After that I felt we had a chance of pulling through: God could not be so cruel as to have saved us just to prolong our agony.

But at present we need not worry about crevasses; for we had not reached the long stretch where the moving Barrier, with the weight of many hundred miles of ice behind it, comes butting up against the slopes of Mount Terror, itself some eleven thousand feet high. Now we were still plunging ankle-deep in the mass of soft sandy snow which lies in the windless area. It seemed to have no bottom at all, and since the snow was much the same temperature as the air, our feet, as well as our bodies, got colder and colder the longer we marched: in ordinary sledging you begin to warm up after a quarter of an hour's pulling, here it was just the reverse. Even now I find myself unconsciously kicking the toes of my right foot against the heel of my left: a habit I picked up on this journey by doing it every time we halted. Well no. Not always. For there was one halt when we just lay on our backs and gazed up into the sky, where, so the others said, there was blazing the most wonderful aurora they had ever seen. I did not see it, being so near-sighted and unable to wear spectacles owing to the cold. The aurora was always before us as we travelled east, more beautiful than any seen by previous expeditions wintering in McMurdo Sound, where Erebus must have hidden the most brilliant displays. Now most of the sky was covered with swinging, swaying curtains which met in a great whirl overhead: lemon yellow, green and orange.

The minimum this night was -65°, and during July 3 it ranged between -52° and -58°. We got forward only 2½ miles, and by this time I had silently made up my mind that we had not the ghost of a chance of reaching the penguins. I am sure that Bill was having a very bad time these nights, though it was an impression rather than anything else, for he never said so. We knew we did sleep, for we heard one another snore, and also we used to have dreams and nightmares; but we had little consciousness of it, and we were now beginning to drop off when we halted on the march.

Our sleeping-bags were getting really bad by now, and already it took a long time to thaw a way down into them at night. Bill spread his in the middle, Bowers was on his right, and I was on his left. Always he insisted that I should start getting my legs into mine before *he* started: we were rapidly cooling down after our hot supper, and this was very unselfish of him. Then came seven shivering hours and first thing on getting out of our sleeping-bags in the morning we stuffed our personal gear into the mouth of the bag before it could freeze: this made a plug which when removed formed a frozen hole for us to push into as a start in the evening.

We got into some strange knots when trying to persuade our limbs into our bags, and suffered terribly from cramp in consequence. We would wait and rub, but directly we tried to move again down it would come and grip our legs in a vice. We also, especially Bowers, suffered agony from cramp in the stomach. We let the primus burn on after supper now for a time—it was the only thing which kept us going—and when one who was holding the primus was seized with cramp we hastily took the lamp from him until the spasm was over. It was horrible to see Birdie's stomach cramp sometimes: he certainly got it much worse than Bill or I. I suffered a lot from heartburn especially in my bag at nights: we were eating a great proportion of fat and this was probably the cause. Stupidly I said nothing about it for a long time. Later when Bill found out, he soon made it better with the medical case.

Birdie always lit the candle in the morning—so called and this was an heroic business. Moisture collected on our matches if you looked at them. Partly I suppose it was bringing them from outside into a comparatively warm tent; partly from putting boxes into pockets in our clothing. Sometimes it was necessary to try four or five boxes before a match struck. The temperature of the boxes and matches was about a hundred degrees of frost, and the smallest touch of the metal on naked flesh caused a frost-bite. If you wore mitts you could scarcely feel anything—especially since the tips of our fingers were already very callous. To get the first light going in the morning was a beastly cold business, made worse by having to make sure that it was at last time to get up. Bill insisted that we must lie in our bags seven hours every night.

In civilization men are taken at their own valuation because there are so many ways of concealment, and there is so little time, perhaps even so little understanding. Not so down South. These two men went through the Winter Journey and lived: later they went through the Polar Journey and died. They were gold, pure, shining, unalloyed. Words cannot express how good their companionship was.

Through all these days, and those which were to follow, the worst I suppose in their dark severity that men have ever come through alive, no single hasty or angry word passed their lips. When, later, we were sure, so far as we can be sure of anything, that we must die, they were cheerful, and so far as I can judge their songs and cheery words were quite unforced. Nor were they ever flurried, though always as quick as the conditions would allow in moments of emergency. It is hard that often such men must go first when others far less worthy remain.

CAMPING AFTER DARK—E. A. WILSON, DEL.

There are those who write of Polar Expeditions as though the whole thing was s easy as possible. They are trusting, I suspect, in a public who will say, "What fine fellow this is! we know what horrors he has endured, yet see, how little e makes of all his difficulties and hardships." Others have gone to the opposite xtreme. I do not know that there is any use in trying to make a -18° temperature ppear formidable to an uninitiated reader by calling it fifty degrees of frost. I rant to do neither of these things. I am not going to pretend that this was anything ut a ghastly journey, made bearable and even pleasant to look back upon by the

qualities of my two companions who have gone. At the same time I have no wis
to make it appear more horrible than it actually was: the reader need not fear th
I am trying to exaggerate.

During the night of July 3 the temperature dropped to -65°, but in the mornir
we wakened (we really did wake that morning) to great relief. The temperatu
was only -27° with the wind blowing some 15 miles an hour with steadily fallir
snow. It only lasted a few hours, and we knew it must be blowing a howling bli
zard outside the windless area in which we lay, but it gave us time to sleep ar
rest, and get thoroughly thawed, and wet, and warm, inside our sleeping-bag
To me at any rate this modified blizzard was a great relief, though we all kne
that our gear would be worse than ever when the cold came back. It was quite in
possible to march. During the course of the day the temperature dropped to -44
during the following night to -54°.

The soft new snow which had fallen made the surface the next day (July 5) a
most impossible. We relayed as usual, and managed to do eight hours' pulling, bi
we got forward only 1½ miles. The temperature ranged between -55° and -61°, ar
there was at one time a considerable breeze, the effect of which was paralysin
There was the great circle of a halo round the moon with a vertical shaft, and mo
moons. We hoped that we were rising on to the long snow cape which marks tl
beginning of Mount Terror. That night the temperature was -75°; at breakfast -7C
at noon nearly -77°. The day lives in my memory as that on which I found out th
records are not worth making. The thermometer as swung by Bowers after lun
at 5.51 P.M. registered -77.5°, which is 109½ degrees of frost, and is I suppose a
cold as any one will want to endure in darkness and iced-up gear and clothes. Tl
lowest temperature recorded by a Discovery Spring Journey party was -67.7°,[1]
and in those days fourteen days was a long time for a Spring Party to be awa
sledging and they were in daylight. This was our tenth day out and we hoped
be away for six weeks.

Luckily we were spared wind. Our naked candle burnt steadily as we trudge
back in our tracks to fetch our other sledge, but if we touched metal for a fractic
of a second with naked fingers we were frost-bitten. To fasten the strap buckl
over the loaded sledge was difficult: to handle the cooker, or mugs, or spoon
the primus or oil can was worse. How Bowers managed with the meteorologic
instruments I do not know, but the meteorological log is perfectly kept. Yet as soc
as you breathed near the paper it was covered with a film of ice through whic
the pencil would not bite. To handle rope was always cold and in these very lo
temperatures dreadfully cold work. The toggling up of our harnesses to the sled
we were about to pull, the untoggling at the end of the stage, the lashing up of o
sleeping-bags in the morning, the fastening of the cooker to the top of the instr
ment box, were bad, but not nearly so bad as the smaller lashings which were no
strings of ice. One of the worst was round the weekly food bag, and those rour
the pemmican, tea and butter bags inside were thinner still. But the real devil w

---

[151] A thermometer which registered -77° at the Winter Quarters of H.M.S. Alert ¢
March 4, 1876, is preserved by the Royal Geographical Society. I do not know whether
was screened.

the lashing of the tent door: it was like wire, and yet had to be tied tight. If you had to get out of the tent during the seven hours spent in our sleeping-bags you must tie a string as stiff as a poker, and re-thaw your way into a bag already as hard as a board. Our paraffin was supplied at a flash point suitable to low temperatures and was only a little milky: it was very difficult to splinter bits off the butter.

The temperature that night was -75.8°, and I will not pretend that it did not convince me that Dante was right when he placed the circles of ice below the circles of fire. Still we slept sometimes, and always we lay for seven hours. Again and again Bill asked us how about going back, and always we said no. Yet there was nothing I should have liked better: I was quite sure that to dream of Cape Crozier was the wildest lunacy. That day we had advanced 1½ miles by the utmost labour, and the usual relay work. This was quite a good march—and Cape Crozier is 67 miles from Cape Evans!

More than once in my short life I have been struck by the value of the man who is blind to what appears to be a common-sense certainty: he achieves the impossible. We never spoke our thoughts: we discussed the Age of Stone which was to come, when we built our cosy warm rock hut on the slopes of Mount Terror, and ran our stove with penguin blubber, and pickled little Emperors in warmth and dryness. We were quite intelligent people, and we must all have known that we were not going to see the penguins and that it was folly to go forward. And yet with quiet perseverance, in perfect friendship, almost with gentleness those two men led on. I just did what I was told.

It is desirable that the body should work, feed and sleep at regular hours, and this is too often forgotten when sledging. But just now we found we were unable to fit 8 hours marching and 7 hours in our sleeping-bags into a 24-hour day: the routine camp work took more than 9 hours, such were the conditions. We therefore ceased to observe the quite imaginary difference between night and day, and it was noon on Friday (July 7) before we got away. The temperature was -68° and there was a thick white fog: generally we had but the vaguest idea where we were, and we camped at 10 P.M. after managing 1¾ miles for the day. But what a relief. Instead of labouring away, our hearts were beating more naturally: it was easier to camp, we had some feeling in our hands, and our feet had not gone to sleep. Birdie swung the thermometer and found it only -55°. "Now if we tell people that to get only 87 degrees of frost can be an enormous relief they simply won't believe us," I remember saying. Perhaps you won't but it was, all the same: and I wrote that night: "There is something after all rather good in doing something never done before." Things were looking up, you see.

Our hearts were doing very gallant work. Towards the end of the march they were getting beaten and were finding it difficult to pump the blood out to our extremities There were few days that Wilson and I did not get some part of our feet frost-bitten. As we camped, I suspect our hearts were beating comparatively slowly and weakly. Nothing could be done until a hot drink was ready—tea for lunch, hot water for supper. Directly we started to drink then the effect was wonderful: it was, said Wilson, like putting a hot-water bottle against your heart. The beats became very rapid and strong and you felt the warmth travelling outwards and downwards. Then you got your foot-gear off—puttees (cut in half and wound round the bottom of the trousers), finnesko, saennegrass, hair socks, and two pair of woollen socks. Then you nursed back your feet and tried to believe you were glad—a frost-bite does not hurt until it begins to thaw. Later came the blisters, and then the chunks of dead skin.

Bill was anxious. It seems that Scott had twice gone for a walk with him during the Winter, and tried to persuade him not to go, and only finally consented on condition that Bill brought us all back unharmed: we were Southern Journey men. Bill had a tremendous respect for Scott, and later when we were about to make an effort to get back home over the Barrier, and our case was very desperate, he was most anxious to leave no gear behind at Cape Crozier, even the scientific gear which could be of no use to us and of which we had plenty more at the hut. "Scott will never forgive me if I leave gear behind," he said. It is a good sledging principle, and the party which does not follow it, or which leaves some of its load to be fetched in later is seldom a good one: but it is a principle which can be carried to excess.

And now Bill was feeling terribly responsible for both of us. He kept on saying that he was sorry, but he had never dreamed it was going to be as bad as this. He felt that having asked us to come he was in some way chargeable with our troubles. When leaders have this kind of feeling about their men they get much better results, if the men are good: if men are bad or even moderate they will try and take advantage of what they consider to be softness.

The temperature on the night of July 7 was -59°.

On July 8 we found the first sign that we might be coming to an end of this soft, powdered, arrowrooty snow. It was frightfully hard pulling; but every now and then our finnesko pierced a thin crust before they sank right in. This meant a little wind, and every now and then our feet came down on a hard slippery patch under the soft snow. We were surrounded by fog which walked along with us, and far above us the moon was shining on its roof. Steering was as difficult as the pulling, and four hours of the hardest work only produced 1¼ miles in the morning and three more hours 1 mile in the afternoon—and the temperature was -57° with a breeze—horrible!

In the early morning of the next day snow began to fall and the fog was dense: when we got up we could see nothing at all anywhere. After the usual four hours to get going in the morning we settled that it was impossible to relay, for we should never be able to track ourselves back to the second sledge. It was with very great relief that we found we could move both sledges together, and I think this was mainly due to the temperature which had risen to -36°.

This was our fourth day of fog in addition to the normal darkness, and we knew we must be approaching the land. It would be Terror Point, and the fog is probably caused by the moist warm air coming up from the sea through the pressure cracks and crevasses; for it is supposed that the Barrier here is afloat.

I wish I could take you on to the great Ice Barrier some calm evening when the sun is just dipping in the middle of the night and show you the autumn tints on Ross Island. A last look round before turning in, a good day's march behind, enough fine fat pemmican inside you to make you happy, the homely smell of tobacco from the tent, a pleasant sense of soft fur and the deep sleep to come. And all the softest colours God has made are in the snow; on Erebus to the west, where the wind can scarcely move his cloud of smoke; and on Terror to the east, not so high, and more regular in form. How peaceful and dignified it all is.

That was what you might have seen four months ago had you been out on the Barrier plain. Low down on the extreme right or east of the land there was a black smudge of rock peeping out from great snow-drifts: that was the Knoll, and close under it were the cliffs of Cape Crozier, the Knoll looking quite low and the cliffs invisible, although they are eight hundred feet high, a sheer precipice falling to the sea.

It is at Cape Crozier that the Barrier edge, which runs for four hundred miles as an ice-cliff up to 200 feet high, meets the land. The Barrier is moving against this land at a rate which is sometimes not much less than a mile in a year. Perhaps you can imagine the chaos which it piles up: there are pressure ridges compared to which the waves of the sea are like a ploughed field. These are worst at Cape Crozier itself, but they extend all along the southern slopes of Mount Terror, running parallel with the land, and the disturbance which Cape Crozier makes is apparent at Corner Camp some forty miles back on the Barrier in the crevasses we used to find and the occasional ridges we had to cross.

In the Discovery days the pressure just where it hit Cape Crozier formed a small bay, and on the sea-ice frozen in this bay the men of the Discovery found the only Emperor penguin rookery which had ever been seen. The ice here was not blown out by the blizzards which cleared the Ross Sea, and open water or open leads were never far away. This gave the Emperors a place to lay their eggs and an opportunity to find their food. We had therefore to find our way along the pressure to the Knoll, and thence penetrate *through* the pressure to the Emperors' Bay. And we had to do it in the dark.

Terror Point, which we were approaching in the fog, is a short twenty miles from the Knoll, and ends in a long snow-tongue running out into the Barrier. The way had been travelled a good many times in Discovery days and in daylight, and Wilson knew there was a narrow path, free from crevasses, which skirted along between the mountain and the pressure ridges running parallel to it. But it is one thing to walk along a corridor by day, and quite another to try to do so at night, especially when there are no walls by which you can correct your course—only crevasses. Anyway, Terror Point must be somewhere close to us now, and vaguely in front of us was that strip of snow, neither Barrier nor mountain, which was our only way forward.

We began to realize, now that our eyes were more or less out of action, how much we could do with our feet and ears. The effect of walking in finnesko is much the same as walking in gloves, and you get a sense of touch which nothing else except bare feet could give you. Thus we could feel every small variation in surface, every crust through which our feet broke, every hardened patch below the soft snow. And soon we began to rely more and more upon the sound of our footsteps to tell us whether we were on crevasses or solid ground. From now onwards we were working among crevasses fairly constantly. I loathe them in full daylight when much can be done to avoid them, and when if you fall into them you can at any rate see where the sides are, which way they run and how best to scramble out; when your companions can see how to stop the sledge to which you are all attached by your harness; how most safely to hold the sledge when stopped; how, if you are dangling fifteen feet down in a chasm, to work above you to get you up to the surface again. And then our clothes were generally something like clothes. Even under the ideal conditions of good light, warmth and no wind, crevasses are beastly, whether you are pulling over a level and uniform snow surface, never knowing what moment will find you dropping into some bottomless pit, or whether you are rushing for the Alpine rope and the sledge, to help some companion who has disappeared. I dream sometimes now of bad days we had on the Beardmore and elsewhere, when men were dropping through to be caught up and hang at the full length of the harnesses and toggles many times in an hour. On the same sledge as myself on the Beardmore one man went down once head first, and another eight times to the length of his harness in 25 minutes. And always you wondered whether your harness was going to hold when the jerk came. But those days were a Sunday School treat compared to our days of blind-man's buff with the Emperor penguins among the crevasses of Cape Crozier.

Our troubles were greatly increased by the state of our clothes. If we had been dressed in lead we should have been able to move our arms and necks and heads more easily than we could now. If the same amount of icing had extended to our legs I believe we should still be there, standing unable to move: but happily the forks of our trousers still remained movable. To get into our canvas harnesses was the most absurd business. Quite in the early days of our journey we met with this difficulty, and somewhat foolishly decided not to take off our harness for lunch. The harnesses thawed in the tent, and froze back as hard as boards. Likewise our clothing was hard as boards and stuck out from our bodies in every imaginable fold and angle. To fit one board over the other required the united efforts of the would-be wearer and his two companions, and the process had to be repeated for each one of us twice a day. Goodness knows how long it took; but it cannot have been less than five minutes' thumping at each man.

As we approached Terror Point in the fog we sensed that we had risen and fallen over several rises. Every now and then we felt hard slippery snow under our feet. Every now and then our feet went through crusts in the surface. And then quite suddenly, vague, indefinable, monstrous, there loomed a something ahead. I remember having a feeling as of ghosts about as we untoggled our harnesses from the sledge, tied them together, and thus roped walked upwards on that ice. The moon was showing a ghastly ragged mountainous edge above us in the fog, and as we rose we found that we were on a pressure ridge. We stopped, looked at one another, and then *bang*—right under our feet. More bangs, and creaks and groans, for that ice was moving and splitting like glass. The cracks went off all round us, and some of them ran along for hundreds of yards. Afterwards we got used to it,

ɪt at first the effect was very jumpy. From first to last during this journey we had
lenty of variety and none of that monotony which is inevitable in sledging over
•ng distances of Barrier in summer. Only the long shivering fits following close
ɪe after the other all the time we lay in our dreadful sleeping-bags, hour after
ɔur and night after night in those temperatures—they were as monotonous as
ɔuld be. Later we got frost-bitten even as we lay in our sleeping-bags. Things are
ɛtting pretty bad when you get frost-bitten in your bag.

There was only a glow where the moon was; we stood in a moonlit fog, and
ɪis was sufficient to show the edge of another ridge ahead, and yet another on
ɪr left. We were utterly bewildered. The deep booming of the ice continued, and
may be that the tide has something to do with this, though we were many miles
ɔm the ordinary coastal ice. We went back, toggled up to our sledges again and
ɪlled in what we thought was the right direction, always with that feeling that
ɪe earth may open underneath your feet which you have in crevassed areas. But
l we found were more mounds and banks of snow and ice, into which we almost
ɪn before we saw them. We were clearly lost. It was near midnight, and I wrote,
t may be the pressure ridges or it may be Terror, it is impossible to say,—and I
ɪould think it is impossible to move till it clears. We were steering N.E. when we
ɔt here and returned S.W. till we seemed to be in a hollow and camped."

The temperature had been rising from -36° at 11 A.M. and it was now -27°;
ɪow was falling and nothing whatever could be seen. From under the tent came
ɔises as though some giant was banging a big empty tank. All the signs were for
blizzard, and indeed we had not long finished our supper and were thawing our
ʳay little by little into our bags when the wind came away from the south. Before
started we got a glimpse of black rock and knew we must be in the pressure
ɪdges where they nearly join Mount Terror.

It is with great surprise that in looking up the records I find that blizzard last-
ɪ three days, the temperature and wind both rising till it was +9° and blowing
ɔrce 9 on the morning of the second day (July 11). On the morning of the third
ɑy (July 12) it was blowing storm force (10). The temperature had thus risen over
ɪghty degrees.

It was not an uncomfortable time. Wet and warm, the risen temperature al-
•wed all our ice to turn to water, and we lay steaming and beautifully liquid, and
ʳondered sometimes what we should be like when our gear froze up once more.
ɪt we did not do much wondering, I suspect: we slept. From that point of view
ɪese blizzards were a perfect Godsend.

We also revised our food rations. From the moment we started to prepare
ɔr this journey we were asked by Scott to try certain experiments in view of the
lateau stage of the Polar Journey the following summer. It was supposed that
ɪe Plateau stage would be the really tough part of the Polar Journey, and no one
ɪen dreamed that harder conditions could be found in the middle of the Barrier
ɪ March than on the Plateau, ten thousand feet higher, in February. In view of
ɪe extreme conditions we knew we must meet on this winter journey, far harder
f course in point of weather than anything experienced on the Polar Journey, we

had determined to simplify our food to the last degree. We only brought pemmi
can, biscuit, butter and tea: and tea is not a food, only a pleasant stimulant, ar
hot: the pemmican was excellent and came from Beauvais, Copenhagen.

**CAMP WORK IN A BLIZZARD, PASSING IN THE COOKER—E. A
WILSON, DEL.**

The immediate advantage of this was that we had few food bags to handle f
each meal. If the air temperature is 100 degrees of frost, then everything in the a
is about 100 degrees of frost too. You have only to untie the lashings of one bag
a -70° temperature, with your feet frozen and your fingers just nursed back aft
getting a match to strike for the candle (you will have tried several boxes—meta
to realize this as an advantage.

The immediate and increasingly pressing disadvantage is that you have r
sugar. Have you ever had a craving for sugar which never leaves you, even whe
asleep? It is unpleasant. As a matter of fact the craving for sweet things never s

iously worried us on this journey, and there must have been some sugar in our
biscuits which gave a pleasant sweetness to our mid-day tea or nightly hot water
when broken up and soaked in it. These biscuits were specially made for us by
Huntley and Palmer: their composition was worked out by Wilson and that firm's
chemist, and is a secret. But they are probably the most satisfying biscuit ever
made, and I doubt whether they can be improved upon. There were two kinds,
called Emergency and Antarctic, but there was I think little difference between
them except in the baking. A well-baked biscuit was good to eat when sledging if
your supply of food was good: but if you were very hungry an underbaked one
was much preferred. By taking individually different quantities of biscuit, pemmican and butter we were able roughly to test the proportions of proteids, fats and
carbo-hydrates wanted by the human body under such extreme circumstances.
Bill was all for fat, starting with 8 oz. butter, 12 oz. pemmican and only 12 oz.
biscuit a day. Bowers told me he was going for proteids, 16 oz. pemmican and 16
oz. biscuit, and suggested I should go the whole hog on carbo-hydrates. I did not
like this, since I knew I should want more fat, but the rations were to be altered as
necessary during the journey, so there was no harm in trying. So I started with 20
oz. of biscuit and 12 oz. of pemmican a day.

Bowers was all right (this was usual with him), but he did not eat all his extra
pemmican. Bill could not eat all his extra butter, but was satisfied. I got hungry,
certainly got more frost-bitten than the others, and wanted more fat. I also got
heartburn. However, before taking more fat I increased my biscuits to 24 oz., but
this did not satisfy me; I wanted fat. Bill and I now took the same diet, he giving
me 4 oz. of butter which he could not eat, and I giving him 4 oz. of biscuit which
did not satisfy my wants. We both therefore had 12 oz. pemmican, 16 oz biscuit
and 4 oz. butter a day, but we did not always finish our butter. This is an extremely
good ration, and we had enough to eat during most of this journey. We certainly
could not have faced the conditions without.

I will not say that I was entirely easy in my mind as we lay out that blizzard
somewhere off Terror Point; I don't know how the others were feeling. The un-
earthly banging going on underneath us may have had something to do with it.
But we were quite lost in the pressure and it might be the deuce and all to get out
in the dark. The wind eddied and swirled quite out of its usual straightforward
way, and the tent got badly snowed up: our sledge had disappeared long ago. The
position was not altogether a comfortable one.

Tuesday night and Wednesday it blew up to force 10, temperature from -7° to
+2°. And then it began to modify and get squally. By 3 A.M. on Thursday (July 13)
the wind had nearly ceased, the temperature was falling and the stars were shining through detached clouds. We were soon getting our breakfast, which always
consisted of tea, followed by pemmican. We soaked our biscuits in both. Then we
set to work to dig out the sledges and tent, a big job taking several hours. At last we
got started. In that jerky way in which I was still managing to jot a few sentences
down each night as a record, I wrote:

"Did 7½ miles during day—seems a marvellous run—rose and fell over several ridges of Terror—in afternoon suddenly came on huge crevasse on one of

these—we were quite high on Terror—moon saved us walking in—it might hav
taken sledge and all."

To do seven miles in a day, a distance which had taken us nearly a week ii
the past, was very heartening. The temperature was between -20° and -30° all day
and that was good too. When crossing the undulations which ran down out of th
mountain into the true pressure ridges on our right we found that the wind whicl
came down off the mountain struck along the top of the undulation, and flowin;
each way, caused a N.E. breeze on one side and a N.W. breeze on the other. Ther
seemed to be wind in the sky, and the blizzard had not cleared as far away as w
should have wished.

During the time through which we had come it was by burning more oil than i
usually allowed for cooking that we kept going at all. After each meal was cooke(
we allowed the primus to burn on for a while and thus warmed up the tent. The;
we could nurse back our frozen feet and do any necessary little odd jobs. More of
ten we just sat and nodded for a few minutes, keeping one another from going to(
deeply to sleep. But it was running away with the oil. We started with 6 one-galloi
tins (those tins Scott had criticized), and we had now used four of them. At first w
said we must have at least two one-gallon tins with which to go back; but by nov
our estimate had come down to one full gallon tin, and two full primus lamps. Ou
sleeping-bags were awful. It took me, even as early in the journey as this, an hou
of pushing and thumping and cramp every night to thaw out enough of mine t(
get into it at all. Even that was not so bad as lying in them when we got there.

Only -35° but "a very bad night" according to my diary. We got away in goo(
time, but it was a ghastly day and my nerves were quivering at the end, for w(
could not find that straight and narrow way which led between the crevasses oi
either hand. Time after time we found we were out of our course by the sud
den fall of the ground beneath our feet—in we went and then—"are we too fa
right?"—nobody knows—"well let's try nearer in to the mountain," and so forth
"By hard slogging 2¾ miles this morning—then on in thick gloom which sudden
ly lifted and we found ourselves under a huge great mountain of pressure ridg(
looking black in shadow. We went on, bending to the left, when Bill fell and pu
his arm into a crevasse. We went over this and another, and some time after go
somewhere up to the left, and both Bill and I put a foot into a crevasse. We sound
ed all about and everywhere was hollow, and so we ran the sledge down over i
and all was well."[152] Once we got right into the pressure and took a longish tim(
to get out again. Bill lengthened his trace out with the Alpine rope now and ofter
afterwards so he found the crevasses well ahead of us and the sledge: nice for u
but not so nice for Bill. Crevasses in the dark *do* put your nerves on edge.

When we started next morning (July 15) we could see on our left front an(
more or less on top of us the Knoll, which is a big hill whose precipitous cliffs t(
seaward form Cape Crozier. The sides of it sloped down towards us, and pressin;
against its ice-cliffs on ahead were miles and miles of great pressure ridges, alon;
which we had travelled, and which hemmed us in. Mount Terror rose ten thou
sand feet high on our left, and was connected with the Knoll by a great cup-lik(

[152] My own diary.

drift of wind-polished snow. The slope of this in one place runs gently out on to the corridor along which we had sledged, and here we turned and started to pull our sledges up. There were no crevasses, only the great drift of snow, so hard that we used our crampons just as though we had been on ice, and as polished as the china sides of a giant cup which it resembled. For three miles we slogged up, until we were only 150 yards from the moraine shelf where we were going to build our hut of rocks and snow. This moraine was above us on our left, the twin peaks of the Knoll were across the cup on our right; and here, 800 feet up the mountain side, we pitched our last camp.

We had arrived.

What should we call our hut? How soon could we get our clothes and bags dry? How would the blubber stove work? Would the penguins be there? "It seems too good to be true, 19 days out. Surely seldom has any one been so wet; our bags hardly possible to get into, our wind-clothes just frozen boxes. Birdie's patent balaclava is like iron—it is wonderful how our cares have vanished."[153]

It was evening, but we were so keen to begin that we went straight up to the ridge above our camp, where the rock cropped out from the snow. We found that most of it was *in situ* but that there were plenty of boulders, some gravel, and of course any amount of the icy snow which fell away below us down to our tent, and the great pressure about a mile beyond. Between us and that pressure, as we were to find out afterwards, was a great ice-cliff. The pressure ridges, and the Great Ice Barrier beyond, were at our feet; the Ross Sea edge but some four miles away. The Emperors must be somewhere round that shoulder of the Knoll which hides Cape Crozier itself from our view.

Our scheme was to build an igloo with rock walls, banked up with snow, using a nine-foot sledge as a ridge beam, and a large sheet of green Willesden canvas as a roof. We had also brought a board to form a lintel over the door. Here with the stove, which was to be fed with blubber from the penguins, we were to have a comfortable warm home whence we would make excursions to the rookery perhaps four miles away. Perhaps we would manage to get our tent down to the rookery itself and do our scientific work there on the spot, leaving our nice hut for a night or more. That is how we planned it.

That same night "we started to dig in under a great boulder on the top of the hill, hoping to make this a large part of one of the walls of the hut, but the rock came close underneath and stopped us. We then chose a moderately level piece of moraine about twelve feet away, and just under the level of the top of the hill, hoping that here in the lee of the ridge we might escape a good deal of the tremendous winds which we knew were common. Birdie gathered rocks from over the hill, nothing was too big for him; Bill did the banking up outside while I built the wall with the boulders. The rocks were good, the snow, however, was blown so hard as to be practically ice; a pick made little impression upon it, and the only way was to chip out big blocks gradually with the small shovel. The gravel was scanty, but good when there was any. Altogether things looked very hopeful when we turned

---

[153] My own diary.

in to the tent some 150 yards down the slope, having done about half one of the long walls."[154]

The view from eight hundred feet up the mountain was magnificent and I got my spectacles out and cleared the ice away time after time to look. To the east a great field of pressure ridges below, looking in the moonlight as if giants had been ploughing with ploughs which made furrows fifty or sixty feet deep: these ran right up to the Barrier edge, and beyond was the frozen Ross Sea, lying flat, white and peaceful as though such things as blizzards were unknown. To the north and north-east the Knoll. Behind us Mount Terror on which we stood, and over all the grey limitless Barrier seemed to cast a spell of cold immensity, vague, ponderous, a breeding-place of wind and drift and darkness. God! What a place!

"There was now little moonlight or daylight, but for the next forty-eight hours we used both to their utmost, being up at all times by day and night, and often working on when there was great difficulty in seeing anything; digging by the light of the hurricane lamp. By the end of two days we had the walls built, and banked up to one or two feet from the top; we were to fit the roof cloth close before banking up the rest. The great difficulty in banking was the hardness of the snow, it being impossible to fill in the cracks between the blocks which were more like paving-stones than anything else. The door was in, being a triangular tent door-way, with flaps which we built close in to the walls, cementing it with snow and rocks. The top folded over a plank and the bottom was dug into the ground."[155]

Birdie was very disappointed that we could not finish the whole thing that day: he was nearly angry about it, but there was a lot to do yet and we were tired out. We turned out early the next morning (Tuesday 18th) to try and finish the igloo, but it was blowing too hard. When we got to the top we did some digging but it was quite impossible to get the roof on, and we had to leave it. We realized that day that it blew much harder at the top of the slope than where our tent was. It was bitterly cold up there that morning with a wind force 4-5 and a minus thirty temperature.

The oil question was worrying us quite a lot. We were now well in to the fifth of our six tins, and economizing as much as possible, often having only two hot meals a day. We had to get down to the Emperor penguins somehow and get some blubber to run the stove which had been made for us in the hut. The 19th being a calm fine day we started at 9.30, with an empty sledge, two ice-axes, Alpine rope, harnesses and skinning tools.

Wilson had made this journey through the Cape Crozier pressure ridges several times in the Discovery days. But then they had daylight, and they had found a practicable way close under the cliffs which at the present moment were between us and the ridges.

As we neared the bottom of the mountain slope, farther to the north than we had previously gone, we had to be careful about crevasses, but we soon hit off the edge of the cliff and skirted along it until it petered out on the same level as the

[154] My own diary.
[155] Ibid.

arrier. Turning left handed we headed towards the sea-ice, knowing that there ere some two miles of pressure between us and Cape Crozier itself. For about alf a mile it was fair going, rounding big knobs of pressure but always managing keep more or less on the flat and near the ice-cliff which soon rose to a very great eight on our left. Bill's idea was to try and keep close under this cliff, along that me Discovery way which I have mentioned above. They never arrived there ear- enough for the eggs in those days; the chicks were hatched. Whether we should ow find any Emperors, and if so whether they would have any eggs, was by no eans certain.

However, we soon began to get into trouble, meeting several crevasses ev- y few yards, and I have no doubt crossing scores of others of which we had knowledge. Though we hugged the cliffs as close as possible we found our- lves on the top of the first pressure ridge, separated by a deep gulf from the e-slope which we wished to reach. Then we were in a great valley between the st and second ridges: we got into huge heaps of ice pressed up in every shape every side, crevassed in every direction: we slithered over snow-slopes and awled along drift ridges, trying to get in towards the cliffs. And always we came against impossible places and had to crawl back. Bill led on a length of Alpine pe fastened to the toggle of the sledge; Birdie was in his harness also fastened to e toggle, and I was in my harness fastened to the rear of the sledge, which was of eat use to us both as a bridge and a ladder.

Two or three times we tried to get down the ice-slopes to the comparatively vel road under the cliff, but it was always too great a drop. In that dim light every roportion was distorted; some of the places we actually did manage to negotiate ith ice-axes and Alpine rope looked absolute precipices, and there were always evasses at the bottom if you slipped. On the way back I did slip into one of these d was hauled out by the other two standing on the wall above me.

We then worked our way down into the hollow between the first and second rge pressure ridges, and I believe on to the top of the second. The crests here rose fty or sixty feet. After this I don't know where we went. Our best landmarks were atches of crevasses, sometimes three or four in a few footsteps. The temperatures ere lowish (-37°), it was impossible for me to wear spectacles, and this was a emendous difficulty to me and handicap to the party: Bill would find a crevasse d point it out; Birdie would cross; and then time after time, in trying to step over climb over on the sledge, I put my feet right into the middle of the cracks. This ay I went well in at least six times; once, when we were close to the sea, rolling to and out of one and then down a steep slope until brought up by Birdie and ll on the rope.

A PROCESSION OF EMPERORS

THE KNOLL BEHIND THE CLIFFS OF CAPE CROZIER

We blundered along until we got into a great cul-de-sac which probab formed the end of the two ridges, where they butted on to the sea-ice. On all sid rose great walls of battered ice with steep snow-slopes in the middle, where v slithered about and blundered into crevasses. To the left rose the huge cliff of Ca Crozier, but we could not tell whether there were not two or three pressure ridg between us and it, and though we tried at least four ways, there was no possibili of getting forward.

And then we heard the Emperors calling.

Their cries came to us from the sea-ice we could not see, but which must ha been a chaotic quarter of a mile away. They came echoing back from the cliffs, we stood helpless and tantalized. We listened and realized that there was nothir for it but to return, for the little light which now came in the middle of the d. was going fast, and to be caught in absolute darkness there was a horrible ide We started back on our tracks and almost immediately I lost my footing and roll down a slope into a crevasse. Birdie and Bill kept their balance and I clamber back to them. The tracks were very faint and we soon began to lose them. Bird was the best man at following tracks that I have ever known, and he found the time after time. But at last even he lost them altogether and we settled we must ju go ahead. As a matter of fact, we picked them up again, and by then were out the worst: but we were glad to see the tent.

The next morning (Thursday, June 20) we started work on the igloo at 3 A. and managed to get the canvas roof on in spite of a wind which harried us a hat day. Little did we think what that roof had in store for us as we packed it in vith snow blocks, stretching it over our second sledge, which we put athwartships across the middle of the longer walls. The windward (south) end came right down o the ground and we tied it securely to rocks before packing it in. On the other hree sides we had a good two feet or more of slack all round, and in every case we ied it to rocks by lanyards at intervals of two feet. The door was the difficulty, and or the present we left the cloth arching over the stones, forming a kind of portico. The whole was well packed in and over with slabs of hard snow, but there was 10 soft snow with which to fill up the gaps between the blocks. However, we felt already that nothing could drag that roof out of its packing, and subsequent events proved that we were right.

It was a bleak job for three o'clock in the morning before breakfast, and we vere glad to get back to the tent and a meal, for we meant to have another go at he Emperors that day. With the first glimpse of light we were off for the rookery again.

But we now knew one or two things about that pressure which we had not known twenty-four hours ago; for instance, that there was a lot of alteration since he Discovery days and that probably the pressure was bigger. As a matter of fact t has been since proved by photographs that the ridges now ran out three-quar-ers of a mile farther into the sea than they did ten years before. We knew also hat if we entered the pressure at the only place where the ice-cliffs came down o the level of the Barrier, as we did yesterday, we could neither penetrate to the rookery nor get in under the cliffs where formerly a possible way had been found. There was only one other thing to do—to go over the cliff. And this was what we proposed to try and do.

Now these ice-cliffs are some two hundred feet high, and I felt uncomfortable, especially in the dark. But as we came back the day before we had noticed at one place a break in the cliffs from which there hung a snow-drift. It *might* be possible to get down that drift.

And so, all harnessed to the sledge, with Bill on a long lead out in front and Birdie and myself checking the sledge behind, we started down the slope which ended in the cliff, which of course we could not see. We crossed a number of small crevasses, and soon we knew we must be nearly there. Twice we crept up to the edge of the cliff with no success, and then we found the slope: more, we got down it without great difficulty and it brought us out just where we wanted to be, be-tween the land cliffs and the pressure.

THE BARRIER PRESSURE AT CAPE CROZIER

Then began the most exciting climb among the pressure that you can imagine. At first very much as it was the day before—pulling ourselves and one another up ridges, slithering down slopes, tumbling into and out of crevasses and holes of all sorts, we made our way along under the cliffs which rose higher and higher above us as we neared the black lava precipices which form Cape Crozier itself. We straddled along the top of a snow ridge with a razor-backed edge, balancing the sledge between us as we wriggled: on our right was a drop of great depth with crevasses at the bottom, on our left was a smaller drop also crevassed. We crawled along, and I can tell you it was exciting work in the more than half darkness. At the end was a series of slopes full of crevasses, and finally we got right in under the rock on to moraine, and here we had to leave the sledge.

We roped up, and started to worry along under the cliffs, which had now changed from ice to rock, and rose 800 feet above us. The tumult of pressure which climbed against them showed no order here. Four hundred miles of moving ice behind it had just tossed and twisted those giant ridges until Job himself would have lacked words to reproach their Maker. We scrambled over and under, hanging on with our axes, and cutting steps where we could not find a foothold with our crampons. And always we got towards the Emperor penguins, and it really began to look as if we were going to do it this time, when we came up against a wall of ice which a single glance told us we could never cross. One of the largest pressure ridges had been thrown, end on, against the cliff. We seemed to be stopped when Bill found a black hole, something like a fox's earth, disappearing into the bowels of the ice. We looked at it: "Well, here goes!" he said, and put his head in, and disappeared. Bowers likewise. It was a longish way, but quite possible to wriggle along, and presently I found myself looking out of the other side with a deep gully below me, the rock face on one hand and the ice on the other. "Put your back against the ice and your feet against the rock and lever yourself along," said Bill, who was already standing on firm ice at the far end in a snow pit. We cut some fifteen steps to get out of that hole. Excited by now, and thoroughly enjoy ing ourselves, we found the way ahead easier, until the penguins' call reached us again and we stood, three crystallized ragamuffins, above the Emperors' home. They were there all right, and we were going to reach them, but where were all the thousands of which we had heard?

We stood on an ice-foot which was really a dwarf cliff some twelve feet high, and the sea-ice, with a good many ice-blocks strewn upon it, lay below. The cliff dropped straight, with a bit of an overhang and no snow-drift. This may have been because the sea had only frozen recently; whatever the reason may have been it meant that we should have a lot of difficulty in getting up again without help. It was decided that some one must stop on the top with the Alpine rope, and clearly that one should be I, for with short sight and fogged spectacles which I could not wear I was much the least useful of the party for the job immediately ahead. Had we had the sledge we could have used it as a ladder, but of course we had left this at the beginning of the moraine miles back.

We saw the Emperors standing all together huddled under the Barrier cliff some hundreds of yards away. The little light was going fast: we were much more excited about the approach of complete darkness and the look of wind in the south than we were about our triumph. After indescribable effort and hardship we were witnessing a marvel of the natural world, and we were the first and only men who had ever done so; we had within our grasp material which might prove of the utmost importance to science; we were turning theories into facts with every observation we made,—and we had but a moment to give.

EMPERORS BARRIER AND SEA ICE—E. A. WILSON, DEL.

The disturbed Emperors made a tremendous row, trumpeting with their curious metallic voices. There was no doubt they had eggs, for they tried to shuffle along the ground without losing them off their feet. But when they were hustled a good many eggs were dropped and left lying on the ice, and some of these were quickly picked up by eggless Emperors who had probably been waiting a long time for the opportunity. In these poor birds the maternal side seems to have necessarily swamped the other functions of life. Such is the struggle for existence that they can only live by a glut of maternity, and it would be interesting to know whether such a life leads to happiness or satisfaction.

I have told[156] how the men of the Discovery found this rookery where we now stood. How they made journeys in the early spring but never arrived early enough to get eggs and only found parents and chicks. They concluded that the Emperor was an impossible kind of bird who, for some reason or other, nests in the middle of the Antarctic winter with the temperature anywhere below seventy degrees of frost, and the blizzards blowing, always blowing, against his devoted back. And they found him holding his precious chick balanced upon his big feet and pressing it maternally, or paternally (for both sexes squabble for the privilege) against a bald patch in his breast. And when at last he simply must go and eat something in the open leads near by, he just puts the child down on the ice and twenty chickless Emperors rush to pick it up. And they fight over it, and so tear it that sometimes it will die. And, if it can, it will crawl into any ice-crack to escape from so much kindness, and there it will freeze. Likewise many broken and addled eggs were found, and it is clear that the mortality is very great. But some survive, and summer comes; and when a big blizzard is going to blow (they know all about the weather), the parents take the children out for miles across the sea-ice, until they reach the threshold of the open sea. And there they sit until the wind comes, and the swell rises, and breaks that ice-floe off; and away they go in the blinding drift to join the main pack-ice, with a private yacht all to themselves.

You must agree that a bird like this is an interesting beast, and when, seven months ago, we rowed a boat under those great black cliffs,[157] and found a disconsolate Emperor chick still in the down, we knew definitely why the Emperor has to nest in mid-winter. For if a June egg was still without feathers in the beginning of January, the same egg laid in the summer would leave its produce without practical covering for the following winter. Thus the Emperor penguin is compelled to undertake all kinds of hardships because his children insist on developing so slowly, very much as we are tied in our human relationships for the same reason. It is of interest that such a primitive bird should have so long a childhood.

But interesting as the life history of these birds must be, we had not travelled for three weeks to see them sitting on their eggs. We wanted the embryos, and we wanted them as young as possible, and fresh and unfrozen that specialists at home might cut them into microscopic sections and learn from them the previous history of birds throughout the evolutionary ages. And so Bill and Birdie rapidly collected five eggs, which we hoped to carry safely in our fur mitts to our igloo upon Mount Terror, where we could pickle them in the alcohol we had brought for

[156] See Introduction, pp. xxxix-xlv.
[157] See p. 82.

e purpose. We also wanted oil for our blubber stove, and they killed and skinned
ree birds—an Emperor weighs up to 6½ stones.

The Ross Sea was frozen over, and there were no seal in sight. There were only
)0 Emperors as compared with 2000 in 1902 and 1903. Bill reckoned that every
urth or fifth bird had an egg, but this was only a rough estimate, for we did not
ant to disturb them unnecessarily. It is a mystery why there should have been so
w birds, but it certainly looked as though the ice had not formed very long. Were
ese the first arrivals? Had a previous rookery been blown out to sea and was this
e beginning of a second attempt? Is this bay of sea-ice becoming unsafe?

Those who previously discovered the Emperors with their chicks saw the pen-
uins nursing dead and frozen chicks if they were unable to obtain a live one. They
so found decomposed eggs which they must have incubated after they had been
ozen. Now we found that these birds were so anxious to sit on something that
me of those which had no eggs were sitting on ice! Several times Bill and Birdie
icked up eggs to find them lumps of ice, rounded and about the right size, dirty
d hard. Once a bird dropped an ice nest egg as they watched, and again a bird
turned and tucked another into itself, immediately forsaking it for a real one,
owever, when one was offered.

Meanwhile a whole procession of Emperors came round under the cliff on
hich I stood. The light was already very bad and it was well that my companions
ere quick in returning: we had to do everything in a great hurry. I hauled up the
ggs in their mitts (which we fastened together round our necks with lampwick
nyards) and then the skins, but failed to help Bill at all. "Pull," he cried, from the
ottom: "I am pulling," I said. "But the line's quite slack down here," he shouted.
nd when he had reached the top by climbing up on Bowers' shoulders, and we
ere both pulling all we knew Birdie's end of the rope was still slack in his hands.
irectly we put on a strain the rope cut into the ice edge and jammed—a very
ommon difficulty when working among crevasses. We tried to run the rope over
n ice-axe without success, and things began to look serious when Birdie, who
ad been running about prospecting and had meanwhile put one leg through a
ack into the sea, found a place where the cliff did not overhang. He cut steps for
imself, we hauled, and at last we were all together on the top—his foot being by
ow surrounded by a solid mass of ice.

We legged it back as hard as we could go: five eggs in our fur mitts, Birdie with
vo skins tied to him and trailing behind, and myself with one. We were roped up,
nd climbing the ridges and getting through the holes was very difficult. In one
lace where there was a steep rubble and snow slope down I left the ice-axe half
ay up; in another it was too dark to see our former ice-axe footsteps, and I could
ee nothing, and so just let myself go and trusted to luck. With infinite patience Bill
aid: "Cherry, you *must* learn how to use an ice-axe." For the rest of the trip my
ind-clothes were in rags.

We found the sledge, and none too soon, and now had three eggs left, more or
ess whole. Both mine had burst in my mitts: the first I emptied out, the second I
ft in my mitt to put into the cooker; it never got there, but on the return journey I

had my mitts far more easily thawed out than Birdie's (Bill had none) and I belie
the grease in the egg did them good. When we got into the hollows under the rid
where we had to cross, it was too dark to do anything but feel our way. We did
over many crevasses, found the ridge and crept over it. Higher up we could s
more, but to follow our tracks soon became impossible, and we plugged straig
ahead and luckily found the slope down which we had come. All day it had be
blowing a nasty cold wind with a temperature between -20° and 30°, which we f
a good deal. Now it began to get worse. The weather was getting thick and thin
did not look very nice when we started up to find our tent. Soon it was blowi
force 4, and soon we missed our way entirely. We got right up above the patch
rocks which marked our igloo and only found it after a good deal of search.

I have heard tell of an English officer at the Dardanelles who was left, blin
ed, in No Man's Land between the English and Turkish trenches. Moving only
night, and having no sense to tell him which were his own trenches, he was fired
by Turk and English alike as he groped his ghastly way to and from them. Thus
spent days and nights until, one night, he crawled towards the English trench
to be fired at as usual. "Oh God! what can I do!" some one heard him say, and
was brought in.

Such extremity of suffering cannot be measured: madness or death may gi
relief. But this I know: we on this journey were already beginning to think of dea
as a friend. As we groped our way back that night, sleepless, icy, and dog-tired
the dark and the wind and the drift, a crevasse seemed almost a friendly gift.

"Things must improve," said Bill next day, "I think we reached bed-rock la
night." We hadn't, by a long way.

It was like this.

We moved into the igloo for the first time, for we had to save oil by usi
our blubber stove if we were to have any left to travel home with, and we did n
wish to cover our tent with the oily black filth which the use of blubber neces
tates. The blizzard blew all night, and we were covered with drift which came
through hundreds of leaks: in this wind-swept place we had found no soft sno
with which we could pack our hard snow blocks. As we flensed some blubb
from one of our penguin skins the powdery drift covered everything we had.

Though uncomfortable this was nothing to worry about overmuch. Some
the drift which the blizzard was bringing would collect to leeward of our hut a
the rocks below which it was built, and they could be used to make our hut mo
weather-proof. Then with great difficulty we got the blubber stove to start, and
spouted a blob of boiling oil into Bill's eye. For the rest of the night he lay, qui
unable to stifle his groans, obviously in very great pain: he told us afterwards th
he thought his eye was gone. We managed to cook a meal somehow, and Bird
got the stove going afterwards, but it was quite useless to try and warm the plac
I got out and cut the green canvas outside the door, so as to get the roof cloth
under the stones, and then packed it down as well as I could with snow, and
blocked most of the drift coming in.

It is extraordinary how often angels and fools do the same thing in this li nd I have never been able to settle which we were on this journey. I never heard n angry word: once only (when this same day I could not pull Bill up the cliff out f the penguin rookery) I heard an impatient one: and these groans were the near-st approach to complaint. Most men would have howled. "I think we reached ed-rock last night," was strong language for Bill. "I was incapacitated for a short ime," he says in his report to Scott.[158] Endurance was tested on this journey under unique circumstances, and always these two men with all the burden of responsi-ility which did not fall upon myself, displayed that quality which is perhaps the only one which may be said with certainty to make for success, self-control.

We spent the next day—it was July 21—in collecting every scrap of soft snow we could find and packing it into the crevasses between our hard snow blocks. It was a pitifully small amount but we could see no cracks when we had finished. To counteract the lifting tendency the wind had on our roof we cut some great flat hard snow blocks and laid them on the canvas top to steady it against the sledge which formed the ridge support. We also pitched our tent outside the igloo door. Both tent and igloo were therefore eight or nine hundred feet up Terror: both were below an outcrop of rocks from which the mountain fell steeply to the Barrier be-hind us, and from this direction came the blizzards. In front of us the slope fell for a mile or more down to the ice-cliffs, so wind-swept that we had to wear crampons o walk upon it. Most of the tent was in the lee of the igloo, but the cap of it came over the igloo roof, while a segment of the tent itself jutted out beyond the igloo wall.

That night we took much of our gear into the tent and lighted the blubber stove. I always mistrusted that stove, and every moment I expected it to flare up and burn the tent. But the heat it gave, as it burned furiously, with the double lin-ing of the tent to contain it, was considerable.

It did not matter, except for a routine which we never managed to keep, wheth-er we started to thaw our way into our frozen sleeping-bags at 4 in the morning or 4 in the afternoon. I think we must have turned in during the afternoon of that Friday, leaving the cooker, our finnesko, a deal of our foot-gear, Bowers' bag of personal gear, and many other things in the tent. I expect we left the blubber stove there too, for it was quite useless at present to try and warm the igloo. The tent floor-cloth was under our sleeping-bags in the igloo.

"Things must improve," said Bill. After all there was much for which to be thankful. I don't think anybody could have made a better igloo with the hard snow blocks and rocks which were all we had: we would get it air-tight by degrees. The blubber stove was working, and we had fuel for it: we had also found a way down to the penguins and had three complete, though frozen eggs: the two which had been in my mitts smashed when I fell about because I could not wear spectacles. Also the twilight given by the sun below the horizon at noon was getting longer.

But already we had been out twice as long in winter as the longest previous journeys in spring. The men who made those journeys had daylight where we had darkness, they had never had such low temperatures, generally nothing approach-

[158] *Scott's Last Expedition*, vol. ii. p. 42.

ing them, and they had seldom worked in such difficult country. The nearest ap
proach to healthy sleep we had had for nearly a month was when during blizzarc
the temperature allowed the warmth of our bodies to thaw some of the ice in ou
clothing and sleeping-bags into water. The wear and tear on our minds was ver
great. We were certainly weaker. We had a little more than a tin of oil to get bac
on, and we knew the conditions we had to face on that journey across the Barrie
even with fresh men and fresh gear it had been almost unendurable.

And so we spent half an hour or more getting into our bags. Cirrus clou
was moving across the face of the stars from the north, it looked rather hazy an
thick to the south, but it is always difficult to judge weather in the dark. There wa
little wind and the temperature was in the minus twenties. We felt no particula
uneasiness. Our tent was well dug in, and was also held down by rocks and th
heavy tank off the sledge which were placed on the skirting as additional securit
We felt that no power on earth could move the thick walls of our igloo, nor dra
the canvas roof from the middle of the embankment into which it was packed an
lashed.

"Things must improve," said Bill.

I do not know what time it was when I woke up. It was calm, with that abso
lute silence which can be so soothing or so terrible as circumstances dictate. The
there came a sob of wind, and all was still again. Ten minutes and it was blowin
as though the world was having a fit of hysterics. The earth was torn in pieces: th
indescribable fury and roar of it all cannot be imagined.

"Bill, Bill, the tent has gone," was the next I remember—from Bowers shoutin
at us again and again through the door. It is always these early morning shock
which hit one hardest: our slow minds suggested that this might mean a peculiar
lingering form of death. Journey after journey Birdie and I fought our way acros
the few yards which had separated the tent from the igloo door. I have never un
derstood why so much of our gear which was in the tent remained, even in the le
of the igloo. The place where the tent had been was littered with gear, and whe
we came to reckon up afterwards we had everything except the bottom piece of th
cooker, and the top of the outer cooker. We never saw these again. The most wor
derful thing of all was that our finnesko were lying where they were left, whic
happened to be on the ground in the part of the tent which was under the lee of th
igloo. Also Birdie's bag of personal gear was there, and a tin of sweets.

Birdie brought two tins of sweets away with him. One we had to celebrate ou
arrival at the Knoll: this was the second, of which we knew nothing, and whic
was for Bill's birthday, the next day. We started eating them on Saturday, howev
er, and the tin came in useful to Bill afterwards.

To get that gear in we fought against solid walls of black snow which flowe
past us and tried to hurl us down the slope. Once started nothing could hav
stopped us. I saw Birdie knocked over once, but he clawed his way back just i
time. Having passed everything we could find in to Bill, we got back into the iglo
and started to collect things together, including our very dishevelled minds.

There was no doubt that we were in the devil of a mess, and it was not alto gether our fault. We had had to put our igloo more or less where we could get rocks with which to build it. Very naturally we had given both our tent and igloo all the shelter we could from the full force of the wind, and now it seemed we were in danger not because they were in the wind, but because they were not sufficiently in it. The main force of the hurricane, deflected by the ridge behind, fled over our heads and appeared to form by suction a vacuum below. Our tent had either been sucked upwards into this, or had been blown away because some of it was in the wind while some of it was not. The roof of our igloo was being wrenched upwards and then dropped back with great crashes: the drift was spouting in, not it seemed because it was blown in from outside, but because it was sucked in from within: the lee, not the weather, wall was the worst. Already everything was six or eight inches under snow.

Very soon we began to be alarmed about the igloo. For some time the heavy snow blocks we had heaved up on to the canvas roof kept it weighted down. But it seemed that they were being gradually moved off by the hurricane. The tension became well-nigh unendurable: the waiting in all that welter of noise was maddening. Minute after minute, hour after hour—those snow blocks were off now anyway, and the roof was smashed up and down—no canvas ever made could stand it indefinitely.

We got a meal that Saturday morning, our last for a very long time as it happened. Oil being of such importance to us we tried to use the blubber stove, but after several preliminary spasms it came to pieces in our hands, some solder having melted; and a very good thing too, I thought, for it was more dangerous than useful. We finished cooking our meal on the primus. Two bits of the cooker having been blown away we had to balance it on the primus as best we could. We then settled that in view of the shortage of oil we would not have another meal for as long as possible. As a matter of fact God settled that for us.

We did all we could to stop up the places where the drift was coming in, plugging the holes with our socks, mitts and other clothing. But it was no real good. Our igloo was a vacuum which was filling itself up as soon as possible: and when snow was not coming in a fine black moraine dust took its place, covering us and everything. For twenty-four hours we waited for the roof to go: things were so bad now that we dare not unlash the door.

Many hours ago Bill had told us that if the roof went he considered that our best chance would be to roll over in our sleeping-bags until we were lying on the openings, and get frozen and drifted in.

Gradually the situation got more desperate. The distance between the taut-sucked canvas and the sledge on which it should have been resting became greater, and this must have been due to the stretching of the canvas itself and the loss of the snow blocks on the top: it was not drawing out of the walls. The crashes as it dropped and banged out again were louder. There was more snow coming through the walls, though all our loose mitts, socks and smaller clothing were stuffed into the worst places: our pyjama jackets were stuffed between the roof and the rocks over the door. The rocks were lifting and shaking here till we thought they would fall.

We talked by shouting, and long before this one of us proposed to try and get the Alpine rope lashed down over the roof from outside. But Bowers said it was an absolute impossibility in that wind. "You could never ask men at sea to try such a thing," he said. He was up and out of his bag continually, stopping up holes, pressing against bits of roof to try and prevent the flapping and so forth. He was magnificent.

And then it went.

Birdie was over by the door, where the canvas which was bent over the lintel board was working worse than anywhere else. Bill was practically out of his bag, pressing against some part with a long stick of some kind. I don't know what I was doing but I was half out of and half in my bag.

The top of the door opened in little slits and that green Willesden canvas flapped into hundreds of little fragments in fewer seconds than it takes to read this. The uproar of it all was indescribable. Even above the savage thunder of that great wind on the mountain came the lash of the canvas as it was whipped to little tiny strips. The highest rocks which we had built into our walls fell upon us, and a sheet of drift came in.

Birdie dived for his sleeping-bag and eventually got in, together with a terrible lot of drift. Bill also—but he was better off: I was already half into mine and all right, so I turned to help Bill. "Get into your own," he shouted, and when continued to try and help him, he leaned over until his mouth was against my ear. "*Please*, Cherry," he said, and his voice was terribly anxious. I know he felt responsible: feared it was he who had brought us to this ghastly end.

The next I knew was Bowers' head across Bill's body. "We're all right," he yelled, and we answered in the affirmative. Despite the fact that we knew we only said so because we knew we were all wrong, this statement was helpful. Then we turned our bags over as far as possible, so that the bottom of the bag was uppermost and the flaps were more or less beneath us. And we lay and thought, and sometimes we sang.

I suppose, wrote Wilson, we were all revolving plans to get back without a tent: and the one thing we had left was the floor-cloth upon which we were actually lying. Of course we could not speak at present, but later after the blizzard had stopped we discussed the possibility of digging a hole in the snow each night and covering it over with the floor-cloth. I do not think we had any idea that we could really get back in those temperatures in our present state of ice by such means, but no one ever hinted at such a thing. Birdie and Bill sang quite a lot of songs and hymns, snatches of which reached me every now and then, and I chimed in somewhat feebly I suspect. Of course we were getting pretty badly drifted up. "I was resolved to keep warm," wrote Bowers, "and beneath my debris covering I paddled my feet and sang all the songs and hymns I knew to pass the time. I could occasionally thump Bill, and as he still moved I knew he was alive all right—what a birthday for him!" Birdie was more drifted up than we, but at times we all had to hummock ourselves up to heave the snow off our bags. By opening the flaps of our gs we could get small pinches of soft drift which we pressed together and put to our mouths to melt. When our hands warmed up again we got some more; we did not get very thirsty. A few ribbons of canvas still remained in the wall er our heads, and these produced volleys of cracks like pistol shots hour after ur The canvas never drew out from the walls, not an inch The wind made just e same noise as an express train running fast through a tunnel if you have both e windows down.

I can well believe that neither of my companions gave up hope for an instant. ey must have been frightened but they were never disturbed. As for me I never d any hope at all; and when the roof went I felt that this was the end. What else uld I think? We had spent days in reaching this place through the darkness in ld such as had never been experienced by human beings. We had been out for ur weeks under conditions in which no man had existed previously for more an a few days, if that. During this time we had seldom slept except from sheer ysical exhaustion, as men sleep on the rack; and every minute of it we had been hting for the bed-rock necessaries of bare existence, and always in the dark. We d kept ourselves going by enormous care of our feet and hands and bodies, by rning oil, and by having plenty of hot fatty food. Now we had no tent, one tin oil left out of six, and only part of our cooker. When we were lucky and not too ld we could almost wring water from our clothes, and directly we got out of our eping-bags we were frozen into solid sheets of armoured ice. In cold tempera- res with all the advantages of a tent over our heads we were already taking more an an hour of fierce struggling and cramp to get into our sleeping-bags—so fro- n were they and so long did it take us to thaw our way in. No! Without the tent e were dead men.

MT. EREBUS

ICE PRESSURE AT A

And there seemed not one chance in a million that we should ever see our te
again. We were 900 feet up on the mountain side, and the wind blew about as ha
as a wind can blow straight out to sea. First there was a steep slope, so hard tha
pick made little impression upon it, so slippery that if you started down in finn
ko you never could stop: this ended in a great ice-cliff some hundreds of feet hig
and then came miles of pressure ridges, crevassed and tumbled, in which y
might as well look for a daisy as a tent: and after that the open sea. The chanc
however, were that the tent had just been taken up into the air and dropped som
where in this sea well on the way to New Zealand. Obviously the tent was gone

Face to face with real death one does not think of the things that torment t
bad people in the tracts, and fill the good people with bliss. I might have specul
ed on my chances of going to Heaven; but candidly I did not care. I could not ha
wept if I had tried. I had no wish to review the evils of my past. But the past d
seem to have been a bit wasted. The road to Hell may be paved with good inte
tions: the road to Heaven is paved with lost opportunities.

I wanted those years over again. What fun I would have with them: wh
glorious fun! It was a pity. Well has the Persian said that when we come to die w
remembering that God is merciful, will gnaw our elbows with remorse for thin
ing of the things we have not done for fear of the Day of Judgment.

And I wanted peaches and syrup—badly. We had them at the hut, sweeter a
more luscious than you can imagine. And we had been without sugar for a mont
Yes—especially the syrup.

Thus impiously I set out to die, making up my mind that I was not going to try and keep warm, that it might not take too long, and thinking I would try and get some morphia from the medical case if it got very bad. Not a bit heroic, and entirely true! Yes! comfortable, warm reader. Men do not fear death, they fear the pain of dying.

And then quite naturally and no doubt disappointingly to those who would like to read of my last agonies (for who would not give pleasure by his death?) I fell asleep. I expect the temperature was pretty high during this great blizzard, and anything near zero was very high to us. That and the snow which drifted over us made a pleasant wet kind of snipe marsh inside our sleeping-bags, and I am sure we all dozed a good bit. There was so much to worry about that there was not the least use in worrying; and we were so *very* tired. We were hungry, for the last meal we had had was in the morning of the day before, but hunger was not very pressing.

And so we lay, wet and quite fairly warm, hour after hour while the wind roared round us, blowing storm force continually and rising in the gusts to something indescribable. Storm force is force 11, and force 12 is the biggest wind which can be logged: Bowers logged it force 11, but he was always so afraid of overestimating that he was inclined to underrate. I think it was blowing a full hurricane. Sometimes awake, sometimes dozing, we had not a very uncomfortable time so far as I can remember. I knew that parties which had come to Cape Crozier in the spring had experienced blizzards which lasted eight or ten days. But this did not worry us as much as I think it did Bill: I was numb. I vaguely called to mind that Peary had survived a blizzard in the open: but wasn't that in the summer?

It was in the early morning of Saturday (July 22) that we discovered the loss of the tent. Some time during that morning we had had our last meal. The roof went about noon on Sunday and we had had no meal in the interval because our supply of oil was so low; nor could we move out of our bags except as a last necessity. By Sunday night we had been without a meal for some thirty-six hours.

The rocks which fell upon us when the roof went did no damage, and though we could not get out of our bags to move them, we could fit ourselves into them without difficulty. More serious was the drift which began to pile up all round and over us. It helped to keep us warm of course, but at the same time in these comparatively high temperatures it saturated our bags even worse than they were before. If we did not find the tent (and its recovery would be a miracle) these bags and the floor-cloth of the tent on which we were lying were all we had in that fight back across the Barrier which could, I suppose, have only had one end.

Meanwhile we had to wait. It was nearly 70 miles home and it had taken us the best part of three weeks to come. In our less miserable moments we tried to think out ways of getting back, but I do not remember very much about that time. Sunday morning faded into Sunday afternoon,—into Sunday night,—into Monday morning. Till then the blizzard had raged with monstrous fury; the winds of the world were there, and they had all gone mad. We had bad winds at Cape Evans this year, and we had far worse the next winter when the open water was at our doors. But I have never heard or felt or seen a wind like this. I wondered why did not carry away the earth.

In the early hours of Monday there was an occasional hint of a lull. Ordinaril in a big winter blizzard, when you have lived for several days and nights with th turmoil in your ears, the lulls are more trying than the noise: "the feel of not to fe it."[159] I do not remember noticing that now. Seven or eight more hours passec and though it was still blowing we could make ourselves heard to one anoth without great difficulty. It was two days and two nights since we had had a mea

We decided to get out of our bags and make a search for the tent. We did s bitterly cold and utterly miserable, though I do not think any of us showed it. In th darkness we could see very little, and no trace whatever of the tent. We returne against the wind, nursing our faces and hands, and settled that we must try an cook a meal somehow. We managed about the weirdest meal eaten north or soutl We got the floor-cloth wedged under our bags, then got into our bags and drev the floor-cloth over our heads. Between us we got the primus alight somehow, an by hand we balanced the cooker on top of it, minus the two members which ha been blown away. The flame flickered in the draughts. Very slowly the snow i the cooker melted, we threw in a plentiful supply of pemmican, and the smell of was better than anything on earth. In time we got both tea and pemmican, whic was full of hairs from our bags, penguin feathers, dirt and debris, but deliciou The blubber left in the cooker got burnt and gave the tea a burnt taste. None of u ever forgot that meal: I enjoyed it as much as such a meal could be enjoyed, an that burnt taste will always bring back the memory.

It was still dark and we lay down in our bags again, but soon a little glow c light began to come up, and we turned out to have a further search for the ten Birdie went off before Bill and me. Clumsily I dragged my eider-down out of m bag on my feet, all sopping wet: it was impossible to get it back and I let it freeze: was soon just like a rock. The sky to the south was as black and sinister as it coul possibly be. It looked as though the blizzard would be on us again at any momen

I followed Bill down the slope. We could find nothing. But, as we searchec we heard a shout somewhere below and to the right. We got on a slope, slippec and went sliding down quite unable to stop ourselves, and came upon Birdie wit the tent, the outer lining still on the bamboos. Our lives had been taken away an given back to us.

We were so thankful we said nothing.

The tent must have been gripped up into the air, shutting as it rose. The bam boos, with the inner lining lashed to them, had entangled the outer cover, an the whole went up together like a shut umbrella. This was our salvation. If it ha opened in the air nothing could have prevented its destruction. As it was, with a the accumulated ice upon it, it must have weighed the best part of 100 lbs. It ha been dropped about half a mile away, at the bottom of a steep slope: and it fell i a hollow, still shut up. The main force of the wind had passed over it, and there was, with the bamboos and fastenings wrenched and strained, and the ends of tw

[159] Keats.

of the poles broken, but the silk untorn.

If that tent went again we were going with it. We made our way back up the slope with it, carrying it solemnly and reverently, precious as though it were something not quite of the earth. And we dug it in as tent was never dug in before; not by the igloo, but in the old place farther down where we had first arrived. And while Bill was doing this Birdie and I went back to the igloo and dug and scratched and shook away the drift inside until we had found nearly all our gear. It is wonderful how little we lost when the roof went. Most of our gear was hung on the sledge, which was part of the roof, or was packed into the holes of the hut to try and make it drift-proof, and the things must have been blown inwards into the bottom of the hut by the wind from the south and the back draught from the north. Then they were all drifted up. Of course a certain number of mitts and socks were blown away and lost, but the only important things were Bill's fur mitts, which were stuffed into a hole in the rocks of the hut. We loaded up the sledge and pushed it down the slope. I don't know how Birdie was feeling, but I felt so weak that it was the greatest labour. The blizzard looked right on top of us.

We had another meal, and we wanted it: and as the good hoosh ran down into our feet and hands, and up into our cheeks and ears and brains, we discussed what we would do next. Birdie was all for another go at the Emperor penguins. Dear Birdie, he never would admit that he was beaten—I don't know that he ever really was! "I think he (Wilson) thought he had landed us in a bad corner and was determined to go straight home, though I was for one other tap at the Rookery. However, I had placed myself under his orders for this trip voluntarily, and so we started the next day for home."[160] There could really be no common-sense doubt: we had to go back, and we were already very doubtful whether we should ever manage to get into our sleeping-bags in very low temperature, so ghastly had they become.

I don't know when it was, but I remember walking down that slope—I don't know why, perhaps to try and find the bottom of the cooker—and thinking that there was nothing on earth that a man under such circumstances would not give for a good warm sleep. He would give everything he possessed: he would give—how many—years of his life. One or two at any rate—perhaps five? Yes—I would give five. I remember the sastrugi, the view of the Knoll, the dim hazy black smudge of the sea far away below: the tiny bits of green canvas that twittered in the wind on the surface of the snow: the cold misery of it all, and the weakness which was biting into my heart.

For days Birdie had been urging me to use his eider-down lining—his beautiful dry bag of the finest down—which he had never slipped into his own fur bag. I had refused: I felt that I should be a beast to take it.

We packed the tank ready for a start back in the morning and turned in, utterly worn out. It was only -12° that night, but my left big toe was frost-bitten in my bag which I was trying to use without an eider-down lining, and my bag was always too big for me. It must have taken several hours to get it back, by beating one foot against the other. When we got up, as soon as we could, as we did every night, for

---

[160] Bowers.

our bags were nearly impossible, it was blowing fairly hard and looked like blizz
ing. We had a lot to do, two or three hours' work, packing sledges and making ₃
depôt of what we did not want, in a corner of the igloo. We left the second sledge
and a note tied to the handle of the pickaxe.

"We started down the slope in a wind which was rising all the time and -15°
My job was to balance the sledge behind: I was so utterly done I don't believe
could have pulled effectively. Birdie was much the strongest of us. The strain anc
want of sleep was getting me in the neck, and Bill looked very bad. At the bot
tom we turned our faces to the Barrier, our backs to the penguins, but after doing
about a mile it looked so threatening in the south that we camped in a big wind
our hands going one after the other. We had nothing but the hardest wind-swep
sastrugi, and it was a long business: there was only the smallest amount of drift
and we were afraid the icy snow blocks would chafe the tent. Birdie lashed the ful
biscuit tin to the door to prevent its flapping, and also got what he called the ten
downhaul round the cap and then tied it about himself outside his bag: if the ten
went he was going too.

"I was feeling as if I should crack, and accepted Birdie's eider-down. It wa:
wonderfully self-sacrificing of him: more than I can write. I felt a brute to take
it, but I was getting useless unless I got some sleep which my big bag would no
allow. Bill and Birdie kept on telling me to do less: that I was doing more than my
share of the work: but I think that I was getting more and more weak. Birdie kep
wonderfully strong: he slept most of the night: the difficulty for him was to ge
into his bag without going to sleep. He kept the meteorological log untiringly, bu
some of these nights he had to give it up for the time because he could not keep
awake. He used to fall asleep with his pannikin in his hand and let it fall: anc
sometimes he had the primus.

"Bill's bag was getting hopeless: it was really too small for an eider-down anc
was splitting all over the place: great long holes. He never consciously slept fo
nights: he did sleep a bit, for we heard him. Except for this night, and the nex
when Birdie's eider-down was still fairly dry, I never consciously slept; excep
that I used to wake for five or six nights running with the same nightmare—tha
we were drifted up, and that Bill and Birdie were passing the gear into my bag
cutting it open to do so, or some other variation,—I did not know that I had beer
asleep at all."[161]

"We had hardly reached the pit," wrote Bowers, "when a furious wind came
on again and we had to camp. All that night the tent flapped like the noise o
musketry, owing to two poles having been broken at the ends and the fit spoilt
I thought it would end matters by going altogether and lashed it down as much
as I could, attaching the apex to a line round my own bag. The wind abated after
1½ days and we set out, doing five or six miles before we found ourselves among
crevasses."[162]

We had plugged ahead all that day (July 26) in a terrible light, blundering ir

[161] My own diary.
[162] Bowers.

1ong pressure and up on to the slopes of Terror. The temperature dropped from 1° to -45°. "Several times [we] stepped into rotten-lidded crevasses in smooth 1nd-swept ice. We continued, however, feeling our way along by keeping always f hard ice-slopes and on the crustier deeper snow which characterizes the hol-vs of the pressure ridges, which I believed we had once more fouled in the dark. e had no light, and no landmarks to guide us, except vague and indistinct sil-ouetted slopes ahead, which were always altering and whose distance and char-ter it was impossible to judge. We never knew whether we were approaching a eep slope at close quarters or a long slope of Terror, miles away, and eventually travelled on by the ear, and by the feel of the snow under our feet, for both the und and the touch told one much of the chances of crevasses or of safe going. We ntinued thus in the dark in the hope that we were at any rate in the right direc-on."[163] And then we camped after getting into a bunch of crevasses, completely st. Bill said, "At any rate I think we are well clear of the pressure." But there were essure pops all night, as though some one was whacking an empty tub.

It was Birdie's picture hat which made the trouble next day. "What do you ink of *that* for a hat, sir?" I heard him say to Scott a few days before we started, olding it out much as Lucille displays her latest Paris model. Scott looked at it ietly for a time: "I'll tell you when you come back, Birdie," he said. It was a com-icated affair with all kinds of nose-guards and buttons and lanyards: he thought was going to set it to suit the wind much as he would set the sails of a ship. We ent a long time with our housewifes before this and other trips, for everybody is their own ideas as to how to alter their clothing for the best. When finished me looked neat, like Bill: others baggy, like Scott or Seaman Evans: others rough d ready, like Oates and Bowers: a few perhaps more rough than ready, and I ill not mention names. Anyway Birdie's hat became improper immediately it as well iced up.

"When we got a little light in the morning we found we were a little north of e two patches of moraine on Terror. Though we did not know it, we were on the oint where the pressure runs up against Terror, and we could dimly see that we ere right up against something. We started to try and clear it, but soon had an 1ormous ridge, blotting out the moraine and half Terror, rising like a great hill on 1r right. Bill said the only thing was to go right on and hope it would lower; all e time, however, there was a bad feeling that we might be putting any number of dges between us and the mountain. After a while we tried to cross this one, but 1d to turn back for crevasses, both Bill and I putting a leg down. We went on for out twenty minutes and found a lower place, and turned to rise up it diagonally, 1d reached the top. Just over the top Birdie went right down a crevasse, which as about wide enough to take him. He was out of sight and out of reach from e surface, hanging in his harness. Bill went for his harness, I went for the bow the sledge: Bill told me to get the Alpine rope and Birdie directed from below hat we could do. We could not possibly haul him up as he was, for the sides of e crevasse were soft and he could not help himself."[164]

---

[163] Wilson in *Scott's Last Expedition*, vol. ii. p. 58.
[164] My own diary.

"My helmet was so frozen up," wrote Bowers, "that my head was encased
a solid block of ice, and I could not look down without inclining my whole boc
As a result Bill stumbled one foot into a crevasse and I landed in it with both mi
[even as I shouted a warning[165]], the bridge gave way and down I went. For
nately our sledge harness is made with a view to resisting this sort of thing, a
there I hung with the bottomless pit below and the ice-crusted sides alongside,
narrow that to step over it would have been quite easy had I been able to see it. I
said, 'What do you want?' I asked for an Alpine rope with a bowline for my fo
and taking up first the bowline and then my harness they got me out."[166] Mea
while on the surface I lay over the crevasse and gave Birdie the bowline: he pu
on his foot: then he raised his foot, giving me some slack: I held the rope while
raised himself on his foot, thus giving Bill some slack on the harness: Bill then he
the harness, allowing Birdie to raise his foot and give me some slack again. I
got him up inch by inch, our fingers getting bitten, for the temperature was -4
Afterwards we often used this way of getting people out of crevasses, and it wa
wonderful piece of presence of mind that it was invented, so far as I know, on t
spur of the moment by a frozen man hanging in one himself.

"In front of us we could see another ridge, and we did not know how ma
lay beyond that. Things looked pretty bad. Bill took a long lead on the Alpine ro
and we got down our present difficulty all right. This method of the leader bei
on a long trace in front we all agreed to be very useful. From this moment our lu
changed and everything went for us to the end. When we went out on the sea-:
the whole experience was over in a few days, Hut Point was always in sight, a
there was daylight. I always had the feeling that the whole series of events h
been brought about by an extraordinary run of accidents, and that after a cert
stage it was quite beyond our power to guide the course of them. When on t
way to Cape Crozier the moon suddenly came out of the cloud to show us a gr
crevasse which would have taken us all with our sledge without any difficulty
felt that we were not to go under this trip after such a deliverance. When we h
lost our tent, and there was a very great balance of probability that we shou
never find it again, and we were lying out the blizzard in our bags, I saw that v
were face to face with a long fight against cold which we could not have survivec
cannot write how helpless I believed we were to help ourselves, and how we we
brought out of a very terrible series of experiences. When we started back I hac
feeling that things were going to change for the better, and this day I had a distir
idea that we were to have one more bad experience and that after that we cou
hope for better things.

---

[165] Wilson.
[166] Bowers.

DOWN A CREVASSE

"By running along the hollow we cleared the pressure ridges, and continued all day up and down, but met no crevasses. Indeed, we met no more crevasses and no more pressure. I think it was upon this day that a wonderful glow stretched over the Barrier edge from Cape Crozier: at the base it was the most vivid crimson it is possible to imagine, shading upwards through every shade of red to light green, and so into a deep blue sky. It is the most vivid red I have ever seen in the sky."[167]

It was -49° in the night and we were away early in -47°. By mid-day we were rising Terror Point, opening Erebus rapidly, and got the first really light day, though the sun would not appear over the horizon for another month. I cannot describe what a relief the light was to us. We crossed the point outside our former track, and saw inside us the ridges where we had been blizzed for three days on

[167] My own diary.

our outward journey.

The minimum was -66° the next night and we were now back in the windles bight of Barrier with its soft snow, low temperatures, fogs and mists, and linge ing settlements of the inside crusts. Saturday and Sunday, the 29th and 30th, w plugged on across this waste, iced up as usual but always with Castle Rock gettin bigger. Sometimes it looked like fog or wind, but it always cleared away. We wei getting weak, how weak we can only realize now, but we got in good marche though slow—days when we did 4½, 7¼ 6¾, 6½, 7½ miles. On our outward jou ney we had been relaying and getting forward about 4½ miles a day at this poin The surface which we had dreaded so much was not so sandy or soft as when w had come out, and the settlements were more marked. These are caused by a cru falling under your feet. Generally the area involved is some twenty yards or s round you, and the surface falls through an air space for two or three inches wit a soft 'crush' which may at first make you think there are crevasses about. In th region where we now travelled they were much more pronounced than elsewher and one day, when Bill was inside the tent lighting the primus, I put my foot into hole that I had dug. This started a big settlement; sledge, tent and all of us droppe about a foot, and the noise of it ran away for miles and miles: we listened to it unt we began to get too cold. It must have lasted a full three minutes.

In the pauses of our marching we halted in our harnesses the ropes of whic lay slack in the powdery snow. We stood panting with our backs against the mour tainous mass of frozen gear which was our load. There was no wind, at any rat no more than light airs: our breath crackled as it froze. There was no unnecessar conversation: I don't know why our tongues never got frozen, but all my teeth, th nerves of which had been killed, split to pieces. We had been going perhaps thre hours since lunch.

"How are your feet, Cherry?" from Bill.

"Very cold."

"That's all right; so are mine." We didn't worry to ask Birdie: he never had frost-bitten foot from start to finish.

Half an hour later, as we marched, Bill would ask the same question. I tell hir that all feeling has gone: Bill still has some feeling in one of his but the other is los He settled we had better camp: another ghastly night ahead. We started to get ou of our harnesses, while Bill, before doing anything else, would take the fur mitt from his hands, carefully shape any soft parts as they froze (generally, howeve our mitts did not thaw on our hands), and lay them on the snow in front of him-two dark dots. His proper fur mitts were lost when the igloo roof went: these wer the delicate dog-skin linings we had in addition, beautiful things to look at an to feel when new, excellent when dry to turn the screws of a theodolite, but to dainty for straps and lanyards. Just now I don't know what he could have don without them.

Working with our woollen half-mitts and mitts on our hands all the time, an our fur mitts over them when possible, we gradually got the buckles undone, an spread the green canvas floor-cloth on the snow. This was also fitted to be use as a sail, but we never could have rigged a sail on this journey. The shovel and the bamboos, with a lining, itself lined with ice, lashed to them, were packed on the top of the load and were now put on the snow until wanted. Our next job was to lift our three sleeping-bags one by one on to the floor-cloth: they covered it, bulging over the sides—those obstinate coffins which were all our life to us.... One of us is off by now to nurse his fingers back. The cooker was unlashed from the top of the instrument box; some parts of it were put on the bags with the primus, methylated spirit can, matches and so forth; others left to be filled with snow later. Taking a pole in each hand we three spread the bamboos over the whole. "All right? Down!" from Bill; and we lowered them gently on to the soft snow, that they might not sink too far. The ice on the inner lining of the tent was formed mostly from the steam of the cooker. This we had been unable to beat or chip off in the past, and we were now, truth to tell, past worrying about it. The little ventilator in the top, made to let out this steam, had been tied up in order to keep in all possible heat. Then over with the outer cover, and for one of us the third worst job of the day was to begin. The worst job was to get into our bags: the second or equal worst was to lie in them for six hours (we had brought it down to six): this third worst was, to get the primus lighted and a meal on the way.

As cook of the day you took the broken metal framework, all that remained of our candlestick, and got yourself with difficulty into the funnel which formed the door. The enclosed space of the tent seemed much colder than the outside air: you tried three or four match-boxes and no match would strike: almost desperate, you asked for a new box to be given you from the sledge and got a light from this because it had not yet been in the warmth, so called, of the tent. The candle hung by a wire from the cap of the tent. It would be tedious to tell of the times we had getting the primus alight, and the lanyards of the weekly food bag unlashed. Probably by now the other two men have dug in the tent; squared up outside; filled and passed in the cooker; set the thermometer under the sledge and so forth. There were always one or two odd jobs which wanted doing as well: but you may be sure they came in as soon as possible when they heard the primus hissing, and saw the glow of light inside. Birdie made a bottom for the cooker out of an empty biscuit tin to take the place of the part which was blown away. On the whole this was a success, but we had to hold it steady—on Bill's sleeping-bag, for the flat frozen bags spread all over the floor space. Cooking was a longer business now. Some one whacked out the biscuit, and the cook put the ration of pemmican into the inner cooker which was by now half full of water. As opportunity offered we got out of our day, and into our night foot-gear—fleecy camel-hair stockings and fur boots. In the dim light we examined our feet for frost-bite.

I do not think it took us less than an hour to get a hot meal to our lips: pemmican followed by hot water in which we soaked our biscuits. For lunch we had tea and biscuits: for breakfast, pemmican, biscuits and tea. We could not have managed more food bags—three were bad enough, and the lashings of everything were like wire. The lashing of the tent door, however, was the worst, and it *had* to be tied tightly, especially if it was blowing. In the early days we took great pains to brush rime from the tent before packing it up, but we were long past that now.

The hoosh got down into our feet: we nursed back frost-bites: and we were al the warmer for having got our dry foot-gear on before supper. Then we started to get into our bags.

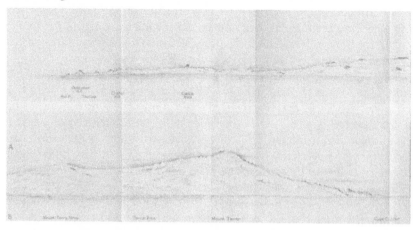

PANORAMA AND MAP OF THE WINTER JOURNEY—COPIED AT HUT POINT BY APSLEY CHERRY-GARRARD FROM A DRAWING BY E. A. WILSON

Birdie's bag fitted him beautifully, though perhaps it would have been a little small with an eider-down inside. He must have had a greater heat supply than other men; for he never had serious trouble with his feet, while ours were constantly frost-bitten: he slept, I should be afraid to say how much, longer than we did, even in these last days: it was a pleasure, lying awake practically all night, to hear his snores. He turned his bag inside out from fur to skin, and skin to fur, many times during the journey, and thus got rid of a lot of moisture which came out as snow or actual knobs of ice. When we did turn our bags the only way was to do so directly we turned out, and even then you had to be quick before the bag froze. Getting out of the tent at night it was quite a race to get back to your bag before it hardened. Of course this was in the lowest temperatures.

We could not burn our bags and we tried putting the lighted primus into them to thaw them out, but this was not very successful. Before this time, when it was very cold, we lighted the primus in the morning while we were still in our bags: and in the evening we kept it going until we were just getting or had got the mouths of our bags levered open. But returning we had no oil for such luxuries, until the last day or two.

I do not believe that any man, however sick he is, has a much worse time than we had in those bags, shaking with cold until our backs would almost break. One of the added troubles which came to us on our return was the sodden condition of our hands in our bags at night. We had to wear our mitts and half-mitts, and they were as wet as they could be: when we got up in the morning we had washer-women's hands—white, crinkled, sodden. That was an unhealthy way to start the day's work. We really wanted some bags of saennegrass for hands as well as et; one of the blessings of that kind of bag being that you can shake the moisture om it: but we only had enough for our wretched feet.

The horrors of that return journey are blurred to my memory and I know they ere blurred to my body at the time. I think this applies to all of us, for we were uch weakened and callous. The day we got down to the penguins I had not cared hether I fell into a crevasse or not. We had been through a great deal since then. now that we slept on the march; for I woke up when I bumped against Birdie, d Birdie woke when he bumped against me. I think Bill steering out in front anaged to keep awake. I know we fell asleep if we waited in the comparatively arm tent when the primus was alight—with our pannikins or the primus in our nds. I know that our sleeping-bags were so full of ice that we did not worry if e spilt water or hoosh over them as they lay on the floor-cloth, when we cooked them with our maimed cooker. They were so bad that we never rolled them in the usual way when we got out of them in the morning: we opened their ouths as much as possible before they froze, and hoisted them more or less flat to the sledge. All three of us helped to raise each bag, which looked rather like squashed coffin and was probably a good deal harder. I know that if it was only 0° when we camped for the night we considered quite seriously that we were ing to have a warm one, and that when we got up in the morning if the tempera- re was in the minus sixties we did not enquire what it was. The day's march was iss compared to the night's rest, and both were awful. We were about as bad as en can be and do good travelling: but I never heard a word of complaint, nor, I lieve, an oath, and I saw self-sacrifice standing every test.

Always we were getting nearer home: and we were doing good marches. We ere going to pull through; it was only a matter of sticking this for a few more ys; six, five, four ... three perhaps now, if we were not blizzed. Our main hut as behind that ridge where the mist was always forming and blowing away, and ere was Castle Rock: we might even see Observation Hill to-morrow, and the iscovery Hut furnished and trim was behind it, and they would have sent some ry sleeping-bags from Cape Evans to greet us there. We reckoned our troubles ver at the Barrier edge, and assuredly it was not far away. "You've got it in the ck, stick it, you've got it in the neck"—it was always running in my head.

And we did stick it. How good the memories of those days are. With jokes out Birdie's picture hat: with songs we remembered off the gramophone: with ady words of sympathy for frost-bitten feet: with generous smiles for poor jests: ith suggestions of happy beds to come. We did not forget the Please and Thank u, which mean much in such circumstances, and all the little links with decent vilization which we could still keep going. I'll swear there was still a grace about s when we staggered in. And we kept our tempers—even with God.

We might reach Hut Point to-night: we were burning more oil now, that e-gallon tin had lasted us well: and burning more candle too; at one time we ared they would give out. A hell of a morning we had: -57° in our present state. ut it was calm, and the Barrier edge could not be much farther now. The surface as getting harder: there were a few wind-blown furrows, the crust was coming p to us. The sledge was dragging easier: we always suspected the Barrier sloped

downwards hereabouts. Now the hard snow was on the surface, peeping out li
great inverted basins on which we slipped, and our feet became warmer for n
sinking into soft snow. Suddenly we saw a gleam of light in a line of darkness ru
ning across our course. It was the Barrier edge: we were all right now.

We ran the sledge off a snow-drift on to the sea-ice, with the same cold strea
of air flowing down it which wrecked my hands five weeks ago: pushed out
this, camped and had a meal: the temperature had already risen to -43°. We cou
almost feel it getting warmer as we went round Cape Armitage on the last thr
miles. We managed to haul our sledge up the ice foot, and dug the drift away fro
the door. The old hut struck us as fairly warm.

Bill was convinced that we ought not to go into the warm hut at Cape Eva
when we arrived there—to-morrow night! We ought to get back to warmth grad
ally, live in a tent outside, or in the annexe for a day or two. But I'm sure we nev
meant to do it. Just now Hut Point did not prejudice us in favour of such abs
nence. It was just as we had left it: there was nothing sent down for us there—n
sleeping-bags, nor sugar: but there was plenty of oil. Inside the hut we pitch
a dry tent left there since Depôt Journey days, set two primuses going in it; s
dozing on our bags; and drank cocoa without sugar so thick that next morning v
were gorged with it. We were very happy, falling asleep between each mouthf
and after several hours discussed schemes of not getting into our bags at all. B
some one would have to keep the primus going to prevent frost-bite, and we cou
not trust ourselves to keep awake. Bill and I tried to sing a part-song. Finally v
sopped our way into our bags. We only stuck *them* three hours, and thankful
turned out at 3 A.M., and were ready to pack up when we heard the wind con
away. It was no good, so we sat in our tent and dozed again. The wind dropped
9.30: we were off at 11. We walked out into what seemed to us a blaze of light.
was not until the following year that I understood that a great part of such twilig
as there is in the latter part of the winter was cut off from us by the mountains u
der which we travelled. Now, with nothing between us and the northern horizc
below which lay the sun, we saw as we had not seen for months, and the iridesce
clouds that day were beautiful.

We just pulled for all we were worth and did nearly two miles an hour: for tw
miles a baddish salt surface, then big undulating hard sastrugi and good goin
We slept as we walked. We had done eight miles by 4 P.M. and were past Glaci
Tongue. We lunched there.

As we began to gather our gear together to pack up for the last time, Bill sa
quietly, "I want to thank you two for what you have done. I couldn't have foun
two better companions—and what is more I never shall."

I am proud of that.

Antarctic exploration is seldom as bad as you imagine, seldom as bad as
sounds. But this journey had beggared our language: no words could express i
horror.

We trudged on for several more hours and it grew very dark. There was a di
cussion as to where Cape Evans lay. We rounded it at last: it must have been t

r eleven o'clock, and it was possible that some one might see us as we pulled towards the hut. "Spread out well," said Bill, "and they will be able to see that there re three men." But we pulled along the cape, over the tide-crack, up the bank to he very door of the hut without a sound. No noise from the stable, nor the bark of dog from the snowdrifts above us. We halted and stood there trying to get ourselves and one another out of our frozen harnesses—the usual long job. The door pened—"Good God! here is the Crozier Party," said a voice, and disappeared.

Thus ended the worst journey in the world.

And now the reader will ask what became of the three penguins' eggs for which three human lives had been risked three hundred times a day, and three human frames strained to the utmost extremity of human endurance.

Let us leave the Antarctic for a moment and conceive ourselves in the year 913 in the Natural History Museum in South Kensington. I had written to say that I would bring the eggs at this time. Present, myself, C.-G., the sole survivor of the three, with First or Doorstep Custodian of the Sacred Eggs. I did not take a verbatim report of his welcome; but the spirit of it may be dramatized as follows:

FIRST CUSTODIAN. Who are you? What do you want? This ain't an egg-shop. What call have you to come meddling with our eggs? Do you want me to put the police on to you? Is it the crocodile's egg you're after? I don't know nothing about no eggs. You'd best speak to Mr. Brown: it's him that varnishes the eggs.

I resort to Mr. Brown, who ushers me into the presence of the Chief Custodian, man of scientific aspect, with two manners: one, affably courteous, for a Person of Importance (I guess a Naturalist Rothschild at least) with whom he is conversing, and the other, extraordinarily offensive even for an official man of science, for myself.

I announce myself with becoming modesty as the bearer of the penguins' ggs, and proffer them. The Chief Custodian takes them into custody without a word of thanks, and turns to the Person of Importance to discuss them. I wait. The emperature of my blood rises. The conversation proceeds for what seems to me considerable period. Suddenly the Chief Custodian notices my presence and eems to resent it.

CHIEF CUSTODIAN. You needn't wait.

HEROIC EXPLORER. I should like to have a receipt for the eggs, if you please.

CHIEF CUSTODIAN. It is not necessary: it is all right. You needn't wait.

HEROIC EXPLORER. I should like to have a receipt.

But by this time the Chief Custodian's attention is again devoted wholly to he Person of Importance. Feeling that to persist in overhearing their conversation would be an indelicacy, the Heroic Explorer politely leaves the room, and establishes himself on a chair in a gloomy passage outside, where he wiles away he time by rehearsing in his imagination how he will tell off the Chief Custodian when the Person of Importance retires. But this the Person of Importance shows no sign of doing, and the Explorer's thoughts and intentions become darker and darker. As the day wears on, minor officials, passing to and from the Presenc look at him doubtfully and ask his business. The reply is always the same, "I a⌐ waiting for a receipt for some penguins' eggs." At last it becomes clear from tⁿ Explorer's expression that what he is really waiting for is not to take a receipt b⌐ to commit murder. Presumably this is reported to the destined victim: at all even⌐ the receipt finally comes; and the Explorer goes his way with it, feeling that he hₐ behaved like a perfect gentleman, but so very dissatisfied with that vapid cons⌐ lation that for hours he continues his imaginary rehearsals of what he would hav⌐ liked to have done to that Custodian (mostly with his boots) by way of teachir⌐ him manners.

Some time after this I visited the Natural History Museum with Captaⁱ Scott's sister. After a slight preliminary skirmish in which we convinced a min⌐ custodian that the specimens brought by the expedition from the Antarctic did n⌐ include the moths we found preying on some of them, Miss Scott expressed a wi⌐ to see the penguins' eggs. Thereupon the minor custodians flatly denied that an⌐ such eggs were in existence or in their possession. Now Miss Scott was her brot⌐ er's sister; and she showed so little disposition to take this lying down that I w⌐ glad to get her away with no worse consequences than a profanely emphasize⌐ threat on my part that if we did not receive ample satisfaction in writing withⁱ twenty-four hours as to the safety of the eggs England would reverberate with tⁿ tale.

The ultimatum was effectual; and due satisfaction was forthcoming in tim⌐ but I was relieved when I learnt later on that they had been entrusted to Profess⌐ Assheton for the necessary microscopic examination. But he died before he cou⌐ approach the task; and the eggs passed into the hands of Professor Cossar Ewa⌐ of Edinburgh University.

His report is as follows:

APPENDIX
PROFESSOR COSSAR EWART'S REPORT

"It was a great disappointment to Dr. Wilson that no Emperor Penguin embryos were obtained during the cruise of the Discovery. But though embryos were conspicuous by their absence in the Emperor eggs brought home by the National Antarctic Expedition, it is well to bear in mind that the naturalists on board the Discovery learned much about the breeding habits of the largest living member of the ancient penguin family. Amongst other things it was ascertained (1) that in the case of the Emperor, as in the King Penguin, the egg during the period of incubation rests on the upper surface of the feet protected and kept in position by a fold of skin from the lower breast; and (2) that in the case of the Emperor the whole process of incubation is carried out on sea ice during the coldest and darkest months of the antarctic winter.

"After devoting much time to the study of penguins Dr. Wilson came to the conclusion that Emperor embryos would throw new light on the origin and history of birds, and decided that if he again found his way to the Antarctic he would make a supreme effort to visit an Emperor rookery during the breeding season. When, and under what conditions, the Cape Crozier rookery was eventually visited and Emperor eggs secured is graphically told in The Winter Journey. The question now arises, Has 'the weirdest bird's-nesting expedition that has ever been made' added appreciably to our knowledge of birds?

"It is admitted that birds are descended from bipedal reptiles which flourished some millions of years ago—reptiles in build not unlike the kangaroo. From Archaeopteryx of Jurassic times we know primeval birds had teeth, three fingers with claws on each hand, and a long lizard-like tail provided with nearly twenty pairs of well-formed true feathers. But unfortunately neither this lizard-tailed bird, nor yet the fossil birds found in America, throw any light on the origin of feathers. Ornithologists and others who have devoted much time to the study of birds have as a rule assumed that feathers were made out of scales, that the scales along the margin of the hand and forearm and along each side of the tail were elongated, frayed and otherwise modified to form the wing and tail quills, and that later other scales were altered to provide a coat capable of preventing loss of heat. But as it happens, a study of the development of feathers affords no evidence that they were made out of scales. There are neither rudiments of scales nor feathers in very young bird embryos. In the youngest of the three Emperor embryos there are, however, feather rudiments in the tail region,—the embryo was probably seven or eight days old—but in the two older embryos there are a countless number of feather rudiments, *i.e.* of minute pimples known as papillae.

"In penguins as in many other birds there are two distinct crops of feathe papillae, viz.: a crop of relatively large papillae which develop into prepennae, th forerunners of true feathers (pennae), and a crop of small papillae which develop into preplumulae, the forerunners of true down feathers (plumulae).

"In considering the origin of feathers we are not concerned with the true feath ers (pennae), but with the nestling feathers (prepennae), and more especially with the papillae from which the prepennae are developed. What we want to know is Do the papillae which in birds develop into the first generation of feathers corre spond to the papillae which in lizards develop into scales?

"The late Professor Assheton, who undertook the examination of some of the material brought home by the Terra Nova, made a special study of the feathe papillae of the Emperor Penguin embryos from Cape Crozier. Drawings were made to indicate the number, size and time of appearance of the feather papillae but unfortunately in the notes left by the distinguished embryologist there is no indication whether the feather papillae were regarded as modified scale papillae or new creations resulting from the appearance of special feather-forming factor in the germ-plasm.

"When eventually the three Emperor Penguin embryos reached me that their feather rudiments might be compared with the feather rudiments of other birds I noticed that in Emperor embryos the feather papillae appeared before the scale papillae. Evidence of this was especially afforded by the largest embryo, which had reached about the same stage in its development as a 16-days goose embryo.

"In the largest Emperor embryo feather papillae occur all over the hind-quarters and on the legs to within a short distance of the tarsal joint. Beyond the tarsa joint even in the largest embryo no attempt had been made to produce the papil lae which in older penguin embryos represent, and ultimately develop into, the scaly covering of the foot. The absence of papillae on the foot implied either that the scale papillae were fundamentally different from feather papillae or that for some reason or other the development of the papillae destined to give rise to the foot scales had been retarded. There is no evidence as far as I can ascertain that in modern lizards the scale papillae above the tarsal joint appear before the scale papillae beyond this joint.

"The absence of papillae below the tarsal joint in Emperor embryos, together with the fact that in many birds each large feather papilla is accompanied by two or more very small feather papillae, led me to study the papillae of the limbs of other birds. The most striking results were obtained from the embryos of Chinese geese in which the legs are relatively longer than in penguins. In a 13-days goose embryo the whole of the skin below and for some distance above the tarsal joint is quite smooth, whereas the skin of the rest of the leg is studded with feather papil lae. On the other hand, in an 18-days goose embryo in which the feather papillae of the legs have developed into filaments, each containing a fairly well-formed feath er, scale papillae occur not only on the foot below and for some distance above the tarsal joint but also between the roots of the feather filaments between the tarsa

ιd the knee joints. More important still, in a 20-days goose embryo a number of
e papillae situated between the feather filaments of the leg were actually devel-
)ing into scales each of which overlapped the root (calamus) of a feather just as
ᐧales overlap the foot feathers in grouse and other feather-footed birds.

"As in bird embryos there is no evidence that feather papillae ever develop
to scales or that scale papillae ever develop into feathers it may be assumed that
.ather papillae are fundamentally different from scale papillae, the difference
ᐧesumably being due to the presence of special factors in the germ-plasm. Just
ᐧ in armadillos hairs are found emerging from under the scales, in ancient birds
ᐧ in the feet of some modern birds the coat probably consisted of both feathers
ιd scales. But in course of time, owing perhaps to the growth of the scales being
ᐧrested, the coat of the birds, instead of consisting throughout of well-developed
ᐧales and small inconspicuous feathers, was almost entirely made up of a count-
ᐧss number of downy feathers, well-developed scales only persisting below the
ᐧrsal joint.

"If the conclusions arrived at with the help of the Emperor Penguin embryos
)out the origin of feathers are justified, the worst journey in the world in the in-
ᐧrest of science was not made in vain."

GLOSSARY

BLIZZARD.

An Antarctic blizzard is a high southerly wind generally accompanied clouds of drifting snow, partly falling from above, partly picked up from the s face. In the daylight of summer a tent cannot be seen a few yards off: in the da ness of winter it is easy to be lost within a few feet of a hut. There is no doubt tha blizzard has a bewildering and numbing effect upon the brain of any one expos to it.

BRASH.

Small ice fragments from a floe which is breaking up.

CLOUD.

The commonest form of cloud, and also that typical of blizzard conditio was a uniform pall stretching all over the sky without distinction. This was logg by us as *stratus*. *Cumulus* clouds are the woolly billows, flat below and round on top, which are formed by local ascending currents of air. They were rare in t south and only formed over open water or mountains. *Cirrus* are the "mare's tai and similar wispy clouds which float high in the atmosphere. These and their lied forms were common. Generally speaking, the clouds were due to stratificati of the air into layers rather than to ascending currents.

CRUSTS.

Layers of snow in a snow-field with air space between them.

FINNESKO.

Boots made entirely of fur, soles and all.

FROST SMOKE.

Condensed water vapour which forms a mist over open sea in cold weathe

ICE-FOOT.

Fringes of ice which skirt many parts of the Antarctic shores: many of th have been formed by sea-spray.

NUNATAK.

An island of land in a snow-field. Buckley Island is the top of a mountain sti ing out of the top of the Beardmore Glacier.

PIEDMONT.

Stretches of ancient ice which remain along the Antarctic coasts.

PRAM.

A Norwegian skiff, with a spoon bow.

SAENNEGRASS.

A kind of Norwegian hay used as packing in finnesko.

SASTRUGI

are the furrows or irregularities formed on a snow plain by the wind. They may be a foot or more deep and as hard and as slippery as ice: they may be quite soft: they may appear as great inverted pudding bowls: they may be hard knots covered with soft powdery snow.

SLEDGING DISTANCES.

All miles are geographical miles unless otherwise stated, 1 statute or English mile = 0.87 geographical mile: 1 geographical mile = 1.15 statute miles.

TANK.

A canvas "hold-all" strapped to the sledge to contain food bags.

TIDE CRACK.

A working crack between the land ice and the sea ice which rises and falls with the tide.

WIND.

Wind forces are logged according to the Beaufort scale, which is as follows:

No.	Description.	Mean velocity in miles per hour.
0.	Calm	0
1.	Light air	1
2.	Light breeze	4
3.	Gentle breeze	9
4.	Moderate breeze	14
5.	Fresh breeze	20
6.	Strong breeze	26
7.	Moderate gale	33
8.	Fresh gale	42
9.	Strong gale	51
10.	Whole gale	62
11.	Storm	75
12.	Hurricane	92

INDEX

A

A. A. Milne *Xlvii*
Activity *Xxiv*, 99, 147
Adélie Land *Xxi*
Adélie Penguin 43, 45, 56, 57
Adélie Penguins *Xxxiii, Xxxiv, Xlix*, 42, 43, 55
Alexander Land *Xx*
Altitude 77, 137
Anchorage 11, 71
Antarctic Adventures *Xlviii*
Antarctic Penguins *Xxxiii, Xlix*, 43, 44
Antarctic Petrel 42
Antarctic Regions *Xxiv*, 137
Anton 120, 157, 158, 164
Appearance *Xxii, L*, 2, 10, 17, 26, 62, 70, 86, 91, 117, 216
Apsley Cherry-Garrard *Iii, V, Vii, X, Li*, 135, 210
Arethusa 4
Arrival Bay *Xxxvii*, 117
Arrival Heights *Iv*, 68, 110, 115, 116, 129
Ascent Of *Xxix*

B

Balloon Bight *Xxix*, 91
Barne Glacier 127, 133
Bay Of Whales *Xxxix*, 90, 91, 93, 94, 155
Beaufort Island 57, 127
Bellingshausen *Xx, Xxi*
Biological Observations 26
Bird Life 25
Black-Breasted Petrel 9
Black Island *Xxiii*
Blacksand Beach 70
Blizzards *Xxxiv*, 39, 57, 66, 75, 79, 85, 95, 96, 116, 127, 128, 129, 132, 154, 170, 179, 181, 186, 192, 195, 196, 201
Blue Whale 47
Bluff Depôt 79, 81, 89, 95

Lector House believes that a society develops through a two-fold approach of continuous learning and adaptation, which is derived from the study of classic literary works spread across the historic timeline of literature records. Therefore, we aim at reviving, repairing and redeveloping all those inaccessible or damaged but historically as well as culturally important literature across subjects so that the future generations may have an opportunity to study and learn from past works to embark upon a journey of creating a better future.

This book is a result of an effort made by Lector House towards making a contribution to the preservation and repair of original ancient works which might hold historical significance to the approach of continuous learning across subjects.

HAPPY READING & LEARNING!

LECTOR HOUSE LLP
E-MAIL: lectorpublishing@gmail.com

9 789353 445225